中国邮政储蓄银行
POSTAL SAVINGS BANK OF CHINA
邮储银行外汇业务
让视野更远 与世界更近
中国邮政储蓄银行为您构建通达境外200多个国家和地区的服务网络，提供境内外，内外贸，本外币，进出口全流程贸易金融综合服务方案，让世界触手可得。

中国外汇指定银行年鉴 2015

China Foreign Exchange Designated Bank Yearbook

主　编　寇亚南
副主编　魏建玲　于　强

中国金融出版社

责任编辑：张智慧　王雪珂
责任校对：李俊英
责任印制：程　颖

图书在版编目（CIP）数据

中国外汇指定银行年鉴.2015（Zhongguo Waihui Zhiding Yinhang Nianjian.2015）/寇亚南主编.—北京：中国金融出版社，2015. 10
ISBN 978 - 7 - 5049 - 8134 - 9

Ⅰ.①中…　Ⅱ.①寇…　Ⅲ.①商业银行—外汇业务—中国—2015—年鉴　Ⅳ.①F832.64-54

中国版本图书馆CIP数据核字（2015）第223001号

出版发行　中国金融出版社
社址　北京市丰台区益泽路2号
市场开发部　（010）63266347，63805472，63439533（传真）
网上书店　http://www.chinafph.com
（010）63286832，63365686（传真）
读者服务部　（010）66070833，62568380
邮编　100071
经销　新华书店
印刷　北京松源印刷有限公司
尺寸　185毫米×260毫米
插页　2
印张　30.5
字数　545千
版次　2015年10月第1版
印次　2015年10月第1次印刷
定价　98.00元
ISBN 978 - 7 - 5049 - 8134 - 9/F.7694
如出现印装错误本社负责调换　联系电话（010）63263947

序

国家外汇管理局国际收支司　温建东

经过三十多年的改革开放，外汇指定银行的内涵多次演变，现在是指经批准办理结售汇业务的银行。外汇指定银行是外汇管理部门借以实施外汇措施、调节外汇供求、传导政策意图、进行统计监测的主要渠道和枢纽。

结售汇业务是银行对客户办理的人民币与外币之间的兑换业务。其中，结汇是指客户将外汇卖给银行的业务，售汇是指客户向银行购买外汇的业务。银行办理结售汇业务的净差额通过银行间外汇市场平盘，对人民币汇率和外汇储备产生影响，并通过基础货币投放影响货币政策和宏观经济政策。

值得指出的是，结汇和售汇业务是政策性、行政性很强的业务，与一般的存贷款等外汇业务有着本质区别，需要进行特殊监管。银行需要依据外汇管理法规为企业和个人办理本外币兑换，对企业和个人结售汇交易背景的真实性和合规性进行审核。银行能否认真贯彻外汇管理规定，直接决定外汇管理政策的执行效力。近年来，因为行政审批制度改革，外汇指定银行甚至被授权实施越来越多的诸如外商投资企业资本金结汇等传统上属于外汇局审批的业务。如果从监管机构分工的角度看，外汇管理部门对银行的监管侧重合规性监管，侧重于是否符合外汇管理政策，最终目的在于保障外汇管理政策的执行。银行监管部门侧重于风险监管，重点是资本充足率，以保证银行清偿能力，最终保障社会公众的利益。

从外汇市场角度，银行结售汇业务属于外汇零售市场，是银行与机构或个人之间进行的柜台式外汇买卖所形成的市场。银行办完结售汇业务并与此相对的是银行间外汇市场，即银行同业之间通过中国外汇交易中心进行结售汇头寸平补和交易的市场。也就是说，银行为客户办理结售汇业务会形成相应的头寸盈缺，多余的头寸需要在银行间外汇市场抛出，短缺的头寸需要补进。2014年，国内外汇市场累计成交12.76万亿美元，较上年增长13.4%。其中，银行对客户市场和银行间外汇市场分别成交3.95万亿美元和8.81万亿美元[①]。

2005年汇率形成机制改革后，银行结售汇业务迎来了迅猛发展，涵盖了即期结售汇、远期结售汇、人民币外汇期权等。远期结售汇、人民币外汇期权等衍生品交易，可以帮助企业锁定成本，规避汇率风险，实现保值增值。2014年，即期和衍生产品分别成交7.25万亿美元和5.51万亿美元。从中我们可以看出，衍生产品在外汇市场交易总量中的比重升至历史新高的43.2%。

办理结售汇业务，应当了解掌握外汇管理政策法规。否则，可能承担《外汇管理条例》规定的法律责任。外汇违法行为主要有逃汇、非法套汇、非法结汇、非法使用外汇、非法买卖外汇等。近年来，外汇局多次对地下钱庄等违反外汇管理行为进行了坚决查处和打击，起到了震慑作用。

本书汇集了全国主要外汇指定银行的名录，并对外汇指定银行常见业务相关外汇管理政策法规和业务流程进行了介绍，可以作为广大银行和企业从业者的参考书。

2015年8月于北京

① 银行对客户市场采用客户买卖外汇总额，银行间外汇市场采用单边交易量，以下同。

目　录

中国外汇指定银行业务发展综述

ZHONGGUO WAIHUI ZHIDING YINHANG YEWU FAZHAN ZONGSHU

1993年12月28日，中国人民银行发布了《关于进一步改革外汇管理体制的公告》，公告中明确了我国外汇管理体制改革的总体思路和具体实施方案。根据公告，我国自1994年1月1日起，实行银行结汇、售汇制度；取消外汇的上缴与留成，实行人民币汇率并轨；并轨后的人民币汇率，实行以市场供求为基础的、单一的、有管理的浮动制；建立全国统一的银行间外汇交易市场。二十二年后的今天，回顾我国的外汇管理体制改革之路，我们可以看到，改革基本上都是按照当年公告中的制度框架来设计、完善和实施的。也正是在此份公告中，第一次出现了“外汇指定银行”的概念，并沿用至今。按照中国人民银行的官方定义，外汇指定银行是指“经批准经营外汇业务的银行”。

1993年底，我国的外汇指定银行屈指可数。在中资银行中，当时仅有中国银行、中国工商银行、中国人民建设银行、中国农业银行、交通银行、中信实业银行、光大银行、投资银行、华夏银行、广东发展银行、福建兴业银行、上海浦东发展银行、深圳发展银行、深圳蛇口招商银行具有外汇指定银行资格。二十余年来，随着改革开放进程和金融体制改革的不断深化，我国外汇指定银行的数量实现了连续跨越式的增长，成绩显著。截止到2015年6月底，我国共有中资外汇指定银行262家。其中，国有政策性银行及全国性股份制商业银行21家，城市商业银行89家，农村商业银行（合作银行、信用联社）152家。然而，令人遗憾的是，市场上一直缺少一幅全国外汇指定银行的“全家福”，这也正是《中国外汇指定银行年鉴（2015）》出版的意义所在。年鉴将成为相关政府机构、银行同业、外贸企业和财经类大专院校不可多得的参考资料和工具书。

对于国有政策性银行及全国性股份制商业银行而言，基于其全国性的市场定位、客户定位和产品定位，通过开展外汇业务实现本外币业务的一体化发展是其业务发展的必然之举。那么，为什么越来越多的地方性商业银行也纷纷向监管机构申请外汇指定银行资格，开办外汇业务呢？我们认为，尽管各家银行的具体情况不同，但其中的原因通常会包括以下几点：

一是为了丰富产品系列，满足客户需要。随着我国外贸体制改革的不断深化，特别是阿里巴巴等大量B2B电子商务网站应用的普及，全国数以百万计的中小企业开始涉足外贸业务，因而会产生大量的国际结算和贸易融资需求，如果其往来银行不能办理外汇业务，实现本外币业务“两条腿”走路，则只能坐失商机，让利于竞争对手；

二是为了增加中间业务收入，改善收益结构。长期以来，我国银行业的主要利润来源是贷款利息收入，而来自中间业务的非利息收入通常不足两成。这种情况一方面不利于银行利润最大化经营目标的实现，另一方面也使得银行的经营业绩会随着宏观经济景气指数的波动，以及信贷风险的集中爆发而出现大幅波动，从而对银行信用评级和长远发展带来负面影响。2015年8月底，国内16家上市银行陆续公布了上半年财务报表，在整体宏观经济GDP增速下滑的背景下，所有银行总共获得了近7000亿元人民币的净利润，但却承担着8000多亿元的不良贷款，其中8家银行的净利润增速跌至个位数，这反映出国内商业银行增加中间业务收入，改善收益结构的战略调整任重而道远；

三是为了有效管理风险，提高经济资本回报率。银行在办理国际结算过程中，通过办理汇款、托收、信用证、保函以及结售汇业务可以赚取可观的手续费收入，而贸易融资产品所具有的自偿性特征使得其相较于一般银行信贷产品如流动资金贷款具有更低的风险系数。因此，外汇业务往往由于其低风险、期限短、高收益的特征而成为“安眠药”式的银行产品，即国际结算和贸易融资业务可以让银行的客户经理们晚上睡得着觉！根据中国银监会现行的《商业银行资本管理办法（试行）》规定，贷款授信业务的信用转换系数为100%，而信用证业务的信用转换系数为20%。因此，在银行资本约束压力增大的情况下，开展外汇业务，有利于银行“少花钱多办事”，提高经济资本回报率。此外，地方性商业银行开办外汇业务还会得到其他一些增值回报，例如有利于提升银行整体形象，有利于吸引境内、外战略投资者，有利于帮助当地政府部门组织、协调境外考察、招商、参展等活动。一位城商行的董事长陪同市长赴境外商务考察归来，曾深受感触地说：“如果我们没有开办外汇业务，就不可能有自己的海外代理行网络，我们的考察也不会完成得如此顺利圆满，更谈不上抢抓商机！”

毫无疑问，银行外汇业务的开展与外贸形势息息相关。2014 年，按照国际收支统计口径，我国货物出口23 541亿美元，同比增长6%；进口18 782 亿美元，同比增长1%；货物贸易顺差为4 760 亿美元，同比增长32%。相应地，2014年1～12月，银行累计结汇116 422亿元人民币（等值18 958亿美元），累计售汇108 737亿元人民币（等值17 700亿美元），累计结售汇顺差7 686亿元人民币（等值1 258亿美元）。多年来，外贸一直是拉动我国经济发展的“三驾马车”之一。在这一背景下，外汇指定银行的外汇业务获得了长足发展，效益显著。然而，具体到不同的银行，则难免会出现苦乐不均、效益参差的情况。因此，要在日趋激烈的同业竞争中脱颖而出，各外汇指定银行必须结合自身的条件，找准定位，制定出具有差异化的竞争策略，并坚定不移地将既定的策略切实贯彻到位。俗话说，“尺有所短，寸有所长”，工、农、中、建、交等大行固然具有先天优势，小行却未必一定在竞争中败北。在一些三四线城市，许多当地城商行、农商行依托自己在本币存贷款、银行网点和结算业务中的优势，大力拓展外汇业务，市场份额已远超一些大行的当地分行，成为所在地区外汇业务的“龙头老大”，未来发展不容小觑。

在外汇业务产品方面，产品同质化的现象依然突出。各行的外汇业务产品基本上以汇款、托收、信用证、保函，以及与之相配套的贸易融资、供应链融资、结售汇业务为主。可喜的是，一些银行已在积极探索新的产品创新方向。

一是配合人民币国际化，推出人民币跨境结算与融资产品。例如，中行把握有利政策机遇，充分发挥其在贸易金融领域的传统优势，在境内所有地区以及境外多个国家和地区成功办理首笔试点人民币业务，率先在跨境人民币结算、海外人民币贷款、离岸人民币债券等领域推出配套产品和服务。

二是抓住汇率改革和利率市场化契机，推出避险类产品，为客户解决后顾之忧。例如，中信银行推出的换汇宝、汇添盈、无忧利率等外汇资金产品，融租通、保汇通、银证通、人民币NRA全额质押融资、上海自贸区与苏州工业园人民币境外借款及国内应收账款质押等创新产品，很好地满足了客户需求，拓宽了收入来源，实现了规模与收益的协同发展。

三是打破部门界限，将外汇业务的拓展重点延伸到个人银行外汇业务领域。近年来，受国内居民境外投资、旅游、移民、留学等消费刺激，以及未来美元升值预期的影响，银行个人客户的购汇需求日趋踊跃，一些银行抓住机遇，“以客户为中心”，打破内部部门界限，为个人客户提供贷款、购汇、汇款等一揽子服务，成效显著。例如，招商银行推出的出国金融系列产品，涵盖了出国留学、出国旅游、商务出行、移民国外等各个方面，甚至可以提供协助客户申请签证服务，深受客户欢迎。

在外汇业务产品价格方面，从全国范围来看，各地情况差异较大。有的地区银行同业间的行业自律氛围较好，或者当地一行独大，竞争不够充分，则各行基本上执行标准的利费率和汇率。而在那些行业自律氛围较差，或者市场竞争激烈的地区，则各行会按照总行授权的利费率和汇率优惠审批权限，结合客户对银行的综合回报，给予客户适当的优惠安排。总体而言，一二线城市的客户会更习惯于与银行议价。

在外汇业务营销渠道方面，银行除了传统的网点营销、团队营销之外，“互联网+外汇业务”的营销模式也日益普及。目前，大多数外汇业务系统已上线的银行均已开通互联网业务处理功能，不仅方便客户办理业务，也便于银行开展营销。尤其值得注意的是，银行开始有意识地依托第三方的大数据系统开展营销活动。2014年7月，中国银行、招商银行、建设银行等多家银行与阿里巴巴集团合作推出“网商贷高级版”，向使用阿里巴巴B2B“一达通”出口基础服务的中小企业提供以出口贸易数据为基础的无抵押、免担保、纯信用的互联网贷款服务，影响深远。

在外汇业务营销促销方面，除了依靠价格手段让利于客户，各行也纷纷探索新的促销手段，如在银行内部设置产品经理，配合客户经理开展营销；对外为客户提供业务培训、帮助客户度身定制本外币一揽子融资安排、银行领导适时拜访重点客户、定期举办客户联谊活动或组织客户境内外考察等，林林总总，不一而足。

展望2015年，银行外汇业务发展的机遇与挑战并存。首先，从宏观层面上看，我国经济增速虽有所回落，但保持在7%上下的中高增速。随着改革红利不断释放，我国经济仍存在较大的发展空间。这是人民币汇率、国际收支运行维持基本稳定的重要支撑。其次，贸易和投资依然是跨境资金流入的稳定来源。随着我国出口产品由劳动密集型转向资本和技术密集型，高铁等重大装备制造业成为出口的新亮点，出口竞争优势依然存在。同时，我国是全球最大的消费市场，随着全面改革措施落地和国内金融市场开放，对外资仍有较强的吸引力，2015 年我国仍将保持吸收外资的大国地位。最后，我国外汇储备充裕，抵御外部冲击的能力较强。当然，由于我国经济对外开放度越来越高，跨境资金流动渠道日益丰富且便利，部分领域的跨境套利投机活动也需要密切关注。

面对市场机遇，外汇指定银行一方面需要面向市场谋发展，另一方面也要练好内功控风险。尤其需要注意的是，与前几年相比，2015年国际经济与金融波动将会加剧，来自于监管机构的政策调整也会更加频繁，银行开展外汇业务所面临的信用风险、操作风险和市场风险均会显著增加，而银行推行的产品创新也有可能会因为市场与预期的逆向发展而暴露风险。据《国家外汇管理局年报 2014》报道，“2014 年，国家外汇管理局抓住跨境资金异常流动重点主体和关键环节，针对虚假转口贸易、虚假贸易融资、远期结汇异常增长等情况，积极组织开展专项检查，严厉打击地下钱庄等外汇违法犯罪活动，取得积极成效，全年共查处外汇违规案件1 900 余起，处行政罚款4.5 亿元人民币。”可见，国家外汇管理局在不断推出一系列促进贸易和跨境投融资便利化政策的同时，检查力度和处罚力度也同样在加强。因此，面对2015年复杂多变的经营环境，以及日益严峻的合规风险，各外汇指定银行应坚持依法合规开展业务，加强制度学习和内部培训，并在实际业务中加强内控和风险预警，必要时还需引入第三方机构开展内审，以确保银行外汇业务的健康可持续发展。

政策性银行及大型商业银行

ZHENGCEXING YINHANG JI DAXING SHANGYE YINHANG

ICBC 中国工商银行 工于至诚 行以致远

中国工商银行股份有限公司

中国工商银行股份有限公司前身为中国工商银行，成立于1984年1月1日。2005年10月28日整体改制为股份有限公司。2006年10月27日成功在上交所和香港联交所同日挂牌上市。

通过持续努力和稳健发展，工商银行已经迈入世界领先大银行行列，拥有优质的客户基础、多元的业务结构、强劲的创新能力和市场竞争力。截至2014年末，工商银行业务跨越六大洲，境外网络扩展至41个国家和地区，并通过持股南非标准银行间接布局非洲20个国家，是覆盖国家和地区范围最广的中资银行。作为全球服务网络的重要补充，外资代理行总数突破1 800家，遍布对华投资和贸易往来95%以上的国家和地区，实现对全球GDP排名前20强、对华贸易400亿美元以上国家和地区前十大代理行的全覆盖，在中资同业中稳固保持代理行数量、布局和营销优势。同时，也是首家拥有横跨亚洲、欧洲、美洲三大时区人民币清算行资格的商业银行，真正构建起全球24小时不间断人民币清算交易业务体系。通过境内、外机构、代理行以及网上银行、电话银行和自助银行等分销渠道，工商银行向509万公司客户和4.65亿个人客户提供广泛的金融产品和服务，形成了以商业银行为主体，综合化、国际化的经营格局，在商业银行业务领域保持国内市场领先地位。

外汇业务开展状况：工商银行重视国际化经营发展，在持续完善境外机构布局的同时，还特别注重同步抓好境外重点产品线建设，全球市场交易业务实现外币债券、外汇买卖、账户贵金属和大宗商品的24小时不间断交易。截至2014年末，境外外汇即期、外币债券、衍生品集中交易量分别增长6倍、7倍和8倍；全球现金管理产品线延伸至近70个国家和地区，与超过4 300家企业客户建立了业务合作关系；私人银行全球理财基金获得卢森堡金融管理局批准，成为首个在国际主流基金市场注册私募基金的中资银行。

外汇业务经营范围：国内外结算、同业拆借买卖、代理买卖外汇、结汇、售汇、提供信用证服务及担保、代理资金清算、各类汇兑业务、代理政策性银行、外国政府和国际金融机构贷款业务、外汇存款、外汇贷款、外汇汇款、外汇借款、发行、代理发行、买卖或代理买卖股票以外的外币有价证券、外汇票据承兑和贴现、自营、代客外汇买卖、外币兑换、外汇担保、资信调查、咨询、见证业务、金融衍生产品交易业务。

特色业务：跨境人民币业务：继工商银行新加坡分行后，卢森堡分行、多哈分行、工银加拿大相继获得中国人民银行授权，担任所在国家或地区的人民币业务清算行，工商银行成为首家拥有横跨亚洲、欧洲、美洲三大时区人民币清算行的金融机构。人民币清算账户持续增加，人民币清算网络覆盖全球75个国家和地区。

工商银行推进业务产品创新，支持离岸人民币市场建设。工银亚洲推动完成首笔国际金融公司（IFC）人民币债券在伦敦交易所发行和交易；新加坡人民币清算行业务量实现大幅增长，“狮城债”承销市场占比达68.5%；工银欧洲成功发行欧洲UCITS基金，成为首家进入欧洲投资基金行业的中资机构。在上海自贸区首创跨境人民币双向资金池、完成首笔跨境人民币借款放款、首笔跨境并购等业务。在深圳前海牵头推动成立前海首只主权基金。截至2014年末，跨境人民币业务总量3.66万亿元，较上年增长65.7%。

Industrial and Commercial Bank of China Limited, formerly known as Industrial and Commercial Bank of China, was established on 1 January 1984. On 28 October 2005, the Bank was wholly restructured to a joint-stock limited company. On 27 October 2006, the Bank was successfully listed on both SSE and SEHK.

Through its continuous endeavor and stable development, the Bank has developed into the top large listed bank in the world, possessing an excellent customer base, a diversified business structure, strong innovation capabilities and market competitiveness. Among all Chinese banks, the Bank enjoys the widest overseas operational coverage. By the end of 2014, the Bank had its presence in six continents, with its overseas network expanding to 41 countries and regions. The Bank has also set foot indirectly in 20 African countries through Standard Bank of South Africa, as its single largest shareholder. As an important supplement for its global services network, the Bank is cooperating with more than 1800 correspondent banks, covering more than 95% of China’s trade and investment partners in terms of geographic distribution. Leveraging on correspondent relationship with all the TOP 10 banks among the world's largest 20 economies with trade volumes exceeding 40 billion USD , the Bank has continuously maintained a privileged correspondent coverage in terms of numbers, layout and marketing advantages among its peers. In addition, by having designated as the RMB clearing bank in Asia, Europe, and the Americas across three main time zones, the Bank has become the first commercial bank offering 24 × 7 global RMB clearing service across the globe. The Bank is committed to providing comprehensive financial products and services to 5090 thousand corporate customers and 465 million personal customers by virtue of the distribution channels of domestic and overseas institutions, along with correspondent banks worldwide, and the E-banking network, which comprises a range of Internet and telephone banking services and self-service banking centers, forming a diversified and internationalized operating structure focusing on commercial banking business and maintaining a leading position in the domestic market in the commercial banking sector.

Valuing the internationalization development, ICBC has been continuously building up global layout and the overseas key product line. The Bank now is capable of offering round-the-clock global market trading services including foreign currency debt, FX trading, precious metal and commodity trading services. By the end of 2014, the trading of FX spot, foreign currency bonds, and derivatives outside China have increased by 6 folds, 7 folds, and 8 folds respectively. The Bank's global cash management product line has been expanded to nearly 70 countries and regions, by establishing business collaboration with over 4300 corporate clients. CSSF, the regulatory authority of Luxembourg has approved the Bank to set up an UCITS in Luxembourg investing in China's onshore bond market, which enabled the Bank to be the first Chinese bank tapping European investment fund industry through its European arm.

ICBC's foreign currency business includes: international settlement, money market, FX trading agent service, exchanges of foreign currencies, L/C and guarantee, agency clearing service, agency loans from policy banks/foreign governments/ international financial institutions, foreign-currency deposit, foreign-currency loan, foreign-currency remittance, foreign currency-denominated securities (stock excluded) issuance/arrangement/trading/trade agent service, foreign exchange bills acceptance and discounting, foreign currency notes exchange, foreign currency guarantee, credit investigation and consultation, witness services, derivatives trading.

Cross-border RMB Business: Followed by ICBC Singapore, ICBC Luxembourg, ICBC Doha, and ICBC Canada successively got designated by the PBoC as the RMB clearing bank in the local markets. Thus, the Bank has become the first commercial bank with an RMB clearing system covering three main time zones across Asia, Europe, and the Americas. With the increase of RMB clearing account customers, RMB clearing network has been spread out to 75 countries and regions.

ICBC is always devoted to innovation and supports the development of off-shore RMB markets. ICBC Asia has been the arranger for IFC to issue its first RMB-denominated bond in London. ICBC Singapore has been enjoying a rapid growth in terms of RMB clearing business, and managed to take 68.5% market share of "Lion City" bonds issuance as arranger and co-arranger. ICBC Europe successfully issued UCITS in Europe, becoming the first Chinese bank tapping European investment fund industry. In addition, the Bank created the first cross-border RMB two-way capital pool in Shanghai FTZ, conducted the first cross-border RMB lending, and the first cross-border M&A. The Bank also led to establish the first sovereign fund in Qianhai, Shenzhen. By the end of 2014, the Bank's cross-border RMB totalled in 3660 billion RMB, increased by 65.7% on a year-on-year basis.

中国农业银行
AGRICULTURAL BANK OF CHINA

中国农业银行股份有限公司

全球视野 融会贯通——中国农业银行贸易金融服务

中国农业银行作为国内主要的综合性金融服务提供商，至今已有60多年的发展历史。农业银行致力于建设“面向‘三农’、城乡联动、融入国际、服务多元”的国际一流大型商业银行，不断提升服务实体经济能力，加强全面风险管控，完善公司治理结构，凭借全面的业务组合、庞大的分销网络、领先的技术平台和差异化的竞争优势，向广大客户提供全方位、多渠道、广覆盖的产品和服务。截至2015年3月末，中国农业银行的资产规模达到16.84万亿元人民币。2014年，农行入选全球系统重要性银行；在英国《银行家》杂志全球银行1 000强排名中，以一级资本排名计，农行列第9位；在美国《财富》杂志全球500强排名中，农行列第47位。

一、贸易金融服务助力企业全球发展

农业银行以满足客户在国际贸易活动中的多样化金融需求为宗旨，形成了“进口融汇通”、“出口融汇通”和“收付通”三大品牌系列下的7大类100余种贸易金融产品，逐渐形成以贸易融资为核心，集国际结算、结售汇、涉外担保、国内信用证等产品于一体，覆盖本外币、内外贸全流程的贸易金融服务体系，务求通过专业而全面的金融服务方案为客户解决融资困难，“全球视野、融会贯通”的贸易金融品牌形象在市场上形成了较强的影响力。

近年来，农业银行积极主动适应客户多样化贸易金融服务需求，加快产品创新步伐，推出应收账款融资、供应链融资、保理等多项产品，为客户度身打造功能强大、方便实用的贸易金融综合服务方案和产品体系；创新研发结构性融资、大宗商品和大宗农产品融资产品，积极拓展出口信贷、并购贷款、对外保函等创新产品，为企业“走出去”提供有力支持。

近年来，农行连续荣获“亚太地区贸易融资最佳对手银行”、“最佳贸易金融

成长银行”和“最佳贸易金融管理银行”等多种社会奖项，市场美誉度不断提升。

二、跨境人民币业务迅猛发展

农行跨境人民币业务发展速度和市场份额处于主流银行地位。目前，已为境外同业开立200多个人民币同业往来账户，服务覆盖100多个国家和地区。2014年，农业银行办理跨境人民币业务超过万亿元，集团累计办理跨境人民币业务量已突破3.7万亿元。

农行积极服务“一带一路”金融合作，建设了境内外一体化的跨境人民币清算平台，率先推出面向欧美和中东地区的“0时差”跨境人民币清算服务；成立“中国—东盟跨境人民币业务中心”，首家发布人民币对东盟货币汇率指数和农银越南盾指数，成功挂牌东盟9个国家货币汇率；农业银行还与塔吉克斯坦农业投资银行签署《农业领域合作协议》，为两国在投资、结算等方面的金融合作奠定了良好的基础。

农行加快创新跨境人民币产品服务，形成了“人民币跨境通”系列，覆盖客户结算、融资、交易、投资领域，30余种跨境人民币产品。推出跨境结汇通、跨境人民币代付、跨境人民币福费廷、跨境人民币保函等多项特色产品，有效满足客户全面跨境业务需求。

农行积极参与离岸人民币市场建设，在台湾首发中资银行宝岛债；在法兰克福发行人民币莱茵债，是中资银行在欧洲大陆发行的首笔人民币债券；在阿联酋发行中资银行首笔人民币债券并在迪拜NASDAQ上市；与伦敦证交所集团（LSEG）签署跨境人民币战略合作协议，合作研发人民币全球存托凭证产品；设立150亿美元本外币中期票据计划，居中资银行全球中期票据计划规模之首。

三、积极打造自贸区金融新优势

农业银行将发展自贸区业务作为实施大城市发展战略和国际战略的重要推手，主动适应自贸区战略实施的新常态，改善自贸区内企业的营商环境。作为第一批在自贸区内设立分行、第一批与区内企业签署合作协议的金融机构之一，农行关注自贸区政策动向，跟随自贸区管理政策落地节奏，成功开展资本金意愿结汇、跨境人民币借款、双向人民币资金池、自贸账户结售汇等业务和产品创新。农业银行一直努力成为自贸区业务的推动者，支持区内跨国公司提高全球资金使用效率，实施“走出去”战略，更好地参与国际竞争。

农行积极开展自贸业务创新。率先实施自贸分账核算体系；首批成功办理分账核算境外融资业务；率先办理首单自贸区航运及大宗商品金融衍生品代理清算业务；成功获得"沪港通"跨境结算银行资格，并托管"沪港通"下境内首只ETF基金；获得黄金交易国际板首批结算银行、上海清算所首批自贸区大宗商品金融衍生品清算会员等资格；创新推出的自贸账户小企业简式快速贷款被作为典型案例推广。

四、全球服务网络日臻完善

近年来，农业银行加快海外机构战略布局，积极拓展境外服务网络。农行在13个国家和地区设有16家境外机构，包括中国香港、新加坡、首尔、纽约、迪拜、东京、法兰克福、悉尼、卢森堡分行，英国子行、莫斯科子行、卢森堡子行、农银国际控股有限公司、农银财务有限公司14家经营性机构，温哥华、河内2家境外代表处，形成了涵盖主要国际金融中心和周边合作密切国家和地区的境外经营网络，能够为客户提供全球范围24小时不间断的金融服务。农行代理行网络覆盖143个国家和地区的1 500余家外资银行，形成了全球营销服务的有效延伸，为企业"走出去"保驾护航。

尽管全球经济总体仍将延续不平衡的缓慢复苏态势，国内外经济金融环境依然复杂，但国内经济发展步入新常态，经济运行稳中有进，"一带一路"战略实施，"引进来"和"走出去"不断推进，自贸区业务扩容升级，对于银行和客户都衍生出大量新的业务机遇。农业银行将主动适应经济新常态，在金融服务过程中实现自身的发展转型，努力提质增效，为服务实体经济发展作出更大贡献。

ABC Trade Finance Services Linking the World Together

As one of the major integrated financial service providers in China, Agricultural Bank of China (the Bank) is blessed with a history of 60 years and committed to catering to the needs of Sannong (Agriculture, Rural Areas and Farmers) and capitalizing on the synergy between the Urban Areas and the County Areas. The Bank strives to expand into the international market and provides diversified services so as to become an international first-class large-scale commercial bank. Capitalizing on the comprehensive business portfolio, extensive distribution network and advanced IT platform, the Bank provides diversified corporate and retail banking products and services for a broad range of customers and conducts treasury operations and asset management. As of the end of March 2015, the Bank had total assets of RMB 16.84 trillion. In 2014, the Bank was included in the list of Global Systemically Important Banks (G-SIBs) for the first time. The Bank ranked No. 9 in The Banker's "Top 1 000 World Banks" list, and ranked No. 47 in Fortune's Global 500 in terms of tier 1 capital.

1. Strong Trade Finance Services Fueling Clients' Global Growth

Aiming at satisfying the customers' diversified trade finance needs, the Bank developed a portfolio of services branded as "Import Finance Express", "Export Finance Express" and "Receipt-Payment Express", covering over 100 trade financing products of 7 kinds. A full-fledged trade finance product line including International Settlement, Guarantees and Domestic L/C was forged, integrating the whole process of international and domestic trade. "Global Vision, Comprehensive Solutions" has strong influence in the market.

In response to the customers' diversified business demands, the Bank has taken great efforts in product innovation, expanded major businesses including account receivables financing, supply chain financing and factoring. Meanwhile, to support the enterprises "Going Global" endeavor, the Bank was actively involved in the R&D of structured financing, Commodities and Agricultural Commodities financing products, expanding its product line to include Export Loans, M&A Loans and Guarantees.

In recent years, the Bank's market reputation was greatly enhanced and was awarded the "Leading Counterparty Bank for the Asia Pacific", "Best Bank for Trade Finance Growth" and "Best Bank for Trade Finance Management".

2. Rapidly Developing Cross-Border RMB Business

ABC is a premium bank in terms of cross-border RMB business in China. Up to now, more than 200 foreign banks from over 100 countries has opened RMB accounts in ABC. In 2014, the cross-border RMB business volume of its domestic branches amounted to over 1 trillion, and that of the whole group (including overseas branches) amounted to over 3.7 trillion.

ABC stands ready to provide financial services to countries alongside "One Belt One Road" economic zone. An integrated cross-border RMB clearing platform was set up to deliver real-time clearing services with "0 time difference" to clients in Europe, America and the Mid-east. The "China-ASEAN Cross-border RMB Business Center" was initiated by ABC to publish "Exchange Rate Index of RMB against ASEAN Currencies" and the "ABC Vietnamese Dong Index", altogether exchange rates of 9 countries were listed in the center. In addition, ABC and OJSC Agroinvestbank (the largest bank in Tajikistan) forged an agreement on co-operation in the agricultural sector, laying a solid foundation for investment and settlement cooperation between the two countries.

The Bank accelerates the innovation of RMB cross-border products and services, and has developed "RMB Cross-Border Express" Brand which includes more than 30 RMB cross-border products related to settlement, financing, treasury, and investment. It rolled out such products as RMB Cross-border Buying Express, RMB Cross-border Refinancing, RMB Cross-border Forfeiting, and RMB Cross-border Guarantees etc., fulfilling the customers' comprehensive cross-border business needs.

The Bank was actively involved in the development of offshore RMB market. After its very first RMB-denominated "Formosa Bond" issuance in Taiwan, ABC issued RMB "Rhine Bond" in Frankfurt, also the first of its kind issued by a Chinese bank. In UAE, the "Emirates Bond" issued by the Bank was later listed on NASDAQ. In the UK, it signed a "Memorandum of Understanding" with the London Stock Exchange Group (LSEG) in an effort to jointly roll out Global Depository Receipt (GDR) Products denominated in RMB. A global MTN program of USD 15 billion was set up, ranking the Bank the top among Chinese banks in terms of the size of the MTN plan.

3. Leveraging on the Advantages of the Free Trade Zone (FTZ)

ABC considers the FTZ business as a key link in implementing its mega-city development initiatives and international strategy, adapting itself to the "new norms" brought about by the FTZ policies, and endeavoring to improve the business environment for the enterprises in FTZ. As one of few financial institutions that established branches in the FTZ and signed cooperation agreements with the enterprises in the FTZ, ABC proactively follows the FTZ policy trends, and successfully launched such products as demand forex sales for capital funds, cross-border RMB loan, Two-way RMB pool, and Free Trade accounts settlement, etc. ABC always makes great effort to become a facilitator of FTZ business and help the global enterprises to improve the use of global funds, implement "Going Global" strategy and better participate in international competition.

ABC takes the lead in conducting product innovation in the pilot FTZ. It was the first Chinese Bank that implemented the "Free Trade Accounting Unit" (FTU) and was among the first to handle the overseas financing business with FTU system. The Bank executed the FTZ shipping and commodity derivative clearing, also the first of its kind by a Chinese local bank. It was qualified as the "Shanghai-HK Stock Connect" Settlement Bank and the first ETF fund in domestic China was under ABC's custody as well. In addition, ABC was successfully granted the qualification as a settlement bank on the Shanghai International Gold Exchange Co., Ltd. and a clearing member of FTZ commodity derivative in the Shanghai Clearing House. The fast & convenient loans for small enterprises in the FTZ, rolled out by the Bank innovatively was regarded as a role model in the region.

4. Improved Global Service Network

In recent years, ABC has actively extended its global reach. The Bank has established 16 overseas affiliates in 13 countries and regions, which comprise 9 branches in Hong Kong, Singapore, Seoul, New York, Dubai, Tokyo, Frankfurt, Sydney and Luxembourg, 3 subsidiaries in UK, Russia and Luxembourg, 2 representative offices in Vancouver and Hanoi, as well as ABC International Holding and China Agricultural Finance.The overseas affiliates locate in major international finance centers and neighboring countries and regions, and could provide 24 hours uninterrupted worldwide financial services.The Bank also has over 1 500 correspondent banks in 143 countries and regions which have become the effective extensions of the bank, providing global services for “Going Global” enterprises.

Despite the slow recovery of global economy and the complicated domestic and external economic & financial environment, Chinese economy is progressing steadily and has entered into a “New Normal” stage. With the implementation of the “One Belt One Road” initiatives, the “Bringing In” and “Going Global” strategies, and the expansion and upgrading of free trade zone business, banks and customers will have plenty of business opportunities. ABC will take the initiative to adapt to New Normal Economy, achieve its own development and transformation, strive to improve quality and efficiency, and contributes more to the development of the real economy.

中国银行
BANK OF CHINA

中国银行股份有限公司

中国银行简介及贸易金融业务发展情况

一、中国银行简介

1912年2月，经孙中山先生批准，中国银行正式成立。从1912年至1949年，中国银行先后行使中央银行、国际汇兑银行和国际贸易专业银行职能，坚持以服务社会民众、振兴民族金融为己任，历经磨难，艰苦奋斗，在民族金融业中长期处于领先地位，并在国际金融界占有一席之地。

1949年以后，中国银行长期作为国家外汇外贸专业银行，统一经营管理国家外汇，开展国际贸易结算、侨汇和其他非贸易外汇业务，大力支持外贸发展和经济建设。改革开放以来，中国银行牢牢抓住国家利用国外资金和先进技术加快经济建设的历史机遇，充分发挥长期经营外汇业务的独特优势，成为国家利用外资的主渠道。1994年，中国银行改为国有独资商业银行。2004年8月，中国银行股份有限公司挂牌成立。2006年6月、7月，中国银行先后在香港联交所和上海证券交易所成功挂牌上市，成为国内首家“A+H”发行上市的中国商业银行。2013年，中国银行再次入选全球系统重要性银行，成为新兴市场经济体中唯一连续3年入选的金融机构。

中国银行是中国国际化和多元化程度最高的银行，在中国、中国香港、中国澳门、中国台湾及37个国家为客户提供全面的金融服务。主要经营商业银行业务，包括公司金融业务、个人金融业务和金融市场业务，并通过全资子公司中银国际控股有限公司开展投资银行业务，通过全资子公司中银集团保险有限公司及中银保险有限公司经营保险业务，通过全资子公司中银集团投资有限公司经营直接投资和投资管理业务，通过控股中银基金管理有限公司经营基金管理业务，通过全资子公司中银航空租赁私人有限公司经营飞机租赁业务。

二、贸易金融业务开展情况

贸易金融业务是中国银行优势业务。中国银行加强境内外机构联动，实现国际结算及贸易融资业务快速发展。中国银行秉持“最好的贸易金融银行”发展目标，在有效防控风险的前提下推进业务创新、完善管理机制，推动贸易金融业务平稳增长，持续巩固市场领先优势。2014年，集团完成国际结算业务量3.92万亿美元，同比增长14.79%，国际贸易结算市场份额继续稳居同业首位，对外担保市场份额继续保持同业领先，出口双保理业务持续位列全球首位。

加快新兴战略性业务发展。积极拓展重点行业供应链金融业务，2014年业务量突破9737亿元人民币。继续加快新加坡大宗商品业务中心建设，推动伦敦和纽约大宗商品融资业务发展；设立上海大宗商品业务平台，与国际能源交易中心签署战略合作协议，协助推进原油期货上市。推出跨国公司总部资金集中运营服务，在担任客户主办银行的数量上处于市场领先地位。

大力推动人民币国际化业务发展。贯彻落实人民币国际化战略，努力担当人民币跨境流通的主渠道、人民币国际化的重要推动者、金融产品和服务创新的引领者。2014年，集团跨境人民币结算量超过5.32万亿元，同比增长34%；跨境人民币结算量2.55万亿元，市场份额稳居第一。积极推动人民币在新兴领域和离岸市场的使用，不断提升人民币全球清算服务能力，率先完成人民币对新西兰元、欧元、新加坡元直接交易，与世界各大交易所合作开发人民币计价的离岸金融产品。持续发布《中国银行人民币国际化业务白皮书》、“中国银行跨境人民币指数（CRI）”和“中国银行离岸人民币指数（ORI）”，保持人民币国际化业务的专业领先地位。

2014年，本行获得国内外知名媒体与机构评选的“最佳贸易融资银行”、“最佳供应链金融银行”、“最佳跨境人民币业务银行”等奖项共计20个，荣获国际保理商联合会（FCI）“最佳进出口保理商”第五名，在中资同业中位列第一。

Bank of China Overview and the Trade Finance Business

Ⅰ Bank of China Overview

Bank of China was formally established in February 1912 following the approval of Dr. Sun Yat-sen. From 1912 to 1949, the Bank served consecutively as the country's central bank, international exchange bank and specialised international trade bank. Fulfilling its commitment to serving the public and developing China's financial services sector, the Bank rose to a leading position in the Chinese financial industry and developed a good standing in the international financial community, despite many hardships and setbacks. After 1949, with a long history as the state-designated specialised foreign exchange and trade bank, the Bank became responsible for managing China's foreign exchange operations and provided vital support to the nation's foreign trade development and economic infrastructure through its offering of international trade settlement, overseas fund transfer and other non-trade foreign exchange services. During China's reform and opening up period, the Bank seized the historic opportunity presented by the government's strategy of capitalising on foreign funds and advanced technologies to boost economic development, and became the country's key foreign financing channel by building up its competitive advantages in foreign exchange business. In 1994, the Bank was transformed into a wholly state-owned commercial bank. In August 2004, Bank of China Limited was incorporated. The Bank was listed on the Hong Kong Stock Exchange and Shanghai Stock Exchange in June and July 2006 respectively, becoming the first Chinese commercial bank to launch an A-Share and H-Share initial public offering and achieve a dual listing in both markets. In 2013, Bank of China was enrolled again as a Global Systemically Important Bank, becoming the sole financial institution from emerging economies to be enrolled for three consecutive years.

As China's most international and diversified bank, the Bank provides a comprehensive range of financial services to customers across the Chinese mainland, Hong Kong, Macau, Taiwan and 37 countries. The Bank's core business is commercial banking, including corporate banking, personal banking and financial markets services.

BOC International Holdings Limited, a wholly owned subsidiary, is the Bank's investment banking arm. Bank of China Group Insurance Company Limited and Bank of China Insurance Company Limited, both wholly owned subsidiaries, run the Bank's insurance business. Bank of China Group Investment Limited, a wholly owned subsidiary, undertakes the Bank's direct investment and investment management business. Bank of China Investment Management Co., Ltd., a controlled subsidiary, operates the Bank's fund management business. BOC Aviation Pte. Ltd., a wholly owned subsidiary, is in charge of the Bank's aircraft leasing business.

Ⅱ Trade Finance

Dedicated to its developmental objective of being best trade finance bank, the Bank continued to strengthen its market dominance by promoting business innovation, improving management mechanisms and driving forward the stable growth of its trade finance business while effectively managing and controlling risks. In 2014, the Group's international settlement volume reached USD 3.92 trillion, an increase of 14.79% compared with the prior year. The domestic institutions of the Bank retained leading position among peers in providing international trade settlement, held the leading market share of overseas guarantee business and ranked the first globally in two-factor export factoring business.

The Bank accelerated the development of its emerging strategic businesses. It actively expanded supply chain finance in key industries, bringing business volumes above RMB973.7 billion during 2014. The Bank stepped up the development of its commodity business unit (Singapore) and realised rapid growth in its commodity financing businesses in London and New York. It has set up a commodity business platform in Shanghai and signed a strategic cooperation agreement with the Shanghai International Energy Exchange to assist in launching crude oil futures. In addition, the Bank provided centralised cross-border fund management services for the headquarters of multinational enterprises, leading the market in terms of the number of customers for which the Bank served as the lead bank.

The Bank also vigorously promoted the development of its RMB internationalisation business. It implemented the RMB internationalisation strategy and strived to serve as the main channel for cross-border RMB fund flows, a key promoter of RMB internationalisation and a leader in RMB-related financial product and service innovation. In 2014, the cross-border RMB settlement volume of the Group exceeded RMB5.32 trillion, an increase of 34% compared with the prior year. The cross-border RMB settlement volume of the domestic institutions of the Bank totalled RMB2.55 trillion, maintaining its leading market share. In addition, the Bank actively promoted the use of RMB products in emerging business and offshore markets, continually improved its RMB global clearing services, took the lead to establishing the direct trading of RMB against New Zealand Dollar, Euro and Singapore Dollar and developed RMB-denominated offshore financial products in cooperation with major exchanges around the world. It continued to publish the White Paper on RMB Internationalisation Business of Bank of China, "BOC Cross-border RMB Index (CRI)" and "BOC Offshore RMB Index (ORI)", thus maintaining its position as a driving force in RMB internationalisation.

In 2014, the Bank received 20 awards granted by well-known local and international media titles and institutions, including "Best Trade Finance Bank", "Best Supply Chain Finance Bank" and "Best Cross-border RMB Business Bank", and ranked fifth among "Export and Import Factors of The Year" as rated by Factors Chain International, ahead of its Chinese peers.

中国建设银行
China Construction Bank

中国建设银行股份有限公司

专业引领、融通国际——中国建设银行贸易金融服务

中国建设银行股份有限公司作为一家全球领先的商业银行，至今已有六十年的辉煌历史。六十年间，建设银行“砥砺奋进，不断发展壮大，为国家经济社会发展作出了积极贡献”，秉承“以客户为中心、以市场为导向”的经营理念，大力支持实体经济发展，加强风险管理与内控建设，积极履行企业社会责任，不断完善公司治理结构、积极创新产品、渠道和服务模式，为客户提供优质、高效、全方位的现代金融服务。截至2014年末，中国建设银行的资产规模达到16.74万亿元人民币，ROA、ROE、资本充足率等多项关键指标处于全球领先水平。在英国《银行家》杂志2014年“世界银行1 000强（按一级资本排名）”中位列第二，在美国《福布斯》2015年全球2 000强上市企业排行榜中位列第二。

一、“贸易金融”品牌深入人心

建设银行致力于为客户提供专业化的贸易金融服务，连续多年国际结算量超万亿美元，贸易融资投放超万亿元人民币。向客户提供涵盖不同结算方式和贸易全流程的贸易金融标准化产品如跨境供应链、国际保理、出口信保融资、应收账款池融资、大宗商品结构性融资等五十余个，可为客户的个性化需求量身定制本外币和境内外一体化的综合金融服务方案。全行统一的“贸易金融”品牌和“专业引领、融通国际”的理念已深入人心。

建设银行贸易融资特色产品的打造来源于客户在国际贸易过程中各个环节的业务诉求。为满足“走出去”客户的跨境融资需要，建设银行通过授信体制创新推出了覆盖全球的跨境供应链金融服务。在全球授信服务体系内，银行利用核心企业的信用延伸，打通上下游、境内外整个供应链条的资金流，从而实现整个产业链上有核心价值资源的整合，改进传统贸易金融服务的模式，提升银行信用对产业链上中

小客户的服务能力。为帮助客户降低融资成本，建设银行通过设计出口应收账款风险参与等一系列创新产品，凭借自身海外网络优势，引入境外资金，让客户获得更低成本的融资便利。为满足客户对大宗商品融资与保值避险的需求，建设银行推出了极具个性化的结构性大宗商品融资，为客户量身打造融资与套保避险一体化的特色服务。

近年来，建设银行相继获得中国银行业协会等机构颁发的“最佳贸易金融产品创新银行”、“最佳供应链融资银行”、“中国最佳贸易融资银行”等奖项。

二、跨境人民币业务频创佳绩

跨境人民币业务发展速度和市场份额处于同业领先地位。2014年，建设银行境内外机构办理跨境人民币业务超过3万亿元，客户数超过16 000个。

成功获任亚洲以外首个人民币清算行。2014年，建设银行获任伦敦人民币清算行并正式投入运营，这是央行首次在亚洲以外的国家（地区）选定人民币清算行，也是中国建设银行首次获任海外人民币指定清算行。

与国际知名交易所的合作取得新突破。2014年，建设银行与香港交易所［包括港交所旗下的伦敦金属交易所（LME）、伦敦证券交易所（LSE）］签署了战略合作谅解备忘录，是继建设银行获得人民币清算行资格后，在英国金融领域拓展业务的又一重大举措，也是建行在“综合性、多功能、集约化”的发展战略下，坚持国际化发展方向的又一里程碑。

积极参与离岸人民币市场建设，离岸人民币债券发行成绩突出。2014年尤其在离岸人民币债券发行方面取得了突出成绩：在香港发行是当时境外单次单年期规模最大的点心债；首家发行在德国证券交易所场内市场交易以及当地的结算托管机构接受非德国法的中资人民币债券；发行首只在场内交易所挂牌交易离岸人民币的大洋债；在瑞士发行当地首只人民币债券，被路透社称为“为全球最大的离岸金融中心之一——苏黎世人民币业务开了先河”；在中国台湾发行亚欧三地同时挂牌交易的有史以来规模最大的“宝岛债”，也是首个在中国香港和欧洲挂牌交易的“宝岛债”。

三、自贸区业务赢得先机

建设银行自贸区业务始终坚持“争先”和“创新”。自2013年中国（上海）自由贸易试验区正式挂牌成立以来，上海自贸区分行陆续成为首批获批成立自由贸易试验区分行、首批获得开办分账核算业务资格、首批试点跨境人民币业务、首批办理跨境人民币境外借款业务和双向人民币资金池业务、首批成功办理外汇资本金意愿结汇业务以及获得首批开展自贸区分账核算业务资格的银行之一。

建设银行长期关注和重视自贸区业务发展，具有良好的业务开展基础。基于上海分行在上海自贸区业务开展过程中积累的成功经验，建行各自贸区分行在自贸区政策研究与运用、分账核算系统建设、跨境投融资业务开展、本外币资金集中运营等方面取得了先发优势。2015年4月，广东、天津、福建自贸区挂牌成立，建设银行再次走在了业界前列，各自贸区分行在自贸区挂牌成立当日同时开业运营并承办首笔业务。

建设银行将紧跟各自贸区相关政策落地步伐，以自贸区金融创新业务为特色和重点，着力在区内基础设施建设、对外投融资、跨境人民币业务、融资租赁业务、保理业务、大宗商品市场以及金融同业市场等多个领域取得突破并发挥引领作用，努力成为自贸区金融业务的推动者，并通过丰富资金运用渠道和手段，更好地服务区内实体经济的发展。

四、海外布局日臻完善

近年来，建设银行加快海外战略的推进，机构布局日臻完善。截至2015年3月，建行已在全球设立了22家（一级）境外机构，网络布局覆盖20个国家和地区，包括：中国香港、新加坡、法兰克福、约翰内斯堡、东京、首尔、纽约、胡志明市、悉尼、中国台北、卢森堡、中国澳门、多伦多和伦敦14家分行，建行亚洲、建行伦敦、建行俄罗斯、建行迪拜、建行欧洲、建行新西兰和建银国际7家全资子公司，在巴西收购了BIC银行。目前，境外机构数量超过110家，能够为客户提供全球范围24小时不间断的金融服务。

尽管面临全球经济复苏进程曲折、国内经济增速放缓的“新常态”，但随着全球经济的逐步企暖，中国经济的平稳运行，改革红利的陆续释放，以及中央力推的“一带一路”战略构想，无论对于客户还是银行而言都存在着大量新的机遇。今后，建设银行将始终坚持“以客户为中心”，充分挖掘客户在每个交易环节的业务需求，依托行业领先优势，持续加大金融创新，切实服务实体经济的发展。

Global Finance of Leading Profession—Trade Finance of China Construction Bank

With a brilliant 60-year history, China Construction Bank Corporation (CCB) is a leading commercial bank in China. In our history, through hard and persevering work, CCB has grown rapidly and made great contribution to boost China's economic and social developments. We have persisted in our philosophy of "customer centered and market oriented", and provided strong support to the growth of the real economy. With strict risk management and internal controls, we have fulfilled our social responsibilities, improved corporate governance, and made great efforts to offer innovative products, channels and service models, so as to deliver to our customers efficient and extensive modern financial services of the highest quality. As of the end of 2014, CCB's total asset exceeds RMB 16.74 trillion, and our key indicators including ROA, ROE, CAR, etc. are among the best in the world. CCB ranked second on The Banker's Top 1000 world bank list in 2014 (by tier 1 capital), and second on Forbes Global 2000 list of the year 2015.

1. Well accepted brand- "Trade Finance"

CCB is dedicated to providing financial service to clients. International settlement and trade finance volume both passed the milestone of a trillion US dollars.

Over 50 trade finance products, such as supply chain finance, international factoring, trade finance based on export insurance, receivables finance and commodity finance and hedging services, are ready to satisfy clients' individual need throughout the whole procedure of international commerce. CCB can also bulid up an overall financial service plan covering home and foreign currency, in or out of the border for each client according to clients' individual financial demand. The slogan of "Trade Finance" and "Global finance of leading profession" have deeply accepted and acknowledged by people.

Shaping of traits of CCB's trade finance products come from the different needs throughout international commerce. Through innovation of internal credit system, CCB presents the "stepping out" clients a global supply chain finance service catering for their across border fund-raising need. CCB extends the credit of core enterprise of supply chain, integrates funds and valuable resources throughout the supply chain and improve the service mode, which promote the ability to finance small and medium-sized enterprise. By designing the product "risk participation for export receivables" and taking the advantage of its extensive overseas network to introduce fund from abroad, CCB remarkably lowers the funding cost. Structured commodity finance serves as an integrated financial solution, which is presented by CCB to provide both finance and risk-hedging function.

In recent years, CCB was awarded prizes "Best Innovation Bank on", "Best Bank For Supply Chain Service", "Best Trade Finance Bank of China" by organizations such as China Banking Association.

2. Brilliant cross-border RMB business accomplishment

Cross-border RMB services of CCB ranks leading position in pace and portion. Volume of the year 2014 exceeds 3 trillion.

In 2014, CCB was inaugurated the title of RMB clearing bank and went into operation, which was the first time CCB was chosen as the RMB clearing bank. CCB became the first RMB clearing bank out of Asia assigned by central bank.

In 2014, CCB signed a memo with HKEx (Hong Kong Exchanges and Clearing Limited),which was another remarkable step of forging through British finance after the qualification of RMB clearing bank in London and also another milestone of the procedure of internationalized development under the guidance of strategy saying "integrity, multi-functional, intensification". CCB accomplished excellent achievement in the issuance of Off-Shore RMB bonds. Firstly, it finished the issuance of dim-sum bonds of top scale. It accomplished the first bank who issues the RMB bonds transacted within German bonds market and supervised by non-German law. In Australia, it issued the first RMB bonds transacted within local bonds market. In Swiss, it issued the first RMB bonds, which commented by Reuter"opening an new era of Swiss RMB business in world's biggest off-shore financial center". In Taiwan, it issued the largest scale of"Island Bonds",which went into transaction in Taiwan, Hong Kong and Europe.

3. Leading position of FTZ business

When it comes to Free Trade Zone business, CCB stinks to innovation and tries its best to hold the leading position. FTZ branch became one of the several banks who were granted the opening qualification at the very beginning of FTZ's foundation. Moreover, it's among the banks who were granted the FTU account, cross-border RMB, two-direction RMB currency pool, capital optional FX settlement business qualification.

Satisfying foundation for FTZ business commanded by CCB comes from the long-lasting attention. Leading advantage is acquired by other FTZ branches of CCB due to the experience accumulated by Shanghai FTZ branch during policy reading, FTU account system build-up, cross-border finance and investment, centralized management of home and abroad currency. Guangdong, Tianjin, Fujian FTZ branch came into operation in this April and worked out first business procedure of each FTZ.CCB has surpassed its peers another time.

CCB will follow the pace of policy in each FTZ, try to feature itself with FTZ innovation financial service, put emphasis on infrastructure construction, cross-border finance and investment, cross-border RMB, financial leasing, international factoring, commodity market and inter-bank business, push itself into the leading position, and give a more satisfying support to real economy by diversify the channels and methods of fund manipulation.

4. Complete Overseas Network

Recent years, CCB has tensed its schedule up for overseas network building and distribution of its branches and subsidiaries is becoming more and more reasonable. By this march, CCB owns 22 overseas institutions (tier 1), which covering 20 countries and regions, including 14 branches: Hong Kong, Singapore, Frankfort, Johannesburg, Tokyo, Seoul, New York, Ho Chi Minh, Sydney, Taipei, Luxembourg, Marco, Toronto, London; 7 subsidiaries: CCB Asia, CCB London, CCB Russia, CCB Dubai, CCB Europe, CCB New Zealand and CCB International. And CCB has finished the procurement procedure of BIC bank in Brazil. By now, overall amount of overseas institutions has climbed to 110. Non-interval financial service can be bought to clients all over the world.

Although the slowdown of domestic economy growth and difficult recovery of global economy shape “China’s new Normal”, both clients and banks are faced plentiful opportunities as domestic and global economy gradually warm up, effects of reform manifest and the effects brought about by “The Belt and Road Initiatives” strategy. CCB will always cling to the philosophy of “clients -centralized”, discover the business demand during every period of business, take advantage of leading advantage, pay more attention to innovation and make contribution to the development of real economy.

交通银行
BANK OF COMMUNICATIONS
您 的 财 富 管 理 银 行

交通银行股份有限公司

交通银行始建于1908年，是中国历史最悠久的银行之一，也是近代中国的发钞行之一。1987年重新组建后的交通银行正式对外营业，成为中国第一家全国性的国有股份制商业银行，总部在上海。2005年6月交通银行在香港联合交易所挂牌上市，2007年5月在上海证券交易所挂牌上市。根据2014年《银行家》杂志发布的全球1 000家大银行报告，交通银行一级资本列第19位，跻身全球银行20强；根据《财富》杂志发布的“世界500强公司”排行榜，交通银行列第217位。

交通银行的发展战略：走国际化、综合化道路，建设以财富管理为特色的一流公众持股银行集团（“两化一行”战略）。截至2014年末，交行境内开办外汇业务网点数量达2 614个，占全行营业网点的95.37%；境外银行机构13家，境外经营网点54个；与全球142个国家和地区的1 658家同业建立代理行关系，开立216个跨境人民币账户，在24个国家和地区的56家境外银行开立17个币种共72个外币清算账户。

国际业务开展状况

国际结算与贸易融资业务。交行通过调动境内外资源，大力推进跨境组合型结算和贸易融资产品，为企业提供个性化、全球化投融资服务。2014年，交行境内分行办理国际结算量37 464.31亿元，同比增长9.95%；国际贸易融资发生量1 830.80亿元。积极运用国际保理帮助中小型外贸企业规避出口收汇风险，提供融资便利，2014年实现国际保理业务量90.38亿元，其中国际保理商联合会（FCI）双保理业务量71.47亿元，同比增长42.61%。连续三年荣膺中国银行业协会贸易金融委员会“最佳贸易企业伙伴银行”奖项。

境内外联动业务。交行不断深化境内外联动内涵，积极打造全球金融服务平台和全球财富管理平台，整合境内外分（子）行、离岸金融、子公司等资源优势，通过“贸易+资本”双轮驱动，为企业客户提供跨境贸易结算与融资、对外担保项下的海外融资、海外投资与并购支持、境外业务咨询等境内外一体化的优质金融服务。2014年共办理联动业务507.40亿美元，累计实现联动业务收入60.78亿元，收入同比增长30.04%。

跨境人民币业务。交行成功获任首尔人民币业务清算行，清算行业务实现安全有序运行，海外机构综合实力进一步提升。首家启用中韩两国货币互换协议资金，成功发放首笔“中新”（中国—新加坡）跨境人民币贷款，服务实体经济发展。推出“融元通”跨境人民币金融服务品牌，为客户提供全方位、一揽子跨境人民币金融服务。成功办理上海自贸区内首笔人民币境外借款、人民币外债、FT账户资金汇划等业务，不断推进区内人民币的跨境使用与创新。持续简化跨境人民币业务流程和手续，促进贸易、投资自由化和便利化。2014年，境内外机构办理跨境人民币结算量达人民币10 997.37亿元，同比增长20.87%。

离岸业务。充分发挥离岸业务优势，通过集团内业务联动和重点开展贸易融资与再融资业务，多渠道吸收境外低成本资金，多途径强化风险管控。夯实离岸客户基础，注重客户分类管理与分层服务，推动客户群实现量增质升。2014年，离岸资产规模127.18亿美元，较年初增长6.87%。离岸客户总数较年初增长31.55%。离岸贸易融资业务量、国际结算量均居中资离岸同业首位。

Founded in 1908, Bank of Communications Co., Ltd. is one of the Banks with the longest history and was one of the note-issuing banks in China in the past. Bank of Communications started its business operation after its re-establishment in 1987. It is the first nationwide state-owned joint-stock commercial bank in China, with its head office located in Shanghai. The Bank was listed on the Hong Kong Stock exchange in June 2005 and on the Shanghai Stock exchange in May 2007. The Bank ranked No. 19 among the global top 1 000 banks in terms of Tier 1 Capital rated by The Banker in 2014, positioning among the top 20 of global banks and ranked No. 217 among the “Fortune 500 Companies”.

The Bank’s development strategy is to become “a first class listed comprehensive banking group focusing on international expansion and specialising in wealth management” (hereinafter referred to as “BoCom Strategy”).The Bank has opened 2 614 foreign exchange business networks in China, which reaches 95.37% of the total business networks, and 13 bank institutions out of china, and 54 overseas business networks. The Bank established agency relationship with 1 658 banks in over 142 countries and regions. And set up 216 cross-border Renminbi inter-bank accounts as well as 72 foreign currency settlement accounts in 17 currencies with 56 overseas financial institutions in over 24 countries and regions.

International settlement and trade finance

By utilising both domestic and overseas resources, the Bank gave great impetus to combined cross-border settlement and trade finance products to provide personalised, global investment and financing services with enterprises. In 2014, domestic branches' international settlement volume increased year-on-year by 9.95% to RMB 3 746.431 billion, and the amount of international trade finance was RMB 183.080 billion. the Bank actively utilised international factoring to help small and medium-sized foreign trade enterprises to avoid the risks from exported exchange collections and provide financing facilities. In 2014, the volume of international factoring was RMB9.038 billion, among which the amount of the dual factoring business of Factors chain international ("FCI") reached RMB 7.147 billion, representing a year-on-year increase of 42.61%. The Bank was awarded the "Best trading Partner Bank" by the Finance committee of china Banking association for three consecutive years.

Domestic and overseas synergy business

The Bank continuously enriched contents of domestic and overseas synergy business and actively built up the global financial service platform and global wealth management platform. the Bank also integrated resource advantages, such as domestic and overseas branches, offshore finance and subsidiaries, and were driven by two wheels, which were "trade + capital", to provide quality financial services integrating domestic and overseas services such as cross-border trade settlement and financing, foreign financing, investment and merger and acquisition, domestic and overseas business consultation and so on. In 2014, the total transaction amount of the synergy business was USD 50.740 billion and its accumulated revenue was RMB 6.078 billion, representing a year-on-year increase of 30.04%.

Cross-border Renminbi transaction

Successfully being appointed as a clearing bank of Renminbi Business in seoul, the Bank conducted its clearing business stably and orderly, with better comprehensive competence of overseas entities. as the first bank to use the funds under the china and south Korea currency swap agreement, the Bank successfully issued the first "China-Singapore" cross-border Renminbi loan to serve the development of real economy. The Bank released a financial service brand, "Rong yuan tong", to provide a full series of cross-border Renminbi financial services in all aspects for customers. The Bank succeeded in first time capital transfer of Ft accounts and businesses such as Renminbi-denominated overseas borrowing and Renminbi-denominated foreign debts within shanghai FtZ, constantly pushing forward cross-border usage and innovation of Renminbi in FtZ. The Bank constantly simplified procedures of Renminbi business for purposes of free and convenient trade and investment. In 2014, the transaction amount of the cross-border Renminbi settlement by domestic and oversea banking institutions increased by 20.87% on a year-on-year basis to RMB 1 099.737 billion.

Offshore financial services

Taking advantage of the offshore business, the Bank absorbed overseas low cost capitals and enhanced risk control in several ways, by means of intra-group business synergy and emphasis on trade financing and refinancing. The Bank reinforced the customer foundation and put great emphasis on the classification management and stratified services to customers, in order to raise the quantity and quality of customer clusters. In 2014, the total amount of offshore assets increased by 6.87% from the beginning of the year to USD 12.718 billion. The total number of offshore customers increased by 31.55% from the beginning of the year. Both offshore trade financing and international settlement were the first in terms of volume among its peers.

中信银行
CHINA CITIC BANK

中信银行股份有限公司
China CITIC Bank Corporation Limited

中信银行成立于1987年，是中国改革开放中最早成立的新兴商业银行之一，是中国最早参与国内外金融市场融资的商业银行，并以屡创中国现代金融史上多个第一而蜚声海内外，为中国经济建设作出了积极的贡献。

中信银行作为国内资本实力最雄厚的商业银行之一，在中国经济发展的浪潮中快速成长，2007年，中信银行实现A+H股同步上市，跻身于国际公众持股银行之列，成为具有强大综合竞争力的全国性商业银行。2014年7月，中信银行在英国《银行家》世界1 000家银行排名中，一级资本排名第37位，总资产排名第48位，位居中国商业银行前列。

截至2014年末，中信银行控股股东为中国中信有限公司，持股比例67.13%。中信银行在全国121个大中城市设有1 230家分支机构，主要分布在东部沿海地区和中西部经济发达城市，拥有员工5万余名。中信银行在中国内地和香港设有中信国际金融控股有限公司、振华国际财务有限公司和浙江临安中信村镇银行股份有限公司等3家附属公司，在英国伦敦设有代表处。中信国际金融控股有限公司子公司中信银行（国际）有限公司在中国香港、中国澳门、纽约、洛杉矶、新加坡和中国境内设有40多家营业网点，拥有员工1 800余名。

CITIC Bank was established in 1987, it is one of the earliest emerging commercial banks in China's reform and opening up, it is also the first Chinese commercial bank involved in financing in domestic and international financial markets. CITIC Bank is well known at home and abroad by creating many records in Chinese modern financial history, and has made a positive contribution to China's economic construction.

CITIC Bank as one of domestics commercial banks which have the most powerful capital, growing fast in the tile of China's economic development. In 2007, CITIC Bank listed A+H shares simultaneously, being an international public shareholding banks and a national commercial bank with a strong comprehensive competitiveness. July 2014, in the British "The Banker" CITIC was 37th in tier one capital ranking and 48th in total assets ranking among top 1 000 world banks, which listed in the forefront of China's commercial bank.

By the end of 2014, CITIC Group takes 67.13% CITIC Bank's stake and be its controlling shareholder. CITIC Bank has 1 230 branches in 121 large and medium cities around China, mainly distributed in the eastern and coastal areas and mid-west economically developed cities, with more than 50 000 staffs. CTIC Bank has CITIC International Financial Holdings Limited, Zhenhua International Finance Limited, Zhejiang Lin'am CITIC Bank Co., Ltd., and other three subsidiaries in Mainland China and Hong Kong. It also has representative offices in London and United Kingdom. CITIC International Financial Holdings Limited, a subsidiary of China CITIC Bank International Limited, has more than 40 outlets in Hong Kong, Macro, New York, Los Angeles, Singapore, and Mainland China, with more than 1 800 staffs.

招商银行
CHINA MERCHANTS BANK

招商银行股份有限公司
China Merchants Bank Co., Ltd.

招商银行成立于1987年4月8日，总行设在深圳，是中国境内第一家完全由企业法人持股的股份制商业银行，也是国家从体制外推动银行业改革的第一家试点银行。

截至2014年12月31日，本公司在中国大陆的120多个城市设有125家分行及1 297家支行，1家分行级专营机构（信用卡中心），1家代表处，2 791家自助银行，10 604台现金自助设备 (其中自助取款机2 364台，自助循环机8 240台），2家子公司——招银租赁和招商基金，1家合营公司——招商信诺；在香港拥有永隆银行和招银国际等子公司，及1家分行（香港分行）；在美国设有纽约分行和代表处；在新加坡设有新加坡分行；在伦敦和台北设有代表处。本公司目前在 110 个国家（含中国）及地区共有境内外代理行1 941家。在英国《银行家》公布的“2014 年全球银行品牌 500 强”排行榜中，列第44位，位居全国性中小型银行之首；在其公布的2014年全球1 000家大银行榜单中，排名第36名。

截至2014年末，本集团资产总额为47 318.29亿元，比年初增长17.81%； 客户存款总额为33 044.38亿元，比年初增长19.07%；贷款和垫款总额为25 139.19亿元，比年初增长14.42%。归属于本行股东的净利润为559.11亿元，同比增长8.06%；归属于本行股东的税后平均净资产收益率为19.28%，同比下降2.94个百分点。成本收入比为30.54%，比上年下降为3.82个百分点。高级法下资本充足率为12.38%，不良贷款率为1.11%，不良贷款拨备覆盖率为233.42%。

China Merchants Bank was established in April 8, 1987, headquartered in Shenzhen. It is the first joint-stock commercial bank wholly owned by business entity. It is also the first pilot bank to promote banking reform from outside the system.

As of December 31 2014, the Company has 125 branched, 1 297 sub-branches, a branch level exclusive institution (Credit Card Center), a representative office, 2 791 self-service banking, 10 604 cash self-service equipment (including 2 364 Automatic Teller Machines and 8 240 self-service circulation machines, two subsidiaries—CMB leasing and investment funds, a joint venture company—CIGNA in over 120 cities in Mainland China; has Wing Lung Bank, China Merchants Bank International, and other subsidiaries, as well as a branch (Hong Kong Branch) in Hong Kong; has a New York Branch and representative offices in the United States; has a Singapore Branch in Singapore; has representatives in London and Taipei. The Company has 1 941 domestic and overseas correspondent bank in 110 countries (including China). In the British "The Banker" released "2014 Top 500 World Banks" ranking list, China Merchants Bank was 44th, ranking first in the national small and medium-sized banks; was 36th in "2014 Top 1 000 World Banks" list.

By the end of 2014, the group total assets is 4 731.83 billion Chinese Yuan (yuan), increasing 17.81% than it in the beginning of that year; total customer deposits is 3 304.44 billion yuan, increasing 19.07% than it in the beginning of that year; total loans and advances is 2 513.92 billion yuan, increasing 14.42% than it in the beginning of that year. Net profit attributable to shareholders belonging the bank is 55.91 billion yuan, an increase of 8.06%; Average return on equity after tax attributable to shareholders belonging the bank is 19.28%, down 2.94 percentage points. Cost to income ratio is 30.54%, compared with the previous year, down 3.82 percentage points. Under the advanced approach, capital adequacy ratio is 12.38%, non-performing loan ratio was 1.11%, non-performing loan coverage ratio is 233.42%.

Bank 中国光大银行
共享阳光 · 创新生活

中国光大银行
China Everbright Bank Company Limited

中国光大银行成立于1992年8月，总部设在北京，是经国务院批复并经人民银行批准设立的金融企业，为客户提供全面的商业银行产品与服务。

自成立以来，伴随着中国金融业的发展进程，中国光大银行不断开拓创新，锐意进取，在为社会提供优质金融服务的同时，取得了良好的经营业绩，在综合经营、公司业务、国际业务、理财业务、电子银行业务等方面培育了较强的比较竞争优势，基本形成了各主要业务条线均衡发展、零售业务贡献度不断提升、风险管理逐步完善、创新能力日益增强的经营格局。2010年8月18日，中国光大银行在上海证券交易所成功上市，走上更有内涵的发展之路；2013年12月20日，中国光大银行在香港联交所主板成功上市，迎来又一个崭新的发展阶段。

截至2014年末，中国光大银行资产总额为27 370.10亿元，负债总额为25 575.27亿元，全年实现营业收入785.31亿元，净利润289.28亿元。在英国《银行家》杂志2014年发布的“世界1 000家大银行”排名中，中国光大银行位列第59。

China Everbright Bank was established in August 1992, headquartered in Beijing. It is a financial enterprise, approved by the State Council and the People's Bank of China, providing customers with comprehensive commercial banking products and services.

Since its inception, with the development of China's financial sector. China Everbright Bank continuous pioneering, innovative, forge ahead, not only providing quality financial services for the community but also achieved good operating results. It cultivates a strong comparative advantage in the comprehensive management, business, international business, financial business, electronic banking, etc.. The basic structure of business formed with the balanced development of the main business lines, the contribution of retail business rising, the gradual improvement of risk management, and the growing ability of innovation. On August 18, 2010, China Everbright Bank successfully listed on the Shanghai Stock Exchange, on the way of more deep developing; On December 20, 2013, China Everbright Bank successfully listed on the Hong Kong Stock Exchange main board, which is a new stage of development.

By the end of 2014, China Everbright Bank's total assets is 2 737.01 billion Chinese yuan (yuan), total liabilities is 2 557.53 billion yuan, full-year operating income is 78.53 billion yuan, net profit is 28.93 billion yuan. In the British "The Banker" released "2014 Top 1 000 World Banks" ranking list, China Everbright Bank was 59th.

华夏银行股份有限公司
Hua Xia Bank Co., Limited

华夏银行1992年10月在北京成立；1995年3月，实行股份制改造；2003年9月，首次公开发行股票并上市交易（股票代码：600015），成为全国第五家上市银行；2005年10月，成功引进德意志银行为国际战略投资者；2008年10月、2011年4月，先后两次顺利完成非公开发行股票。

截至2014年末，华夏银行在80 个地级以上城市设立了34家一级分行、38家二级分行和10家异地支行，营业网点达到590家，与境外1 000多家银行建立了代理业务关系，代理行网络遍及五大洲115个国家和地区的329个城市，建成了覆盖全球主要贸易区的结算网络；资产规模稳步增长，盈利能力持续提升，业务结构不断优化，服务质效进一步提高，规范运营扎实推进，保持了良好的发展势头。在2014年7月出版的英国《银行家》杂志世界1 000家大银行评选中，华夏银行按资产规模排名第90名；在2014年中国企业500强中排名第158、中国服务业企业500强排名第58。

Hua Xia Bank was established in Beijing in October 1992; in March 1995, implementing a joint-stock transformation; in September 2003, it became the fifth listed bank because of the initial public offering and listing transaction (stock code:600015）; in October 2005, the successful introduction of Deutche Bank for International strategic investors; in October 2008 and April 2011, has successfully completed non-public offering respectively.

By the end of 2014, Hua Xia Bank set up 34 primary branches, 38 secondary branches, 10 branches in different places, and 590 outlets in 80 prefecture-level cities. It built a settlement network covering the major global trade zones across 329 cities in over 115 countries and region in five continents by establishing correspondent banking relationships with more than 1 000 overseas banks. Hua Xia Bank maintained a good momentum of development based on the steady growth in asset size, continuing improvement in profitability, constantly optimization in business structure, further improvement in service quality, and solid progress in standardize operations. In July 2014, the British “The Banker” released “Top 1 000 World Banks” ranking list, Hua Xia Bank was 90th in assets; in 2014, ranked 158th among Top 500 Chinese Enterprises and ranked 58th among Top 500 Chinese Service Industry Enterprises.

广发银行|CGB

广发银行股份有限公司
China Guangfa Bank Co., Ltd

广发银行成立于1988年，是国内首批组建的股份制商业银行之一。2014年，在英国《银行家》杂志全球1 000家大银行排名中，本行按一级资本排名第108。

截至2014年末，广发银行资产1.65万亿元，在境内16个省（直辖市、自治区）76个地级及地级以上城市和澳门特别行政区设立了36家分行、700家营业机构、220家“小企业金融中心”、27家智能银行，个人网银客户规模超1 300万户，信用卡发卡量3 450多万张，与全球125个国家和地区的1 671家银行总部及其分支机构建立了代理行关系，是首家与中国银联开展多渠道多应用电子支付战略合作的金融机构。

China Guangfa Bank Co., Ltd. was establish in 1988, is one of the first joint-stock commercial banks in China. In 2014, in the British “The Banker” released “Top 1000 World Banks” ranking list, it was 108th in tier one capital ranking.

By the end of 2014, China Guangfa Bank’s total assets is 1.65 trillion Chinese Yuan. In the 76 prefecture-level and above prefecture-level cities across territory of 16 provinces (municipalities directly under the central government, autonomous regions) and Macao Special Administrative Region, there are 36 branches, 700 business organizations, 220 “small business financial center”, 27 smart banking, over 1,300 million personal online banking customers, issuing more than 34.5 million credit cards. Guangdong Development Bank established correspondent bank relationship with 1,671 bank headquarters and their branches in 125 countries and regions, being the first financial institution has strategic cooperation with China UnionPay to carry our multi-channel and multi-application electronic payment.

平安银行股份有限公司
Ping An Bank Co., Ltd.

平安银行股份有限公司（股票代码：000001）是由原深圳发展银行股份有限公司以吸收合并原平安银行股份有限公司的方式完成两行整合并更名而来，是中国首家向公众发行股票并公开上市的全国性股份制商业银行，总部设于深圳。中国平安保险（集团）股份有限公司及其子公司为平安银行的控股股东。截至2014年12月末，本行共有43家分行，747家营业机构，其中，社区支行 129家。

截至2014年12月末，本行资产总额21 864.59亿元，较年初增长15.58%；各项存款余额15 331.83亿元，较年初增加3 161.81亿元，增幅25.98%，增量为上年全年增量的1.6倍，增速居同业领先地位，市场份额提升；各项贷款（含贴现）余额突破万亿元，达10 247.34亿元，较年初增长20.94%；营业收入734.07亿元，同比增长40.66%，其中非利息净收入203.61亿元，同比增长77.04%；准备前营业利润412.57亿元，同比增长53.69%；净利润198.02亿元，同比增长30.01%；资本充足率10.86%、一级资本充足率8.64%、核心一级资本充足率8.64%。

Ping An Bank Corporation Limited (abbreviation: Ping An Bank, stock abbreviation: Ping An Bank (Stock Code: 000001) is the integration of the former Shenzhen Development Bank absorbing and merging the former Ping An Corporation Limited, headquartered in Shenzhen. It is the first national joint-stock commercial bank that issuing public offering and publicly listed in the stock market. China Ping An Insurance (Group) Corporation Limited and its subsidiaries are the controlling shareholder of Ping An Bank. At the end of December 2014, the bank has 43 branches, 747 business organizations, including 129 community branches.

At the end of December 2014, the bank's total assets is 2 186.46 billion Chinese Yuan (yuan), increasing 15.58% than the beginning of that year; the balance of deposits is 1 533.18 billion yuan, representing an increase of 316.18 billion yuan and 25.98% compared with it in the beginning of that year, the increment is 1.6 times than that of the previous year, the growth rate is in leading position in the whole industry and market share increased; the balance of loans (including discount) exceeds trillion, up to 1 024.73 billion yuan, increases 20.94% than it in the beginning of that year; operating income is 73.41 billion yuan, increases 40.66% year-on-year, of which non-interest net income is 20.36 billion yuan. Increases 77.04% year-on-year; prepare before operating profits is 41.26 billion yuan, increases 53.69% year-on-year; net profit is 19.8 billion yuan, increases 30.01% year-on-year; capital adequacy ratio is 10.86%, tier one capital adequacy ratio is 8.64%, and core tier one capital adequacy ratio is 8.64%.

兴业银行
INDUSTRIAL BANK CO.,LTD.

兴业银行股份有限公司
Industrial Bank Co., Ltd.

兴业银行成立于1988年8月，是经国务院、中国人民银行批准成立的首批股份制商业银行之一，总行设在福建省福州市，2007年2月5日正式在上海证券交易所挂牌上市（股票代码：601166），注册资本190.52亿元。

兴业银行主要经营范围包括：吸收公众存款；发放短期、中期和长期贷款；办理国内外结算；办理票据承兑与贴现；发行金融债券；代理发行、代理兑付、承销政府债券；买卖政府债券、金融债券；代理发行股票以外的有价证券；买卖、代理买卖股票以外的有价证券；资产托管业务；从事同业拆借；买卖、代理买卖外汇；结汇、售汇业务；从事银行卡业务；提供信用证服务及担保；代理收付款项及代理保险业务；提供保管箱服务；财务顾问、资信调查、咨询、见证业务；经中国银行业监督管理机构批准的其他业务。

开业二十多年来，兴业银行始终坚持“真诚服务，相伴成长”的经营理念，致力于为客户提供全面、优质、高效的金融服务。根据2014年业绩快报，截至2014年12月31日，兴业银行资产总额达4.41万亿元，股东权益2 450亿元，全年实现归属于母公司股东的净利润471.08亿元。

目前，兴业银行已在全国各主要城市设立了108家分行、1 435家分支机构；旗下拥有兴业国际信托、兴业金融租赁、兴业基金、兴业消费金融、兴业财富和兴业国信资产管理等子公司，形成以银行为主体，涵盖信托、租赁、基金、消费金融、期货、资产管理等在内的现代金融服务集团。建立了网上银行“在线兴业”（www.cib.com.cn）、电话银行“95561”、手机银行“无线兴业”（wap.cib.com.cn）和直销银行（http://directbank.cib.com.cn/），与全球1 600多家银行建立了代理行关系。

外汇业务开展状况

兴业银行于2013年度和2014年度连续两年荣获“最佳跨境金融服务银行”和“最佳外汇金融银行”称号，在全球拥有1 600多家代理行；交易币种除美元、港元、日元、欧元等主要贸易结算币种外，还提供澳元、瑞士法郎、加拿大元、英镑、瑞典克朗、新加坡元等币种的结算、融资及资金交易等服务。2014年全年，本行本外币国际结算量已超1 100亿美元，国际贸易融资额超470亿美元，结算融资率高达42.72%。

兴业银行拥有一个专业能力强、从业经验丰富的外汇业务资深团队，已有从业人员200余人。总行层面，在贸易金融部下设国际业务中心，全面协调推进全行国际业务的发展；在支付结算部设立单证处理中心，负责全面外汇单证业务的集中处理；在金融市场部设立外汇资金交易团队，负责外汇即远期外汇买卖、结售汇、货币掉期与利率掉期等各种外汇衍生品交易。在分行方面，分行贸易金融部内嵌国际业务团队，具体负责分行层面的营销推进、国际结算和客户服务。

外汇业务经营范围

国际结算（包括汇款、托收、信用证、兴业单证通、兴业E通关）、对外担保（海关税费电子支付担保、付款保函、融资性保函、留置金保函、履约保函、融资租赁保函、投标保函、现汇偿还的补偿贸易保函、预付款保函、质量/维修保函）、国际贸易融资（打包贷款、出口押汇、出口信保项下押汇、出口单保理、出口双保理、出口订单融资、出口退税质押融资、福费廷、进口控货融资、提货担保、进口押汇、进口保理、进口代付）、外汇资金类业务（即期结售汇、远期结售汇、外汇买卖、人民币与外汇期权、人民币与外汇掉期、外币利率互换）。

特色业务

兴业银行为客户提供全门类跨境金融服务，产品结构个性化突出，秉承传统，不断超越，先后为数家境外法人提供本外币跨境项目贷款，并成为首家跨境项目独立融资银行；以客为本，客户需求即我行动力，为制造型、交易型企业的贸易融资及投融资量身定制结构化应付应收账款融资方案，成为首家与境外代理行合作开展此项业务的银行；精诚合作，善用境外分行和代理行网络，为客户提供全方位跨境金融服务。兴业银行利用自身在外汇资金交易、代理行网络、境外香港分行以及上海自贸区分行的平台优势以及融资领域的专业服务能力，为各种类型的企业提供了有针对性的涵盖跨境融资、结算、存款、资金交易等服务的金融服务方案，满足该类型企业个性化需求。例如，向进出口量较大的进料加工企业提供本外币资金收付管理支持，并通过资产负债管理、外币间或本外币间的资金交易产品实现财务上规避汇率风险实现保值增值的服务方案；向出口型企业提供较低成本的跨境人民币信用证交叉币种融资、外保直贷等产品并辅以外币掉期等产品，为企业节约财务成本。

Founded in August 1988 and headquartered in Fuzhou, Fujian Province, Industrial Bank (CIB) is one of the first groups of joint-stock commercial banks approved by the State Council and the People's Bank of China. On February 5, 2007, CIB was listed on Shanghai Stock Exchange (Stock Code: 601166) with registered capital amounting to RMB 19.052 billion.

The main business scope of CIB covers: deposits taking; provision of short-medium- and long-term loans; domestic and international settlement; bills acceptance and discounting; issue of financial bonds; agency issue, cashing and underwriting of government bonds; trading of government bonds and financial bonds; agency issue of negotiable securities except stock; trading and agency trading of negotiable securities except stock; asset custody; inter-bank borrowing and lending; trading or agency trading of foreign exchange; settlement and sales of foreign exchange; bank card business; L/C services and guarantee; agency collections and payments and agency insurance; safe-box services, financial consulting, credit investigation, consulting, witness business and other banking activities approved by the China's Banking Regulatory Commission.

For over 20 years since its establishment, CIB has been advocating the business philosophy of "Growing Together with Sincere Service" and endeavoring to offer comprehensive, top-quality, and efficient financial services for customers. According to the 2014 performance bulletin, by December 31, 2014, the total assets of CIB hit RMB 4.41trillion, the shareholders' equity RMB 245 billion, and the realized net profits attributable to shareholders of the parent company RMB 47.108 billion.

Now, CIB has established 108 branches and 1 435 sub-branches in major cities across China. With a number of subsidiaries and affiliates, including Industrial

International Trust, Industrial Financial Leasing, Industrial Fund, Industrial Consumer Finance, Industrial Wealth Management and Industrial Asset Management, CIB has grown into a modern financial service group focusing on the principal banking businesses and covering trust, lease, fund, securities, consumer finance, futures and assets management. CIB has established an online banking platform "Online CIB" (www.cib.com.cn), a telephone banking platform "95561", a mobile banking system "Wireless CIB" (wap.cib.com.cn) and a direct banking platform (http://directbank.cib.com.cn/), and has formed correspondent relationships with over 1 600 banks worldwide.

CIB kept improving its market position and brand image steadily in 2014, and made its presence stably in the Global Top 50 Banks (ranking of the British magazine, The Banker), and Fortune Global 500 (ranking of the US magazine, Fortune), and the global top 200 of listed companies (the ranking of US magazine, Forbes). In various appraisals organized by authoritative institutions both at home and abroad, CIB has also won a number of honors successively, such as the Best Chinese-funded ban, the Best Bank of Strategic Innovation, the Best Green Bank, the Bank with the Best Internet Finance Platform, the Best Bank in Inclusive Finance Practices, the Best Listed Company for Contribution in Social Responsibility, China Charity Award for Outstanding Contribution (Organization), and China Best Employer.

The Industrial Bank has won "The Best Cross-Border Financial Services Bank" and "The Best Foreign Exchange Bank" for the year of 2013 and 2014. It has more than 1 600 corresponding banks in the world, and provides the cross—border settlement, financing and capital trading services in Australian dollar, the SWISS Franc, Canadian dollar, the GBP, the SEK and the Singapore dollar except the US dollar, the HK dollar, the Yen, the EURO dollar as the major trading currency. In the year of 2014, the amount of the cross-border trading has exceeded 110 billion US dollars, and the International trade financing amount has over 47 billion US dollars, which is accounted for 42.72% of the whole cross-border trading amount.

The Industrial Bank has a strong professional and rich experience foreign exchange business senior team which has more than 200 employees now. In the head office, there is a international business center of the trade financing.

Department, which coordinates and promotes the comprehensive development of the cross-border trade business of the bank; The documents processing center of the payment and settlement department is responsible for processing all business exchange documents of the bank. Meanwhile, the foreign exchange transaction team of the financial market department is in charge of the foreign exchange forward trading.

Foreign exchange, currency swaps, the interest rate swaps and other foreign exchange derivatives trading. In the branch, the international business team embedded in the trade financing department is responsible for the marketing, International.

Settlement and customer servives.

Business Scope

International Settlement (including remittance, collection, credit, Industrial Easy trade, IB E-customs clearance), Guarantee (Guarantee for Electronic payment of Customs Tariffs and Fees, Payment guarantee, Financing guarantee, Retention Money Guarantee, Performance guarantee, Guarantee for financing lease, tender guarantee, Guarantee for Compensation Trade with Spot Exchange Repayment guarantee, Advance Payment Guarantee, Quality/Maintenance Guarantee), International trade financing (Package Loan, Export bill purchase, Export credit insurance bill purchase, Export Factoring, Export two factor, Export order financing, Export Tax Rebate Pledged Financing, Forfaiting, Import Goods Control Financing, Guarantee for Delivery, Import bill purchase, Import Factoring, Import Refinancing), Foreign exchange fund business (Spot foreign exchange, Forward foreign exchange, RMB and foreign exchange option, RMB and foreign exchange swap, Foreign currency interest rate swap).

Industrial bank provides all categories of cross-border financial services for customers, the financial instruments of IB are individual, the tradition has been carried on and transcend. It has offered RMB and foreign currency cross-border loans for numbers of overseas customers, and it is the first independent cross-border project financing bank.

Customer-oriented, the customer demand is our action, we do tailor-making structured receivable payable accounts financing scheme for manufacturing and trading enterprise, has become the first bank that cooperated with overseas corresponding bank to carry out this business. Sincerely cooperation, we provide full range of cross-border financial services for customers with overseas branches and corresponding banks net.

The Industrial Bank provides targeted financial services to meet the personalized needs for all type of enterprises with its own platform advantages in foreign exchange transactions, corresponding network, Hong Kong branch and Shanghai branch of the FTA, and also the professional financing services capabilities. Including Cross-border financing, settlement, deposit, and other services.

For example, It provides the RMB and foreign currency payment management supporting to the bigger import and export feed processing enterprises, realizing keeping value and avoid exchange rate risks through asset liability management or RMB and foreign currency transactions. We also provides low cost of cross-border RMB credit of cross currency financing, foreign direct loan to the export-oriented enterprises, supplemented by foreign currency swap and other products, for the enterprise financial cost savings.

中国民生银行股份有限公司
China Minsheng Banking Corp., Ltd.

中国民生银行于1996年1月12日在北京正式成立，是中国首家主要由非公有制企业入股的全国性股份制商业银行。多种经济成分在中国金融业的涉足和实现规范的现代企业制度，使中国民生银行有别于国有银行和其他商业银行，而为国内外经济界、金融界所关注。

2000年12月19日，中国民生银行A股股票（600016）在上海证券交易所挂牌上市。2003年3月18日，中国民生银行40亿元可转换公司债券在上交所正式挂牌交易。2004年11月8日，中国民生银行通过银行间债券市场成功发行了58亿元人民币次级债券，成为中国第一家在全国银行间债券市场成功私募发行次级债券的商业银行。2005年10月26日，民生银行成功完成股权分置改革，成为国内首家完成股权分置改革的商业银行。2009年11月26日，中国民生银行在香港交易所挂牌上市。

截至2014年末，中国民生银行实现净利润445.46亿元，加权平均净资产收益率达到20.41%。截至2014年末，中国民生银行在全国38个城市设立了39家分行，机构总数量为 1 021个。

China Minsheng Bank was officially established in Beijing on January 12, 1996. It is the first national joint-stock commercial bank that most of shareholders are non-public enterprises. A variety of economic sectors involved in China's financial industry and achieves a standardized modern enterprise system, makes China Minsheng Bank different from the state-owned banks, drawing more economic and financial attention at home and abroad.

On December 19, 2000, China Minsheng Bank A share (600016) listed on the Shanghai Stock Exchange. On March 18, 2003, China Minsheng Bank 4 billion Chinese Yuan (yuan) convertible bonds officially listed on the Shanghai Stock Exchange. On

November 8, 2004, China Minsheng Bank became the first commercial bank that successfully issuing 5.8 billion yuan subordinated bonds through inter-bank bond market. On October 26, 2005, China Minsheng Bank became the first commercial bank that successfully completed the split share reform. On November 26, 2009, China Minsheng Bank listed on the Hong Kong Stock Exchange.

By the end of 2014, China Minsheng Band's net profit is 44.55 billion Chinese Yuan, the weighted average return on equity reached 20.41%.

By the end of 2014, China Minsheng Bank set up 39 branches, and 1 021 agencies in 38 cities across the country.

上海浦东发展银行

Shanghai Pudong Development Bank Co., Ltd.

上海浦东发展银行股份有限公司是1992年8月28日经中国人民银行批准设立、1993年1月9日开业、1999年在上海证券交易所挂牌上市（股票代码：600000）的全国性股份制商业银行，总行设在上海。目前，注册资本金186.53亿元。

截至2014年12月末，公司总资产规模达41 959亿元，各项贷款余额20 284亿元，各项存款余额27 240亿元，2014年实现归属于上市公司股东的净利润470.26亿元。目前，浦发银行已在全国设立了40家一级分行、逾1 200家营业机构，拥有超过4.2万名员工。

2014年2月，英国《银行家》杂志发布“全球银行品牌500强”榜单，浦发银行排名第75位，列中资银行第10位；同年5月，《福布斯》杂志发布全球企业2 000强榜单，浦发银行居榜单第130位，居上榜中资企业第16位，居上榜中资银行第9位；6月，英国《银行家》杂志发布世界银行1 000强排名，根据核心资本，浦发银行排名全球第44位，位居上榜中资银行第8位；同时，浦发银行标普评级：长期信用评级“BBB+”、短期信用评级“A-2”、长期大中华区信用体系评级“cnA+”以及短期大中华区信用体系评级“cnA-1”；7月，美国《财富》杂志发布财富世界500强排行，浦发银行列第383位，居上榜中资企业第81位和上榜中资银行第9位；12月，穆迪投资者服务公司（穆迪）发布浦发银行信用评级报告，长期存款评级上调至Baa1，短期存款评级上调至Prime-2，财务实力评级由D上调至D+（对应的基础信用评估由ba2上调至ba1），评级前景展望均为稳定。

2012年7月，RepuTex（崇德）发布“恒生内地上市公司可持续发展指数十强”，浦发银行居第3位，可持续发展评级A；2014年6月浦发银行获评中国银行业协会“2013年度最佳绿色金融奖”；2014年12月，浦发银行先后荣获2014年中国企业公民评选“最佳股东回馈奖”、2014年中国银行业企业公众透明度评价“最佳社会责任报告奖”；2014年12月，润灵环球责任评级发布《2014A股上市公司企业社会责任报告评级数据库》，浦发银行评级等级为AA，评级展望为积极。

Shanghai Pudong Development Bank Corporation Limited was approved the establishment by the People's Bank of China on August 28, 1992, opened on January 9, 1993, listed on the Shanghai Stock Exchange (stock code: 600000) in 1991. It is a national joint-stock commercial bank, headquartered in Shanghai. At present, the registered capital is 18.65 billion Yuan.

To the end of December 2014, the company's total asset is 4195.9 billion Chinese Yuan (yuan), the balance of loans is 2 028.4 billion yuan, the balance of deposits is 2 724 billion yuan, and attributing net profit to shareholders of listed companies is 47.03 billion yuan. At present, Shanghai Pudong Development Bank has set up 40 primary branches, more than 1 200 business organization, with more than 42 000 employees.

In February 2014, in the British "The Bank" released " Top 500 World Banks" ranking list, Shanghai Pudong Development Bank was 75th and 10th in Chinese banks; in May of the same year, "Forbes" released "Global 2 000 Companies", Shanghai Pudong Development Banks was 130th, 16th in Chinese enterprises, and 9th in Chinese banks; in June, in the in the British "The Bank" released " Top 1 000 World Banks" ranking list, Shanghai Pudong Development Banks was 44th according to the core capital, and 8th in Chinese banks; at the same time, Shanghai Pudong Development Band Standard & Poor's rating: long-term credit rating is "BBB+", short-term credit rating is "A-2", long-term credit rating system in greater China rate it as "cnA+:, and short-term credit rating system in greater China rate it as "cnA-1"; in July, the United States "Fortune" published wealth ranking of the world top 500, Pudong Development Bank was 383rd, 81st in Chinese enterprises, and 9th in Chinese banks; in December, Moody's Investor Service (Moody's) issued Shanghai Pudong Development Bank credit rating report—raised long-term deposit rating to Baa1, raised short-term deposit rating Prime-2, financial strength rating by D to D+ (corresponding to raise the basis of credit assessment by ba2 to ba1), the rating oulook is stable.

In July 2012, ReuTex (Zonta) issued the "Hang Seng mainland listed top 10 companies sustainable development index", Shanghai Pudong Development was 3rd, the sustainable development rating A grade; in June 2014, Shanghai Pudong Development Banks won the "2013 Best Green Finance Award"; in December 2014, Shanghai Pudong Development Bank won the 2014 China Corporate Citizen awarded "Best For Shareholders", 2014 China banking corporate publicly and transparently evaluate it as "Best Social Responsibility Reporting Award"; in December 2014, Run Ling global responsibility rating issued "2014 social responsibility report rating database of A share listed companies corporate", Shanghai Pudong Development Bank was rated AA, and rating outlook is positive.

HF EGF 恒丰银行

恒丰银行股份有限公司
Evergrowing Bank Co., Limited

恒丰银行于2003年经中国人民银行批准，经过整体股份制改造，成为一家全国性股份制商业银行，英文名称为Evergrowing Bank Co., Ltd.，总部设在山东省烟台市。目前，设有青岛分行、济南分行、南京分行、杭州分行、成都分行、重庆分行、烟台分行、福州分行、昆明分行、西安分行、宁波分行等11家一级分行，在苏州、绍兴、东营、义乌、济宁、滨州、乐山、温州、无锡、达州、南充、聊城、德州、潍坊、南通等地设立15家二级分行，共148家分支机构。2008年6月成功引进新加坡大华银行为战略投资者。

截至2014年末，公司总资产8 486亿元；一般存款余额4 766亿元；各项贷款余额2 390亿元；实现净利润71.70亿元。平均总资产收益率0.87%，加权平均净资产收益率19.54%，成本收入比29.85%，资产流动性比例（人民币）55.04%，资本充足率（新口径）11.14%，存贷款比例50.14%，不良贷款率0.94%，拨备覆盖率266.61%，拨贷比2.51%。

Evergrowing Bank is a national joint-stock commercial bank by overall shareholding system reform and approved by the people's bank of China in 2003. Evergrowing Bank is its English name. It headquartered in Yantai, Shandong. At present, there are 11 primary branches located in Qingdao, Jinan, Nanjing, Hangzhou, Chengdu, Chongqing, Yantai, Fuzhou, Kunming, Xi'an, and Ningbo respectively; there are 15 secondary branches located in Suzhou, Shaoxing, Dongying, Yiwu, Jining, Binzhou, Leshan, Wenzhou, Wuxi, Dazhou, Nanchong, Liaocheng, Dezhou, Weifang, and Nantong respectively, and 148 total branches. In June 2008, Evergrowing Bank sucessfully introduced UOB Singapore as a strategic investor.

By the end of 2014, the company's total asset is 848.6 billion Chines Yuan (yuan), the balance of general deposits is 476.6 billion yuan; the balance of loans is 239 billion yuan, and net profit is 7.17 billion yuan. Average return on assets yields 0.87%, weighted average net assets yields 19.54%, cost-to-income ratio is 29.85%, liquidity ratio (RMB) is 55.04%, capital adequacy ratio (new standard) is 11.14%, loan-to-deposit ratio is 50.14%, non-performing loan ratio is 0.94%, provision coverage is 266.61%, and loans ratio is 2.51%.

浙商银行
CHINA ZHESHANG BANK

浙商银行股份有限公司
China Zheshang Bank Co., Ltd.

浙商银行是经中国银监会批准设立的全国性股份制商业银行，全称为浙商银行股份有限公司，英文全称为China Zheshang Bank Co.，Ltd.，英文简称CZB。浙商银行前身为浙江商业银行，是一家于1993年在宁波成立的中外合资银行，2004年6月30日，经中国银监会批准，重组、更名、迁址，改制为现在的浙商银行，并于2004年8月18日正式开业，总行设在浙江省杭州市。截至2014年末，浙商银行注册资本115亿元，监管资本410亿元，总资产6 700亿元，各项存款3 600亿元，各项贷款2 600亿元。在2014年英国《银行家》杂志公布的“全球银行业1 000强”榜单中列第208位。中诚信国际给予浙商银行AAA主体信用评级，在同类银行中居先进水平。浙商银行目前已在 11个省市和浙江省内全部省辖市设立（筹建）了130余家机构，全国性机构体系初步形成。国际业务方面，积极拓宽境外机构合作渠道，目前已有海外代理行逾950家，并与多家境外同业建立了战略合作关系。国际结算量和跨境人民币等业务实现了快速增长。截至2014年末，全行不良贷款率为0.88%，居同业优秀水平；贷款拨备覆盖率292.89%，贷款拨备率2.59%，拨备充足。

China Zheshang Bank is a national joint-stock commercial bank approved by the China Banking Regulatory Commission (CBRC), called the China Zheshang Bank Corporation Limited, referred to as CZB. Zheshang bank, formerly known as Zhejiang Commercial Bank which is a joint venture bank established in 1993 in Ningbo. On June 30, 2014, CBRC approved it restructuring, changing its name, moving to a new location and became China Zheshang Bank. China Zheshang Bank officially opened on August 18, 2004, headquartered in Hangzhou, Zhejiang. By the end of 2014, China Zheshang

Bank's registered capital is 11.5 billion Chinese Yuan (yuan), regulatory capital is 41 billion yuan, total assets is 670 billion yuan, the balance of deposits is 360 billion yuan, the balance of loans is 260 billion yuan. In 2014, the British "The Bank" released "Top 1000 World Banks" ranking list, China Zheshang Bank was 208th. CCXI gave Zheshang Bank AAA credit rating, which is in the advanced level in similar banks. Zheshang bank set up (setting up) more than 130 institutions in 11 provinces and cities in Zhejiang, and national institutions system has a initial formation. International business, China Zheshang Bank actively expand cooperation methods with overseas institutions, there are more than 950 overseas agents, and built a strategic partnership with a number of foreign peers. Therefore, it achieved a rapid grownth on international settlement, cross-border RMB business, and so on. By the end of 2014, non-performing loan ratio is 0.88% in the whole bank, which is in the excellent level in the industry, loan provision coverage is 292.89%, loan-loss provisioning ratio is 2.59%, having adequate reserve.

渤海银行股份有限公司
China Bohai Bank Co., Ltd.

渤海银行是1996年以来获国务院批准新设立的第一家全国性股份制商业银行，是第一家在发起设立阶段就引入境外战略投资者的中资商业银行，也是第一家总部设在天津的全国性股份制商业银行。本行由天津泰达投资控股有限公司、渣打银行（香港）有限公司、中国远洋运输（集团）总公司、国家开发投资公司、宝钢集团有限公司、天津信托有限责任公司和天津商汇投资（控股）有限公司等7家股东发起设立，注册资本总额85亿元人民币。2005年12月30日成立，2006年2月正式对外营业。

截至2014年末，本行资产总额6 671.48亿元，比年初增长17.41%；负债总额6 376.51亿元，比年初增长17.21%；实现净利润50.31亿元，比上年增长10.28%；不良贷款率为1.20%。

China Bohai Bank (the Bank) is the first national joint-stock commercial bank founded with the approval of the State Council since 1996. It is also the first Chinese-funded commercial bank introducing overseas strategic investors at the establishment stage and the first national joint-stock commercial bank headquartered in Tianjin. The Bank was set up by its seven shareholders, namely, TEDA Investment Holding Co., Ltd., Standard Chartered Bank (Hong Kong) Limited, China Ocean Shipping (Group) Company, State Development & Investment Corporation, Baosteel Group Corporation, Tianjin Trust Co., Ltd. and Tianjin Shanghui Investment (Holding) Co., Ltd., with the total registered capital of RMB8.5 billion. The Bank was established on December 30, 2005 and was officially opened in February, 2006.

As at the end of 2014, the Bank's total assets and total liabilities amounted to RMB 667.148 million and RMB 637.651 million respectively, representing a respective increase of 17.41% and 17.21% over the beginning of the year. Net profit stood at RMB 5.031 million, up by10.28% over the previous year. NPL ratio stood at 1.20%.

中国进出口银行
The Export-Import Bank of China

中国进出口银行成立于1994年，是直属国务院领导的、政府全资拥有的国家银行，其国际信用评级与国家主权评级一致。中国进出口银行总部设在北京。截至2014年末，在国内设有24家营业性分支机构；在境外设有巴黎分行、东南非代表处和圣彼得堡代表处；与境内外1 355家银行的总分支机构建立了代理行关系，代理行网络覆盖全球160多个国家和地区。

中国进出口银行的主要职责是为扩大我国机电产品、成套设备和高新技术产品进出口，推动有比较优势的企业开展对外承包工程和境外投资，促进对外关系发展和国际经贸合作，提供金融服务。

Founded in 1994, the Export-Import Bank of China is a state bank solely owned by the Chinese government and under the direct leadership of the State Council. Its international credit ratings are the same as China's sovereign ratings. The Bank is headquartered in Beijing. By the end of 2014, the Bank has established 24 domestic business branches, and three overseas institutions, namely, the Paris Branch, Representative Office for Southern and Eastern Africa, and St. Petersburg Representative Office. It has established correspondent banking relationship with more than 1 355 banks in over 160 countries and regions worldwide.

The Bank's main mandate is to facilitate the export and import of Chinese mechanical and electronic products, complete sets of equipment and new-and high-tech products, assist Chinese companies with comparative advantages in their offshore project contracting and outbound investment, and promote international economic cooperation and trade.

中国农业发展银行
Agricultural Tural Development Bank of China

中国农业发展银行是直属国务院领导的我国唯一的一家农业政策性银行，1994年11月挂牌成立。主要职责是按照国家的法律、法规和方针、政策，以国家信用为基础，筹集资金，承担国家规定的农业政策性金融业务，代理财政支农资金的拨付，为农业和农村经济发展服务。全系统共有31个省级分行、300多个二级分行和1 800多个营业机构，服务网络遍布中国大陆地区。

Agricultural Tural Development Bank of China is the only agricultural policy bank and directly under the leadership of the State Council of China, established in November 1994. Its main responsibilities are raising funds based on national credit, undertaking state prescribed finance business under agricultural policies, being an agent that appropriating financial funds for supporting agriculture, and servicing for the development of agricultural and rural economy, in accordance with national laws, regulations, and guidelines. There are 31 provincial branches, more than 300 secondary branches and more than 1 800 business organizations, leading to the service network throughout Mainland China.

国家开发银行
CHINA DEVELOPMENT BANK

国家开发银行
China Development Bank Corporation

国家开发银行成立于1994年，经中华人民共和国国务院批准，于2008年12月11日改制为国家开发银行股份有限公司。

2014年，本行稳步推进内部流程梳理和组织架构调整，住宅金融事业部获批成立，加拉加斯代表处顺利开业。截至2014年末，本行境内分支机构包括一级分行37家，二级分行2家；境外分支机构包括1家分行和4家代表处；主要控股子公司4家。

境外代理行网络进一步发展，国际业务代理行全球分布初具规模，已与106个国家和地区的707家银行建立代理行关系，服务能力稳步提高。

截至2014年末，总资产10.3万亿元，同比增长26%，贷款余额7.94万亿元，不良贷款率0.65%，连续39个季度控制在1%以内，净利润977亿元，ROA1.06%，ROE15.63%，资本充足率11.88%，可持续发展和抗风险能力进一步增强。

China Development Bank was established in 1994. On December 11, 2008, in accordance with approval from the State Council of the People's Republic of China, China Development Bank was incorporated as China Development Bank Corporation.

In 2014, the Bank continued to support the enhancement of internal processes and its organizational structure. CDB Housing Finance as a business unit was established and the representative office in Caracas was opened. As of the end of 2014, the Bank had 37 tier-1 branches and two tier-2 branches within Mainland China and one branch and four representative offices in overseas locations. In addition, the Bank maintained controlling shareholder positions within four subsidiaries.

With correspondent banking relationships established with 707 banks in 106 overseas markets, the Bank has maintained a global network of correspondent banks that underpins steady improvements in the Bank's service capability.

As of the end of 2014, CDB's total assets had grown 26% year-on-year to RMB 10.3 trillion. The bank had an outstanding loan book of RMB 7.94 trillion, with a non-performing loan ratio of only 0.65%, maintaining an NPL of under 1% for a thirty-ninth consecutive quarter. CDB earned RMB 97.7 billion in net profits, with an ROA of 1.06%, an ROE of 15.63%, a capital adequacy ratio of 11.88%, and an increasingly robust capacity for sustainable business development and risk containment.

中国邮政储蓄银行
POSTAL SAVINGS BANK OF CHINA

中国邮政储蓄银行

中国邮政储蓄银行简介及贸易金融业务发展情况

一、中国邮政储蓄银行简介

2007年3月20日，根据国务院金融体制改革的总体安排，中国邮政储蓄银行有限责任公司正式成立。2012年1月21日，经国务院同意并经中国银监会批准，中国邮政储蓄银行有限责任公司依法整体变更为中国邮政储蓄银行股份有限公司（以下简称邮储银行）。

邮储银行自成立以来，在各级政府、金融监管部门以及社会各界的关心和支持下，坚持服务“三农”、服务中小企业、服务社区的市场定位，走出了一条普惠金融的商业可持续发展之路。目前，邮储银行已成为全国网点规模最大、覆盖面最广、服务客户数量最多的商业银行。通过近4万个营业网点，6.6万台ATM以及包括网上银行、手机银行、电话银行、电视银行、微博银行、微信银行和易信银行在内的电子金融服务网络，邮储银行为中国4.78亿客户提供丰富多样的金融产品和服务。截至2014年末，邮储银行资产总额达到6.3万亿元，资本回报率、利润增长率、不良贷款率、拨备覆盖率和经济利润率等关键指标达到银行同业优秀或良好水平。邮储银行始终坚持以客户为中心，不断创新产品和提升服务水平，“普惠金融先行者”的品牌形象深入人心。

近年来，邮储银行持续推进改革，完善公司治理架构，优化组织流程；抓住机遇谋求发展，用创新驱动业务增长，盈利能力在银行业中处于较高水平；同时，坚守服务“三农”、小微、社区的战略定位，践行普惠金融商业可持续发展的行动和成果，从而赢得了社会各界充分肯定。2014年，评级机构对中国邮政储蓄银行的主体信用评级和债券信用评级均为“AAA”。在英国《银行家》杂志“2014年全球银行1 000强排名”评选中，邮储银行按资产总额居第28位。由于邮储银行在履行社会责任方面所做出的成绩，荣获“年度社会责任引领人物”“最佳社会责任特殊贡献网点”“最佳普惠金融服务银行”等诸多奖项。

未来，邮储银行将继续依托网络优势，按照公司治理架构和商业银行管理要求，不断丰富业务品种，拓展营销渠道，提升服务能力，为广大客户提供更全面、更便捷、更高效的金融服务，打造成为一家资本充足、内控严密、营运安全、品牌卓越、竞争力强的大型零售商业银行。

二、贸易金融业务开展情况

邮储银行贸易金融业务自开展以来，不断丰富产品种类，充分发挥本外币联动和内外贸一体化优势，继续扩大业务规模，推出以进口代付、押汇、打包贷款、内保外贷、外保内贷、售后回租/回购中涉及的跨境担保业务、信用证融资为代表的跨境贸易融资产品体系，以财贷惠、信保、出口退税、银承质押为代表的本外币组合产品体系及以开证、托收、汇款、跨境人民币、NRA、边贸通、保函为代表的结算及中间业务产品体系，以应收账款质押、国内保理、保兑仓、先款/票后货、订单融资、动产质押为代表的供应链金融体系，开发了境外项目直接贷款、海外银团、跨境人民币融资等新产品，有力推动了本外币一体化的进程，提升了对客户精细化服务水平，配合了中国企业“走出去”的发展战略。通过跨境专项融资，实现了与企业的强强合作。为推动边贸结算特色业务发展，中国邮政储蓄银行以中国—东盟自贸区为服务重点，充分利用政策支持，加快跨境人民币业务的创新发展，与越南银行同业签订了边贸协议，建立了“边贸通”，并支持120多种小币种汇款业务。邮储银行为进一步加强同业合作，与境内外近800家银行建立了代理行关系，基本覆盖了境内外大型商业银行，涵盖了亚太地区、欧洲、北美、非洲、大洋洲等主要国家与地区，为国际业务的发展奠定了重要基础。

Postal Savings Bank of China Overview and the Trade Finance Business

I Postal Savings Bank of China Overview

In accordance with the master plan of the State Council for financial system reform, Postal Savings Bank of China was officially established on 20 March 2007. On 21 January 2012, with the approval of the State Council and China Banking Regulatory Commission (CBRC), Postal Savings Bank of China Limited Liability Company was restructured in its entirety into Postal Savings Bank of China Co., Ltd. (hereinafter referred to as PSBC).

Since PSBC established, with the support of different levels of the government, financial regulators and across the social spectrum, by committing its resources to focus on delivering services to support agricultural development, rural areas and farmers, promote small and medium-sized enterprises and serve the communities, PSBC has embarked on a route of "Inclusive Financial Services" that is also commercially sustainable. Currently, PSBC has become a commercial bank having outlets with the largest scale and widest coverage and serving maximum number of customers. PSBC provides a wide variety of financial products and services to 478 million customers throughout China via nearly 40 000 banking service outlets, more than 66 000 ATM machines, and technology-based online banking, mobile banking, telephone banking, TV banking, microblog banking, We Chat banking and ease credit banking options. At the end of 2014, PSBC has total assets of more than RMB 6.3 trillion, with the key indexes of return on capital, profit growth rate, non-performing loan ratio, provision coverage and rate of economic profit etc. reaching the level of excellent or good of banks. PSBC adheres to the tenet of focusing on customers, and is committed to product innovation and service level improvement, with an enduring brand image of "Pioneer of Inclusive Financial Services" deeply rooted in the minds of its customers.

In recent years, PSBC have kept pursuing the reform to improve the corporate governance structure and constantly deepen the organization process, and seizing opportunities to promote our development and creatively drove the business growth, with the profitability remaining at a higher level in banking industry; otherwise, PSBC were committed to the strategic positioning of serving agricultural development, rural areas and farmers, communities, actively engaged in the commercially sustainable "Inclusive Financial Services", and won full affirmation from the public.

In 2014, the corporate credit rating and bond credit rating of PSBC were given "AAA" by rating agencies, and PSBC ranked 28th in the banker's Top 1 000 World Banks list for 2014 in terms of total assets. PSBC has received a number of awards for its contributions, including "Leading Figure in Social Responsibility Management", "Best Social Responsibility Special Contribution Outlet", "Best Bank of Inclusive Financial Services", etc..

Relying on its network advantages, PSBC will be committed to forging ahead as a distinctive and competitive large retail commercial bank that is adequately capitalised, properly controlled, safely operating and offers full range of services through its continuous investments and efforts in diversifying its businesses and products, improving its service channels and enhancing its service capabilities in accordance with the governance structure of the company and management requirements of commercial banks, so as to better provide more comprehensive and convenient financial services to its valued clients across China.

Ⅱ Trade financing

PSBC constantly enriched product types and gave full play to advantages of linkage between RMB and foreign currencies as well as integration of internal and international trade, thus its business scale continued to expand. PSBC launched cross-border trade finance product system represented by cross-border guarantee business and financing by letter of credit (L/C) which are involved in agency payment for import, documentary bill, packing loan, overseas loan under domestic guarantee, domestic loan under overseas guarantee and after-sale leaseback/buy-back, RMB and foreign currency combination product system represented by Caidaihui, export credit insurance, export rebate and silver pledge, as well as settlement and intermediary service product system represented by issuing of L/C, collection, remitting, cross-border RMB settlement,

NRA, Bianmaotong and letter of guarantee and Supply chain finance system represented by pledging of accounts receivable, demosticfactor, bonded warehouse, prepayment, purchase-order financing, movable propertyand it developed new products such as overseas project direct loan, overseas bank consortium and cross-border RMB financing, which pushed forward integration of RMB and foreign currencies, improved delicacy services to our customers and promoted Chinese enterprises to “Go Global”. PSBC achieved strong cooperation with enterprises through special cross-border financing. PSBC promoted the development of distinctive business of border trade settlement. With emphasis on China-ASEAN FTA, PSBC made the best of policy support, accelerated the innovation and development of cross-border RMB business, entered into border trade agreement with the banks in Vietnam to establish Bianmaotong. Till now PSBC can serve the remittance business denominated in 120 minor foreign currency. It further enhanced interbank cooperation. As at the end of the reporting period, PSBC has established agent bank relationship with nearly 800 domestic and foreign banks, basically covering all the domestic and foreign large-scale commercial banks and encompassing major countries and regions in Asia Pacific, Europe, North America, Africa and Oceania, which laid a solid foundation for international business development.

城市商业银行

CHENGSHI SHANGYE YINHANG

北京银行
BANK OF BEIJING

北京银行股份有限公司
Bank of Beijing Co., Ltd.

北京银行成立于1996年，是一家中外资本融合的新型股份制银行。目前，已在北京、天津、上海、西安、深圳、杭州、长沙、南京、济南及南昌等十余个中心城市设立近400家分支机构，发起设立北京延庆、浙江文成及吉林农安北银村镇银行，成立香港和荷兰阿姆斯特丹代表处，发起设立国内首家消费金融公司——北银消费金融公司，首批试点合资设立中荷人寿保险公司，设立中加基金管理公司、北银金融租赁公司。

截至2014年12月末，北京银行资产达到1.52万亿元，实现净利润156亿元，成本收入比仅24.65%。ROA1.09%，ROE17.96%，不良贷款率0.86%，拨备覆盖率为324.22%，资本充足率11.08%，各项经营指标均达到国际银行业先进水平，公司价值排名中国区域性发展银行首位，品牌价值201.36亿元，一级资本排名全球千家大银行99位，首次跻身全球银行业百强，被誉为中国最具创新能力和发展潜力的中小银行。

Bank of Beijing Established in 1996, Bank of Beijing is a Sino-foreign joint stock commercial bank. Currently, the Bank has set up over 400 branches in Beijing, Tianjin, Shanghai, Xi'an, Shenzhen, Hangzhou, Changsha, Nanjing, Jinan and Nanchang. The Bank also initiated the establishment of BOB Yanqing Village Bank, BOB Wencheng Village Bank and BOB Nong'an Village Bank, set up representative offices in Hong Kong and Amsterdam, initiated Bank of Beijing Consumer Finance Company—the first consumer finance operation in China, established insurance joint venture ING-BoB Life Insurance as one of the first pilot, set up Bank of Beijing Scotiabank Asset Management Company and BoB Financial Leasing Company.

As of 2014 Dec-end, Bank of Beijing's total assets balance was RMB 1.52 trillion.

Net profit achieved 15.6 billion yuan, with a cost/income ratio at only 24.65%. It's ROA and ROE was 1.09% and 17.96% respectively. NPL ratio was 0.86% while provision coverage ratio was 324.22% and CAR 11.08%. The Bank holds a brand value of 20.136 billion yuan and ranks No.99 in terms of tier1 capital on the latest World Top 1 000 Banks list, becoming the world Top-100 for the first time. It creates leading performance of all financial indicators internationally. The Bank has built its excellence in terms of profit per capita and asset quality.

上海银行
Bank of Shanghai

上海银行股份有限公司
Bank of Shanghai Co., Ltd.

上海银行成立于1995年12月29日，是一家由国有股份、中资法人股份、外资股份及个人股份共同组成的股份制商业银行，总行位于上海。

近年来，上海银行以“精品银行”为战略愿景，以“精诚至上，信义立行”为企业核心价值观，以“总体形成特色、区域兼顾差异、局部凸显亮点”为指导思想，持续推进专业化经营和精细化管理，经营实力和发展能力明显提升。根据市场和自身优势，上海银行形成了“中小企业综合金融服务”、“城市居民财富管理和养老金融服务”、“金融市场领先交易服务”、“两岸三地跨境金融服务”以及“最佳在线金融服务”等特色定位，通过培育和塑造经营特色，推动结构调整和转型发展，增强可持续发展能力。

目前，上海银行在上海、宁波、南京、杭州、天津、成都、深圳、北京、苏州、无锡、绍兴、南通等地拥有分支机构和营业网点311个，设有自助银行211个，布放自助服务类终端设备2 167台，初步形成了覆盖长三角、环渤海、珠三角、中西部重点城市的网络布局框架。上海银行还发起设立闵行上银、衢江上银、江苏江宁上银和崇州上银村镇银行，发起成立上银基金管理有限公司，在香港地区设立上海银行（香港）有限公司，并与全球130多个国家和地区近1 600多家境内外银行及其分支机构建立了代理行关系。

成立20年来，上海银行市场竞争力和影响力不断提高，在英国《银行家》全球前1 000家银行中排名持续提升，2014年列全球银行业第130位，较2013年排名上升28位。多次被《亚洲银行家》杂志评为“中国最佳城市零售银行”，先后荣获“上海市著名商标”、“小企业优秀客户服务银行”、“全国再就业先进单位”、“全国银行间市场优秀交易成员”、“全国敬老模范单位”、“最佳企业形象奖”、“银团贷款最佳机构奖”等荣誉称号。

Bank of Shanghai Founded on December 29, 1995 and headquartered in Shanghai, Bank of Shanghai (hereinafter “the Bank”) is a joint-stock commercial bank formed by state-owned shares, Chinese corporation-owned shares, foreign corporation-owned shares, and individually-owned shares.

Since its foundation, the Bank has implemented sound operations, standardized management, regarded “sincerity and honesty foremost, and keeping good faith” as the enterprise’s core concept, “boutique bank” as its development vision, and “constructing general business characteristics considering regional differences, while forming unique business advantages” as its business guideline. The Bank has been speeding up on its way of distinctive development and striding on the road to form its own service characteristics. Based on its market position, the Bank has gradually formed its unique market position as “Comprehensive Financial Service for SMEs”, “Wealth Management and Pension Service for Citizens”, “Financial Market Transaction Service”, and “Best Financial Service Platform covering the Mainland, Hong Kong and Taiwan”. Besides, through cultivating and shaping the operation features, it boosts the structure adjustment and transformation development, and strengthens the sustainable development capability.

At present, the Bank has 311 branches and outlets in Shanghai, Ningbo, Nanjing, Hangzhou, Tianjin, Chengdu, Shenzhen, Beijing, Suzhou, Wuxi and Shaoxing, Nantong, with 211 self-service banking, and 2 167 self-service terminals, preliminarily forming the service network covering the Yangtze River Delta, the Pearl River Delta, the Bohai Bay, and the key cities in central and western regions. Besides, the Bank also has set up Minhang BOS Rural Bank, Qujiang BOS Rural Bank, Jiangsu Jiangning BOS Rural Bank, and Chongzhou BOS Rural Bank, and initiated Bank of Shanghai Asset Management Co., Ltd., and set up Bank of Shanghai (Hong Kong) Co., Ltd. in Hong Kong, and maintains correspondent banking relations with over 1 600 domestic and foreign banks and their affiliated agencies in over 130 countries and regions.

Since its foundation 20 years ago, the market competitiveness and influence of the Bank have been improving. The Bank ranks No.130 in 2014 in the list of the “Top 1 000 Banks in the world” released by the British magazine The Banker, exceeding the former 28 banks compared with 2013. The Bank had also been crowned by the Asian Banker as

“China’s Best Urban Retail Bank” for several times. The Bank has successively received numerous honorary titles such as “Shanghai Famous Brand”, “Outstanding Bank for Customer Service to Small Business”, “National Outstanding Unit for Re-employment”, “National Outstanding Trading Member of the Inter-bank Market”, ”National Model Unit for Respecting the Elders”, “Best Corporate Image Award”, and “Best Organization Award of Syndicated Loans”, etc..

天津银行股份有限公司
Bank of Tianjin Co., Ltd.

天津银行股份有限公司前身天津城市合作银行成立于1996年，是中国首批获准组建的5家城市合作银行之一，1998年8月按照国务院要求更名为天津市商业银行，2007年4月4日，天津市商业银行更名为天津银行。目前设有6家分行、2家二级分行、6家中心支行、262个营业机构，注册资本为51.26亿元。截至2014年12月末，全行资产总额为4 775亿元；各项存款余额2 885亿元；各项贷款余额1 701亿元；在英国《银行家》全球1 000家大银行最新排名中，排在第290位。

Bank of Tianjin the predecessor of Bank of Tianjin was Tianjin City Cooperation Bank, founded in 1996. It is one of the five city cooperation banks that were the first batch to get the establishment approval in China. In August, 1998, its name was changed to Tianjin City Commercial Bank according to the requirements of the State Council. On April 4th, 2007, its name was changed to Bank of Tianjin. At present, it has 6 branches, 2 secondary branches, 6 central banks, and 262 business institutions, with RMB 5.126 billion of registration capital. Up to the end of 2014, its total asset was RMB 477.5 billion; the deposit balance was RMB 288.5 billion; the loan balance was RMB 170.1 billion. Besides, in the latest ranking of TOP 1 000 Banks in British “The Banker”, it was ranked 290.

重庆银行
BANK OF CHONGQING

重庆银行股份有限公司
Bank of Chongqing Co., Ltd.

重庆银行是中国西部和长江上游地区成立最早的地方性股份制商业银行。截至2014年12月31日，重庆银行共设4家分行，123 家分支机构，775台自助终端。截至2014年末，重庆银行资产总额2 745.31亿元，同比增长32.8%；存款总额1 679.32亿元，同比增长12.9%；贷款总额1 064.49亿元；同比增长17.6%；实现净利润人民币28.27亿元，比上年增长21.4%。2014年，重庆银行在英国《银行家》公布的全球银行业1 000强中综合排名370位。在中国《银行家》公布的2014年度“资产规模2 000亿元以上城商行综合排名”中列第3位。

Bank of Chongqing is the earliest local joint-stock commercial bank in upper reaches of Yangtze River and the southwest region. Up to the end of 2014, it established 4 branches, 123 sub-branches, and 775 self-service terminals. Besides, the total asset was RMB 274.531 billion, which increased by 32.8% on year-on-year growth; the deposit amount was RMB 167.932 billion, which increased by 12.9% on year-on-year growth; the loan amount was RMB 106.449 billion, which increased by 17.6% on year-on-year growth. It realized RMB 2.827 billion of the net profit, which increased by 21.4% compared with last year. In 2014, Bank of Chongqing ranked 3 in 2014 “Comprehensive Ranking of City Commercial Bank with over RMB 200 Billion of Assets” issued by China’s “The Banker” .

重庆三峡银行股份有限公司
Chongqing Three Gorges Bank Co., Ltd.

重庆三峡银行是经中国银监会批准，于2008年2月在原万州商业银行基础上重组而成的城市商业银行，注册资本23.54亿元。截至 2014 年 12 月末，全行资产总额1 008.92亿元，各项存款余额 678.55 亿元，各项贷款余额 268.45 亿元，在全市营业网点达到67个。2014年，重庆三峡银行在英国《银行家》杂志全球1 000家大银行排名中列第711位。

Chongqing Three Gorges Bank is a City Commercial Bank established based on the original Wanzhou Commercial Bank in February of 2008 after approval from China Banking Regulatory Commission, with RMB 2.353 billion of the registration capital. Up to the end of 2014, the total asset was RMB 100.892 billion; deposit balance was RMB 67.855 billion; loan deposit was RMB 26.845 billion. It also had 67 service points in the whole city. In 2014, it ranked 711 among Global Top 1 000 Banks (British Magazine—The Banker).

河北银行股份有限公司
Bank of Hebei Co., Ltd.

河北银行成立于1996年5月28日，是全国首批五家城市合作银行试点之一，也是目前河北省成立最早、规模最大的城市商业银行。2012年7月，河北省委、省政府为加快经济强省、和谐河北建设，做大做强地方金融产业，正式将河北银行纳入省级管理，河北银行成为河北省纳入省级管理的唯一一家地方法人银行。在2014年英国《银行家》杂志公布的全球1 000家大银行中河北银行排名第492位。到2014年末，河北银行在全省11个设区市和天津、青岛设立了13家分行级机构，营业网点总数达到177家。

截至2014年12月末，河北银行资产总额1 818.98亿元，较年初增长19.56%。存款余额1 371.45亿元，较年初增长17.92%。贷款余额752.05亿元，较年初增长21.05%。全年实现主营业务收入101.4亿元。

The Bank of Hebei Co., Ltd., formerly Shijiazhuang City Commercial Bank established with the approval of the China Banking Regulatory Commission, founded on May 28th, 1996, is known as one of the first five pilot urban cooperative banks in China and the oldest city commercial bank in Hebei Province. In July, 2012, to speed up the economy and construction in Hebei, Heibei Provincial Party Committee and Provincial Government paid great attention to the local financial industry, formally listed Bank of Heibei into provincial management. Bank of Hebei has become the only local legal bank incorporated into the provincial management in Heibei. It ranked 492 in Global Top 1 000 Bankers issued by British magazine named the Banker. By the end of 2014, it established 13 branches and 177 service points in 11 cities of Hebei, Tianjin, and Qingdao.

Up to the end of 2014, its total asset was RMB 181.898 billion, which increased by

19.56% compared with the beginning of the year; the deposit balance was RMB 137.145 billion, which increased by 17.92%; the loan balance was RMB 75.205 billion, which increased by 21.05%. In the whole year, it realized RMB 10.14 billion of the main business income.

BOTS 唐山银行

唐山银行股份有限公司

Bank of Tangshan Co., Ltd.

唐山银行是唐山市唯一具有独立法人资格的地方性股份制银行，成立于1998年6月，总部位于唐山市，其前身可追溯至20世纪八九十年代的金融服务所与城市信用社，现有1 200余名正式员工，2014年开办了外汇业务，年末营业网点总数达 43家。截至2014年末，全行资产总额达到572.64亿元，各项贷款余额223.88亿元，各项存款总额500.55亿元。

Bank of Tangshan, founded in June of 1998, is the only local joint-stock bank with the independent legal entity in Tangshan City. Its head office is located in Tangshan. Its predecessor can be traced back to the financial service agency and urban credit cooperative in 1980s and 1990s. At present, it has about 1 200 employees. In 2014, it opened foreign exchange transaction. By the end of 2014, it had 43 service points. Its total asset reached RMB 57.264 billion; its loan balance reached RMB 22.388 billion; its deposit balance reached RMB 50.055 billion.

廊坊银行
BANK OF LANGFANG

廊坊银行股份有限公司
Bank of Langfang Co., Ltd.

廊坊银行股份有限公司于2000年12月29日正式成立，是廊坊市政府唯一出资设立的国家法定金融机构，2008年12月，正式更名为廊坊银行。目前，廊坊银行下辖1个营业部、2家分行和30家支行，员工1 100余人。2014年末，全行资产达到571亿元，存款361亿元，贷款190亿元。

Bank of Langfang Co., Ltd. was established on December 29, 2000, which is the only national statutory financial institutions funded by the Langfang government. In December 2008, officially changed its name to Bank of Langfang. At present, Bank of Langfang has a a sales department, two branches, thirty sub-branches, and more than 1 100 employees. At the end of 2014, the total assets reached RMB 57.1 billion, the balance of deposits is RMB 36.1 billion, and the balance of loans is RMB 19 billion.

邯郸银行

BANK OF HANDAN

邯郸银行股份有限公司

Bank of Handan Co., Ltd.

邯郸银行是一家区域性股份制商业银行，2007年10月在邯郸市城信社基础上筹建邯郸市商业银行，2008年7月10日正式挂牌；2010年11月26日更名为邯郸银行。2014年6月末有员工1 528人，有1家分行、57家支行、1家村镇银行。截至2014年末，总资产为816.5 亿元，年末存款 595.2 亿元，年末账面贷款 241.6 亿元。在英国《银行家》杂志公布的“2014 年度世界1 000强银行”榜单中，列第780 位。在《亚洲银行家》杂志“2014 亚洲银行 500 强”两项排名中，资产排名为第326位，同时进入实力排名（评价指标 12 项）30 强，居中国入选银行第 11 位。在中国《银行家》 杂志组织的“2014中国商业银行竞争力评价”中，荣获“最佳风险管理城市商业银行” 。

Bank of Handan Co., Ltd. is a regional joint-stock commercial bank with investment mainly from Handan Municipal Government. Authorized in October, 2007, Handan Commercial Bank formerly known as the Handan City Credit Union had been formally opened on July 10, 2008; the bank was renamed as “Bank of Handan” on November 26, 2010. By end of June in 2014, it has 1 528 employees, a branch, 57 sub-branches, and a village bank. Up to the end of 2014, the total assets amounted to RMB 81.65 billion, and the deposit was RMB 59.52 billion, and the bookkeeping loan was RMB 24.16 billion. It also ranked No. 780 in 2014 World Top 1 000 Banks by the English magazine The Banker. In the magazine The Asian Banker – 2014 Asian Banks Top 500, its asset ranking ranked 326. Meanwhile, it entered into Top30 in Power Ranking (12 evaluation indexes), and ranked 11 in the selected banks of China. In “2014 China Commercial Bank Competitiveness Evaluation” organized by China Banker, it was honored as “the Best Risk Management City Commercial Bank”.

晋商银行股份有限公司
Jinshang Bank Co., Ltd.

晋商银行股份有限公司经中国银监会批准于2009年2月28日正式挂牌成立，是一家总行设在山西太原的股份制商业银行。全行现有在岗职工3 136人。在太原市内，晋商银行设有68家营业网点（含14家社区、小微支行）；省内设有9家异地分行和30家异地支行（含16家社区、小微支行）。截至 2014 年末，全行总资产为1 435.2755万元人民币，各项存款9 107.7777万元，各项贷款人民币509.7186万元。

Jinshang Bank was formally established on February 28th, 2009 after being approved by China Banking Regulatory Commission. It is a joint-stock commercial bank, with its head office located in Taiyuan of Shanxi. At present, it has 3 136 employees. In Taiyuan, it has 68 service points (including 14 communities and branches). In the province, it has 9 offsite branches and 30 offsite sub-branches (including 16 communities and branches). By the end of 2014, its total asset was RMB 1 435 275 550 000; its deposit was RMB 910 777 770 000; its loan was RMB 50 971 860 000.

bsb 包商银行

包商银行股份有限公司
Baoshang Bank Co., Ltd.

包商银行成立于1998年12月，是内蒙古自治区最早成立的股份制商业银行，前身为包头市商业银行，2007年9月经中国银监会批准更名为包商银行。目前，包商银行在内蒙古自治区内的包头、赤峰、巴彦淖尔、通辽、鄂尔多斯、锡林郭勒、呼伦贝尔、呼和浩特、兴安盟、乌兰察布、乌海、阿拉善和自治区外的宁波、深圳、成都、北京设立了16家分行、173个营业网点，员工7 400多人。此外，还成立了达茂旗包商惠农贷款公司，发起设立了北京昌平、天津津南、江苏南通、大连金州、四川广元、贵州毕节、吉林九台、河南鄢城、山西清徐等27家村镇银行；机构遍布全国16个省、市、自治区。2014年末，资产总额3 029亿元，各项存款余额1 601亿元，各项贷款余额863亿元。

Founded in December of 1998, Baoshang Bank was a joint-stock commercial bank, founded at the earliest in the Nei Monggol Autonomous Region. Its predecessor is Baotou City Commercial Bank. In September of 2007, its name was approved by China Banking Regulatory Commission to be Baoshang Bank. At present, it has established 16 branches and 173 service points in Baotou, Cifeng, Bayannur, Tongliao, Erdos, Xilingol, Hulun Buir, Hohhot, Hinggan League, Ulan Qab, Wuhai, Alxa, Ningbo, Shenzhen, Chengdu, and Beijing, with more than 7 400 employees. In addition, it established Concessionaire Huinong Loan Company, as well as 27 village banks in Changping of Beijing, Jinnan of Tianjin, Nantong of Jiangsu, Jinzhou of Dalian, Guangyuan of Sichuan, Bijie of Guizhou, Jiutai of Jilin, Yancheng of Henan, Qingxu of Shanxi. Its institutions spread over 16 provinces, cities and municipalities over the country. By the end of 2014, its total asset reached RMB 302.9 billion; its deposit balance reached RMB 160.1 billion; its loan balance reached RMB 86.3 billion.

内蒙古银行股份有限公司
Bank of Inner Mongolia Co., Ltd.

内蒙古银行（原名呼和浩特市商业银行）成立于1999年11月19日，是经中国人民银行批准，由呼和浩特市地方财政、原呼和浩特市13家城市信用社股东和其他企业法人共同以发起方式设立的股份制商业银行。2009年9月8日，经中国银监会批准，更名为内蒙古银行股份有限公司（简称内蒙古银行）。

目前机构总数达到107个，包括总行机关、营业部、区外的哈尔滨分行和区内的9家分行、95家支行和1家小企业金融服务中心。其中，在北京、上海设立金融市场分部，在北京设立投资银行部，员工总数3 000多人。该行共主发起设立31家村镇银行，区内22家，区外9家，在国贫、省贫旗县设立11家。截至2014年末，资产规模达到816亿元，所有者权益82.35亿元，各项存款余额达到581.55亿元，各项贷款余额达到361.7 亿元。

Bank of Inner Mongolia (predecessor: Hohhot City Commercial Bank), founded in November 19th, 1999, is a joint-stock commercial bank established by the local finance of Hohhot City, the original 13 city credit cooperative shareholders in Hohhot, and other enterprise legal persons, after approval from People's Bank of China. On September 8th, 2009, after being approved by China Banking Regulatory Commission, its name was changed into Bank of Inner Mongolia.

At present, it has 107 institutions in total, including 9 branches, 95 sub-branches and 1 small enterprise finance service center, as well as the head office, service points and Harbin branches. It has established financial market branch in Beijing and Shanghai, and investment banking division in Beijing, with more than 3 000 employees. Besides, its collective masters initiate to establish 31 village banks (22 banks inside the city and 9 banks outside the city). By the end of 2014, its asset scale reached RMB 81.6 billion. The owner's equity was RMB 8.235 billion. The deposit balance reached RMB 58.155 billion, and the loan balance reached RMB 36.17 billion.

鞍山银行股份有限公司
Bank of Anshan Co., Ltd.

鞍山银行的前身是鞍山市城市信用联社，成立于1991年，1996年12月正式组建为鞍山城市合作银行，1998年9月更名为鞍山市商业银行，2010年12月中国银监会正式批准更名为鞍山银行。截至2014年12月末，全行下辖19家一级支行、77家二级支行；资产总额达到805.73亿元，各项存款达到681.3亿元，贷款总额达到433.9亿元。

Founded in 1991, Bank of Anshan's predecessor is Anshan City Credit Union. In December of 1996, it was formally established as Anshan City Cooperative Bank. In September of 1998, its name was changed to Anshan City Commercial Bank. In December of 2010, its name was changed to Bank of Anshan after being approved by China Banking Regulatory Commission. By the end of 2014, it has 19 first sub-branches, and 77 secondary sub-branches. Its total asset reached RMB 80.573 billion; its deposit balance reached RMB 68.13 billion; its loan amount reached RMB 43.39 billion.

锦州银行
BANK OF JINZHOU

锦州银行股份有限公司
Bank of Jinzhou Co., Ltd.

锦州银行股份有限公司成立于1998年，是一家由国家股、国内企业法人股以及部分个人股组成的股份制商业银行。截至2014年末，资产规模达2 467亿元，在锦州、北京、天津、沈阳、大连、哈尔滨、丹东、抚顺、鞍山、朝阳、阜新、辽阳设立12家分行。目前，与70多个国家及地区500多个金融机构开展业务，代理行网络遍及世界各地。

Bank of Jinzhou Co., Ltd. was established in 1998, which is a joint-stock commercial bank composed of state-owned shares, legal person shares of domestics companies, and some individual shares. At the end of 2014, the bank reached RMB 246.7 billion in assets. There are 12 branches in Jinzhou, Beijing, Tianjin, Shenyang, Dalian, Harbin, Dandong, Fushun, Anshan, Chaoyang, Fuxin, and Liaoyang. Currenty. Its agency network throughout the world by carrying our business with more than 500 financial institutions in more than 70 countries.

抚顺银行股份有限公司
Bank of Fushun Co., Ltd.

抚顺银行前身为抚顺市商业银行，成立于1998年6月，2011年6月更名为抚顺银行，成为跨区域经营的商业银行。截至2014年末，总资产规模达到388亿元，存款余额实现272亿元，贷款余额实现170亿元。设有营口分行及6家一级支行，机构营业网点达到60家。

Bank of Fushun was founded in June, 1998. Its predecessor is Fushun City Commercial Bank. In June, 2011, its name was changed into Bank of Fushun, and became a commercial bank with trans-regional operation. By the end of 2014, its total asset reached RMB 38.8 billion, and its deposit balance realized RMB 27.2 billion, and its loan balance realized RMB 17 billion. Besides, it has established Yingkou Branch, 6 primary sub-branch, and 60 service points.

辽阳银行
BANK OF LIAOYANG

辽阳银行股份有限公司

Bank of Liaoyang Co., Ltd.

辽阳银行是一家由国有股、企业法人股、自然人股组成的具有独立法人资格的股份制商业银行，在本地和沈阳、鞍山、葫芦岛、抚顺、丹东等地区设有分、支行60家，从业人员总计1 000余人，其中研究生以上学历80余人。做“中小微企业的伙伴银行，市民最亲近的银行和服务‘三农’的银行”，是辽阳银行快速发展的市场定位。秉承着“贴心服务、相伴成长”的经营理念，辽阳银行一直把服务中小微企业摆在重要位置，2009年4月，率先成立了东北地区第一家“小企业信贷服务中心”，积极开展小企业金融服务月活动，全力支持中小微企业的发展。服务市民是辽阳银行不变的承诺，营业网点遍布全市两县五区，方便市民金融服务。家庭电视银行、网上银行、网上支付等电子银行系统的全面推广，扩大了银行业务受理渠道，极大地促进了中间业务拓展与服务手段提升。特别是在全省率先开办了家庭电视银行业务，使得客户真正实现了足不出户办理业务。目前已开办包括水、电、煤气、通讯、供暖等在内的23项代理缴费业务，是全市同业代理缴费业务品种最全、业务量最大的银行，极大地方便了市民生活。为切实践行“服务‘三农’的银行”。2010年5月，该行先后发起成立了辽宁首山村镇银行、辽宁灯塔村镇银行；2010年12月，在佟二堡地区成立了服务农村经济的佟二堡支行，积极服务农村经济发展。同时，辽阳银行沈阳分行成立，实现了跨区域经营；2011年12月，又发起成立了营口宏诚村镇银行和设立了沈阳分行和平支行；2012年，跨区域发展战略深入实施，分别设立沈阳分行沈河支行、铁西支行，同时，辽阳银行葫芦岛分行、鞍山分行隆重开业。2014年1月，设立丹东分行和抚顺分行，大连、营口分行获批即将开业，全行网点布局进一步优化，服务触角进一步延伸。

坚持以人为本，凝聚团队力量，打造独具特色的企业文化是辽阳银行快速发展的力量源泉。全面、深入地推进企业文化建设，确立了“贴心服务、相伴成长”的经营理念，把全面建设风险合规文化、创新发展文化、服务文化、精英团队文化，培育“敬业、拼搏、创新、奉献”的企业精神和“诚信、责任、价值、拼搏、成长”的核心价值观作为企业文化建设的根本任务，始终坚持资本先行、内控先行、科技先行、人才先行。在经营管理过程中，不断加快人才引进，加大人才招聘、培养、选拔力度。近年来，面向高等院校招聘研究生、本科生200余人，成为了辽阳银行发展的人才保证。营销部门贯彻“不把贷款当权力，只把贷款当产品，更把贷款当服务”的营销理念，使独具辽阳银行特色的企业文化成为促进全行发展的有力保证，并不断提升着该行的风险控制能力、创新能力、发展能力、盈利能力和核心竞争力，成为了传承先进理念的有效载体，成为了推动该行持续、稳健、快速发展，全力打造精品银行的力量源泉。

不断进取、沿着五年战略发展规划阔步前行，是辽阳银行快速发展的崇高追求。不断深化“贴心服务、相伴成长”的理念，以强化内控、防范风险为重点，以深化改革和科技进步为动力，以建设优秀企业文化为目标，解放思想、更新观念、锐意改革、开拓创新，不断提升精细化管理水平，全力打造特色化业务体系，社会形象、社会地位不断提高，客户满意度、忠诚度持续增强，已成为辽阳市银行业中资产规模最大、经济效益最佳、支持地方经济建设力度最强的第一银行品牌。

截至2014年底，全行资产规模已突破800亿元，较年初增加71亿元，与规划目标比增加262亿元；各项存款余额660亿元，较年初增加31亿元，与规划目标比增加160亿元；实现净利润8亿元，比上年增加0.82亿元，与规划目标比增加1.4亿元；上缴税金5亿元，提前一年实现“双80”发展目标。在全市同业中，以存款余额占比36% 以上（不含域外机构，下同），贷款余额占比 32% 以上，开户数占 40% 以上，代理业务占 70% 以上的成果稳居全市首位。连续四年监管评级达到“二级”，位居全省及全国城商行前列。根据英国《银行家》杂志最新排名，在全球银行业排名第633名，在全国银行业排名第75名。荣获“2013年度最佳小微金融服务中小银行”奖（是东北地区唯一一家获奖单位），“全国工人先锋号”、“全国三八红旗集体”、“全国巾帼文明岗”、“中国银行业文明规范服务示范单位”等多项国家级荣誉，“辽宁五一奖状”、“辽宁省政治思想工作先进单位”、“优秀经营单位”等省级荣誉50余项。连续多年被市委、市政府授予“发展经济优质服务单位”、“纳税十强单位”、“促进就业和社会保障工作先进单位”、“扶贫开发先进单位”荣誉称号。

放眼未来，辽阳银行将进一步增强责任感、使命感和紧迫感，履行“对存款人负责，实现银行、股东、客户、员工共同成长，创造良好的经济效益和社会效益”的使命，紧紧围绕五年战略发展规划和“双80”目标，站在全地区的高度，站在整个行业发展的高度，走差异化、特色化的道路，向着管理精细化、经营特色化、财务成果好、社会信誉佳、达到上市标准的精品银行目标不断迈进!

外汇业务开展状况：辽阳银行外汇业务于2009年底正式开办，采取“全行营销，统一管理、集中操作”的经营管理模式。总行国际业务部内设外汇会计、外汇资金、国际结算和贸易融资等多个条线，产品涉及国际结算、国际贸易融资、跨境人民币和国内信用证等三十多个品种，当地客户群的覆盖率已超过70%，很好地服务了地方的涉外经济的发展。

外汇业务经营范围：外汇存款、外汇贷款、外汇汇款、外币兑换、国际结算、外币票据的承兑和贴现、外汇借款、外汇担保、自营外汇买卖和代客外汇买卖、资信调查、咨询与见证、同业外汇拆解、结售汇、跨境人民币结算。

Bank of Liaoyang is a joint-stock commercial bank with independent legal person qualification, composed of state-owned shares, enterprise legal person shares and natural person shares, with 60 branches and sub-branches in Liaoyang, Shenyang, Anshan, Huludao, Fushun, Dandong, etc. with a total of more than one thousand staff, among which more than 80 of them has obtained master degree or above. The market positioning for the rapid development of Bank of Liaoyang is to become “a partner bank of micro, small and medium enterprises, the closet bank of the public and a bank serving the agriculture, farmer and rural area”. Holding the operation principle of “thoughtful service, grow together”, Bank of Liaoyang has always been making it the priority to serve micro, small and medium enterprises. In April, 2009, the first “small business credit service center” in Northeast China was established in Bank of Liaoyang, and an activity called small business financial service month was conducted to fully support the development of micro, small and medium enterprises. Serving the public has always been the promise of Bank of Liaoyang. Branches throughout five districts in two counties provides convenient financial service to the public. Family TV banking, internet banking, online payment and other comprehensive promotion of electronic banking system has expanded the banking channels and greatly promoted the development of intermediate business and the improvement of service methods. In particular, family TV banking business has been conducted within the province, even throughout the country, which makes it possible for the clients to conduct business in their homes. At present, 23 proxy payment services including the payment for water, electricity, gas, communications, heating, etc. has been provided, which makes the bank the largest bank in the city in terms of the proxy payment services and business volume among the banks who provide proxy services, and so the life of the public has been greatly facilitated. In order to truly practice the idea of becoming "a bank who serves agriculture, farmer and rural area", the bank established Liaoning Shoushan Village Bank and Liaoning Dengta Village Bank in May, 2010 successively. In December, 2010, Tongerbu branch was established in Tongerbu to serve the rural economy and promote the development of rural economy; meanwhile, the establishment of Shenyang branch of Bank of Liaoyang has realized cross-district operation; in December, 2011, the bank established Yingkou Hongcheng Village Bank and set up Shenyang Branch and Heping sub-branch; in 2012, cross-district development strategy has been implemented and Shenyang Branch Shenhe sub-branch, Tiexi sub-branch were set up; meanwhile, Huludao Branch, Anshan Branch of Bank of Liaoyang have been grandly started. In January, 2014, Dandong branch and Fushan branch were set up, and Daliang branch and Yingkou branch has been approved and will soon start their businesses. So the branches of the bank has been further optimized and its services has been further expanded.

Adhere to the principle of people-oriented, gathering team strength and creating a unique enterprise culture is the source of power for the rapid development of Bank of Liaoyang. To comprehensively and deeply promote the construction of enterprise culture, the operation principle of "thoughtful services, grow together" has been established and the basic tasks for the construction of enterprise culture is to comprehensively establish risk compliance culture, innovation and development culture, service culture, elite team culture and cultivate the enterprise spirit of "dedication, perseverance, innovation and contribution" and the core values of "integrity, responsibility and value, perseverance, growth", and always adhere to the principle of capital first, internal control first, technology first, and talents first. In the process of operation and management, it is important to accelerate the talent introduction, intensify talent recruitment, training and selection. In recent years, more than 200 undergraduates and graduates has been recruited and have taken up management positions, which ensures the development of Bank of Liaoyang in terms of personnel. The marketing department has been carrying out the operation principle of "not taking loan as a power, but a product, and more a service". This unique enterprise culture of Bank of Liaoyang greatly reinforced the development of the whole bank and constantly promotes the risk control ability, innovative ability, development ability, profitability and core competitiveness, which makes the bank the effective carrier of inheriting advanced concept and facilities the continuous, stable and rapid development of the bank and become the source of power for establishing a competitive bank.

The pursuit of the Bank of Liaoyang is to take big strides forward according to the five-year development strategy. Bank of Liaoyang keeps deepening the concept of "thoughtful service, grow together" and taking strengthening internal control, preventing risk as the key, and regarding deepening the reform and scientific progress as impetus, taking establishing distinctive enterprise culture as objective and continuously improving its delicacy management through emancipating the mind, renew the idea, reforming keen determination and innovation, so as to establish as distinctive business system and improve its social image and status and increase its customer satisfaction and loyalty. Bank of Liaoyang has become the No.1 Bank in the banking system of Liaoyang city with largest assets size, best economic benefit and the most powerful bank in supporting the development of local economy.

Up to the end of 2014, the assets size of the bank has exceeded RMB 80 billion, an increase of RMB 7.1 billion compared with that of the beginning of the year and an increase of RMB 26.2 billion than its planned objective; RMB 66 billion outstanding of deposits has been realized, an increase of RMB 3.1 billion compared with that of the beginning of the year and an increase of RMB 16 billion than its planned objective;

RMB 500 million taxes has been paid, and the "double 80" objective has been achieved one year in advance. With its outstanding of deposits taking up more than 36% (excluding banks outside the field), outstanding loan taking up more than 32%, number of accounts taking up more than 40% and agent service taking up more than 70%, Bank of Liaoyang has remained to be the top bank among the banks of the same trade in the city. The supervision rating of the bank has been rated as "second grade" for four years continuously. According to ranking made by the magazine, "The Bankers", Bank of Liaoyang has been listed No.633 among the banks around the world, and No.75 among banks in China. Bank of Liaoyang has won the national award of "The Best Small and Medium Bank Providing Micro and Small Financial Service Award in 2013" (the only awarded unit in Northeast China), "The National Worker Pioneer", "National Advanced Women Unit", "National Women Civilization Post", "Civilized Norms Service Demonstration Unit in China's Banking Sector" and more than 50 provincial awards including "Liaoning May 1 Award", "Political and Ideological Work Advanced Unit in Liaoning", "Outstanding Operation Unit" etc. and has won the honoring title of "Outstanding Service Unit in Developing Economy", "Top 10 Enterprises in Paying Taxes", "Advance Unit in Promoting Employment and Social Security", "Advance Unit in Anti-poverty and Development" awarded by the municipal party committee and the municipal government .

Looking to the future, Bank of Liaoyang will further enhance its sense of responsibility, sense of mission and sense of urgency, and fulfill the mission to "being responsible for depositors, and realized the growth of the bank, shareholders, customers and the staff and create favorable economic and social benefit" and closely adhere to the five-year strategic development plan and "double 80" objective and keep moving toward the objective of becoming a competitive bank reaching the listing standard with delicate management, distinctive operation, outstanding financial result and great social reputation through standing at the height of the whole region, standing at the height of the whole industry and taking a differentiating and characterized road.

Bank of Liaoyang started its foreign exchange business at the end of 2009 with the operation and management mode of "whole bank marketing, unified management and centralized operation". The international business department of the head office provides services including foreign exchange accounting, foreign liquid assets, international settlement and trade financing etc., whose products are more than 30 in kind, involving international settlement, international trade financing, cross-border RMB and domestic L/C etc. With fraction of coverage of the local customer base having exceeded 70%, the bank has provided great service in the development of foreign-related business in the local area.

Scope of business of foreign exchange transactions: foreign exchange deposits, foreign exchange loans, foreign exchange remittance, foreign currency exchange, international settlement, the acceptance and discount of foreign currency bill, foreign exchange borrowing, foreign exchange guarantee, proprietary trading foreign exchange purchase and sale and conduct foreign exchange purchase and sale for the customers, credit investigation, consultant and witness, foreign exchange lending among the same trade, foreign exchange settlement and sale, cross border RMB settlement.

营口银行
BANK OF YINGKOU

营口银行股份有限公司
Bank of Yingkou Co., Ltd.

营口银行前身——营口市商业银行，作为中国一家地方性股份制商业银行，成立于1997年4月1日。2008年1月14日，经中国银行业监督管理委员会批准，营口市商业银行正式更名为“营口银行”，实现了一个地方性股份制商业银行向区域性股份制商业银行的转变。

Bank of Yingkou was formerly known as Yingkou City Commercial Bank, which was founded in April 1, 1997, as a local joint-stock commercial bank in China. On January 14, 2008, approved by the China Banking Regulatory Commission, Yingkou City Commercial Bank officially changed its name to “Bank of Yingkou”, achieving the transformation form a local joint-stock commercial bank to a regional joint-stock commercial bank.

丹东银行
BANK OF DANDONG

丹东银行股份有限公司

Bank of Dandong Co., Ltd.

丹东银行成立于1993年12月，是经中国人民银行批准设立的地方性股份制商业银行。其前身为丹东城市信用联社，1997年1月组建成立丹东城市合作银行，1998年，更名为丹东城市商业银行。2010年9月，经中国银监会批准，正式更名为丹东银行。截至2014年末，丹东银行下设外埠分行2家，支行90家，营业网点总数达到93个，全行在岗员工人数1 674人。截至2014年末，全行资产总额达到411.42亿元，各项存款余额为348.40亿元，各项贷款余额187.24亿元。

Founded in December of 1993, Dandong is a local joint-stock commercial bank established after the approval of the People's Bank of China. Its predecessor is Dandong City Credit Union. In January of 1997, it was established into Dandong City Cooperative Bank. In 1998, its name was changed into Dandong City Commercial Bank. In September of 2010, its name was officially changed into Bank of Dandong after the approval of China Banking Regulatory Commission. By the end of 2014, Bank of Dandong established 2 branches in other cities, 90 sub-branches, 93 service points, with 1 674 staffs. Besides, its total asset reached RMB 41.142 billion, and its deposit balance realized RMB 34.84 billion, and its loan balance realized RMB 18.724 billion.

盛京银行股份有限公司
Shengjing Bank Co., Ltd.

盛京银行股份有限公司是东北地区成立最早、规模最大、实力雄厚的总部银行，成立于1997年9月，其前身是沈阳市商业银行，2007年2月经中国银监会批准更名为盛京银行，并实现跨区域经营。截至2014年末，盛京银行已在北京、上海、天津、长春等中心城市和辽宁省内沈阳、大连、营口、鞍山、本溪、盘锦、葫芦岛、朝阳、抚顺、锦州、阜新、丹东等地设立了16家分行，机构网点已达150家；在上海宝山、宁波江北、沈阳沈北、新民、辽中、法库等地发起设立了6家富民村镇银行，并入股丹东、本溪等城市商业银行。

截至2014年末，盛京银行资产总额达5 033.71亿元，各项存款余额达3 159.44亿元。2014年在英国《银行家》杂志的排名中，盛京银行的一级资本回报率在全球排名中列第83位，在中国银行业中列第7位，资产回报率在全球排名中列第214位，在中国银行业中列第25位；在中国《银行家》杂志发布的《2014年中国商业银行竞争力评价报告》中，盛京银行被评为“最佳城商行”并在2013年度资产规模2 000亿元以上的城市商业银行综合排名中位列第一；2013年，在《亚洲周刊》所组织的排名中，盛京银行的净资产回报率在全亚洲列第6位，在中国银行业中列第4位。近年来先后荣获“中国服务业企业500强”、“中国最具区域竞争力城市商业银行”、“最具影响力中小银行”、辽沈地区“最受百姓喜爱的银行”等荣誉称号。

Shengjing Bank was founded in September of 1997 at the earliest in the northeastern part with the largest scale and power. Its predecessor is Shengyang City Commercial Bank. In February of 2007, its name was changed into Shengjing bank after the approval from China Banking Regulatory Commission, and it realized the trans-regional operation. By the end of 2014, Shengjing Bank has established 16 branches in Beijing, Shanghai, Tianjin, Changchun, Shenyang, Dalian, Yingkou, Anshan, Benxi,

Panjin, Huludao, Zhaoyang, Fushun, Jinzhou, Fuxin, Dandong, etc. It also has 150 service points. Moreover, it has established 6 village banks in Baoshan of Shanghai, Jiangbei of Ningbo, Shenbei of Shengyang, Xinmin, Liaozhong, Faku, etc., and become a shareholder of Dandong City Commercial Bank and Benxi City Commercial Bank.

By the end of 2014, its total asset reached RMB 503.371 billion, and its deposit balance reached RMB 315.944 billion. In 2014, In the rankings organized by the British magazine The Banker, the tier one capital return rate of Shengjing Bank ranked 83 over the world, and ranked 7 among the Chinese banks. Its asset return rate ranked 214 over the world, and ranked 25 among the Chinese banks. In Competitiveness Evaluation Report of Chinese Commercial Banks in 2014 issued by the Chinese magazine The Banker, it was rated as the best city commercial bank and it ranked 1 among the comprehensive rankings of the city commercial banks with over RMB 200 billion assets in 2013. In 2013, in the rankings organized by Asian Week, the net asset return rate of Shengjing Bank ranked 6 in Asia, and ranked 4 in the Chinese banking industry. In recent years, it was honored as “TOP 500 Service Enterprises in China”, “City Commercial Bank with the Most Regional Competitiveness in China”, “Small and Medium-sized Banks with the Most Influence”, “Favorite Bank in Public” in Liaoning and Shenyang, etc..

阜新银行
BANK OF FUXIN

阜新银行股份有限公司
Bank of Fuxin Co., Ltd.

阜新银行是在阜新城市信用社基础上组建的城市商业银行。1994年12月，阜新市政府整合25家分散的信用社，组建城市信用社中心社；1997年6月4日，更名为阜新市城市信用联合社；2001年8月27日，组建为阜新市商业银行股份有限公司；2009年12月3日，中国银监会正式批准阜新市商业银行更名为“阜新银行”，这标志着该行正式步入区域性股份制商业银行行列。截至 2014 年 6 月末，本公司分支机构共计 60 家，包括 3 家分行和 57 家支行。

Bank of Fuxin is a city commercial bank established on the basis of Fuxin City credit cooperatives. In December 1994, Fuxin City government formed urban credit cooperatives community center by integrating 25 decentralized credit cooperatives; On June 4, 1997, changed its name to Fuxin City credit union; On August 27, 2001, formed the Fuxin City Commercial Bank Co., Ltd.; On December 3, 2009, the China Banking Regulatory Commission officially approved the Fuxin City Commercial Bank changed its name to “Bank of Fuxin”, which marks the bank has formally entered the ranks of regional joint-stock commercial banks. As of the end of June 2014, the company has a total of 60 branches, including 3 branches and 57 sub-branches.

葫芦岛银行股份有限公司
Bank of Huludao Co., Ltd.

葫芦岛银行是辽宁省葫芦岛市的一家地方商业银行，前身是葫芦岛市商业银行，成立于2001年9月25日，2009年12月21日中国银行业监督管理委员会正式批准更名为葫芦岛银行，总部在辽宁省葫芦岛市。

Bank of Huludao is a local commercial bank in Huludao City, Liaoning Province, formerly known as Huludao City Commercial Bank, which was established on September 25, 2001. On December 21, 2009, the China Banking Regulatory Commission officially renamed Bank of Huludao, headquartered in Huludao City, Liaoning Province.

大连银行
BANK OF DALIAN

大连银行股份有限公司
Bank of Dalian Co., Ltd.

大连银行前身大连市商业银行成立于1998年3月28日，是一家由大连市国有股份、中资法人股份及个人股份共同组成的地方性股份制商业银行。2007年2月17日更名为大连银行。在天津、北京、沈阳、成都、营口、上海、丹东和重庆设立8家异地分行。

大连银行秉承“稳健经营、科学发展”的经营理念，以完善法人治理结构、增强风险控制能力和建立资本约束机制为手段，以支持东北老工业基地振兴和地方经济发展为己任，进一步明确了“服务地方、服务中小、服务市民”的市场定位，先后为大连市基础设施改造、区域经济发展提供了一揽子金融支持，实现了中小企业融资的一站式服务。

在2014年7月出版的英国《银行家》杂志全球前1 000家大银行排名中，大连银行列第391位，在中国的银行中排名第42位。

截至2014年末，大连银行共有代理行905家，网络覆盖99个国家和地区，在境外开有美元、日元、港元、欧元、加元、澳元6大币种21家账户行，其中美元账户行有花旗、摩根大通、汇丰等10家。设立上海、大连两大单证中心，借助先进的国际结算系统为客户资金汇划提供便利，国际结算量超过百亿美元。

大连银行外汇业务经营范围包括：外汇存款；外汇贷款；外汇汇款；国际结算；结汇、售汇；代客及自营外汇买卖；外汇同业拆借；资信调查、咨询、见证；国外保函；国际保理业务。

特色业务：本外币联动、内外贸联动的未来货权开证及融资解决方案；跨境供应链贸易融资解决方案。

Dalian City Commercial Bank, the predecessor of the Bank of Dalian, established on March 28th 1998, was a local joint-stock commercial bank comprising government-owned shares, and shares held by corporations and individuals. Dalian City Commercial Bank was renamed 'Bank of Dalian' on February 17 2007. Bank of Dalian has established eight 'cross-region' branches in Tianjin, Beijing, Shenyang, Chengdu, Yingkou, Shanghai, Dandong and Chongqing.

Firmly adhering to the management philosophy of "steady operations and scientific development", Bank of Dalian aims to support the revitalization of North-eastern Old Industrial Bases and local economic development by improving the corporate governance structure, strengthening risk control capabilities and establishing capital constraint mechanism. Meanwhile, Bank of Dalian further defines the market orientation of "serving local economic development, serving small and medium enterprises, and serving the citizens", and has successively provided a package of financial support for the infrastructure reconstruction of Dalian City and regional economic development, and meanwhile realized the one-stop financial service for small and medium enterprises.

Among the world's top 1000 banks released by The Banker magazine in July 2014, Bank of Dalian ranked the 391th place in the world, and ranked the 42th place amongst domestic banks in China.

International Business

By the end of 2014, Bank of Dalian has established the correspondent banking relationship with 905 banks, covering 99 countries and regions in the world. It has opened 21 settlement accounts which can help to clear USD , JPY, HKD, EUR, CAD and AUD. Its main USD settlement accounts are opened in some well-known banks including Citi bank, J.P.Morgan bank, HSBC bank etc. In respect of international business, Bank of Dalian sets two Trade Services Centers located in both Dalian and Shanghai and has advanced international settlement system. It is very convenient for the customers to transfer fund. The volume of Bank of Dalian's international business has reached more than ten billion USD .

International Business Scope

The international banking services of Bank of Dalian are authorized to provide include: foreign exchange deposit, foreign exchange loan, foreign exchange remittance, international settlement, buying and selling foreign exchange, foreign exchange borrowing from and lending to financial institutions, credibility investigation, consultant, certification, international guarantee, and international factoring.

Special Business

Bank of Dalian can issue L/C under future goods ownership and provide finance services for the customers through RMB and foreign currency coordination and domestic and foreign trade linkage. It can also help customers to provide cross-border trade finance solutions.

朝阳银行股份有限公司

Bank of chaoyang Co., Ltd.

朝阳银行股份有限公司是经中国银行业监督管理委员会批准组建的股份制银行业金融机构。前身是朝阳市商业银行，2011年4月正式更名为朝阳银行，下辖1家直属营业部，13家一级支行，42家二级支行，3家域外分行——沈阳分行、抚顺分行、本溪分行。

朝阳银行主要从事吸收存款；发放贷款；办理国内外结算；办理票据承兑与贴现；发行金融债券；代理发行、兑付、承销、买卖各种债券；从事同业拆借；提供信用证服务及担保；代理收付款项及代理保险业务；提供保险箱服务及经中国银行业监督管理机构批准的其他业务。

Bank of Chaoyang Co., Ltd. is a joint-stock financial institution approved by the China Banking Regulatory Commission. Formerly known as Chaoyang City Commercial Bank, in April 2011, officially changed its name to Bank of Chaoyang, has 1 immediate business department, 13 primary branches, 42 secondary branches, and 3 branches outside—Shenyang Branch, Fushun Branch, and Benxi Branch.

Bank of Chaoyang is mainly engaged in absorbing deposits; issuing loans; handling domestic and international settlement; handling acceptance and discounting; issuing financial bonds; being a agency to issue, pay, underwrite, trading all kinds of bonds; interbank lending; providing letters of credit and guarantee; acting receipts and payments and insurances agents; providing safe service and other business approved by the China Banking Regulatory Agencies.

吉林银行
BANK OF JILIN

吉林银行股份有限公司
Bank of Jilin Co., Ltd.

吉林银行成立于2007年10月10日，是经中国银行业监督管理委员批准，长春市商业银行与吉林市商业银行、辽源市城市信用社（后又吸收合并白山、通化、四平、松原等四个地区的城信社）合并而成立的股份有限公司，目前在吉林省内9个市州和大连、沈阳拥有11家分行，全行共364个营业网点。2014年7月，吉林银行在英国《银行家》杂志全球1 000强银行排名中列第322位，居中国地区银行第35位。

Bank of Jilin was established on October 10, 2007, by merging Changchun, Jilin, and Liaoyuan City Commercial Banks (it further absorbed Baishan, Tonghua, Siping, and Songyuan Commercial Banks), approved by the China Banking Regulatory Commission. Currently, it has 11 branches in nine cities in Jinlin province, Dilian, and Shenyang, as well as 364 outlets. In the British “The Banker” released “2014 Top 1 000 World Banks” ranking list, Bank of Jilin was 322th, and 35th in Chinese banks.

哈尔滨银行 HRBanK HARBIN BANK

哈尔滨银行股份有限公司
Harbin Bank Co., Ltd.

哈尔滨银行成立于1997年7月，总部位于中国黑龙江省哈尔滨市。现已在天津、重庆、大连、沈阳、成都、哈尔滨、大庆等地设立了17家分行，在北京、广东、江苏、吉林、黑龙江等14个省及直辖市设立了24家村镇银行，并作为战略投资者投资重组广东华兴银行，发起设立哈银金融租赁有限责任公司。目前，拥有营业机构332家，在职员7 408人，分支机构遍布全国六大行政区。截至2014年12月31日，资产总额人民币3 436.416亿元，存款总额人民币2 321.972亿元，贷款总额人民币1 239.303亿元。在英国《银行家》杂志2014年全球1 000家大银行排行中列第282位，居中资银行第32位。在美国《环球金融》杂志2014年“中国之星”评选中被评为“2014年最佳城市商业银行”，同时被新浪财经授予“2014年度最佳城市商业银行”，均是国内唯一获此殊荣的城商行。在《亚洲银行家》杂志“亚洲银行家500强（AB500）2014年度中国最具实力银行”榜单被评为“2014年度中国最具实力银行（黑龙江省）”。在亚洲品牌协会等机构联合主办的第9届亚洲品牌评选中，成功跻身“2014亚洲品牌500强”。

Harbin Bank was founded in July 1997, headquartered in Harbin, Heilongjiang Province, with 17 branches in Tianjin, Chongqing, Dalian, Shenyang, Chengdu, Harbin, Daqing etc., and 24 village and town banks in 14 provinces and autonomous cities such as Beijing, Guangdong, Jiangsu, Jilin and Heilongjiang. Furthermore, it has invested to restructure Guangdong Huaxing Bank as a strategic investor. Currently Harbin Bank has 332 functional business bodies employing 7 408 staffs with branching in six administrative regions in China. Up to December 31st, 2014, it has a total asset of 343.6416 billion Yuan, total deposit of 232.1972 billion Yuan, total loan of 123.9303 billion Yuan. According to ’Global 1 000 Banks’ issued by UK’s “Banker” magazine in

2014, Harbin Bank ranked No. 282 in terms of first-class total capital, ranking No. 32 among the Chinese-funded banks. In the election of “Star of China 2014” in American magazine “Global Finance”, it was listed as “The Best City Commercial Bank in 2014”. Meanwhile, it was honored as “The Best City Commercial Bank in 2014” by Sina Finance and Economics. It is the only such bank to gain such honor. It was listed in Asian Bankers “Top 500 Asian Bankers (AB500) in 2014 – The Bank with the Greatest Power in China” in Heilongjiang Province. In the election of the 9th Asian Brands held by Asian Brand Association and institutions, it was successfully listed in Top 500 Asian Brands in 2014.

龙江银行股份有限公司
Longjiang Bank Co., Ltd.

龙江银行股份有限公司是经中国银行业监督管理委员会于2009年11月27日批准，在重组原大庆市商业银行、齐齐哈尔市商业银行、牡丹江市商业银行和七台河市城市信用社的基础上，引进黑龙江省大正投资集团、中粮集团、黑龙江交通发展公司、上海（上实）集团等国内一流的战略投资者，组建成立的股份制商业银行，总行设在哈尔滨市，下设13家分行，现有网点200多个。

Bank of Longjiang Co., Ltd. is a joint-stock commercial bank by restructuring Daqing, Qiqihaer, Mudanjiang Commercial Banks and Qitarihe City credit cooperatives, meanwhile, introducing Helongjiang Dazheng Investment Group, COFCO, Helongjiang Transport Development Corporation, Shanghai (SIIC) Group, and other domestic first-class strategic investors, approved by the China Banking Regulatory Commission. It headquartered in Harbin, with 13 branches, and more than 200 outlets.

南京银行
BANK OF NANJING

南京银行股份有限公司
Bank of Nanjing Co., Ltd.

南京银行成立于 1996 年 2 月 6 日，是一家由国有股份、中资法人股份、外资股份及众多个人股份共同组成的股份制商业银行，实行一级法人体制。历经两次更名，先后于2001 年、2005 年引入境外战略投资者国际金融公司和法国巴黎银行，在全国城商行中最先启动上市辅导程序并于 2007 年成为首家在上海证券交易所上市的城商行。目前注册资本为 29.69 亿元，下辖 13 家分行，129 家营业网点。在英国《银行家》杂志发布的 2014 年度全球1 000 家大银行排名中居第 214 位。

Bank of Nanjing was established on February 6, 1996, which is a joint-stock commercial bank, composed of state-owned shares, legal person shares, foreign shares, and many individual shares, implementing a corporate structure. After twice changed its name, in 2001 and 20015, it is successful introduction of foreign strategic investors IFC and BNP Paribas. Bank of Nanjing is the first city firm that starting listing counseling program and became the first city firm listed on the Shanghai Stock Exchange. Currently, its registered capital reached RMB 2.97 billion. It also has 13 branches and 129 outlets. In the British “The Banker” released “2014 Top 1 000 World Banks” ranking list, Bank of Nanjing was 214th.

融你我　融无限

江苏银行股份有限公司
Bank of Jiangsu Co., Ltd.

江苏银行是由江苏省内十家城市商业银行合并成立的股份制商业银行。2007年1月24日成立，总部位于江苏省南京市。截至2014年末，江苏银行下辖总行营业部和无锡、苏州、南通、常州、淮安、徐州、扬州、镇江、盐城、连云港、宿迁、泰州、上海、深圳、北京、杭州16家分行，共营业网点512个，员工总数13 733名。总资产达10 550亿元人民币。年实现国际结算795亿美元，已与全球1 790家银行及其分支机构建立了代理行关系。

外汇业务经营范围：提供信用证服务及担保；外汇存款、贷款；外汇汇款；外币兑换；国际结算；自营及代客外汇买卖；同业外汇拆借；买卖或代理买卖股票以外的外币有价证券。

特色业务：连续两年分别获得中国银行业协会颁发的2012年度“贸易金融最佳合作伙伴”和2013年度“贸易金融最佳城商行”殊荣。

Bank of Jiangsu, made up of ten city commercial banks in Jiangsu Province, was formally opened on January 24, 2007. The head office is located in Nanjing, Jiangsu Province, China. By the end of 2014, Bank of Jiangsu had one head office, 16 branches, 512 sub-branches and 13 733 employees. Total assets reached RMB 1 055 billion.The network can cover the whole Jiangsu Province, which is the most developed province in China. Along with the opening of Shanghai Branch, Shenzhen Branch, Beijing Branch and Hangzhou Branch, Bank of Jiangsu started the step to the whole country.

The volume of international settlement was USD 79.5 billion. By the end 2014, Bank of Jiangsu has established corresponding relationships with 1 790 bank unities in the world, which makes it easy and smooth to develop international business very quickly.

Issuing Letter of Credit and Bank Guarantee; Payments collecting; Foreign currency deposits and loans; Foreign currency remittance; Foreign exchange; International settlement; Inter-bank foreign currency borrowing and lending; Transacting foreign currency securities (except stocks).

In consecutive two years, named the “Best Cooperation Partner on Trade Finance” for 2012Y and “Best City Commercial Bank on Trade Finance” for 2013Y by China Banking Association.

苏州银行股份有限公司

Bank of Suzhou Co., Ltd.

苏州银行，全称苏州银行股份有限公司，经中国银行业监督管理委员会批准，于 2010 年 9 月 28 日正式挂牌开业，成为苏州地区唯一一家总部设在苏州的城市商业银行。苏州银行现拥有 141 个服务网点，下辖总行营业部，苏州、宿迁、淮安、常州、南京和南通 6 家分行，8 家直属支行，85 家二级支行、34 家分理处、3 家社区支行和 4 家小微支行，机构覆盖苏州大市；同时发起设立 4 家村镇银行；入股 2 家农商行。成立之时，注册资本 30 亿元。截至2014 年末，苏州银行总资产达 2 013.20 亿元，本外币存款余额达 1 204.61 亿元，本外币贷款余额达 685.81 亿元，主要监管指标优良，发展态势良好。

Bank of Suzhou (Suzhou Bank Co., Ltd.) was formally established on September 28th, 2010 after approval from China Banking Regulatory Commission. It becomes the only city commercial bank with the head office in Suzhou. It has 141 service points, 6 branches in Suzhou, Suqian, Huaian, Changzhou, Nanjing and Nantong, 8 sub-branches directly subordinated, 85 secondary sub-branches, 34 sub-branches, 3 community sub-branches and 4 tiny sub-branches. Its institutions spread over Suzhou. Meanwhile, it has established 4 village banks and become a shareholder of 3 rural commercial banks. During its foundation, its registration capital was RMB 3 billion. By the end of 2014, its total asset reached RMB 201.320 billion; its foreign currency deposit balance reached RMB 120.416 billion; its foreign currency loan balance reached RMB 68.581 billion. Its major supervision indexes are good and its development trend is positive.

杭州银行股份有限公司
Bank of Hangzhou Co., Ltd.

杭州市商业银行成立于1996年9月26日，是一家具有独立法人资格的地方性股份制商业银行。总部位于中国杭州，有百余家分支机构，在北京、上海、深圳、南京、合肥、舟山、宁波、绍兴、温州金华、衢州、嘉兴、湖州等地都设立了分行。发起设立一家缙云村镇银行，和澳洲联邦银行共同投资设立3家村镇银行，投资入股石嘴山银行。

Hangzhou City Commercial Bank was established on September 26, 1996, which is an independent legal personality of local joint-stock commercial bank. It headquartered in Hnagzhou, China, with hundreds of branches in Beijing, Shanghai, Shenzhen, Nanjing, Hefei, Zhoushan, Ningbo, Shaoxing, Wenzhou, Jinhua, Quzhou, Jiaxing, Huzhou, and other places. Bank of Hangzhou initiated the establishment of a Jinyun village bank, jointly set up three village banks with the Common wealth Bank of Australia, and also invested Shizuishan Bank in shares.

绍兴银行股份有限公司
Bank of Shaoxing Co., Ltd.

绍兴银行股份有限公司是一家由地方财政及企业单位参股、具有一级法人资格的股份制商业银行。1997年12月由9家城信社和农信社组建而成，1998年5月由绍兴城市合作银行更名为绍兴市商业银行，2009年12月又更名为绍兴银行。

Bank of Shaoxing Co., Ltd. is a legal personality joint-stock commercial bank, with local governments and enterprises unites participated. In December 1997, it composed of 9 city credit cooperatives and rural credit cooperatives. In May 1998, Shaoxing Urban Cooperative Bank was renamed Shaoxing City Commercial Bank. In December 2009, changed its name to Bank of Shaoxing.

湖州银行股份有限公司
Bank of Huzhou Co., Ltd.

湖州银行注册设立于1998年，是在5家城市信用社和5家农村信用社的基础上，由地方财政、企业和个人参股组建的地方性、股份制商业银行，股本总额为6.08亿元。截至2014年末，湖州银行总资产295.59亿元，各项存款余额为250.85亿元，各项贷款余额为168.28亿元，有46个分支机构，47个营业网点。

Bank of Huzhou, founded in 1998, is a local and joint-stock commercial bank established by the local finance, enterprises and individuals based on five city cooperatives and five rural cooperatives, with RMB 0.608 billion of the capital stock amount. By the end of 2014, its total asset was RMB 29.559 billion; its deposit balance was RMB 25.085 billion; its loan balance was RMB 16.828 billion. Besides, it has 46 branches and 47 service points.

金华银行股份有限公司
Bank of Jinhua Co., Ltd.

金华银行是一家地方性股份制商业银行，成立于1997年12月，2010年6月10日由金华市商业银行更名而来，目前在杭州、温州、金华、衢州四地设有营业网点68家，是一家资本充足、资产质量优良、管理规范的现代商业银行。

Bank of Jinhua is a local joint-stock commercial bank, founded in December 1997. On June 10, 2010, it changed its name from Jinhua Commercial Bank. Currently, it has 68 outlets in Hangzhou, Wenzhou, Jinhua, and Quzhou. Bank of Jinhua is a capital adequacy, asset quality, standardize the management of modern commercial bank.

嘉兴银行
BANK OF JIAXING

嘉兴银行股份有限公司
Bank of Jiaxing Co., Ltd.

嘉兴银行成立于1997年12月，是嘉兴市第一家具有法人资格的地方性股份制商业银行。原名嘉兴市商业银行，2009年12月10日更名为嘉兴银行。嘉兴银行目前注册资本10.15亿元，内设20个部门，下辖分支机构45个，其中跨区分支机构7家，嘉兴辖内县市区一级支行9家，二级支行27家。另外，在浙江浦江、安徽歙县主发起成立了两家村镇银行。到2014年11月末，嘉兴银行总资产达到361.93亿元，本外币各项存贷款余额分别为300.29亿元和214.52亿元。

Founded in December, 1997 Bank of Jiaxing corporation limited is the first local commercial bank of shareholding system with legal corporation in Jiaxing city. Its former name is Jiaxing City Commercial Bank, and changed its name to Bank of Jiaxing in December 10, 2009. At the present, its registered capital is up to RMB 1.01 billion. There are 20 departments and 45 branches, including 7 cross branches, 9 primary branches and 27 secondary branches in Jiaxing. IN addition, Bank of Jiaxing set up 2 village banks in Pujiang, Zhejiang province and Shexian, Anhui province.By the end of November, 2014, the total value of the assets of Bank of Jiaxing has reached RMB 36.19 billion, the balance of deposits and loans reached RMB 30.023 billion and RMB 21.45 billion respectively.

温州银行
BANK OF WENZHOU

温州银行股份有限公司
Bank of Wenzhou Co., Ltd.

温州银行股份有限公司前身—温州市商业银行成立于1998年12月17日，2007年温州银行顺利更名并启动跨区域经营，相继在衢州、宁波、杭州、上海、丽水、台州等地设立了分行，舟山分行即将完成筹建，现辖属112家营业网点（含总行营业部），员工2 500余人，逐步形成“立足温州、布局浙江、进军长三角”的跨区域经营发展服务格局。截至2014年末，该行总资产1 263.71亿元，本外币存款余额800.06亿元，本外币贷款余额584.43亿元。2014年，温州银行在英国《银行家》杂志2013年全球1 000强银行评选中列第671位。

Wenzhou Bank Co., Ltd. was founded on December 17th, 1998. It predecessor is Wenzhou City Commercial Bank. In 2007, its name was successfully changed and it initiated the trans-regional operation. It has established sub-branches in Quzhou, Ningbo, Hangzhou, Shanghai, Lishui, Taizhou, etc. Its Zhoushan Branch is nearly finished. Now, it has 112 service points (including the sales department of the head office) and over 2 500 employees. It gradually forms the trans-regional operation development service pattern of “keeping a foothold in Wenzhou, carrying out layout in Zhejiang, and walking to the Yangtze River Delta”. By end of 2014, its total asset reached RMB 126.371 billion; its foreign currency deposit balance reached RMB 80.006 billion; its foreign currency loan balance reached RMB 58.443 billion. In 2014, Bank of Wenzhou ranked 671 in the bank selection of TOP 1 000 over the world in 2013 (the British Magazine—The Banker).

台州银行
TZB 简单 方便 快捷

台州银行股份有限公司
Taizhou Bank Co., Ltd.

台州银行始建于1988年6月6日，由城市信用社发展而来，总行地处浙江省台州市。2002年3月，以市场化方式发起成立了全国首家政府不控股的城市商业银行——台州市商业银行，2010年9月更名为台州银行。截至目前，拥有员工7 000余人。设有7家分行，同时主发起设立了浙江三门银座村镇银行、深圳福田银座村镇银行、北京顺义银座村镇银行、江西赣州银座村镇银行、重庆渝北银座村镇银行、重庆黔江银座村镇银行、浙江景宁银座村镇银行等7家“银座”系列的村镇银行。截至2014年末，全行资产总额1 025.35亿元，各项存款余额为832.95亿元，各项贷款余额为674.59亿元，不良贷款率仅为0.39%。在英国《银行家》杂志公布的“2014年全球1 000家银行”排名中，列第523名。

Taizhou Bank, founded on June 6th, 1988, was developed from the city cooperative. Its head office is located in Taizhou City of Zhejiang Province. In March of 2002, it established the first city commercial bank without holding in China with the way of marketization—Taizhou City Commercial Bank. In September of 2010, its name was changed to Taizhou Bank. Till now, it has about 7 000 staffs. It has established 7 sub-branches, and 7 village banks with “Yinzuo” series, such as Zhejiang Sanmeng Yinzuo Village Bank, Shenzhen Futian Yinzuo Village Bank, Beijing Shunyi Yinzuo Village Bank, Jiangxi Ganzhou Yinzuo Village Bank, Chongqing Yubei Yinzuo Village Bank, Chongqing Qianjiang Yinzuo Village Bank, Zhejiang Jingning Yinzuo Village Bank, etc. By the end of 2014, its total asset reached RMB 102.535 billion; its deposit balance reached RMB 83.285 billion; its loan balance reached RMB 67.459 billion; its non-performing loan ratio was only 0.39%. In the ranking of Global 1 000 Banks in 2014 issued by the British magazine The Banker, it ranked 523.

宁波银行股份有限公司
Bank of Ningbo Co., Ltd.

宁波银行成立于1997年4月10日，截至2015年第一季度末，已设立11家分行，营业网点251家。穆迪给宁波银行的评级为Baa2，英国《银行家》杂志2014年全球1 000强银行排行榜中，宁波银行排名列第220位；英国《银行家》杂志发布“2014年全球银行品牌500强排行榜”，宁波银行居第264位，品牌评级为A+；中国《银行家》杂志、新浪财经等专业机构举办的银行业评选中，宁波银行多次获得“中国最佳城市商业银行”称号。截至2015年第一季度末，宁波银行总资产6 084.84亿元，各项存款3 495.90亿元，各项贷款2 205.60亿元；2015年第一季度实现净利润17.52亿元，同比增长16.61%；不良贷款率0.89%，与2014年年初持平。资本充足率为11.98%，一级资本充足率及核心一级资本充足率均为9.90%。

Bank of Ningbo was established on April 10, 1997. By the end of the first quarter of 2015, there are 11 branches, and 251 outlets. Moody's rated Bank of Ningbo as Baa2; In the British "The Banker" released "2014 Top 500 World Banks" ranking list, Bank of Ningbo was 264th, and brand rating was A+; Chinese "Banker" magazine, Sina Finance and other professional institutions awarded Bank of Ningbo "The Best Chinese City Commercial Bank" in the bank industry. By the end of the first quarter of 2015, the total assets of the Bank achieved RMB 608.48 billion, the balance of deposits was RMB 349.59 billion, and the balance of loans is RMB 220.56 billion; the net profit in first quarter of 2015 was RMB 1.75 billion which has an increase of 16.61% compared with that in the first quarter of 2014; Non-performing loan ratio was 0.89% which was the same as that at the beginning of 2014. Capital adequacy ratio was 11.98%, and tier one capital adequacy ratio and core tier one capital adequacy rate were 9.90%.

浙江稠州商业银行
ZHEJIANG CHOUZHOU COMMERCIAL BANK

浙江稠州商业银行股份有限公司
Zhejiang Chouzhou Commercial Bank Co., Ltd.

浙江稠州商业银行初创于1987年，注册地在全球最大的小商品集散中心——义乌，2006年改制为股份制商业银行。经过20余年的发展，该行已成为一家注册资本30.64亿元、资本净额超120亿元、资产总额超1 200亿元、分支行及村镇银行网点130余家的区域性股份制商业银行。目前该行设有分行（管理部）13家，发起设立村镇银行9家，网点遍布长三角和福建、广东、重庆、四川、江西、云南等全国9省（直辖市），与全世界70多个国家和地区有业务往来。2014年，该行国际结算量达58.5亿美元，市场份额迈入浙江省城市商业银行三甲行列；全行本外币各项业务实现利润总额近20亿元，缴纳各项税收近9亿元，近5年利润总额年均增长率超30%。该行已连续多年跻身国际权威财经媒体英国《银行家》杂志“全球1 000家大银行”榜单，2014年成功跻身全球银行500强，在上榜中资银行中列第56位。

Zhejiang Chouzhou Commercial Bank Co., Ltd. was founded in 1987 and registered YIWU, the largest commodity distribution market in the word. It was incorporated to a shareholding commercial bank in 2006.

Up to 2014, the registered capital of our bank has reached 3.064 billion RMB with net capital more than 120 billion RMB.

We have more than 130 branches covering 9 provinces and 2 municipality cities, including Fujian, Guangdong, Chongqing, Yunnan, Sichuan, Jiangxi, etc.. Besides, we have business connection with over 70 countries and regions across the word.

In 2014, our amount of intemational settlement has achieved 5.85 billion dollars and we successfully step in the top 3 city commercial bank in Zhejiang.

In 2014, we was ranked 500th out of the top 1 000 banks in the word according to THE BANKER.

浙江泰隆商业银行股份有限公司
Zhejiang Tailong Commercial Bank Co., Ltd.

浙江泰隆商业银行成立于2006年，前身是1993年成立的台州市泰隆城市信用社。1993年6月28日，台州市泰隆城市信用社正式成立。2006年8月15日，台州市泰隆城市信用社成功改建成浙江泰隆商业银行。服务范围涵盖浙江、上海、苏州等长三角区域。

Zhejiang Tailong Commercial Bank was establish in 2006, formerly known as Taizhou Tailong City Credit Cooperative founded in 1993. On June 28, 1993, Taizhou Tailong City Credit Cooperative officially founded. On August 15, 2006, Taizhou Tailong City Credit Cooperative converted into Tailong Commercial Bank. Services covering the Yangze River Delta region, such as Zhejiang, Shanghai, Suzhou, and so on.

浙江民泰商业银行
MTB ZHEJIANG MINTAI COMMERCIAL BANK

浙江民泰商业银行股份有限公司
Zhejiang Mintai Commercial Bank Co., Ltd.

浙江民泰商业银行前身是创建于1988年5月的温岭城市信用社，总部位于浙江台州温岭市，2006年8月18日，经中国银行业监督管理委员会批准，更名为浙江民泰商业银行，是具有独立法人资格的股份制商业银行。民泰银行现有员工5 500多人，内设20个职能部门，下设一个营业部，设有台州管理部及杭州、舟山、成都、宁波、上海、义乌、嘉兴、绍兴、温州、衢州、丽水等11家分行和116家支行（含筹），在浙江、江苏、重庆、广州等地主发起设立了9家民泰村镇银行。

Zhejiang Mintai Commercial Bank was formerly known as Wenling City Credit cooperative founded in May 1998, headquartered in Taizhou. On August 18, 2006, changed its name to Zhejiang Mintai Commercial Bank approved by the China Banking Regulatory Commission. It is an independent legal personality joint-stock commercial bank. Mintai Bank has more than 5 500 staffs, 20 functional departments, a sales department, a management department in Taizhou, 11 branches and 116 sub-branches (including chips) in Hangzhou, Zhoushan, Chengdu. Ningbo, Shanghai, Yiwu, Jiaxing, Shaoxing, Wenzhou, Quzhou, and Lishui, as well as 9 Mintai Village Banks in Zhejiang, Jiangsu, Chongqing, Guangzhou, and so on.

宁波东海银行股份有限公司
Ningbo Donghai Bank Co., Ltd.

宁波东海银行是中国浙江省东部的一所城市商业银行，总部位于宁波市，其前身为1988年成立于象山县的绿叶城市信用合作社。2012年3月29日，宁波银监局正式批准该社改制为宁波东海银行，注册资本5.09亿元，由宁波市、象山县两级政府国资企业、多家民营大型企业和上市公司以及其他法人单位和个人股东共同出资组建，为中国最后一家改制的城市信用社。2012年7月16日正式开业。

Ningbo Donghai Bank is a city commercial bank in eastern Zhejiang province, China, headquartered in Ningbo. Its predecessor is Lvye urban city credit cooperative in Xiangshan County founded in 1988. On March 29, 2012, it restructured to Bingbo Donghai Bank approved by Ningbo Municipal Bureau of CBRC. Its registered capital is RMB 0.51 billion. It is a joint venture with state owned enterprises in Ningbo and Xiangshan, many large private enterprises, listed companies and other legal entities, as well as individual shareholders.

徽商银行
HUISHANG BANK

徽商银行股份有限公司
Huishang Bank Co., Ltd.

徽商银行是全国首家由城市商业银行、城市信用社联合重组成立的区域性股份制商业银行，总部设在安徽省合肥市，1997年4月4日注册成立，2005年11月30日更名为徽商银行股份有限公司。2006年1月1日正式对外营业。本行主要经营范围包括在中国吸收公司和零售客户存款，利用吸收的存款发放贷款，以及从事资金业务，包括货币市场业务，投资和交易业务及代客交易等。截至2014年末，徽商银行注册资本110.50亿元。截至2014年12月31日，徽商银行在岗员工6 697人；设有17家分行及250个对外营业机构（包括8家分行营业部和242家支行），498家自助服务区；两家附属公司（金寨徽银村镇银行有限责任公司和无为徽银村镇银行有限责任公司），并参股奇瑞徽银汽车金融股份有限公司。入选英国《银行家》杂志“世界银行1 000强”前200位，排名第194位。

Huishang Bank is the first regional joint-stock commercial bank composed of city commercial banks. Urban credit cooperatives, headquartered in Hefei, Anhui Province. It was registered on April 4, 1997. On November 30, 2005, it changed name its to Huishang Bank Corporation Limited. Huishang Bank officially opened on January 1, 2006. The Bank’s main business scope includes absorbing corporate and retail customers deposits, and using them to loan, as well as engaging in business capital, including money market operations, investment and trading, valet transactions, and so on. As of December 31, 2014, Huishang Bank has 6 697 staffs; 17 branches and 250 foreign business institutions (including 8 branches and 242 sub-branches), 498 self-service area; two subsidiaries (Jinzhai Huiyin Village Bank Co., Ltd. and Wuwei Huiyin Village Bank Co., Ltd.), and shares of Chery Huishang Bank Auto Finance Co., Ltd. In the “The Banker” released “Top 1 000 World Banks” ranking list, Huishang Bank was 194th.

福建海峡银行股份有限公司
Fujian Haixia Bank Co., Ltd.

福建海峡银行的前身是福州市商业银行，成立于1996年12月27日，是在福州市原14家城市信用社和城市信用社联社的基础上，由地方财政、企业法人和个人共同参股组建，具有独立法人资格的福州市第一家地方性股份制商业银行，2009年12月7日正式更名为福建海峡银行。目前下辖温州、漳州、龙岩、宁德、泉州、莆田、三明、福清、南平9家分行、60家支行和1家营业部，网点覆盖福建省各地市，并辐射至浙江省温州市。截至2014年末，资产总额突破千亿元，达1 078亿元，存款余额635.62亿元，贷款余额459.9亿元，各项指标均符合或优于监管要求。近年来先后获得了权威机构授予的“中国最具投资价值高成长银行”、“全国小企业金融服务先进单位”、“全国厂务公开民主管理先进单位”、“最具特色中小银行”、“全国模范劳动关系和谐企业”、“全国青年文明号”、“全国巾帼文明岗”、“全国模范职工之家”以及“福建省文明单位”等各种荣誉称号。

Founded on December 27th, 1996, Fujian Haixia Bank is the first local joint-stock commercial bank with the independent legal qualification established by the local finance, enterprise legal person and individuals based on the original 14 city cooperative and city cooperative associations in Fuzhou. Its predecessor is Fuzhou City Commercial Bank. On December 7th, 2009, its name was formally changed into Fujian Haixia Bank. At present, it has 9 branches in Wenzhou, Zhangzhou, Longyan, Ningde, Quanzhou, Putian, Sanming, Fuqing and Nanping, 60 sub-branches and a sales department. It covers all cities of Fujian Province, and even expands to Wenzhou of Zhejiang Province. By the end of 2014, its total asset broke through hundreds of billions, reaching RMB 107.8 billion. Its deposit balance reached RMB 63.562 billion, and its loan balance reached RMB 45.99 billion. Each index meets or is superior to the supervision requirements.

Recently, it has been awarded many honors and titles endowed by the authoritative organizations, such as “Bank with the most investment value and high growth in China”, “advanced unit of the financial service of the national small enterprises”, “small and medium-sized banks with the most characteristics”, “enterprise with national harmonious model labor relationship”, “national youth civilization”, “national civilization post”, “home of national model staffs”, “civilization units in Fujian Province”, etc..

泉州银行
BANK OF QUANZHOU

泉州银行股份有限公司
Bank of quanzhou Co., Ltd.

泉州银行股份有限公司是经中国人民银行批准，于1997年6月组建成立的股份制商业银行，前身是泉州市商业银行，总行设于福建省泉州市。2009年经中国银监会批准，泉州市商业银行正式更名为“泉州银行”。目前下辖漳州、龙岩、福州3家分行，67家支行（含社区支行）和1家直属营业部。截至2014年末，全行资产总额607.79亿元。

Bank of Quanzhou set up the establishment of joint-stock commercial banks in June 1997, approved by the People's Bank of China. It headquartered in Quanzhou, Fujian Province, was formerly known as Quanzhou City Commercial Bank.In 2009, the China Banking Regulatory Commission officially approved the Quanzhou City Commercial Bank changed its name to "Bank of Quanzhou".

At present, Bank of Quanzhou has owned Zhangzhou ,Longyan, Fuzhou 3 branches, and 67 sub branches (including community branch) and 1 direct sales department. As the end of 2014, total assets reached 60,779 million yuan.

厦门银行
Xiamen Bank

厦门银行股份有限公司
Xiamen Bank Co., Ltd.

厦门银行成立于1996年11月30日，是经中国人民银行批准、具有独立法人资格的股份制商业银行，现有注册资本15.87亿元，2008年，厦门银行成功引进具有台资背景的富邦（香港）银行作为战略投资者，成为大陆首家（也是迄今为止唯一一例）具有台资背景的商业银行。截至2014年底，厦门银行总资产近1 200亿元。经中国银监会审核，厦门银行监管评级连续三年保持二级；同年，外部资信评级提升至AA级。全行现有50个现代化经营网点，已在重庆和福建省内福州、泉州、漳州、南平、莆田、三明等地市设立分行，龙岩分行已获批筹建，今年有望实现福建省内分行网点全覆盖。近年来，厦门银行致力于打造成为“闽台合作样板银行”，开设大陆银行业首个台商业务部、新兴金融部，为台商提供“资金大三通”、“人民币直航”等个性化金融产品。

Established on November 30, 1996, Xiamen Bank is a shareholding commercial bank with independent legal personality, which is approved by the People’s Bank of China. Its registered capital is RMB 1.59 billion. In 2008, Xiamen Bank has successfully introduced Fubin Bank (Hong Kong) as a strategic investor which has Taiwanese background. It became the first mainland commercial bank (and so far the only one) has the Taiwan-funded background. A of the end of 2014, Xiamen Bank’s assets totaled about RMB 120 billion. Xiamen Banking Regulation keep secondary rating in three consecutive years; The same year, the external credit rating raised to AA level. It has 50 business outlets, and has set up branches in Chongqing, as well as Fuzhou, Quanzhou, Zhangzhou, Nanping. Putian, Sanming and other cities in Fujian Province. Moreover, it has been approved to build a branch in Longyan. It is expected to achieve that branches has coverage of Fujian Province in this year. In recent years, Xiamen Bank is committed to create a “model of cooperation between Fujian and Taiwan Bank”. It is the first mainland bank has a business department and emerging financial department, providing “Big Three Links”, “RMB Direct” and other personalized financial products for Taiwanese businessmen.

南昌银行股份有限公司
Bank of Nanchang Co., Ltd.

南昌银行由南昌市地方财政发起，成立于1997年12月。现注册资本27.82亿股。截至2014年12月末，全行总资产1 547.62亿元，较上年末增长23.06%；一般性存款余额1 048.54亿元，较上年末增长15.70%；各项贷款余额600.99亿元，较上年末增长22.93%；实现税前利润22.87亿元，较上年末增长0.23%；上缴各项税收突破10亿元。2014年，南昌银行发行资产证券化产品15.945亿元，成为全国首批27个具有信贷资产证券化业务资格的银行，走在同业前列。目前，南昌银行拥有包括广州、苏州、赣州、九江在内的25家一级分（支）行和1家小企业信贷中心，营业网点达到100多家，基本覆盖全省设区市，并出资设立了5家村镇银行。

Nanchang Bank, founded in December of 1997, was initiated by the local finance of Nanchang City. Currently, its registration capital is RMB 2.782 billion of shares. By the end of 2014, its total asset was RMB 154.762 billion, which was increased by 23.06% compared with last year; the generalized deposit balance was RMB 104.854 billion, which was increased by 15.7% compared with last year; its loan balance reached RMB 60.099, which increased by 22.93%. It realized RMB 2.287 billion of pre-tax profit, which increased by 0.23%. Besides, it paid over RMB 1 billion of tax revenue. In 2014, Nanchang Bank issued RMB 1.5945 billion of asset securitization products, and became the bank among the first lot of 27 banks with securitization of credit assets qualification in China, and walked in front of the industry. At present, it has 25 first-level branches (sub-branches) in Guangzhou, Suzhou, Ganzhou and Jiujiang, and a small enterprise credit center, and over 100 service points. It basically covers the cities of the province, and invests in establishing 5 village banks.

九江银行
BANK OF JIUJIANG

九江银行股份有限公司
Bank of Jiujiang Co., Ltd.

九江银行原名九江市商业银行，于2000年11月18日经中国人民银行武汉分行批准，由九江市8家城市信用社主发起设立，总部设在九江市，总行下辖10家分行（其中省外分行2家、省内分行8家）、85家支行（部）、3个中心（重点客户中心、小企业信贷中心、国际业务中心）。

Bank of Jiujiang was formerly known as Jiujiang City Commercial Bank. Eight urban credit cooperatives in Jiujiang City initiated its establishment, headquartered in Jiujiang City. There are 10 branches (including 2 branches out province and 8 branches in province), 85 sub-branches (department), and 3 centers. (Key Custome Center, Small Business Credit Center, and International Business Center)

赣州银行股份有限公司
Bank of Ganzhou Co., Ltd.

赣州银行前身为赣州市商业银行，是在原赣州市两家城市信用社基础上，经中国人民银行总行批准，由地方财政、企业法人、自然人共同出资发起，于2001年1月18日成立，是赣州市具有独立法人资格的股份制商业银行。2008年11月18日，经中国银监会批准，更名为赣州银行。截至2014年底，已在新余、宜春、南昌、厦门、萍乡、吉安设立6家分行，机构总数达到73家。至2014年末，全行资产总额达到724.76亿元，各项存款余额550.81亿元，各项贷款余额380亿元。

Founded in January 18th, 2001, Bank of Ganzhou is a joint-stock commercial bank with independent legal personality, established by the local finance, enterprise legal person and natural person after the approval from the People's Bank of China on the basis of the original two city cooperatives in Ganzhou. Its predecessor is Ganzhou City Commercial Bank. On November 18th, 2008, after the approval from China Banking Regulatory Commission, its name was changed into "Bank of Ganzhou". By the end of 2014, it established 6 branches in Xinyu, Yichun, Nanchang, Xiamen, Pingxiang, and Ji'an, and 73 institutions. Besides, its total asset reached RMB 72.476 billion; its deposit balance reached RMB 55.081 billion; its loan balance reached RMB 38 billion.

齐鲁银行股份有限公司

Qilu Bank Co., Ltd.

齐鲁银行股份有限公司成立于1996年6月，是全国首批设立的城市商业银行，也是山东省首家、全国第4家与外资银行实现战略合作的城商行，辖有天津、青岛、聊城、泰安、德州5家分行。全行网点数102家，在岗员工2 700余人，齐鲁银行是山东省首家开办国际业务、首家获得跨境贸易人民币结算资格的银行，与全球100多个国家和地区的10 000多家银行建立了代理行关系，截至2014年末，总资产1 222亿元，存款1 002亿元。

Founded on June 6, 1996, Jinan City Cooperation Bank is a city commercial bank established among the first lot of the banks in China. Besides, it is the first one in Shandong and the fourth one in China to realize the strategic cooperation with the foreign-funded banks. It has 5 branches in Tianjin, Qingdao, Liaocheng, Tai'an and Dezhou. It has 102 service points and over 2 700 employees. Qilu Bank is the first bank to deal with the international business and gain Renminbi settlement qualification of the trans-national trade. It has established agent bank relationship with over 10 000 banks in over 100 countries and regions over the world. By the end of 2014, its total asset was RMB 122.2 billion and its deposit was RMB 100.2 billion.

临商银行股份有限公司
Linshang Bank Co., Ltd.

临商银行全称临商银行股份有限公司，是一家总部设在山东省临沂市的跨区域经营的股份制商业银行；前身临沂市商业银行成立于1998年2月18日，2008年11月22日经中国银监会批准，正式更名为临商银行。现辖76家分支机构，横跨鲁浙两省，共有员工2 000余人。截至2014年末，全行总资产637亿元，各项存款533亿元，各项贷款468亿元。

Linshang Bank (Linshang Bank Co., Ltd.) is a joint-stock commercial bank with trans-regional operation. Its head office is located in Linyi of Shandong Province. Its predecessor Linyi City Commercial Bank was established on February 18th, 1998. On November 22nd, 2008, its name was changed to Linshang Bank after approval from China Banking Regulatory Commission. At present, it has 76 branches crossing Shandong and Zhejiang, with over 2 000 employees. By the end of 2014, its total asset was RMB 63.7 billion; deposit was RMB 53.3 billion; loan was RMB 46.8 billion.

BQD 青岛银行

青岛银行股份有限公司
Bank of Qingdao Co., Ltd.

青岛银行成立于1996年11月，是经中国人民银行批准，我国首批设立的城市商业银行之一，山东省资产规模最大的城市商业银行，总部在山东省青岛市。目前已在青岛、济南、东营、威海、淄博、德州、枣庄、烟台等8个城市设立80家分支机构，65家自助银行，358台自助设备，员工2 500余人。截至2015年第一季度末，总股本为31.12亿股，总资产为1 561.63亿元，各项存款1 044亿元，各项贷款余额630亿元。按照总资产计算，青岛银行2014年入围英国《银行家》杂志（*The Banker*）世界银行500强，居第474位。

Bank of Qingdao was established in November 1996, approved by the People's Bank of China, which is one of the city commercial bank in China. It is the city commercial bank which has the largest size of assets in Shandong Province. Currently, Bank of Qingdao has set up 80 branches, 65 self-service banking, and 358 self-service equipment with more than 2 500 people in Qingdao, Jinan, Dongying, Weihai, Zibo, Dezhou, Zaozhuang, and Yantai City. By the end of the first quarter of 2015, the total share capital of RMB 3.112 billion shares, the total assets of RMB 156.163, the balance of deposits was RMB 104.4 billion, and the balance of loans was RMB 63 billion. In the British "The Banker" released "2014 Top 500 World Banks" ranking list, Bank of Qingdao was 474th in total assets.

日照银行
BANK OF RIZHAO

日照银行股份有限公司
Bank of rizhao Co., Ltd.

日照银行前身日照市商业银行，成立于2000年12月28日，是一家由国有股份、企业法人股份及自然人股份共同组成的具有独立法人资格的股份制商业银行。2004年实现本外币一体化经营，与世界上80多个国家和地区的550家银行建立了代理行关系。2009年更名为日照银行，先后在青岛、济南、临沂、潍坊设立了4家分行，在海南三亚、陵水和山东济宁发起设立了3家村镇银行。现辖4家分行、38家支行、1家营业部、1家小企业信贷中心、16个部室，注册资本24.98亿元，从业人员1 198名。

Bank of Rizhao, formerly known as Rizhao City Commercial Bank, was established on December 28, 2000. It is an independent legal personality joint-stock commercial bank composed of state-owned shares, corporate shares, and the natural person shares. Bank of Rizhou achieved the integration of the foreign currency business in 2004, with 550 banks in more than more than 80 countries and regions, by having correspondent banking relationship.

威海市商业银行
Weihai City Commercial Bank Co., Ltd.

威海市商业银行成立于1997年8月1日，现辖济南、天津、青岛、烟台、德州、临沂、济宁、潍坊等60多家分支机构。自成立以来，威海市商业银行始终坚持“正德守信，和谐共进”，始终坚持“严谨规范，务实高效”，始终坚持“真诚相伴，携手超越”，全力打造“学习型快乐银行”“区域性领先银行”“区域性蓝色银行”“社会责任银行”和“科技金融银行”，在服务环渤海区域经济社会建设、追求和谐共赢的过程中，走出了一条独具特色的发展道路。截至2014年年底，全行资产总额达到1 170亿元，各项存款余额达到795亿元，各项贷款余额达到446亿元，各项监管指标全面达标并持续向好改善，连续多年被评为二级行。

外汇业务开展状况：该行贸易金融业务自2009年着手筹备，于2010年5月正式营业，并得到较快发展。2010年国际结算量2.61亿美元，2011年为12.55亿美元，2012年为20.45亿美元，2013年为36.90亿美元，2014年为36.93亿美元。

外汇业务经营范围：外汇汇款、授信开证、进口押汇、发票融资、打包贷款、提货担保、开立国内证、买方押汇等。

Weihai City Commercial Bank was founded on 1st August 1997. Now it has more than 60 branches in Weihai, Jinan, Tianjin, Qingdao, Yantai, Dezhou, Linyi, Jining, Weifang and other cities in China. During the development process, Weihai City Commercial Bank always adheres to different ideas such as “Justness, Morality and Honesty Can Lead to Harmonious Development”, “Rigorous and Normative Standards Result in Practical and Efficient Behavior” and “Sincere Cooperation May Lead to Win-win Development”. Determined to be a “Learning–oriented Pleasant Bank”, “Regionally Leading Bank”, “Socially Responsible Bank” and “Technologically Financial Bank”, the bank has formed its own unique development mode. By the end of March 2014, the bank's total assets, the total deposit and the loan balance has respectively amounted to RMB 117 billion, RMB 79.5 billion and RMB 44.6 billion. Fully complying with regulatory requirements, all the monitoring indicators of the bank are up to the standard and have been improved continually. The bank has been ranked the second rating level by CBRC for many years, which is the highest rating level for city commercial banks in China.

Our bank's trade finance business was prepared since 2009, and launched officially in May 2009. The amount of international in recent four years is respectively $1.5 billion in 2011, $2 billion in 2012, $4 billion in 2013 and $5 billion in 2014.

Foreign exchange loans, L/C, bills of draft, invoice financing, packing credit, dilivery guaranteeand etc..

潍坊银行股份有限公司
Bank of Weifang Co., Ltd.

潍坊银行是经中国人民银行批准设立的山东省潍坊市唯一一家具有独立法人资格的地方性股份制商业银行，总行坐落于潍坊金融街内，注册资本为30 788万元人民币，组织形式为股份有限公司，实行“一级法人、统一核算”的体制。

截至2014年末，潍坊银行全辖78家网点，其中，在潍坊区域设立59家支行和5家社区支行，在青岛、聊城、滨州地区分别成立1家异地分行，其中青岛地区下设8家支行和2家社区支行，控股青岛胶南海汇村镇银行。截至2014年末，全行总资产达到813亿元，本外币存款余额551亿元，各项贷款余额415亿元。

Bank of Weifang is the only local joint-stock commercial bank with the independent legal qualification in Weifang City of Shandong Province after approval of People's Bank of China. Its head office is located in the financial street of Weifang, with the registration capital of RMB 307 880 000. Its organization form is a limited liability company, with the system of “first legal person and uniform accounting”.

By the end of 2014, Bank of Weifang had 78 service points. It established 59 sub-branches and 6 community sub-branches in Weifang. Besides, it established 1 remote branch in Qingdao, Liaocheng and Bingzhou respectively. Among them, it established 8 sub-branches and 2 community sub-branches in Qingdao, and became a shareholder of Qingdao Jiaonan Haihui Village Bank. By the end of 2014, its total asset reached RMB 81.3 billion; its foreign currency deposit balance reached RMB 55.1 billion; its loan balance reached RMB 41.5 billion.

烟台银行股份有限公司
Yantai Bank Co., Ltd.

烟台银行成立于1997年11月12日，2009年3月25日由烟台市商业银行股份有限公司更名为烟台银行股份有限公司，设立21个职能部室，下辖78处经营机构。其中，65处分布于烟台市七区内，县域在龙口、招远、莱州、蓬莱、海阳、栖霞、莱阳、长岛共设有13家支行。截至2014年12月末，全行资产总额479.66亿元，各项存款余额415.8亿元，贷款余额280.72亿元，实现净利润4.13亿元。

Yantai Bank was founded on November 12th, 1997. On March 25th, 2009, Yantai City Commercial Bank was changed into Yantai Bank. It has established 21 functional departments, and 78 operation institutions. Among them, 65 institutions are located in seven districts of Yantai City. Besides, it has established 13 sub-branches in Longkou, Zhaoyuan, Laizhou, Penglai, Haiyang, Qixia, Laiyang and Changdao. By the end of 2014, its total asset reached RMB 47.966 billion; its deposit balance reached RMB 41.58 billion; its loan balance reached RMB 28.072 billion, and reached RMB 0.413 billion of net profit.

齐商银行
QISHANG BANK

齐商银行股份有限公司
Qishang Bank Co., Ltd.

齐商银行的前身是淄博市商业银行，是全国第四批由城市信用社组建的地方性股份制商业银行，成立于1997年8月28日，总部位于山东省淄博市。2009年2月13日，经中国银监会批准，淄博市商业银行更名为齐商银行。齐商银行现有注册资本金17.04亿元，辖属淄博管理中心、高新区支行以及西安、滨州、东营、潍坊、济宁、威海6家分行，控股发起设立了1家村镇银行。

自成立以来，齐商银行按照现代公司治理制度的要求，建立了股东大会、董事会、监事会和高级管理层为主体的“三会一层”组织框架及其运行程序与规则，始终坚持“务实、创新、精细、卓越”的企业精神，立足“市民银行”和“中小企业主办行”的市场定位，遵循“坚持改革、锐意创新，加强内控、稳健发展，完善管理、提高效益”的经营方针，持续调整经营结构、转变发展方式，走“差异化、特色化、精细化”发展道路，经营领域不断延展，创新能力不断增强，资金实力不断壮大，盈利水平不断提高，风险管控机制不断完善，实现了持续健康快速发展，综合经营水平及盈利能力均居省内城商行前列。截至2014年12月底，全行资产总额达到698.2亿元，较年初增长15.2%；各项存款余额579.1亿元，较年初增长12.8%；各项贷款余额375.8亿元，比年初增长13.5%，各项主要监管指标持续达标，实现了规模、质量和效益的协调发展。获评“2014全国支持中小企业发展十佳商业银行”、“2014中国中小企业首选服务商”、“中国小微企业金融服务客户满意十佳典范奖”、“山东省银行业服务‘三农’十佳金融产品奖”等称号。2012年、2013年、2014年连续三年在全市纳税企业500强中名列前6位，为地方经济建设作出了突出贡献，荣获“淄博市工业经济发展突出贡献单位”称号。2011年、2012年度在全省182家地方金融企业绩效评价中，获得AAA优秀等级，名列山东省第4位；被中国银监会评为“全国银行业金融机构小企业贷款工作先进单位”，多次被山东银监局授予“良好银行”称号，先后荣获“山东省文明单位”、“中国优秀企业（品牌）形象十佳单位”、“淄博慈善事业突出贡献奖”等荣誉称号，连续6年入选“全国服务业500强”，行内多家分支机构先后多次被评为“全国青年文明号”、“全国文明规范服务示范窗口”等。2010年至2013年，在中国银监会的监管评级中，连续被评为3A等级。

外汇业务开展状况：齐商银行自2003年6月10日经中国人民银行济南分行批准，取得开办外汇业务资格，2003年8月28日开始办理外汇业务，经历了从无到有、从小到大、从弱到强的蜕化过程。十余年里，我们始终以“合规、发展”作为工作重心，总分支行上下联动、共同努力，在市场开拓、综合收益、内部管理等方面取得显著成绩，各类结算产品不断丰富，服务质效不断提升，国际业务结算量快速发展，连续多年位居山东省城商行前列。经过几年的发展壮大，目前与60多个国家和地区的500多家银行建立代理行关系。2014年国际结算量30亿美元，外汇交易金额83亿美元，外汇条线中间业务收入占全行中间业务收入比例达49%。

外汇业务经营范围：外汇存款、外汇贷款、结售汇、外币兑换、国际结算、外汇买卖、跨境人民币业务、各类贸易融资、保函、担保、同业拆放等。

特色业务：跨境人民币、个人留学汇款。

Qishang Bank Co., Ltd. hereinafter referred to as Qishang bank formerly known as Zibo City Commercial Bank, is the fourth installment of local joint-stock commercial banks established by urban credit cooperatives, which was founded in August 28, 1997 and headquartered in Zibo city, Shandong Province. In February 13, 2009, approved by the China Banking Regulatory Commission, Zibo City Commercial Bank changed its name to “Qishang Bank Co., Ltd.”. Qishang Bank has a registered capital of 1.704 billion yuan, manages Zibo management center, High-Tech Zone Sub-branch and Xian branch，Bizhou branch，Dongying branch, Weifang branch, Jining Branch, Weihai branch, and one holding village bank.

Since establishment, in accordance with the requirements of a modern corporate governance system, Qishang Bank set up organization framework of “shareholders” meeting, Board of Director, Board of Supervisors and top management” and program and rules, always adhering to enterprise’s spirit of “pragmatic, innovation, fine, excellence”, based on the market positioning of “bank for citizens” and “leading bank for small and medium-sized enterprises", following the management policy of "insisting on reform, keeping innovation, tightening internal control, steady development, improving management, raising benefits", continuously adjusting business structure, changing development manner, stepped on a "characteristic and differentiated" development path, continuously extending business field, continuously strengthening innovation ability, continuously expanding capital, continuously improving profit-earning ability, continuously improving risk management mechanism, realized the sustainable healthy and rapid development, comprehensive management level and profit-earning ability ranked the top among all city commercial banks in the province. By the end of 2014, the total assets reached RMB 69.82 billion, increasing by 15.2 %, compared with the beginning of the year. The balances of various deposits were RMB 57.91billion, increasing by 12.8 %, the balances of various loans were RMB 37.58 billion, increasing by 13.5%, all major regulatory indicators met the standards, realized the coordinated development of scale, quality and benefit. The bank was awarded "China Top Ten City Commercial Bank to Support Small and Medium-sized Enterprises in 2014" "China small and medium-sized enterprises preferred provider in 2014" "Golden Award for China top Ten Best Model of Financial Service for Small and Micro Enterprises" "Financial Products Award for Shandong Top Ten service to agriculture, rural areas and farmers", etc.. The bank ranked top six among the top 500 tax payment enterprise in 2012, 2013 and 2014. It made outstanding contributions to local economic development, and was awarded "Unit with Outstanding Contribution in Zibo Industrial Economic Development".

In performance evaluation on 182 local financial enterprises in 2011, 2012, it won grades AAA, ranked top four in Shandong province. It was given the title of "Good Bank" by Shandong banking Regulatory Bureau repeatedly, and was awarded "Civilized Units in Shandong Province" "China Top Ten excellent enterprises image", "Outstanding Contribution Award to Philanthropy", etc.. It was selected "Top 500 service enterprises in China" for six consecutive years, many of its branches and sub-branches were awarded "the National Youth Civilization". It ranked 3A for three consecutive years in the China Banking Regulatory Commission ratings from 2010 to 2013.

In June 10, 2003, approved by People's Bank of China, Shandong Branch, Qishang Bank get the foreign exchange business qualification and start handing foreign exchange business in August 28, 2003, has experienced degeneration process from small to large, from weak to strong. We always take the "compliance and development" as the focus of work, head office and branch have made significant achievements in a concerted effort in market development, comprehensive income, internal management, etc.. All kinds of settlement products were continued to be enriched, service quality was continued to be improved, international settlement amount developed rapidly, which was at the forefront of Shandong Province for many years. After development for many years, up to now it established correspondent relationships with more than 500 banks among more than 60 countries and regions. The balances of international settlement and EX trade were USD 3 billion and USD 8.3 billion respectively, foreign exchange business line income accounted for 49% of the total intermediate business income of the whole bank.

Scope of business of foreign exchange transactions: Foreign currency deposits, foreign currency loans, foreign exchange, foreign currency exchange, international settlement, foreign exchange trading cross-border RMB business, all kinds of trade financing, letter of guarantee, guarantee, correspondent loan, etc..

Characteristic business: Foreign exchange trading cross-border RMB business, personal remittance.

东营银行股份有限公司
Dongying Bank Co., Ltd.

东营银行股份有限公司前身为东营市商业银行股份有限公司，是根据中国银行业监督管理委员会下发的《关于筹建东营市商业银行的批复》（〔2005〕27号文）批准设立的股份制商业银行，2005年8月5日取得山东省工商行政管理局注册号为370000018084402的企业法人营业执照，2005年8月5日取得中国银行业监督管理委员会山东监管局批准的许可证号为B0172H237050001的金融许可证。2011年11月17日经中国银行业监督管理委员会批复（银监复〔2011〕505号）东营市商业银行股份有限公司变更为东营银行股份有限公司，于2012年2月17日经山东省工商行政管理局核准名称变更，企业法人营业执照号及金融许可证号维持不变。截至2014年12月31日止，注册资本为人民币1 783 799 919.00元，总资产461.58亿元，实现净利润6.91亿元，注册地址为山东省东营市东营区井冈山路808号，法定代表人为石子强。

该行于2007年7月正式开办国际业务，七年来，该行始终坚持“内控先行、审慎发展”的理念，以体制改革激发动力，以产品创新开拓市场，东营银行国际业务发展实现了从无到有、从小到大的历史性转变，呈现出持续、健康、快速发展的良好势头，各项指标在山东省城商行系统和东营市外汇指定银行系统中居于前列，跨境人民币业务自2012年底开办以来发展迅猛，2013年和2014年跨境人民币业务结算量在山东省城商行中分别居第三位和第一位。2008年、2010—2012年先后四次被国家外汇管理局山东省分局授予“国际收支优秀申报单位”荣誉称号，2009—2014年连续6年被当地外汇管理部门评为“执行外汇管理法规考核A类行”。

外汇业务经营范围：外汇存款；外汇贷款；外汇汇款；外汇同业拆借；国际结算；外汇票据的承兑及贴现；外汇担保；代客外汇买卖；资信调查、咨询、见证业务；经批准的其他外汇业务。

特色业务：一、国际结算业务：汇款业务、托收业务、信用证业务、保函业务（融资性及非融资性）、合作办理远期结售汇业务、跨境人民币结算业务、国内信用证业务、NRA业务、合作办理跨境人民币转收款业务；

二、贸易融资业务：打包放款、出口押汇、进口押汇、福费廷、出口商业发票贴现、出口信保融资、国内证项下买方融资、国内证项下卖方融资、国内证福费廷转卖、买方付息贴现、换币种转通知。

Dongying Bank Co., Ltd. (hereinafter refers to as "the bank"), originally known as Dongying Commercial Bank Co., Ltd., is a joint-stock commercial bank established through the approval of China Banking Regulatory Commission with the document *On the Approval of Establishing Dongying Commercial Bank* 〔2005〕 No.27). On August 5, 2005, the bank obtained the License of the business corporation (registration No.:370000018084402) from Industrial and Commercial Administration Bureau of Shandong Province. On August 5, 2005, the bank obtained the Financial Business Operation License (license No.: B0172H237050001) from Shandong Supervision Bureau of China Banking Regulatory Commission. On November 17, 2011, with the approval of China Banking Regulatory Commission (YJF 〔2011〕 No.505), Dongying Commercial Bank Co., Ltd. was altered into Dongying Bank Co., Ltd. and its registration number of the License of the business corporation and the license number of Financial Business Operation License remain the same. Up to December, 31, 2014, the registered capital of the bank is RMB 1 783 799 919.00 with RMB 46.158 billion of total asset and RMB 0.691 billion of net profit. Its registered address is No.808, Jinggangshan Road, Dongying District, Dongying City, Shandong Province. Its legal representative is Shi Ziqiang.

This bank started its international business from July, 2007. During the past seven years, the bank has been persisting in its idea of "internal control first and cautiously developing" and stimulate motivation with structural reform, expand the market with innovative products. With this idea in mind, the international business of the bank has made the transition of growing from nothing and from small to big. It can be demonstrated that the development trend of the bank has been sustainable, healthy and rapid, with various indexes has been among the top in commercial bank system in the province and the appointed banking system in conducting foreign exchange in Dongying city. Its cross-border RMB transactions has been developing rapidly from its opening at the end of 2012. Its cross-border RMB settlement transaction volume has been ranked as No. 3 and No.1 in 2013 and 2014 respectively among the commercial banks in Shandong province. In 2008, 2010, 2011 and 2012, the bank has been honored the title of "Distinctive Declare Unit in International Balance of Payment" four times by Shandong Branch of the State Administration of Foreign Exchange. And from 2009 to 2014, the bank has been ranked as "A Level Bank in Executing Foreign Exchange Management Regulation" for six years successively by the local foreign exchange administration department.

Scope of business of foreign exchange transactions: foreign exchange deposits, foreign exchange loans, foreign exchange remittance, foreign exchange lending among the same trade, international settlement, foreign exchange bill acceptance and discount, foreign exchange guarantee, foreign exchange purchase and sale for the customers, credit investigation, consultant and witness, and other foreign exchange transaction approved.

Characteristic business: 1. International settlement business: deposit, collection, L/C, L/G (financing and non-financing), cooperative handling of future foreign exchange settlement, cross-border RMB settlement, domestic L/C, NRA, cooperative handling of RMB payment;

2. Trade financing: packing credit, outward documentary bill, inward documentary bill, Forfaiting, export commercial invoice discount, Export Credit Insurance financing, domestic letter of credit-related buyer financing, domestic letter of credit-related seller financing, Domestic letter of credit-related Forfaiting resale, buyer interest paid note discount, notification on change of currency.

德州银行
DEZHOU BANK

德州银行股份有限公司
Dezhou Bank

德州银行原名德州市商业银行，成立于2004年12月7日。德州银行主营传统商业银行业务，包括公司业务、个人业务、国际业务和金融市场业务。公司业务基于银行的核心信贷产品，为客户提供个性化、创新的金融服务。个人业务主要针对个人客户的金融需求，提供基于银行卡之上的系统服务。国际业务为有外汇业务需求的企业和个人提供国际结算、外汇资金和贸易融资，金融市场业务主要是为其他银行或机构提供国际汇兑、资金清算、同业拆借和托管等全面服务。德州银行将秉承“以客户为中心，以市场为导向，强化公司治理，追求卓越效益”，为客户提供全方位、高品质的银行服务，与广大客户携手共创美好未来。

Dezhou Bank was founded in Dec.7, 2014 which was ever named Dezhou City Commercial Bank, the bank is mainly engaged in commercial banking, including corporate and retail banking, international banking and treasury business. Corporate banking is built upon credit products, to provide customers with personalized and innovative financial services. Retail banking serves the financial needs of the Bank's individual customers, focusing on providing them with such services as savings deposit, consumer bankcard and wealth management business. International banking is to provide international settlement, foreign exchange as well as trade finance to companies or individuals in need.Treasury business includes domestic and foreign-currency trading and investment, fund management, wealth management, value-secured debt business, domestic and overseas financing and other fund operation and management services. Being customer-centered and market-oriented, Dezhou bank will improve corporate governance in pursuit of mutual benefits, it is dedicated to offering customers with a full range of high-quality banking services.

济宁银行股份有限公司
Bank of Jining Co., Ltd.

济宁银行即原济宁市商业银行，于2005年12月31日经中国银监会批准筹建，2006年6月成立，2006年8月26日开业，2009年12月更名为济宁银行，是济宁市唯一一家地方性股份制商业银行。始终坚持“服务地方经济、服务中小企业、服务城市居民”的市场定位，实现了各项业务的跨越式发展。截至2014年末，济宁银行共设4家跨区域分行，38家支行；全行员工1 335人；资产总额达到335亿元，存款余额279亿元，贷款余额207亿元；存贷比74%；各项经营指标在国内同行业均处于领先水平。

济宁银行2010年4月成立国际业务部，目前已与境内外 66个国家或地区的370余家银行建立代理行关系；在11家境外银行开立了清算账户，是中国国际商会、银行家年鉴及外汇交易中心的会员；实行“单证中心”模式，为客户提供“一站式”服务，致力于更贴心、更高效、更便捷的服务。

外汇业务经营范围：外汇存款；外汇贷款；外汇汇款；外币兑换；国际结算；同业外汇拆借；外汇票据的承兑和贴现；外汇借款；外汇担保；自营外汇买卖或者代客外汇买卖；资信调查、咨询、见证业务。

特色业务：挂单结售汇业务（国际业务）、小微信贷业务。

Bank of Jining Co., Ltd. Was formerly named as Jining City Commercial Bank. Upon the approval of the China Banking Regulatory Commission (CBRC), funds were raised to start the Bank’s Business in December, 2005. Approved by the CBRC, the Bank officially opened in August, 2006, and changed its name as Bank of Jining Co., Ltd. (Shortened Form: Bank of Jining) in December, 2009. Bank of Jining is the only locally joint-stock commercial bank in Jining City. Bank of Jining always adhere to the ‘service the local economy, service for small and medium-sized enterprises, service city residents'as market positioning, which has achieved the spanning development of the business. By the end of 2014, Bank of Jining opened four cross-regional branches, with a total of 38 branches. It has 1 335 employees；Total assets are 33.5 billion yuan, Balance of deposit are 27.9 billion yuan, balance of loans are 20.7 billion yuan. The LDR is 74%. Business indicators of Bank of Jining is in the leading level in the domestic industry.

The International business Department of Bank of Jining was established in April 2010. Bank of Jining has established corespondence banking relationship with more than 370 banks in 66 countries. Bank of Jining opened settlement clearing account in 11 foreign banks.Bank of Jining is a member of China International Chamber of Commerce, Bankers Almanac and Foreign Exchange Trading Center. Bank of Jining implementing the 'document center' to provide clients with 'one-stop' service, committed to more intimate, more efficient, more convenient services.

Scope of business of foreign exchange transactions: Foreign exchange deposits; Foreign exchange loans; Foreign exchange remittance; Foreign exchange; The international settlement; Trade foreign currency lending; Foreign exchange bill acceptance and discount; Foreign borrowing; Foreign exchange guarantee; Foreign exchange trading or valet foreign exchange trading; Credit investigation, consultation, to witness the business.

Characteristic business: Pending the settlement and sale of foreign exchange business, micro credit business.

莱商银行股份有限公司
Laishang Bank Co., Ltd.

莱商银行是2005年7月经中国银行业监督管理委员会批准设立的股份制商业银行。目前，莱商银行在总行设有职能部室20个，在徐州、济南等7个地市设有分行，在莱芜本部设有3家管辖行，营业网点共计62家，在职员工1 600余人。截至2014年末，莱商银行各项存款余额达到366亿元，贷款余额265亿元，资产总额516亿元。在英国《银行家》杂志2014年“全球1 000家银行排名”中列第672位。

Laishang Bank is a joint-stock commercial bank established after the approval from China Banking Regulatory Commission in July, 2005. At present, Laishang bank has established 20 functional departments, and branches in 7 cities, such as Xuzhou, Jinan, etc. Besides, it has established 3 jurisdiction banks in the head office of Laifu, and 62 service points, with over 1 600 employees. By the end of 2014, its deposit balance reached RMB 36.6 billion; loan balance reached RMB 26.5 billion; total asset reached RMB 51.6 billion. Moreover, it ranked 672 among “rankings of 1 000 banks over the world in 2014” in the British magazine the Banker.

郑州银行
BANK OF ZHENGZHOU

郑州银行股份有限公司
Bank of Zhengzhou Co., Ltd.

郑州银行的前身郑州市商业银行成立于2000年2月，是总部位于郑州市的一家具有独立法人资格的跨区域经营的股份制银行。2009年12月正式更名为郑州银行。截至2014年12月底，郑州银行在职员工2 941人，分支行94家，其中省内分行6家；发起设立村镇银行3家；资产规模2 042.89亿元，存款余额1 325.61亿元，贷款余额779.86亿元。

Founded in February of 2000, Bank of Zhengzhou is a joint-stock bank with trans-national operation with the independent legal person qualification. Its predecessor is Zhengzhou City Commercial Bank. Its head office is located in Zhengzhou. In December of 2009, its name was officially changed into “Bank of Zhengzhou”. By the end of 2014, it had 2 941 employees and 94 sub-branches and branches. Among them, it had 6 branches in the province. It established 3 village banks, with the asset scale of RMB 204.289 billion, the deposit balance of RMB 132.561 billion, and the loan balance of RMB 77.986 billion.

洛阳银行
BANK OF LUOYANG

洛阳银行股份有限公司

Bank of Luoyang Co., Ltd.

洛阳银行是1997年成立的河南省一家具有独立法人资格的股份制商业银行。2009年3月，经中国银监会批准，更名为洛阳银行，共下辖7家分行、77家支行，4家子公司（洛银金融租赁公司、深圳宝生村镇银行、栾川民丰村镇银行、孟津民丰村镇银行），形成了覆盖全市，辐射全省，迈向全国的服务网络。

截至2014年末，洛阳银行总资产1 119亿元，各项存款余额707.57亿元，各项贷款余额466.26亿元，实现税后利润15.73亿元，资本充足率11.19%，不良贷款率0.7%。

2014年10月开办国际结算业务，仅仅两个月时间，外币结算量已达6 000万美元，累计办理贸易融资3 000万美元，结售汇2 500万美元。2015年外币结算量预计达到2亿美元。

经过一年的筹备，2014年6月洛阳银行正式对外开办业务，成为河南省第二家开办外汇业务的城市商业银行，为支持地方经济建设又增添新的抓手。SWIFT代码为：BOLYCNBJXXX。

外汇业务经营范围：外汇存款、外汇贷款、外汇汇兑、外汇汇款、结售汇、国际结算等。

特色业务：结算速度快，决策联调短，方便灵活。

Bank of Luoyang was founded as an independent joint-stock commercial Bank in 1997 in Henan province. The bank was renamed as “Bank of Luoyang Co., Ltd.” in March 2009, approved by China Banking Regulatory Commission. The Bank has set up 7 branches, 77 sub-branches, 4 subsidiaries (Luoyang Financial Lease Company, Shenzhen Baosheng Rural Bank, Luanchuan Minfeng Rural Bank, Mengjin Minfeng Rural Bank), and has outlet throughout Luoyang City, Henan province and other areas.

In the end of 2014, the bank's total asset increased to CNY111.9 billion, with CNY70.76 billion in deposits balance, CNY46.62 billion in loan balance, and CNY1.57 billion in profits after tax. The Capital adequacy ratio is 11.19% and the non-performing loan ratio is 0.7%.

The bank's foreign currency settlement amount reached to 60 million dollars within only two months since the international settlement business was operated in December 2014. The trade finance was 30 million dollars and money exchange reached to 25 million dollars. The bank's exchange settlement is expected to be 200 million in 2015.

Ban of Luoyang's international business was formally operated in June 2014 after a whole year preparation. The bank becomes the second city commercial bank that operates international business in Henan province. The bank's SWIFT CODE is BOLYCNBJXXX.

Scope of business of foreign exchange transactions: Foreign currency deposits, loans, remittance, money exchanges, and clearing settlement.

Characteristic business: Fast and Flexible.

HKB 漢口銀行

汉口银行股份有限公司
Hankou Bank Co., Ltd.

汉口银行成立于1997年12月，是一家总部位于武汉的区域性股份制商业银行。注册资本41.28亿元。现有各类分支机构112家，机构基本覆盖湖北省，在省内武汉、黄石、襄阳、荆州、宜昌、十堰、孝感、荆门、鄂州、恩施等10个市州设有分行，在重庆市设有1家省外分行，发起组建了阳新、枝江2家村镇银行。根据英国《银行家》杂志“2014年全球银行1 000家”排名，汉口银行一级资本、总资产、资本利润率、资产回报率等指标均进入全球银行400强。

Hankou Bank was established in December 1997, headquartered in Wuhan, which is a regional joint-stock commercial bank. Its registered capital is RMB 4.13 billion. It has 112 various types of branches, and those branches have a basic coverage of Hubei Province. Hankou Bank has set up branches in Wuhan, Huangshi, Xiangyang, Jinzhou, Yichang, Shiyan, Xiaogan, Jingmen, and Ezhou City in Wuhan Province. It also has a branch in Chongqing, which initiated the formation of Yangxin, and Zhijang Village Bank. According to the British “The Banker” released “2014 Top 1 000 World Banks” ranking list, Hankou Bank is one of top 400 global banks in tier one capital, total assets, capital profit margin, return on assets, and other indicators.

湖北银行股份有限公司
Hubei Bank Co., Ltd.

湖北银行是一家拥有深厚历史底蕴和文化传承意义的银行，最早可追溯到1928年，湖北省银行在汉口成立，这也是如今湖北银行的前身。2011年2月27日，湖北银行在原宜昌、襄阳、荆州、黄石、孝感五家城市商业银行的基础上，采取新设合并的方式正式成立，总部设在武汉，现辖9家分行，140余家支行。截至2014年底，湖北银行资产总额达到1 251亿元，存款余额915亿元，贷款余额716亿元。

Hubei Bank has rich historical details and cultural inheritance significance. It can be traced back to 1928 at the earliest. Hubei Province Bank was founded in Hankou, which is the predecessor of today's Hubei Bank. On February 27th, 2011, Hubei Bank was officially founded through the consolidation way based on five city commercial banks in Yichang, Xiangyang, Jinzhou, Huangshi and Xiaogan. Its head office is located in Wuhan, with 9 branches and over 140 sub-branches. By the end of 2014, its total asset reached RMB 125.1 billion; deposit balance reached RMB 91.5 billion; loan balance reached RMB 71.6 billion.

长沙银行股份有限公司
Bank of Changsha Co., Ltd.

长沙银行成立于1997年5月，是湖南首家区域性股份制商业银行，现拥有包括广州、株洲、湘潭、常德、娄底、郴州、益阳、怀化在内的24家分支机构、101个营业网点，控股发起湘西、祁阳、宜章3家村镇银行。截至 2014 年末，全行资产总额达到 2 120.96亿元，一般性存款 1 551.02 亿元，各项贷款余额为 709.35 亿元。在英国《银行家》杂志评选的“2014 全球银行 1 000强”中列第 489 位，较 2013 年攀升 57 位，在中国《银行家》杂志评选的“年度城市商业银行财务评价”（资产规模1 000亿～2 000 亿元）中名列第4位。

Founded in May, 1997, Bank of Changsha is the first regional joint-stock commercial bank in Hunan. At present, it has 24 sub-branches in Guangzhou, Zhuzhou, Xiangtan, Changde, Loudi, Chenzhou, Yiyang and Huanhua, and 101 service points. It is a shareholder of 3 village banks in Xiangxi, Qiyang and Yizhang. By the end of 2014, its total asset reached RMB 212.096 billion; generalized deposit reached RMB 155.102 billion; loan balance reached RMB 70.935 billion. It ranked 489 in the “annual financial evaluation of city commercial bank” elected by the Chinese magazine The Banker. Besides, It ranked 4 in “annual financial evaluation of the city commercial bank” (asset scale: RMB 100～200 billion) elected by the China magazine The Banker.

华融湘江银行
HUARONG XIANGJIANG BANK

华融湘江银行股份有限公司
Huarong Xiangjiang Bank Co., Ltd.

华融湘江银行是经中国银监会批准设立，由中国华融资产管理股份有限公司注资并控股，在重组湖南原湘潭、株洲、岳阳、衡阳市商业银行和邵阳市城市信用社的基础上新设的股份制商业银行。2010年10月12日正式挂牌开业，总行设在湖南长沙。截至2014年末，公司下辖总行营业部，以及长沙、湘潭、株洲、衡阳、岳阳、邵阳、郴州、常德、怀化、益阳、娄底、永州、张家界、湘西 14 家分行，共 161 个营业网点。

Huarong Xiangjinag Bank is a joint-stock commercial bank established on the basis of Hunan Xiangtan, Zhuzhou, Yueyang, Quyang City Commercial Bank, and Shaoyang City Credit Cooperative, by the China Huarong Asset Management Co., Ltd. injecting capital and holding, approved by the China Banking Regulatory Commission. It officially opened on October 12, 2010, headquartered in Changsha, Hunan Province. By the end of 2014, the company administered Head Office, as well as 14 branches in Changsha, Xiangtan, Zhuzhou, Hengyang, Yueyang, Shaoyang, Chenzhou, CHangde, Huaihua, Yiyang, Loudi, Yongzhou, Zhangjiajie, and Xiangxi, totaled 161 outlets.

CRBC 珠海華潤銀行

珠海华润银行股份有限公司

China Resources Bank of Zhuhai Co., Ltd.

珠海华润银行前身为珠海市商业银行，1996年12月28日经中国人民银行总行批准正式开业，是具有一级法人资格的城市商业银行。2010年1月，华润股份有限公司和珠海市政府对珠海市商业银行成功实施战略重组，注册资本56.38亿元。目前，珠海华润银行已拥有4家异地分行、1家总行营业部、63家支行以及2家控股村镇银行。1997年12月经国家外汇管理局批准，开办外汇业务，是全国城市商业银行中首批获准办理外汇业务的城市商业银行。截至2014年末，本行总资产规模达到1 075.34 亿元，贷款总额为 471.57 亿元，存款总额为 647.90 亿元。

The predecessor of China Resources Bank of Zhuhai Co., Ltd. is Zhuhai Commercial Bank which was officially approved and opened by the Head Office of People's Bank of China on December 28, 1996. The Zhuhai City Commercial Bank is a city commercial bank with the first class corporate capacity. In January of 2010, China Resources Co., Ltd. and Zhuhai Municipal Government implemented the strategic restructuring in Zhuhai City Commercial Bank successfully, and the registered capital of which was 5.638 billion yuan. At present, China Resources Bank has four branches in different places, a Head Office, 63 sub-branches and two holding rural banks. In December of 1997, approved by the State Administration of Foreign Exchange, it began offering foreign exchange business which made itself the first city commercial banks in China that is allowed to transact foreign exchange business. Until the end of 2014, the total assets of this bank has reached 107.534 billion yuan, the total loans has reached 47.157 billion yuan, and the total deposits has reached 64.79 billion yuan.

广州银行股份有限公司
Bank of Guangzhou Co., Ltd.

广州银行是由广州市政府控股的股份制商业银行，其前身为在46家城市信用合作社的基础上组建的广州城市合作银行，成立于1996年9月17日。后更名为广州市商业银行股份有限公司。2009年9月，获准更名为广州银行股份有限公司。现有105个机构网点，包括分行7家、支行98家，3 100多名员工，注册资本金83亿元。

截至2014年底，资产总额为3 311.64亿元；资本充足率11.54%，核心资本充足率11.02%，不良贷款率0.3%，不良资产率0.15%，拨备覆盖率超过351%，是国内资产质量最好的银行之一；2014年实现利润44.32亿元，经营管理绩效不断提升。

Bank of Guangzhou was a controlled joint-stock commercial bank whose stock was held by the Guangzhou municipal government. Its predecessor is the Urban Cooperative Bank of Guangzhou which was established in the formation of 46 urban credit cooperatives. It was founded in September 17, 1996. Then it changed its name into Guangzhou City Commercial Bank Co., Ltd. In September 2009, it was allowed to change its name into Bank Of Guangzhou Co., Ltd. It has 105 business locations, including seven branches, 98 sub-branches, and more than 3 100 employees. Its registered capital has reached 8.3 billion yuan.

Until the end of 2014, the total assets of this bank has reached 331.164 billion yuan. The capital adequacy ratio is 11.54%. The core capital adequacy ratio is 11.02%, the NPL ratio is 0.3%, the non-performing assets ratio is 0.15%, and the provision coverage is more than 351%, which makes itself as one of the best asset quality banks in China. In 2014 its profit has reached 4.432 billion yuan, and its management performance has been improving constantly.

广東南粵銀行
GUANGDONG NANYUE BANK

广东南粤银行股份有限公司
Guangdong Nanyue Bank Co., Ltd.

广东南粤银行的前身为湛江市商业银行，成立于1998年1月，注册地和总行所在地均在湛江市。2011年9月，获中国银监会批准更名为广东南粤银行股份有限公司，简称广东南粤银行，是一家区域性股份制商业银行。截至2014 年末，分行级机构14 个，营业网点 88 家。业务范围涵盖公金业务、零售业务、贸易融资、小微金融、投资银行、资金业务、国际业务等七大板块。截至 2014 年末，资产总额达到 1 427.58 亿元，一般性存款余额 923.82 亿元，各项贷款 533.66 亿元。

The predecessor of Guangdong Nanyue Bank is Zhanjiang City Commercial Bank which was established in January，1998. The registered and head office locations were all in Zhanjiang City. In September of 2011, it was approved by the China Banking Regulatory Commission to change its name into “Guangdong Nanyue Bank Co., Ltd.”，which was referred to as “Guangdong Nanyue Bank”. It is a regional joint-stock commercial bank. Until the end of 2014, it has 14 branch-level agencies and 88 business outlets. Its business scope covers seven sectors such as public accumulation funds business, retail business, trade finance, small and micro finance, investment banking, treasury services, international business, etc. Until the end of 2014, its total assets has reached 142.758 billion yuan, the general outstanding of deposits is 92.382 billion yuan, and the loan is 53.366 billion yuan.

东莞银行

BANK OF DONGGUAN

东莞银行股份有限公司

Bank of Dongguan Co., Ltd.

东莞银行股份有限公司是经中国人民银行批准，在东莞市工商行政管理局登记注册的股份制商业银行，成立于1999年9月8日。截至目前，该行下辖总行营业部、11 家分行（东莞分行、广州分行、深圳分行、惠州分行、长沙分行、佛山分行、合肥分行、清远分行、珠海分行、韶关分行、中山分行）、香港代表处、45 家一级支行、73 家二级支行、5 家社区支行，拥有2家子公司（开县泰业村镇银行股份有限公司、东源泰业村镇银行股份有限公司）。截至2014年12月31日（审计后合并报表数），该行总资产达1 869.92亿元，各项存款余额为1 135.68亿元，贷款余额为782.12亿元。

Bank of Dongguan Co., Ltd. is approved by the People's Bank of China for the registration of being a joint-stock commercial bank under Dongguan City Administration. It was established on September 8, 1999. Until present, the Bank has a Head Office, 11 branches (which are Dongguan Branch, Guangzhou Branch, Shenzhen Branch, Huizhou Branch, Changsha Branch, Foshan branch, Hefei Branch, Qingyuan branch, Zhuhai Branch, Shaoguan Branch, Zhongshan Branch), a Hong Kong Representative Office, 45 first class branches, 73 second class branches, 5 community branches, and 2 subsidiaries (which are Kaixian Thaiye Rural Bank Co., Ltd., and Dongyuan Thaiye Rural Bank Co., Ltd.). Until December 31, 2014 (according to the number of consolidated audited), the Bank's total assets has amounted to 186.992 billion yuan, the outstanding of deposits has reached 113.568 billion yuan, and the outstanding loan has reached 78.212 billion yuan.

广东华兴银行股份有限公司
Guangdong Huaxing Bank Co., Ltd.

广东华兴银行股份有限公司是经中国银行业监督管理委员会正式批复同意，于2011年8月依法创新组建的一家股份制商业银行。注册资本为50亿元，注册地为汕头经济特区，运营总部设在广州市，目前已在汕头、广州、佛山、深圳、东莞、江门设立6家分行和9家支行，15家营业网点。截至2014年12月31日，该行资产总额达682.39亿元，存款余额 391.72 亿元，贷款余额 237.82 亿元。

Guangdong Huaxing Bank, founded in August of 2011, is a joint-stock commercial bank established according to the law after approval from China Banking Regulatory Commission, with the registration capital of RMB 5 billion. The registration place is Shantou special economic zone. The operation headquarter is located in Guangzhou. At present, it has established 6 branches, 9 sub-branches and 15 service points in Shantou, Guangzhou, Foushan, Shenzhen, Dongguan, and Jiangmen. By the end of 2014, its total asset was RMB 68.237 billion; deposit balance was RMB 39.172 billion; the loan balance was RMB 23.782 billion.

柳州银行
BANK OF LIUZHOU

柳州银行股份有限公司
Bank of Liuzhou Co., Ltd.

柳州银行成立于1997年3月28日，原名柳州商业银行，是一家由地方财政、地方优势骨干企业发起组建、众多企业和个人投资入股成立的具有独立法人资格的股份制商业银行，注册资本为33 740万元。目前，柳州银行已在广西设立74家分支机构。截至2014年末，柳州银行及其控股村镇银行总资产达到861.44亿元；存款余额564.61亿元；贷款余额275.05亿元。截至2014 年末，全年实现国际业务量31 532.07万美元，结售汇业务量 14 590.62 万美元，国内信用证业务量 204 283.46 万元人民币，实现业务收入超 4 070.40 万元。

Founded on March 28th, 1997, Bank of Liuzhou is a joint-stock commercial bank with the independent corporate capacity established by the local finance, local advantageous cadre enterprises, and invested by many enterprises and individuals. Its predecessor is Liuzhou City Commercial Bank. Its registration capital is RMB 337.4 billion. At present, Bank of Liuzhou has established 74 branches in Guangxi. By the end of 2014, the total assets of Bank of Liuzhou and its holding village banks reached RMB 96.144 billion; deposit balance reached RMB 56.461 billion; loan balance reached RMB 27.505 billion. Moreover, it realized USD 315.3207 million of the international business scale, and USD 145.9062 million of the foreign exchange settlement and sale, RMB 20 428.346 billion of the domestic letter of credit, and also realized over RMB 40.704 million of the sales.

桂林银行股份有限公司
Guilin Bank Co., Ltd.

桂林银行成立于1997年，原为桂林市商业银行，2010年11月改为现名，是一家区域性股份制城市商业银行，可为社会各界提供存贷款、结算、票据、理财、外汇、银行卡及电子银行等优质、高效的本外币金融服务。目前，桂林银行已在广西设立了51家分支机构，业务范围覆盖南宁、柳州、桂林、梧州、贺州、防城港等区域，同时在广西区内和广东深圳控股设立了7家村镇银行。

近年来，桂林银行走特色化、差异化发展之路，坚持“中小企业伙伴银行、市民银行”为市场定位，努力打造“先进的小额信贷银行、优秀的社区银行、旅游金融服务银行和‘三农’金融服务平台”四大特色，为地方经济社会发展作出了积极贡献。截至2014年11月末，桂林银行及其控股村镇银行总资产1 089.76亿元，同比增长20.9%；存款余额 705.41亿元，同比增长18.46%；贷款余额 298.75亿元，同比增长25.96%；2014年1～11月实现经营利润18.31亿元，同比增长15.01%；上缴各类税金6.33亿元，同比增长18.97%。各项监管指标全部达标。桂林银行总资产已进入全国140多家城商行的中上游行列；2013年纳税在广西国税部分列第16位、在桂林列第2位。

桂林银行着力塑造“漓水春风”服务品牌，为客户提供如“漓水般清澈、春风般温暖”的服务。目前，全行共有各级青年文明号30个、“中国银行业文明规范服务示范千家单位”2个。

桂林银行以人才支撑发展，重视员工培训、培养，完善员工职业发展通道，不断增强人才吸引力。目前，全行及控股村镇银行共有职工3 000多人，拥有一支朝气蓬勃、进取向上的员工团队。

桂林银行的发展得到了社会各界的肯定，在网易财经发布的“2013中国金融500强”中列第96位；连续三年被广西企业与企业家联合会评为“广西优秀企业”，列“2014广西企业100强”第42位；在全球权威金融媒体英国《银行家》杂志发布的2014年“全球银行1 000强”榜单中列第717位；在《亚洲银行家》杂志发布的“亚洲银行家500强”（2013—2014年度）竞争力排名中列亚洲区第12位、中国区第4位。

未来，桂林银行将继续以“好山水　好银行”为愿景，进一步增强资本实力，深化“四大特色”，稳步实施“走出去”发展战略，努力打造“服务领先的银行、最具创新力的银行、最具竞争力的银行”，提升政府、企业、市民和股东的满意度，力争成为桂林纳税排头兵，建成国内一流精品银行。

外汇业务开展状况：桂林银行从2010年12月开始正式对外开办国际业务，经营范围包括外汇汇款、进出口信用证、出口托收、进口代收、结售汇、国际贸易融资等业务，业务币种包括美元、港元、日元、欧元、英镑、澳元等。

几年来，桂林银行国际业务以全球快汇、国际贸易融资等产品以及免收结算手续费等惠民措施服务广大进出口企业及个人，业务规模不断扩大，逐步树立了桂林银行国际业务品牌优势，外汇业务服务覆盖桂林、南宁、梧州、柳州、贺州、防城港等经济区域。

外汇业务经营范围：国际结算、国际贸易融资、对外担保、外汇存取款、结售汇、外币兑换等。

特色业务：个人外汇服务（留学、旅游），对公外汇结算及贸易融资服务（贸易融资与衍生产品组合）。

Guilin Bank Co., Ltd. founded in 1997 is a city commercial bank in Guangxi autonomous region, China, owing 51 branches in Guangxi as well as 7 rural holding bank companies in Guangxi and Guangdong province at present. There have been more than 3000 staffs. At the end of 2014, the total asset has been up to CNY109 billion and risen by 11% compared with that last year; the balance of deposit has been to CNY68 billion, risen by 9.74%; the balance of loan has been up to CNY 26 billion, risen by 30.04%. In a word, the operation has met all the supervising standards all the time. In the respects of total assets, Guilin bank ranks forefront among the 140 city commercial banks in China. In 2013, the total amount of taxation ranked second in Guilin City.

In recent years, Guilin bank has focused on providing considerate service to their customers, which has impressed their customers increasingly. In the same time, the bank frequently holds a number of necessary training for their employees, in order to promote their employees' quality and capacity.

Therefore, the society has spoken highly of the bank's development and image as well. Among "Top 500 of Chinese financial institutions" published by NetEase in 2013, Guilin bank ranked 96th; in "Top 100 of Guangxi enterprises in 2014", Guilin bank ranked 42th. Even in The Bankers, Guilin bank ranked 717th among the top 1 000 banks all over the world in 2014 and in The Asian Bankers (2013 to 2014), Guilin bank ranked 12th in Asia and 4th in China in regards to competiveness.

International business: Guilin bank began to conduct foreign exchange business in 2010 on the currency of USD , HKD, EUR, GBP, JPY and AUD. The bank has developed the service for individuals and companies in Guilin, Nanning, Wuzhou, Liuzhou, Hezhou, Fangchenggang.

International business range: International settlement, International trade financing, foreign guarantee, foreign currency deposit and withdrawal and foreign exchange.

Featured service: service for individual (studying aboard, travelling aboard), service for exporting and importing companies (financing and financial derivative products).

广西北部湾银行
GUANGXI BEIBU GULF BANK

广西北部湾银行股份有限公司
Guangxi Beibu Gulf Bank Co., Ltd.

广西北部湾银行股份有限公司是一家具有独立法人资格的股份制商业银行，曾用名包括南宁城市合作银行和南宁市商业银行股份有限公司，总部设在中国广西南宁市，业务以中国广西市场为主。截至 2014 年 12 月 31 日，本行共设有直管分支机构 20 家，县域支行 6 家，二级支行 50家，营业网点67个。主营业务范围包括吸收公众存款；发放短期、中期和长期贷款；办理国内结算；办理票据承兑贴现；发行金融债券；代理发行、代理兑付、承销政府债券；买卖政府债券；从事同业拆借；提供担保；代理收付款项及代理保险业务；提供保管箱业务；经中国银行业监督管理部门批准的其他业务。

Guangxi Beibu Gulf Bank is a joint-stock commercial bank with an independent legal personality based on restructuring of Nanning City Cooperation Bank and Naning City Commercial Bank. It headquartered in Nanning, Guangxi Province, China, and its business Guangxi market-oriented. By the end of December 31, 2014, there are 20 branches, 6 county branches, 50 secondary branches, and 67 outlets. Its main business scope includes absorbing deposits from the public; short-term, medium-term and long-term lending; dealing with domestic settlement; handling acceptance and discounting; issuing financial bonds; being an agent to issue, underwrite, and guarantee government bonds; buying and selling government bonds; interbank lending; providing guarantee; acting receipts and payments and insurance agents; providing safe service, and other businesses approved by China Banking Regulatory Authorities.

成都银行股份有限公司
Bank of Chengdu Co., Ltd.

成都银行股份有限公司的前身为成都市城市信用社，1996年12月30日组建成立，1998年更名为成都市商业银行，2008年更为现名。成都银行是一家以国有股本为主、股权多元化的地方性股份制商业银行，马来西亚丰隆银行作为境外战略投资合作伙伴。目前，注册资金32.5亿元，在岗员工5 000余名，实行一级法人体制。截至2014年12月31日，全行下设162家分支机构，包括9家分行、32家直属支行及121家网点级营业机构。

截至2014年末，总资产为3 002.3亿元，一般性存款2 192.5亿元，各项贷款1 248.9亿元。在2014年英国《银行家》公布的最新排名中，成都银行居全球前1 000家商业银行第319位，中资商业银行第36位，全国城市商业银行第12位，西部地区城市商业银行第1位。截至2014年末，国际结算量为14.33亿美元；贸易融资发放量3.77亿美元。

The predecessor of Bank of Chengdu is Chengdu City Cooperative, founded on December 30th, 1996. In 1998, its name was changed to Chengdu City Commercial Bank. In 2008, its name was changed to Bank of Chengdu. It is a local joint-stock commercial bank with the state-owned capital stock and equity diversity. Besides, it regards Hong Leong Bank Berhad as the overseas strategy investment cooperation partner. At present, it has RMB 3.25 billion registration capital, and over 5 000 employees. It carries out the provincial legal system. By the end of 2014, it has established 162 branch organizations, including 9 branches, 32 directly subordinated sub-branches and 121 service points.

By the end of 2014, its total asset, generalized deposit and loans were RMB 300.23 billion, RMB 219.25 billion and RMB 124.89 billion respectively. In the latest rankings of British magazine The Banker in 2014, Bank of Chengdu ranked 319 among Global TOP 1 000 Banks, and ranked 36 among the Chinese commercial banks, ranked 12 among the city commercial banks in China, and ranked 1 among the city commercial banks in the western areas. Moreover, its international settlement amount was USD 1.433 billion, and its trade financing issuing amount was USD 0.377 billion.

乐山市商业银行
LESHAN CITY COMMERCIAL BANK

乐山市商业银行股份有限公司
Leshan City Commercial Bank Co., Ltd.

乐山市商业银行成立于1997年2月，是经中国人民银行总行批准成立的首批地市级城市商业银行。截至目前，全行资产规模623亿元，各项存款余额359亿元，各项贷款余额179亿元，注册资本18.19亿元，员工近千人。截至目前，全行共有6家分行，控股3家“民富”村镇银行，营业网点共计70个，覆盖了乐山、眉山、成都、自贡、资阳、南充等地23个县（区、市）。

Leshan City Commercial Bank was established in February 1997, which is the first “municipal” city commercial bank approved by the People’s Bank of China. Up to now, its total assets reached RMB 62.3 billion, the balance of deposits is RMB 35.9 billion, the balance of loans is RMB 17.9 billion, and registered capital is RMB 1.82 billion with nearly 1 000 employees. Up to now, the bank has 6 branches, holding 3 “Minfu” Village Banks, 70 outlets covering Leshan, Meishan, Chengdu, Ziyang, Nanchong and other 23 counties (districts, cities).

德阳银行股份有限公司
Bank of Deyang Co., Ltd.

德阳银行股份有限公司是德阳地区唯一一家地方性法人股份制商业银行。其前身德阳市商业银行成立于1998年，注册资本37 138万元。2010年10月1日，德阳市商业银行股份有限公司正式更名为德阳银行股份有限公司。截至 2014 年末，员工共计 1 092 人，全行资产规模达 564.44亿元，各项存款余额 366.19亿元，各项贷款余额达 250.5亿元。截至 2014年 12月 31日，共拥有机构网点 46个，其中德阳地区 35个，德阳以外的异域城市 11个。

Bank of Deyang is the only local joint-stock commercial bank in Deyang. Its predecessor was Deyang City Commercial Bank, founded in 1998, with the registration capital of RMB 371.38 million. On October 1st, 2010, the name of Deyang City Commercial Bank Co., Ltd. was changed into Deyang Bank Co., Ltd. By the end of 2014, it had 1 092 employees, RMB 56.444 billion assets, RMB 36.619 billion deposit and RMB 25.05 billion loans. Besides, it possesses 46 service points, among which, 35 points are located in Deyang, and 11 points are located outside Deyang.

南充市商业银行

Nanchong City Commercial Bank Co., Ltd.

南充市商业银行成立于2001年12月27日，位于四川省第二大金融、交通枢纽、人口、消费、教育中心南充市。截至2014年12月末，共有管理部门18个，事业部13个，营业网点67个。截至2014年12月末，资产总额达到1 284.85亿元，各项存款余额（含同业）达到1 015.17亿元，各项贷款355.27亿元。

Founded on December 27th, 2001, Nanchong City Commercial Bank is located in Nanchong City, which is the second largest finance, transportation junction, population, consumption, and education center in Sichuan Province. By the end of 2014, it has 18 administration departments 13 business divisions, and 67 service points. Besides, total asset reached RMB 128.485 billion, and the deposit balance reached RMB 101.517 billion; the loans reached RMB 35.527 billion.

贵阳银行股份有限公司
Bank of Guiyang Co., Ltd.

贵阳银行（原名贵阳市商业银行）成立于1997年4月，是一家总行设在贵阳市的大型区域性股份制商业银行。截至 2014 年末，共有营业网点 174 个，在成都、毕节、遵义、凯里、都匀、安顺、铜仁、六盘水和兴义共开设有9家异地分行，在贵阳市域内有26家经营管理行和1家营业部，控股子公司广元市贵商村镇银行营业网点达 14 个。截至 2014 年 12 月 31 日，全行总资产1 529.42 亿元，各项存款余额 1 274.45 亿元，各项贷款余额 681.25 亿元。

Founded in April, 1997, Bank of Guiyang (predecessor “Guiyang City Commercial Bank”) is a large regional joint-stock commercial bank. Its head office is located in Guiyang. By the end of 2014, it has 174 service points, and 9 remote branches in Chengdu, Bijie, Zunyi, Kaili, Duyun, Anshun, Tongren, Liupanshui and Xingyi. In Guiyang, it has 26 administration banks and a business division. It has 14 village banks in Guangyuan City, which are the holding subsidiaries of Bank of Guiyang. By the end of 2014, its total asset reached RMB 152.942 billion; its deposit balance reached RMB 127.445 billion; its loan balance reached 68.125 billion.

富滇银行股份有限公司
Fudian Bank Co., Ltd.

富滇银行股份有限公司成立于2007年12月30日，前身是成立于1996年12月的昆明市商业银行，是经中国银监会批准的，在对昆明市商业银行进行增资扩股和处置不良资产的基础上成立的云南省第一家省级地方性股份制商业银行，注册资本47.5 亿元。富滇银行现有机构 116 家（含总行），此外，与老挝外贸大众银行合资设立老中银行股份有限公司，发起设立 4 家村镇银行。本公司员工总数为 2 769 人。截至 2014 年底，本公司本外币资产总额 1 436 亿元，负债总额 1 308 亿元，所有者权益127 亿元，本外币全口径存款余额 1 080 亿元，本外币各项贷款余额 685 亿元，实现净利润 16.34 亿元。

Fudian Bank was founded on December 30th, 2007. Its predecessor is Kunming City Commercial Bank founded in December of 1996. It is the first provincial local joint-stock commercial bank founded based on the capital and share increasing and non-performing loan disposal on Kunming City Commercial Bank in Yunnan, with the registration capital of RMB 4.75 billion. At present, Fudian Bank has 116 institutions (including the head office). In addition, it cooperated with Laos Foreign Trade Public Bank to establish Laos-Sino Bank and 4 village banks. It has 2 769 employees. By the end of 2014, its foreign currency asset amount reached RMB 143.6 billion; the total liabilities reached RMB 130.8 billion; the owner's equity reached RMB 12.7 billion; the full aperture deposit of the foreign currency reached RMB 108 billion; the loan amount of the foreign currency reached RMB 68.5, and it realized the net profit of RMB 1.634 billion.

西安银行
BANK OF XI'AN

西安银行股份有限公司
Bank of Xi'an Co., Ltd.

西安银行是西安市政府、中国信达资产管理公司、加拿大丰业银行、地方大中型企业参股的城市商业银行，成立于1997年，原名为西安城市合作银行，2000年更名为西安市商业银行。2009年底圆满完成战略引资和财务重组工作，注册资本达30亿元，2010年9月更名为西安银行。控股2家村镇银行，下辖榆林分行、宝鸡分行、总行营业部、10家区域支行、11家直属支行，共117个营业网点，59家自助银行，现有员工2 300余人。2014 年末，总资产达到1 512.82 亿元，总存款余额达到1 120 亿元，各项贷款余额达到 723.96 亿元。

Xi'an Bank, founded in 1997, is a city commercial bank shared by Xi'an Government, China Cinda Asset Management Corporation, the Bank of Nova Scotia, and the local large and medium-size enterprises. Its predecessor is Xi'an City Cooperative Bank. In 2002, its name was changed to Xi'an City Commercial Bank. By the end of 2009, it successfully completed the strategic investing absorbing and financial reconstructing, with the registration capital of RMB 3 billion. In September of 2010, its name was changed into Bank of Xi'an, holding 2 village banks, Yulin Branch, Baoji Branch, busincss office of the head quarter, 10 regional sub-branches, 11 directly subordinated sub-branches, 117 service points, and 59 self-help banks. Now, it has over 2 300 employees. By the end of 2014, its total asset reached RMB 151.282 billion; its total deposit balance reached RMB 112 billion; the loan balance reached RMB 72.396 billion.

长安银行股份有限公司
Chang'an Bank Co., Ltd.

长安银行是由中国银行业监督管理委员会批准，由宝鸡市商业银行、咸阳市商业银行、渭南城市信用社、汉中城市信用社和榆林城市信用社5家地方法人银行业金融机构通过新设合并，联合其他发起人共同发起设立的一家地方性法人股份制商业银行，2009年7月31日开业。注册资本金42.32亿元，总行设在陕西省西安市，下辖9家分行，目前共有110个对外营业网点。截至 2014 年末，员工共计 3 446 人，全行资产规模达 1 258.90亿元，各项存款余额 772.03亿元，各项贷款余额达 523.77亿元。

Chang'an Bank, opened on July 31st, 2009, is a local joint-stock commercial bank with legal personality established by Baoji City Commercial Bank, Xianyang City Commercial Bank, Weinan City Cooperative, Hanzhong City Cooperative and Yulin City Cooperative with other people through the merger after approval from China Banking Regulatory Commission. It was open on July 31st, 2009, with the registration capital of RMB 4.232 billion. Its head office is located in Xian City of Shaanxi Province. It has 9 branches. At present, it has 110 service points. By the end of 2014, it had 3 446 employees. The total asset of the bank reached RMB 125.89 billion. The deposit balance reached RMB 77.203 billion. The loan balance reached RMB 52.377 billion.

兰州银行股份有限公司
Bank of Lanzhou Co., Ltd.

兰州银行股份有限公司成立于1997年，总部位于甘肃省省会兰州市，是甘肃省第一家具有法人资格的股份制商业银行。前身为兰州市商业银行，2008年5月，经中国银监会批准更名为兰州银行。兰州银行目前共有分支机构124家，村镇银行6家。营业网点基本实现对全省主要地区的覆盖。

截至 2014 年末，全行资产总额达到 1 551.62 亿元，2014 年，兰州银行再次入选英国《银行家》（The Banker）杂志“全球银行1 000 强”排行榜，按一级资本排名，列第 520 名；按总资产排名，列第 502 名，入选《亚洲银行家》（*The Asian Banker*）杂志“亚太银行 500 强”排行榜，按综合实力排名，列第 144 位；按总资产排名，列第 247 位。

Lanzhou Bank Co., Ltd., founded in 1997, is the first joint-stock commercial bank with the legal personality in Gansu Province. Its head office is located in Lanzhou City of Gansu Province. In May, 2008, its name was changed into “Bank of Lanzhou” after approval from China Banking Regulatory Commission. At present, it has 124 branches and 6 village banks. Its service points basically cover the major areas in the whole province.

By the end of 2014, its total asset reached RMB 155.162 billion. In 2014, Bank of Lanzhou was re-selected among “Top 1 000 Banks over the World” in the British magazine “The Banker”. According to the tier one capital ranking, it ranked 520. According to the total asset ranking, it ranked 502. According to the comprehensive strength, it ranked 144. According to the total asset, it ranked 247.

甘肃银行股份有限公司

Bank of Gansu Co., Ltd.

甘肃银行股份有限公司是经中国银行业监督管理委员会批准，通过合并重组原平凉市商业银行和原白银市商业银行，联合其他发起人共同设立的，由甘肃省政府直接管理的省级法人股份制商业银行。2011年11月19日正式挂牌营业，总部设在甘肃省省会兰州市，注册资本为34.86亿元。成立之初，资产总额125.94亿元，存款余额54.75亿元，贷款余额37.78亿元，下辖总行营业部以及平凉分行、白银分行2家分行和平凉市静宁成纪村镇银行，全行共有41家营业网点，从业人员616人。

在甘肃省委、省政府的高度关注和大力支持下，在监管部门的指导和帮助下，甘肃银行自成立以来，坚持以支持地方经济发展为己任，一手抓业务经营，一手抓规范发展，全力做大资产规模，加快机构网点和信息科技系统建设，扎实推进各项重点工作，各项工作呈现出了良好的发展态势。

截至2014年末，全行资产总额1 547.96亿元，是成立之初的22.17倍；负债总额1 441.61亿元，是成立之初的20.88倍。一般性存款余额1 066.72亿元，是成立之初的19.49倍，当年新增510.7亿元，增长幅度91.85%；贷款余额达562.04亿元，是成立之初的14.87倍，当年新增263.84亿元，增长幅度88.48%；实现净利润10.53亿元，当年上缴税金5.57亿元，三年累计上缴税金10.04亿元。全行全年共新设机构78家，全省营业网点达到155家，机构基本覆盖了全省县域。提前7个月完成了省政府下达的“力争从挂牌营业时起3年内使资产总额达到1 000亿元”的任务目标，并在成立三周年前夕圆满实现了“成立三年存款超千亿”的战略目标，在社会各界树立了良好的企业形象，社会信任度不断提高。

2014年，该行完成了外汇业务系统建设、市场准入、业务准备等基础工作，现已具备外汇存贷款、国际结算及贸易融资、跨境人民币、担保、即期结售汇等基础外汇业务的办理渠道和能力，并于2014年7月全面开办外汇业务。目前，该行外汇业务发展尚处于起步阶段，近期重点工作以围绕完善系统建设、做好业务铺垫、扩大客户储备开展各项工作。

外汇业务经营范围：外汇存贷款、国际结算及贸易融资、跨境人民币、担保、即期结售汇等业务。

With the approval of China Banking Regulatory Commission, Bank of Gansu Co., Ltd. was jointly established through the merger and restructuring of the original Pingliang Commercial Bank and original Baiyin Commercial Bank and the association of other initiators. It is a joint-stock commercial bank of provincial legal person, which is under the direct administration of Gansu government. Its business was started on November 19, 2011 with the head office locating in Lanzhou, Gansu province. Its registered capital is RMB 3.486 billion. At the beginning of its establishment, its total assets reached RMB 12.594 billion, outstanding of deposits RMB 5.475 billion and outstanding loan RMB 3.778 billion. There are 41 branches in the bank, including the Business Department of the Head Office, two branches, including Pingliang Branch and Baiyin Branch, and Pingliang Jingning Chengji Village Bank with 616 employees.

Under the close concern and strong support of Gansu provincial Party committee and provincial government, and under the guidance and assistance of the supervision department, Bank of Gansu has been regarding supporting the development of local economy as its own mission and working for business operation and at the same time for regulated development, and strive to enlarge its assets size and speed up the construction of branches and science and technology system and solidly carry forward the various businesses and the bank is moveing forward with a healthy developing trend.

Up to the end of 2014, the total assets of the bank is RMB 154.796 billion, which is 22.17 times as large as the assets when it was established; its total indebtedness is RMB 144.161 billion, which is 20.88 times as large as the amount when it was established. Its general outstanding of deposit has reached RMB 106.672 billion, which is 19.49 times as large as the amount when it was established. The newly increased general outstanding of deposit of that year has reached RMB 51.07 billion, with a growth rate of 91.85%; its outstanding loan has reached RMB 56.204 billion, which is 14.87 times as large as the amount when it was established. The newly increased outstanding loan of that year has reached RMB 26.384 billion, with a growth rate of 88.48%; RMB 1.053 billion net profits has been realized, and RMB 0.557 billion taxes has been paid that year, and the taxed paid in the recent three years has reached RMB 1.004 billion. The bank has newly established 78 branches in that year, and the branches in the province has reached 155 branches, which has basically covered the whole province. The bank has achieved the objective of "realizing RMB 100 billion total assets within three years from the day of its establishment" set by the provincial government seven months in advance, and has successfully achieved the strategic objective of "realizing RMB 100 billion of deposits within three years from the day of its establishment" prior to the three year's anniversary, and has established a healthy enterprise image in all sectors of society and its social credibility has been increasing day by day.

In 2014, the bank has completed the foundation work of establishing foreign exchange transaction system, market admittance and business preparation and has obtained the handling channel and ability to conduct basic foreign exchange transactions, including foreign exchange deposits and loans, international settlement and trade financing, cross-border RMB transactions, guarantee, at sight settlement, sale and purchase of foreign exchange etc. and has started comprehensive foreign exchange transactions in July, 2014. At present, the development of foreign exchange transactions of the bank is still in its initial stage. Recently, the key emphasis in work has been conducting various tasks surrounding the improvement of system construction, preparation for businesses and enlarge the number of customers.

Scope of business of foreign exchange transactions: foreign exchange deposits, foreign exchange loans, international settlement and trade financing, cross-border RMB transactions, guarantee, at sight settlement, sale and purchase of foreign exchange etc..

青海银行股份有限公司
Bank of Qinghai Co., Ltd.

青海银行原名西宁市商业银行，成立于1997年12月，是青海省首家法人股份制商业银行，由青海省、西宁市两级政府，企业法人和个人共同出资成立，2008年更名为青海银行，总部设在青海省西宁市。截至2014年底，全行资产规模突破500亿元，达到533.25亿元，各项存款余额396.5亿元，各项贷款余额289.27亿元，主要业务范围包括公司业务、个人业务和资金业务等。目前，青海银行在职员工共1 465人。总行设有20个部室，下设12家分支行（其中，西宁6家，格尔木、玉树、海南、海东、海西、海北各1家）和1家小企业金融服务中心，营业网点共73个（包括社区银行和自助银行），经营机构已覆盖全省主要经济区域，金融服务辐射效应不断增强。青海银行已连续6年跻身“青海企业50强”，2014年排名提升至第16位；被中国企业联合会和中国企业家协会评为中国服务业500强企业。

青海银行自2008年正式开办国际业务，一直秉承着“真诚、贴心、精细、高效”的服务理念，业务品种不断丰富，业务量逐年增加。青海银行是青海地区同业中唯一一家SWIFT一级成员单位，清算速度快捷，在主要货币清算中心开立有美元、欧元、港元等清算账户。业务范围包括：外币兑换、外币存款、国际结算、贸易融资、结售汇、人民币跨境结算。作为一级法人金融机构，机制灵活，决策高效，可为客户提供高效优质的服务。

Formerly named Xining Commercial Bank and founded in December, 1997, the Bank of Qinghai is the first juristic person stock commercial bank in Qinghai Province, was jointly established by governments of Qinghai Province and Xining City, corporate juristic persons and individuals, was renamed the “Bank of Qinghai” in 2008 and is headquartered in Xining City of Qinghai Province. Till the end of the year 2014, asset scale of the Bank is more than 50 billion yuan, and reaches 53.325 billion yuan, with deposit balance of 39.65 billion yuan and loan balance of 28.927 billion yuan, and scope of business covering corporate business, personal business and fund business etc. At present, the Bank of Qinghai carries 1 465 employees. The head office is composed of 20 sectors, with 12 branches and sub-branches (6 of which located in Xining, and 1 of which located in Golmud, Yushu, Hainan, Haidong, Haixi and Haibei respectively), 1 small-enterprise financial service center and 73 business networks (including community banks and self-service banks). Its operation organizations have covered all economic regions in the Province, and radiation effects of financial services have been enhanced. The Bank of Qinghai has been ranking "Top 50 of enterprises in Qinghai Province" for consecutive 6 years, and ranks No.16 in 2014; and is awarded "Top 500 Enterprises in Service Industry of China" by the Chinese Enterprise Association and the Chinese Entrepreneur Association.

The Bank of Qinghai starts international business in 2008, adheres to the service ideas of "sincerity, dedication, elaboration and high efficiency", enriches business range and increases business volume. The Bank of Qinghai is the only SWIFT tier-1 membership units in Qinghai, featuring liquidation rate, and the main currency liquidation center accepts USD , Euro, HKD and other liquidation accounts. The scope of business includes: foreign currency exchange, foreign currency deposit, international settlement, trade financing, foreign currency settlement and sales and RMB cross-border settlement. As a tier-1 juristic person financial institution, it has flexible mechanism, efficient decision-making and provides efficient and high-quality services to customers.

宁夏银行股份有限公司
Bank of Ningxia Co., Ltd.

宁夏银行成立于1998年10月28日，是由宁夏回族自治区、银川市两级政府及企业入股组建的一家股份制商业银行。截至目前，全行拥有员工近2 500人，目前，全行下辖58家分支机构, 其中，区内48家（含1家营业部和2家小企业信贷专营机构），西安4家支行、1家营业部；天津4家支行、1家营业部；发起设立1家隆德六盘山村镇银行。宁夏银行国际业务于2003年12月8日开通，网上银行于2009年7月成功上线，服务功能逐步完善。截至2014年末，全行资产总额1 038亿元，各项存款余额827亿元，贷款余额494亿元，分别是成立时的139倍、192倍和156倍；资本充足率12.32%。

Founded on October 28th, 1998, Bank of Ningxia is a joint-stock commercial bank established by the Ningxia Hui Autonomous Region and Yinchuan two-stage government and enterprises. So far, it has 2 500 employees, and 58 branches. Among them, 48 branches are within the district (including a service point and 2 small enterprise credit institutions）; 4 branches and a service point in Xi’an; 4 sub-branches and a service point are in Tianjin; it initiates establishing a Longde Liupanshan Village Bank. The international service of Bank of Ningxia was open on December 8th, 2003. The online banking was successfully on line in July, 2009. The service function was gradually improved. By the end of 2014, its total asset reached RMB 103.8 billion; its deposit balance reached RMB 8.27 billion; its loan balance reached RMB 49.4 billion. All of them were 139, 192 and 156 times more than its foundation. The capital adequacy ratio was 12.32%.

ئۈرۈمچى شەھەرلىك سودا بانكىسى
乌鲁木齐市商业银行
URUMQI CITY COMMERCIAL BANK

乌鲁木齐市商业银行
Urumqi City Commercial Bank

乌鲁木齐市商业银行，全称乌鲁木齐市商业银行股份有限公司，是经中国人民银行批准，由自治区、乌鲁木齐市两级财政、企业、个人共同入股组建的地方性股份制商业银行，于1997年12月20日挂牌开业。1998年，根据国务院有关规定，更名为乌鲁木齐市商业银行股份有限公司，成为新疆自治区第一家具有独立法人资格的地方性股份制商业银行。

The full name of Urumqi City Commercial Bank is Urumqi City Commercial Bank Co., Ltd., which is a local joint-stock commercial bank and joint invested by the autonomous region, Urumqi municipal government, enterprises and individuals. It officially opened on December 20, 1997. According to the relevant provisions is the State Council, it changed its name to Urumqi City Commercial Bank Co., Ltd., and became the first local joint-stock commercial bank with qualification of independent legal person in Xinjiang Autonomous Region.

昆仑银行
Bank of Kunlun

昆仑银行股份有限公司
Bank of Kunlun Co., Ltd.

昆仑银行的前身是克拉玛依市商业银行，2006年6月6日由克拉玛依市城市信用社改制成立。2009年4月中国石油集团通过增资控股对克拉玛依市商业银行进行重组，2010年4月正式更名为昆仑银行。截至2014年末，昆仑银行共有6家分行，发起设立了2家村镇银行，新成立国际业务结算中心，分支机构总数达到62家，已同22个国家的58家金融同业建立了代理行关系。截至2014年末，该行资产总额2 782.99亿元，各项存款余额1 131.03亿元，各项贷款余额730.63亿元。

The predecessor of Bank of Kunlun is Karamay City Commercial Bank. It was restructured by Karamay City Cooperative on June 6th, 2006. In April of 2009, China Petroleum Group reorganized Karamay City Commercial Bank through capital increase and holding. In April, 2010, its name was formally changed into Bank of Kunlun. By the end of 2014, it had 6 branches, and established 2 village banks, and newly built international settlement center. The total number of the branches reached 62. It has established agency relationship with 58 financial institutions with the same trade from 22 countries. Besides, by the end of 2014, its total asset was RMB 278.299 billion; its deposit balance was RMB 113.103 billion; its loan balance was RMB 73.063 billion.

新疆汇和银行股份有限公司

Xinjiang Huihe Bank Co., Ltd.

新疆汇和银行股份有限公司是经中国银监会批准，由地方财政、自治区境内企业法人等投资入股组建的，具有独立法人资格的股份制商业银行。新疆汇和银行前身为奎屯市商业银行，2010年12月31日正式更名为新疆汇和银行。

Xinjiang Huihe Bank Co., Ltd. is joint-stock commercial bank with an independent legal personality, approved by the China Banking Regulatory Commsion. It is set up by the investment from local finance, domestic enterprise as a legal person in autonomous region. Formerly known as Xinjaing Kuitun City Commercial Bank, Xinjiang Huihe changed its name on December 31, 2010.

农村商业银行

NONGCUN SHANGYE YINHANG

北京农村商业银行股份有限公司
Beijing Rural Commercial Bank Company Limited

北京农商银行改制成立于2005年10月19日，是国务院批准组建的首家省级股份制农村商业银行，拥有694家网点，是唯一一家金融服务覆盖全市所有182个乡镇的金融机构，并建成北京市首家持牌社区银行。

截至2014年末，全行资产总额达到5 222亿元，其中，各项存款余额4 214.3亿元，各项贷款余额2 634亿元。全行五级不良贷款率为0.98%，明显优于全国商业银行1.25%的平均水平。不良贷款拨备覆盖率达374.41%，优于全国商业银行232.06%的平均水平，抵御风险能力不断强化。全行核心一级资本充足率、一级资本充足率均为11.49%，资本充足率为14.11%，较2009年末大幅提升。在英国《银行家》杂志最新全球银行业排名中，一级资本位列全球1 000家银行第262位，同比上升了23位，资产规模全球排名第198位。

Beijing Rural Commercial Bank was restructured and founded on October 19, 2005. It was the first provincial level joint-stock rural commercial bank established on the approval of the State Council. With 694 branches, Beijing Rural Commercial Bank is the only financial institute whose financial service covers 182 villages and towns of the whole city and has become the first licensed community bank in Beijing.

By the end of 2014, the total assets of the bank have reached RMB 522.2 billion, which include RMB 421.43 billion balance of deposits and RMB 263.4 billion balance of loans. The fifth grade bad loan ratio of the bank is 0.98%, apparently better than the average level of the commercial banks in China, which is 1.25%. Its bad loan provision coverage has reached 374.41%, better than the average level of the commercial banks in China, which is 232.06%. So its capability to withstand risks is increasing. The core tier one capital adequacy ratio and tier one capital adequacy ratio of the bank is both

11.49%, and its capital adequacy ratio is 14.11%, which is a big improvement compared with that of the end of 2009. According to the rank of banks provided by the Banker, a Britain published magazine, the tier one capital of this bank ranks as No.262 among the 1 000 banks around the world, increased by 23 ranks compared with that of the last year. Its capital scale ranks as No. 198 around the world.

上海农商银行 SRCB

上海农村商业银行股份有限公司
Shanghai Rural Commercial Bank Company Limited

上海农商银行成立于2005年8月25日，是全国首家在省级农信社基础上整体改制成立的股份制商业银行。公司总股本50亿元，由上海国资控股，澳新银行参股。截至2014年末，全行总资产4 666.01亿元，各项存款余额3 751.25亿元，各项贷款余额2 397.57亿元，当年实现净利润47.05亿元。2014年末不良贷款率1.32%，监管评级连续多年保持在二级B档的较高水平，共有机构网点407家，员工总数近6 000人。在上海布设107家金融便利店，挂牌“社区金融服务中心”40家；在全国多个地区批量化布设35家村镇银行。在2014年度全球1 000家大银行中，上海农商银行排名189位，在国内所有入围银行中，排名第20位。

Shanghai Rural Commercial Bank Company Limited, established on August 25, 2005, is the first joint-stock commercial bank which was restructured from a rural credit cooperative of provincial level in China. Its total equity is RMB 5 billion, which was held by Shanghai State-owned assets and Australia and New Zealand Bank holds its shares. By the end of 2014, the total assets of the bank have reached RMB 466.601 billion, which include RMB 375.125 billion balance of deposits and RMB 239.757 billion balance of loans, and RMB 4.705 billion net profits has been realized that year. The bad loan ratio by the end of 2014 was 1.32%. The supervision rating has been remaining at a relatively high level for several years successively, which is Grade Two Level B. The bank has 407 branches, with nearly 6 000 staff. It has set up 107 financial convenient stores, 40 licensed “community financial service centers”; 35 village banks in total has been set up in many regions around the state. Among 1 000 banks around the world in 2014, Shanghai Rural Commercial Bank ranks No.189, and No.20 among all the banks in China.

TRC BANK 天津农商银行

天津农村商业银行股份有限公司
Tianjin Rural Commercial Bank Company Limited

天津农村商业银行股份有限公司的前身是有着近60年发展历史的农村信用社。2010年6月，天津农商银行正式挂牌成立。成立之初，天津农商银行便依靠雄厚的资本金实力成功跻身中国银行50强和世界银行500强行列，是经中国银监会批准成立的一家省级股份合作制地方金融机构，是天津市最大的一家地方性总部商业银行。2014年末，资产达2 215亿元，存款总量1 733亿元，贷款总量 1 119亿元。

Tianjin Rural Commercial Bank Company Limited (short for “Tianjin Rural Commercial Bank”) was restructured from rural credit cooperative of nearly 60 years of history. Tianjin Rural Commercial Bank was established in June, 2010. At the beginning of its establishment, Tianjin Rural Commercial Bank has successively rose to the top 50 banks in China and top 500 banks around the world with its abundant capital. It is a joint-stock cooperative regional banking institution of provincial level established on the approval of CBRC, the biggest regional head office commercial bank in Tianjin. By the end of 2014, its capital has reached RMB 221.5 billion, with total deposits of RMB 173.3 billion and total loans of RMB 111.9 billion.

天津滨海农村商业银行
TIANJIN BINHAI RURAL COMMERCIAL BANK

天津滨海农村商业银行股份有限公司

Tianjin Binhai Rural Commercial Bank Company Limited

天津滨海农村商业银行股份有限公司于2007年12月24日成立，是国内第一家在发起阶段就引入境外战略投资者的农村商业银行，是第一家总部设在滨海新区和天津自贸区的农村商业银行，是第一家在全国跨省区设立分支机构的农村商业银行。截至2015年3月，天津滨海农商银行共有员工2 045人，营业网点总数109家，全面覆盖滨海新区和天津各区县，还在新疆喀什、库尔勒、阿克苏和浙江绍兴等地设立了分支机构；作为主发起行设立了北辰村镇银行，参与发起设立了河南南阳村镇银行。

Tianjin Binhai Rural Commercial Bank Company Limited (hereinafter refer to as “Tianjin Binhai Rural Commercial Bank), established on December 24, 2007, is the first domestic commercial bank which attracted foreign strategic investors during the launch stage. It is also the first rural commercial bank whose head office is located in New Zone of Binhai and Tianjin Free Trade Area, and the fist rural commercial bank that set up branch office across province in China. By March, 2015, Tianjin Binhai Rural Commercial Bank has a staff of 2 045 and 109 outlets in total, which has covered New Zone of Binhai and districts and towns of Tianjin. Branch offices has also been set up in Kashi, Korla, Aksu in Xinjiang province and Shaoxin, etc. in Zhejiang province, etc.. As the main originator, the bank also established Beichen Village Bank and participated in the establishment of Henan Nanyang Village Bank.

重庆农村商业银行
CHONGQING RURAL COMMERCIAL BANK

重庆农村商业银行股份有限公司
Chongqing Rural Commercial Bank Company Limited

重庆农村商业银行股份有限公司的前身为重庆市农村信用社，成立于1951年，至今已有60余年的历史。2003年，重庆成为全国首批农村信用社改革试点省市之一。2008年，组建全市统一法人的农村商业银行。目前，重庆农商行下辖1家分行，42家支行，1 772个分支机构，从业人员1.6万人。截至2014年末，重庆农商行资产规模突破6 000亿元，达6 188.89亿元，居全国农商系统第1位；存款余额突破4 000亿元，达4 097.20亿元，存款总量和增量均居重庆市银行业第1位；贷款余额突破2 400亿元；达2 421.98亿元，不良贷款率保持1%以内；资本充足率12%以上，经营业绩和资产质量持续向好，入围全球银行品牌价值200强、中国企业500强。

Chongqing Rural Commercial Bank Company Limited (hereinafter refer to as "Chongqing Rural Commercial Bank"), was restructured from Chongqing Rural Credit Cooperative, which was founded in 1951, with a history of more than 60 years. In 2003, Chongqing became one of the earliest provinces/cites to conduct pilot reform on rural credit cooperatives. In 2008, rural commercial bank of unified legal person in Chongqing was established. At present, Chongqing Rural Commercial Bank has 1 branch, 42 sub-branches and 1 772 branch offices with 16 000 staff. By the end of 2014, Chongqing Rural Commercial Bank has exceeded RMB 600 billion, reached RMB 618.889 billion, which is the No.1 in the national commercial bank system; its outstanding of deposit has exceeded RMB 400 billion, reached RMB 409.72 billion, whose total deposits and increment is the No.1 in Chongqing banking industry; its balance of loans has exceeded RMB 240 billion, reached RMB 242.198 billion, with bad loan ratio remains below 1%; its capital adequacy ratio is above 12% and its business performance and quality of assets have been improving. It ranks top 200 banks around the world and top 500 banks in China in terms of brand value.

山西尧都农村商业银行股份有限公司
Shanxi Yaodu Rural Commercial Bank Co., Ltd.

尧都农商银行成立于2010年12月21日，是由原尧都区农村信用合作联社改制而成的农村商业银行。注册资本23.5亿元，内设25个部室，92家支行，共有员工1 607人。截至2015年4月末，资产总额574.1亿元，各项存款余额342.9亿元，各项贷款余额240.7亿元，1～4月实现各项收入12亿元，实现利润总额3.3亿元，上缴税费1.2亿元，不良贷款占比1.88%，监管评级连续5年达到二级标准，特别是2014年监管评级由2C上升到2B，是全省唯一的一家，连续3年被银监会选树为标杆银行。改制以来，尧都农商银行在省联社、临汾办事处和各级党委政府的正确领导下，在人行、银监部门的指导监管和社会各界的鼎力支持下，围绕“打造现代金融企业集团”的奋斗目标，坚持“服务‘三农’，微小中企业和优质客户”的市场定位，以科学治理为第一保障，建立“三会一层”法人治理架构，启动流程银行建设，构建全面风险管理体系，形成规范化管理的“八零机制”，治理能力全面提升；以服务客户为第一使命，在全国农合系统首家建立e融九州互联网金融服务平台；在全省农合系统首家开办国际业务、网银业务，发行天河贷记卡、公务卡、社保卡；在全省首家成立小微企业贷款中心，布设延芳社区金融服务站，运营汽车、房产、城建专营支行，试水延时、零币、流动网点；启动贷记卡微信系统，上线客户关系管理系统；推出“丰利宝”系列理财产品、“彩虹易贷”微贷系列产品，服务渠道更加畅通；以强核亮星为第一要务，在全省首家发行二级资本债和中小企业私募债；在省内外发起设立22家村镇银行，战略入股黑河农商银行和海口联合农商银行，在全国唯一一家央行票据未兑付的浮山县信用联社注资改制农商银行，在全国唯一一个没有农合机构的汾西县启动设立汾西支行，金融服务贯通4省13市22县，形成了“立足尧都、辐射三晋、服务全国”的战略格局；以企业文化为第一引领，深入开展商行核心价值观建设，全面导入VI、SI视觉识别系统和终端识别系统，创作《尧都农商银行之歌》，摄制《耕耘梦想》商行形象宣传片，大力实施“伞、家、桥”工程，“四逢文化”、“五子精神”在传承中落地深植。改制至今，尧都农商银行连续三年被银监会选树为全国农村商业银行标杆银行；连续四年荣膺省级“平安单位”、“文明和谐单位”荣誉称号，是山西省百强企业。

2011年4月28日，山西尧都农村商业银行股份有限公司第一届董事会第四次会议上通过了《山西尧都农村商业银行股份有限公司申请开办外汇业务的方案》的决议。2011年11月24日中国银行业监督管理委员会批复同意开办外汇业务。2012年5月21日国家外汇管理局批复同意开办即期结售汇业务。2012年7月6日批准成为上海外汇交易中心即期会员单位。2012年12月3日正式加入SWIFT（环球银行金融电讯协会）。

外汇业务经营范围：外汇存款业务、外汇贷款业务、结售汇业务、国际结算业务、贸易融资业务。

Yaodu Rural Commercial Bank was established on December 21, 2010, which was a rural commercial bank restructured from Yaodu District Rural Credit Cooperative Association. Its registered capital is RMB 2.35 billion, with 25 department offices, 92 branches and 1 607 employees. Up to the end of April, 2015, its total assets has reached RMB 57.41 billion and total deposit balance of RMB 34.29 billion and total loan balance of RMB 24.07 billion. From January to April of 2015, its various income has reached RMB 1.2 billion with total profit of 0.33 billion and has turn in taxes for 0.12 billion. Its bad loans takes up 1.88%. Its supervision rating has been rated as secondary standard for five years successively. In particular, its ratings has been improved from 2C to 2B in 2014 and has been elected as the only bank in the province as a benchmark bank by China Banking Regulatory Commission for three years successively. Since the restructuring, under the right leadership of Provincial Rural Credit Cooperatives, Linfen Office and party committees at all levels and under the guidance and supervision of The People's Bank of China and Banking Supervision Department and the support of all sectors of society, Yaodu Rural Commercial Bank aims at “building a modernized financial enterprise group”, and insists on the market positioning of “serving issues of agriculture, farmer and rural area, micro, small or medium enterprises and high-quality clients”. With scientific management as the first protection, the corporate governance framework of “stockholders’ meeting, board of directors, board of supervisors and senior management” has been established. With the launching of workflow bank, comprehensive risk management system has been built and its governance capacity has been greatly improved through the formation of the “eight zero mechanism” of standardized management; taking serving clients as its first mission, Yaodu Rural Commercial Bank has established the first E Internet financial service platform in the rural cooperative system in China; it is also the first bank who provides international business, Smart E-Bank business, and issues Tianhe credit card, business card and social security card in the provincial rural cooperative system; it is the first bank who established micro and small businesses loaning center in the province and set up Yanfang Community Financing Service Station, starting specialized branch in automobile, real estate and city construction and try delayed, charges and circulating branches; launch Wechat system of credit card, on-line customer relationship management system; launch finance products of “Fenglibao” series, micro-loan products of “Caihong Yidai” series to smoothen service channel; taking “strengthen core service” as the first mission, Yaodu Rural Commercial Bank became the first bank in the province who issue tier 2 capital debt and small and medium sized enterprises private debt; through establishing 22 rural banks in and outside the provide, strategically holding shares of Heihe Rural Commercial Bank and Haikou United Rural Commercial Bank, investing in Fushan County Credit Cooperative Association and restructured into rural commercial bank and setting up a branch in Fenxi County, which is the only county who did not have agriculture cooperation association and with its financial service covering 22 counties, 13 cities and 4 provinces, the strategic pattern of “locating in Yaodu, radiating Shanxi and serving the nation” has been established. Led by enterprise culture, the establishment of core values in commercial banks has been deeply developed, and VI, SI visual identification system and terminal identification system has been introduced comprehensively; “the Song of Yaodu Rural Commercial Bank” has been composed and the image publicity film of the commercial bank called “Ploughing Dreams” has been shot so as to deepen the “umbrella, home, bridge” project, “Sifeng Culture” and “Wuzi Spirit”. Ever since the restructuring, Yaodu Rural Commercial Bank has been elected as the benchmark bank of national rural commercial bank by China Banking Regulatory Commission for three years successively and has been winning the awards as “safe unit”, “civilized and harmonious unit” of the provincial level for four years successively and has become the top one hundred enterprises in Shanxi province.

On November 24, 2011, China Banking Regulatory Commission has approved Yaodu Rural Commercial Bank to conduct foreign exchange businesses. On May 21, 2012, State Administration of Foreign Exchange approved the bank to conduct at sight settlement, sale and purchase of foreign exchange business. On July 6, 2012, the bank was approved as on demand membership unit of Shanghai Foreign exchange trading center. On December 3, 2012, the bank has formally joined in SWIFT (Society for Worldwide Interbank Financial Telecommunications).

Scope of business of foreign exchange transactions: foreign exchange deposits, foreign exchange loans, foreign exchange settlement and sale, international settlement transactions, trade financial transactions.

吉林九台农村商业银行
JILIN JIUTAI RURAL COMMERCIAL BANK

吉林九台农村商业银行股份有限公司
Jilin Jiutai Rural Commercial Bank Company Limited

九台农商银行全称为吉林九台农村商业银行股份有限公司，前身为九台市农村信用合作联社，始建于20世纪50年代。2008年12月，经中国银监会批准，正式改制为东北首家农村商业银行，现有员工1 378人，下辖49家支行和1个营业部。2010年以来，在全国9省全资或控股设立了26家村镇银行以及3家农商银行。目前是东北地区资产规模前列、网点覆盖范围最广的农商银行。

The full name of Jiutai Rural Commercial Bank is Jilin Jiutai Rural Commercial Bank Company Limited, which was restructured from Jiutai City Rural Credit Cooperative Union established in the 1950s. With the approval of CBRC, it was restructured into the first rural commercial bank in Northeast China in December, 2008. Now it has a staff of 1 378 and 49 branches and 1 business department. Since 2010, it has established 26 village banks and 3 commercial banks in 9 provinces either wholly-owned or have holdings. At present, it is a commercial bank whose capital scale is among the top banks and whose overage area of outlets is the largest in Northeast China.

珲春农村商业银行
Hunchun Rural Commercial Bank

吉林珲春农村商业银行股份有限公司
Jilin Hunchun Rural Commercial Bank Company Limited

吉林珲春农村商业银行是一家股份制银行，也是珲春市最大的一家县域总部商业银行。吉林珲春农村商业银行前身是珲春市农村信用合作联社。吉林珲春农村商业银行总行机关设14个职能部门，下辖1家营业部、4家支行、24家分理处。目前是珲春市营业网点最多、服务范围最广、资金规模最大的综合性银行业金融机构，也是全省首家卢布现钞兑换金融机构。

Jilin Hunchun Rural Commercial Bank is a joint-stock bank and also the largest commercial bank in Hunchun whose Head Office is located within the county. Jilin Hunchun Rural Commercial Bank was restructured from Hunchun City Rural Credit Cooperative Union. The Head Office of Jilin Hunchun Rural Commercial Bank has set up 14 functional departments, 1 business department, 4 branches and 24 sub-branches. At present, it is the largest comprehensive banking financial institution in Hunchun in terms of the number of outlet, range of services and capital scale and it is also the first financial institution which offers the service of exchanging rouble into cash.

延边农村商业银行股份有限公司
YanBian Rural Commercial Bank Co., Ltd.

延边农村商业银行股份有限公司是由延边农村合作银行改制而成，是吉林省延边朝鲜族自治州唯一一家由自然人、企业法人和其他经济组织共同发起，具有独立法人资格的股份制农村商业银行，并且在实施股份制改造的同时，有计划、分步骤地吸收合并了原延边州26家城市信用社，有效化解了地方区域性金融风险。延边农村商业银行总部位于延边朝鲜族自治州州府延吉市，2011年11月28日正式挂牌运营，目前注册资本12亿元人民币。延边农村商业银行下设1家总行营业部，5家支行，48家分理处，15家储蓄所。同时控股2家农村商业银行，参股1家农村商业银行，并作为全国最早发起设立村镇银行的主发起行之一已经在全国发起设立16家村镇银行。

延边农村商业银行自2008年5月开办外汇业务以来，先后已在美国、日本、韩国、德国、俄罗斯等多个国家开立了外币结算账户，与13个国家的64家境外银行建立了代理行关系，开立国际结算账户24 898户，其中：外币账户1 504户，人民币境外汇入汇款账户23 394户。累计完成国际结算 7亿美元，结汇43亿元人民币。

外汇业务经营范围：外汇存款、外汇贷款、外汇汇款、国际结算、同业外汇拆借和资信调查、咨询、见证等业务。

特色业务：韩币和卢布结算业务。

YanBian Rural Commercial Bank Co., Ltd.（short for YanBian Rural Commercial Bank） was restructured from YanBian Rural Cooperative Bank, which is the only rural stock commercial bank with independent legal qualification in Yanbian Korean autonomous prefecture, Jilin province. It was started by natural person, enterprise legal person and other economic organizations together. Furthermore, during the shareholding restructuring, it has effectively obviated local regional risks through consolidation by merger with original 26 urban credit unions in Yanbian Prefecture step by step according to plan. The head office of YanBian Rural Commercial Bank Co., Ltd. is located in Yanji city, Yanbian Korean Autonomous Prefecture State, whose operation started on November 28, 2011 with a registered capital of RMB 1.2 billion. YanBian Rural Commercial Bank consists of one business department of the head office, five branches, 48 sub-branches and 15 savings bank. At the same time, it holds over two rural commercial banks and holds share in one rural commercial bank. As one of the earliest major banks who started rural bank, YanBian Rural Commercial Bank has established 16 rural Banks in China. Since it started to conduct foreign exchange transactions in May 2008, Yanbian rural commercial bank has opened foreign currency settlement accounts in many countries, including the United States, Japan, Korea, Germany, Russia etc. and other countries successively and has established correspondent banking relationship with 64 foreign Banks in 13 countries, and has opened 24 898 international settlement account, among which 1 504 accounts are foreign currency accounts, 23 394 accounts are RMB inward remittance accounts with a total of US$700 million international settlements and RMB 4.3 billion exchange settlements having been conducted.

Scope of business of foreign exchange transactions: foreign exchange deposits, foreign exchange loans, foreign exchange remittance, international settlement, foreign exchange inter banking lending in the same trade and credit investigation, consultation and attestation, etc..

Characteristic businesses: settlement business of South Korean Won and rouble.

长春农村商业银行股份有限公司
Changchun Rural Commercial Bank Company Limited

长春农村商业银行股份有限公司前身为长春市农村信用合作社联合营业部，始建于1994年11月，是一家立足城区，集存款、贷款、结算于一体的一级法人金融机构。2009年7月29日，长春农村商业银行正式挂牌成立。2010年8月更名为长春农商银行。截至目前，长春农商银行拥有49家分支机构。其中，长春市区有43家支行（1家自助银行），大连3家支行和黑龙江肇东1家支行；黑龙江阿城、兰西2家全资村镇银行。

Changchun Rural Commercial Bank Company Limited was restructured from Changchun City Rural Credit Cooperative United Business Department in November, 1994. It is a first grade legal personal financial institution rooted on urban areas and combining deposit, loan and settlement. Changchun Rural Commercial Bank was officially opened on July 29, 2009 and was renamed into Changchun Nongshang Bank in August, 2010. So far, Changchun Nongshang Bank has set up 49 branches, among which, 43 branches (1 self-service bank) are located in Changchun city, 3 braches in Dalian and 1 branch in Zhaodong of Heilongjiang; as well as 2 villiage banks in Acheng and Lanxi of Heilongjiang.

黑河农村商业银行
HeiHe Rural Commercial Bank

黑河农村商业银行股份有限公司
Heihe Rural Commercial Bank Company Limited

黑河农村商业银行前身是爱辉区农村信用合作联社合社，成立于1993年，2007年7月，正式更名为黑河市爱辉区农村信用合作联社，2011年1月28日正式改制更名为黑河农村商业银行股份有限公司。

Heihe Rural Commercial Bank was restructured from Aihui District Rural Credit Cooperative Union. It was established in 1993 and was renamed into Heihe City Aihui District Rural Credit Cooperative Union in July, 2007. On January 28, 2011, it was officially renamed into Heihe Rural Commercial Bank Company Limited.

江苏常熟农村商业银行股份有限公司
Jiangsu Changshu Rural Commercial Bank Company Limited

江苏常熟农村商业银行股份有限公司总部设在江苏省常熟市，是一家具有60多年悠久历史的金融机构。2001年11月28日，由常熟市农村信用合作联社改制而来，是全国首批组建的股份制农村金融机构。目前，常熟农商银行在全国共有营业网点133家，其中常熟本地107家，异地26家。同时，开设了17家“常农商”系村镇银行，并参股6家农村金融机构。截至2014年末，全行总资产986.20亿元，存款余额715.61亿元、贷款余额459.42亿元。据英国《银行家》杂志2014年公布的全球1 000家银行排名，居国际第627位。

Jiangsu Changshu Rural Commercial Bank Company Limited has its head office set up in Changshu city, Jiangsu province. It is a financial institution with more than 60 years of history. It was restructured from Changshu Rural Credit Cooperative Union on November 28, 2001, which is one of the earliest joint-stock rural financial institutions established in China. At present, Jiangsu Changshu Rural Commercial Bank has set up 133 outlets, with 107 branches located in Changshu, and 26 branches located outside Changshu. Meanwhile, Jiangsu Changshu Rural Commercial Bank has set up 17 village bank of “Jiangsu Changshu Rural Commercial Bank” series and hold shares in 6 rural financial institutions. By the end of 2014, the total assets of the bank is RMB 98.62 billion, with outstanding deposits of RMB 71.561 billion and balance of loans of RMB 45.954 billion. According to the rank of banks provided by the Banker, a Britain published magazine, this bank ranks No.627 among the 1 000 banks around the world.

ZRC BANK 张家港农村商业银行 RURAL COMMERCIAL BANK OF ZHANGJIAGANG

江苏张家港农村商业银行股份有限公司
Jiangsu Zhangjiagang Rural Commercial Bank Company Limited

张家港农村商业银行成立于2001年11月27日，是全国首家由农村信用社改制组建的股份制商业银行。目前拥有36家支行、1家营业部、56家分理处，其中在省内镇江、南通、宿迁、徐州、连云港和山东青岛设有8家异地支行，机构网点总数93家，并在山东寿光、江苏东海各发起设立1家控股村镇银行。截至2014年末，全行资产总额719.70225亿元，本外币各项存款余额533.20130亿元，各项贷款余额382.99882亿元。

Zhangjiagang Rural Commercial Bank, established on November 27, 2001, was the first joint-stock commercial bank restructured from rural credit cooperative. At present, this bank has set up 36 branches, 1 business department, 56 sub-branches and has set up 8 offsite branches in Zhenjiang, Nantong, Suqian, Xuzhou, Lianyungang within the province and Qingdao in Shandong province. This bank has set up 93 outlets and has hold over 1 village bank in Shouguang, Shandong province and Donghai in Jiangsu province respectively. By the end of 2014, the total assets of the bank is RMB 71.970225 billion with RMB 53.32013 billi total balance of deposits of both domestic and foreign currency and RMB 38.299882 billion total balance of loans.

江苏江阴农村商业银行股份有限公司

Jiangsu Jiangyin Rural Commercial Bank Company Limited

江阴农商银行前身江阴市信用合作社联合社，是在原江阴市35家法人信用合作社和3家城市信用社的基础上，经国务院、中国人民银行总行批准，由江阴企业、自然人入股组建的地方性股份制商业银行，是全国首批三家股份制农村商业银行之一。目前，在江阴县域范围内共有支行级网点25 个，分理处 48 家，助农便民取款点 131 个。截至 2014 年末，全行资产总额为 835.87 亿元，全行各项存款余额为630.83 亿元，各项贷款余额为483.92亿元。

Jiangyin Rural Commercial Bank was originally known as Jiangyin City Credit Cooperative, which was set up on the basis of former 35 legal person credit cooperatives and 3 city credit cooperatives. It was as regional joint-stock commercial bank established by the investment of enterprises in Jiangyin and natural persons through the approval of the State Council and the Head Office of the People's Bank of China. It is one of the earliest three joint-stock commercial banks in China. At present, Jiangyin Rural Commercial Bank has set up 25 outlets, 48 sub-branches and 131 convenience withdraw spots for farmers in Jiangyin county。By the end of 2014, the total assets of the bank is RMB 83.587 billion, with RMB 63.083 billion of total balance of deposits and RMB 48.392 billion balance of loans.

江苏紫金农村商业银行股份有限公司
Jiangsu Zijin Rural Commercial Bank Company Limited

江苏紫金农村商业银行股份有限公司是经中国银行业监督管理委员会批准筹建，由南京市辖区内原4家农村中小金融机构（南京市区农村信用合作联社、南京市江宁区农村信用合作联社、南京市浦口区农村信用合作联社、南京市六合区农村信用合作联社）按照市场化原则组建而成的股份制农村商业银行。2011年3月28日正式挂牌开业。目前注册资本22亿元，下辖9家一级支行，125家营业网点，员工总数2 200余人。截至2014年末，资产总额707.95063亿元，存款总额596.49024亿元，贷款总额430.01284亿元。

Jiangsu Zijin Rural Commercial Bank Company Limited is a joint-stock rural commercial bank restructured from four medium and small financial institutions in Nanjing (including Nanjing City Rural Credit Cooperative Union, Nanjing City Jiangning District Rural Credit Cooperative Union, Nanjing City Pukou District Rural Credit Cooperative Union and Nanjing City Liuhe District Rural Credit Cooperative Union) with the approval of CBRC according to the principle of marketization. It was officially opened on March, 28, 2011 with a registered capital of RMB 2.2 billion. It has set up 9 tier one branches and 125 outlets with a staff of more than 2 200. By the end of 2014, its total assets have reached RMB 70.795063 billion with RMB 59.649024 billion of deposit and RMB 43.001284 billion of loan.

江苏邳州农村商业银行股份有限公司
Jiangsu Pizhou Rural Commercial Bank Company Limited

江苏邳州农村商业银行是徐州市首家由农村信用社改制组建的地方性股份制商业银行，现辖47家支行，1家营业部，500多名干部职工。

Jiangsu Pizhou Rural Commercial Bank is the first regional joint-stock commercial bank restructured from rural credit cooperative with 47 branches, 1 business department and a staff of more than 500.

丹阳农商银行
DANYANG RURAL COMMERCIAL BANK

江苏丹阳农村商业银行股份有限公司
Jiangsu Danyang Rural Commercial Bank Company Limited

江苏丹阳农村商业银行前身为丹阳市农村信用合作联社，成立于1995年9月，总行在丹阳市。丹阳农村商业银行是在丹阳市境内依法设立的、由辖区内农民、农村工商户、企业法人和其他经济组织共同发起成立的地方性合作金融机构，其上级主管部门是江苏省农村信用社联合社和镇江市农村信用合作联社。2007年2月5日，改制为江苏丹阳农村合作银行。2011年9月23日，更名为江苏丹阳农村商业银行。

Jiangsu Danyang Rural Commercial Bank was restructured from Danyang City Rural Credit Cooperative, which was established in September, 1995 with the Head Office in Danyang. Danyang Rural Commercial Bank is a regional cooperative financial institution legally established in Danyang which was jointly founded by the peasants, rural industrial and commercial units, enterprises legal person and other economic organizations. Its higher authority is Jiangsu Province Rural Credit Cooperative Union and Zhenjiang City Rural Credit Cooperative Union. It was restructured into Jiangsu Danyang Rural Cooperative Bank on February 5, 2007 and was renamed into Jiangsu Danyang Rural Commercial Bank on September 23, 2011.

江苏海安农村商业银行股份有限公司
Jiangsu Haian Rural Commercial Bank Company Limited

海安农村商业银行是经中国银行业监督管理委员会批准，在原江苏海安农村合作银行基础上改制组建的股份制商业银行，2011年2月28日正式挂牌对外营业。海安农村商业银行注册资本金8.5亿元，总行内设16个部室、10个中心，现有在职员工727人，下设1家营业部、57家支行以及1家异地支行（盱眙支行），主发起成立2家村镇银行（贵阳小河科技村镇银行、修文江海村镇银行），是海安地区历史最悠久、网点最密集、业务规模最大的金融机构。2014年12月《英国银行家年鉴》杂志公布的国内银行排名中（以2013年末报表为基础的统计口径），列国内银行第139位，上榜农商行第29位。截至2014年末，全行资产总额428.61亿元，存款总额达323.95亿元，贷款总额达228.55亿元。

Haian Rural Commercial Bank is a joint-stock commercial bank restructured from Jiangsu Haian Rural Credit Cooperative with the approval of CBRC. It started its business from February 28, 2011. The registered capital of Haian Rural Commercial Bank is RMB 0.85 billion, with 16 department offices in the Head Office and 10 centers and a staff of 727. It has set up 1 business department, 57 branches and 1 offsite branch (Xuyi Branch). The 2 village banks (Guiyang Xiaohe Keji Village Bank and Xiuwen Jianghai Village Bank) which the bank established, are the biggest financial institutions in Haian with longest history, densest outlets and largest scale. According to the ranking (ranked according to the statistics of the statement at the end of 2013) in the yearbook of bankers, released by The Banker, a British magazine, Haian Rural Commercial Bank was ranked No. 139 among the banks in China, and No.29 among the rural banks in China. By the end of 2014, the total asset of the bank is RMB 42.861 billion, with total balance of deposits of RMB 32.395 billion and balance of loans of RMB 22.855 billion.

江苏盱眙农村商业银行股份有限公司
Jiangsu Xuyi Rural Commercial Bank Company Limited

江苏盱眙农村商业银行股份有限公司成立于2012年4月26日，是由境内906名股东注资16 000万元共同发起设立的独立法人金融机构，是在有着逾50年历史的盱眙县农村信用社基础上整体改制而成的永久存续的股份制商业银行。盱眙农村商业银行是盱眙地区业务规模最大、服务领域最广、机构人员最多的银行。截至2014年末，各项存款余额达87.09亿元，各项贷款余额达77.93亿元；注册资本19 712万元，营业网点32个，员工400多人。

Jiangsu Xuyi Rural Commercial Bank Company Limited was established on April 26, 2012. It was a financial institution of independent legal person jointly established by 906 shareholders with RMB 160 000 000. It was a long-standing joint-stock commercial bank restructured from Xuyi Rural Credit Cooperative, with over 50 years of history. Xuyi Rural Commercial Bank is the largest bank in Xuyi in terms of business scale, range of service and staff. By the end of 2014, its total balance of deposits has reached RMB 8.709 billion and its balance of loans has reached RMB 7.793 billion. Its registered capital is RMB 197 120 000, with 32 outlets and a staff of more than 400.

江苏江都农村商业银行股份有限公司
Jiangsu Jiangdu Rural Commercial Bank Company Limited

江苏江都农村商业银行股份有限公司的前身为江都市农村信用合作联社，2010年4月改制成江苏江都农村商业银行股份有限公司。总部设在江苏省扬州市江都区龙城路21号。现设有18个部门，下辖1家营业部、50家支行和4家分理处，干部职工735名，担负着全区各农工商企事业单位和全区居民及农户个体私营经济户的金融服务工作。截至2014年12月末，全行资产总额为251.05亿元，各项存款余额206.94亿元，各项贷款余额146.07亿元，存贷款余额均列江都区各金融机构之首。

Jiangsu Jiangdu Rural Commercial Bank Company Limited was restructured from Jiangdu Rural Credit Cooperative Union in April, 2010. Its Head Office is located at No.21, Longcheng Road, Jiangdu District, Yangzhou City, Jiangsu Province. Jiangdu Rural Commercial Bank has set up 18 departments, 1 business department, 50 branches and 4 sub-branches with a staff of 735 and has been providing financial services for enterprises and public institutions in agriculture, industrial and commercial sectors, all the citizens and self-employed peasant households. By the end of 2014, its total assets have reached RMB 25.105 billion, with total balance of deposits of RMB 20.694 billion and total balance of loans of RMB 14.607 billion. Its balance of deposits and balance of loans are the largest among the financial institutions in Jiangdu District.

江苏海门农村商业银行股份有限公司
Jiangsu Haimen Rural Commercial Bank Company Limited

海门农商银行前身为海门市农村信用合作联社，是生于海门、长于海门的本土金融机构。2010年12月23日，经中国银行业监督管理委员会批准，成功改制为海门农商银行，实现了由农信社向股份制银行的历史性转变。在做大传统业务的同时，海门农商银行加快新兴业务的发展步伐，逐步形成了投资、票据、电子银行、国际业务、理财产品齐头并进的多元化格局。42家经营网点遍布城乡，430家助农取款服务点覆盖全市所有行政村，528名员工倾情服务广大市民，是海门地区经营规模最大，从业人员最多，服务范围最广的商业银行，成为服务社会公众、支持地方建设、构建和谐社会的重要金融力量。

Haimen Rural Commercial Bank was restructured from Haimen City Rural Credit Cooperative Union. It is a local financial institution which was established and developed in Haimen. On December 23, 2010, with the approval of CBRC, it was successfully restructured into Haimen Rural Commercial Bank, which realized the historical transformation from rural credit cooperative into a joint-stock bank. Other than expanding its traditional businesses, Haimen Rural Commercial Bank has sped up its development pace in newly-developing businesses and has gradually formed a diversified pattern combining investment, bills, electronic banking, international businesses and finance products. With 42 outlets covering the urban and rural areas and 430 withdraw service centers covering all the administrative villages in the city and 528 staff passionate in service the public, it is now the largest commercial bank in Haimen in terms of business scale, staff and range of service and it has become an important financial power in providing service for the public, supporting local construction and building a harmonious society.

启东农商银行
QIDONG RURAL COMMERCIAL BANK

江苏启东农村商业银行股份有限公司
Jiangsu Qidong Rural Commercial Bank Company Limited

启东农商银行前身为启东市农村信用合作联社。2011年12月，经中国银行业监督管理委员会批准，成功改制为启东农商银行。启东农商银行现有64家经营网点，240个金融服务站，719名员工。在启东市各金融机构中，连续多年存、贷款总量、增量稳居第一，是启东地区经营规模最大、从业人员最多、服务范围最广的银行业金融机构，是服务社会公众、支持地方建设、构建和谐社会的重要金融力量。该行外汇业务于2013年12月22日取得银监局批复，2014年8月28日取得外汇局的即期结售汇批复，2014年9月正式成为SWIFT会员和外汇交易市场成员，2015年2月成为外汇拆借市场会员。2014年11月28日正式开办外汇业务。

外汇业务经营范围：国际结算，外汇存款，外汇贷款，外汇汇款，外币兑换，外汇担保，外汇同业拆借，资信调查、咨询和见证业务等。

特色业务：本外币一体化服务，可以为客户提供本外币存款、结算、融资理财等服务。

Qidong Rural Commercial Bank was originally called Qidong Rural Credit Cooperative Association. It was successfully restructured into Qidong Rural Commercial Bank upon the approval of China Banking Regulatory Commission in December, 2011. Currently, Qidong Rural Commercial Bank has 64 branches, 240 financing service stations, 719 employees. Among the financial institutions in Qidong, Qidong Rural Commercial Bank has the largest deposit and loan amount for many years continuously with its increment remaining to be No.1. With the largest operation scale, largest staff and broadest range of services in the banking financial institution in Qidong, Qidong Rural Commercial Bank become an important financial power in providing service to the public, supporting local construction and building a harmonious society. The foreign exchange transaction of this bank has been approved by Banking Supervision Bureau on December 22, 2013. The at sight settlement, sale and purchase of foreign exchange has been approved by the State Administration of Foreign Exchange on August 28, 2014. In September, 2014, Qidong Rural Commercial Bank has formally won the membership of SWIFT and become a member in the foreign exchange transaction market. In February, 2015, Qidong Rural Commercial Bank became a member in the foreign exchange lending market and started to conduct foreign exchange transactions on November 28, 2014.

Scope of business of foreign exchange transactions: international settlement, foreign exchange deposits, foreign exchange loans, foreign exchange remittance, foreign currency exchange, foreign exchange guarantee, foreign exchange lending among the same trade, credit investigation, consultation and attestation etc..

Characteristic businesses: integration service of domestic and foreign currency, providing deposit, settlement and financing and financial management of domestic and foreign currency to clients.

江苏如东农村商业银行股份有限公司
Jiangsu Rudong Rural Commercial Bank Company Limited

江苏如东农村商业银行股份有限公司是经中国银行业监督管理委员会批准设立，由原如东县农村信用合作联社进行整体改制而成的股份制商业银行，2012年7月26日正式挂牌对外营业。如东农商银行注册资本6.5亿元，是县内金融机构中营业网点最多、服务覆盖面最广、资金实力最强的金融企业。总行内设16个职能部门，下设1家营业部、48家支行，拥有从业人员近700名，6个离行式自助服务点，105台自助服务设备。截至2014年12月末，全行各项存款总额200.89亿元，各项贷款总额108.12亿元，存贷款总量及市场份额连续多年位居全县各金融机构首位。

Jiangsu Rudong Rural Commercial Bank Company Limited is a joint-stock commercial bank restructured from Rudong Rural Credit Cooperative Union through the approval of CBRC. It started its business on July 26, 2012. The registered capital of Rudong Rural Commercial Bank is RMB 0.65 billion, which is the financial enterprise with largest number of outlets, most extensive services and strongest capital strength. Its Head Office have set up 16 functional departments, 1 business department, 48 branches, 6 self-service center and 105 self-service devices, with a staff of nearly 700. By the end of 2014, its total balance of deposits has reached RMB 20.089 billion and total balance of loans have reached RMB 10.812 billion. Its total balance of deposits and balance of loans as well as its market share have been ranked the top among the financial institutions in the county for many years successively.

江苏如皋农村商业银行
JIANGSU RUGAO RURAL COMMERCIAL BANK

江苏如皋农村商业银行股份有限公司
Jiangsu Rugao Rural Commercial Bank Company Limited

江苏如皋农村商业银行股份有限公司成立于2010年12月，是经中国银行业监督管理委员会批准成立的股份制银行，公司注册地址：如皋市如城镇海阳路l95号，注册资本5亿元人民币。公司内设董监事会办公室和16个职能部门，下设1家营业部、56家支行、6个离行式自助服务点；拥有从业人员664人，自助服务设备93台。江苏如皋农村商业银行是"长三角"票据业务联席会议成员单位的首家县级金融机构，是苏中、苏北地区首家开办贵金属业务和理财业务的农村商业银行，是南通地区首家开办国际业务的农村商业银行。

Jiangsu Rugao Rural Commercial Bank Company Limited is a joint-stock bank established in December, 2010 with the approval of CBRC. The address of the bank is No.195, Haiyang Road, Rucheng Town, Rugao City. Its registered capital is RMB 0.5 billion. The company has set up a Board of Director Office and 16 functional department, 1 business department, 56 branches and 6 off-bank self-service banking centers with 93 self-service devices and a staff of 664. Jiangsu Rugao Rural Commercial Bank is the first financial institution of county level in "Yangtze River Delta" bill business joint session member units, the first rural commercial bank in conducting precious metal business and financial services in middle and north of Jiangsu province and the first rural commercial bank in providing international business in Nantong.

昆山农村商业银行
Kunshan Rural Commercial Bank Company Limited

昆山农村商业银行，全称江苏昆山农村商业银行股份有限公司，是经中国银行业监督管理委员会批准成立的股份制金融机构，成立于2005年1月8日，前身为昆山市农村信用合作社联合社。昆山农村商业银行现有员工700多人，下设1家营业部、26家支行、9家异地支行、17个分理处、1家村镇银行，是昆山市首家通过ISO 9001质量体系认证的金融企业。昆山农村商业银行现已成为环球银行财务电讯协会（SWIFT组织）和全国外汇交易中心会员。

The full name of Kunshan Rural Commercial Bank, is “Jiangsu Kunshan Rural Commercial Bank Company Limited”. It is a joint-stock financial institution restructured from Kunshan City Rural Credit Cooperative Union With the approval of CBRC, and was established on January 8, 2005. Kunshan Rural Commercial Bank has a staff of more than 700 with 1 business department, 26 branches, 9 offsite branches, 17 sub-branches and 1 village bank. It is a first financial enterprise which has passed the ISO9001 Quality System Certification in Kunshan. Kunshan Rural Commercial Bank has become a member of Society for Worldwide Interbank Financial Telecommunications (SWIFT) and China Foreign Exchange Trading System.

太仓农村商业银行
Taicang Rural Commercial Bank

江苏太仓农村商业银行股份有限公司
Jiangsu Taicang Rural Commercial Bank Company Limited

太仓农村商业银行，前身为太仓农村信用合作联社，经中国银行业监督管理委员会批准，于2005年1月12日正式开业，为股份制商业银行，位于江苏省东南部太仓市。截至2014年末，全行在编员工712名，下设53个网点，注册资本7.2亿元，总资产339.35亿元，各项存款余额227.69亿元、各项贷款余额160.40亿元。

Taicang Rural Commercial Bank, restructured from Taicang Rural Credit Cooperative Union, was officially opened on January 12, 2005 with the approval of CBRC. It is a joint-stock commercial bank located in Taicang in southeast Jiangsu province. By the end of 2014, it has a staff of 712 and 53 outlets with RMB 0.72 billion registered capital, RMB 33.935 billion total assets, RMB 22.769 billion balance of deposits and RMB 16.04 billion balance of loans.

江苏吴江农村商业银行股份有限公司
Jiangsu Wujiang Rural Commercial Bank Company Limited

吴江农村商业银行，全称江苏吴江农村商业银行股份有限公司，是由自然人和法人共同发起设立的股份制金融机构。2004年8月，经中国银行业监督管理委员会批准由原吴江市农村信用合作社联合社改制成立，是自银监会成立后新监管框架下全国第一家挂牌开业的农村商业银行。截至2014年底，吴江农村商业银行有支行40家，分理处27家，总行营业部1家。全行共有员工1 212名，截至2014年底，全行总资产619.45亿元，各项存款余额519.18亿元，各项贷款余额380.44亿元。

Wujiang Rural Commercial Bank, with its full name as Wujiang Rural Commercial Bank Company Limited, is a joint-stock financial institution which was jointly established by natural persons and legal persons. In August, 2004, with the approval of CBRC, Wujiang Rural Commercial Bank was restructured from Wujiang Rural Credit Cooperative. It is the first rural commercial bank established under the new supervision framework upon the establishment of CBRC. By the end of 2014, Wujiang Rural Commercial Bank has set up 40 branches, 27 sub-branches, 1 business department of the Head Office with a staff of 1 212. By the end of 2014, its total assets have reached RMB 61.945 billion, with total balance of deposits of RMB 51.918 billion and total balance of loans of RMB 38.044 billion.

江苏姜堰农村商业银行股份有限公司
Jiangsu Jiangyan Rural Commercial Bank Company Limited

江苏姜堰农村商业银行是一家股份制商业银行，下设46个营业网点，在职员工561人，是姜堰地区历史最悠久、网点最密集、业务规模最大的金融机构。

Jiangsu Jiangyan Rural Commercial Bank is a joint-stock commercial bank with 46 outlets and a staff of 561. It is a financial institution with longest history, densest outlets and largest business scale in Jiangyan.

江苏靖江农村商业银行股份有限公司
Jiangsu Jingjiang Rural Commercial Bank Company Limited

靖江位于江苏省的中南部、长江中下游的北岸，靖江市是江苏省新兴的港口工业城市，靖江是苏中苏北地区GDP最高的城市，外向型经济高度运行，年进出口总额达50多亿美元。江苏靖江农村商业银行成立于2009年11月，是在有着逾50年历史的靖江农村信用合作联社基础上整体改制成立的股份制地方性金融机构。目前在全市各乡镇及城区布设32家物理网点、45个自助网点及3家分理处，1家异地支行（在南京浦口区设立村镇银行），入股1家农村商业银行（金湖农商行）。国际业务于2012年10月22日取得银监会批准，2014年1月8日获得开办即期结售汇业务的批复，2014年2月1日正式加入SWIFT会员组织，2014年3月3日正式成为外汇交易市场会员。

外汇业务经营范围：国际结算、外汇存款、外汇贷款、外汇汇款、外汇兑换；外汇票据承兑与贴现；外汇担保；经中国银行业监督管理委员会批准的其他业务。

特色业务：本外币一站式服务，可以向客户提供本外币存款、结算、融资、理财等服务。

Jingjiang is located in the middle south of Jiangsu Province, the north bank of the middle and lower reaches of Changjiang River. Jingjiang city is a newly-developed harbor city of industry in Jiangsu Province. Jingjiang is a city who enjoys the highest GDP in middle and north of Jiangsu Province. Its export-oriented economy is highly developed with total annual volume of foreign trade of over 5 billion USD dollars. Jiangsu Jingjiang Rural Commercial Bank was established in November, 2009, which is as regional financial institute of joint-stock system restructured on the basis of Jingjiang Credit Cooperative Association who has a history of more than 50 years. Currently, the bank has 32 physical branches, 45 self-service branches, 3 sub-branches and one offsite branch (a country bank established in Pukou District, Nanjing City) in towns and districts within the city and holds share in a rural commercial bank (Jinhu Rural Commercial Bank). Its international business has been approved by Banking Supervision Bureau on October 22, 2012 and its at sight settlement, sale and purchase of foreign exchange business has been approved on January 8, 2014. It has joined in SWIFT on February 1, 2014 and has become a member in foreign exchange transactions market on March 3, 2014.

Scope of business of foreign exchange transactions: international settlement, foreign exchange deposits, foreign exchange loans, foreign exchange remittance, foreign currency exchange, foreign exchange bill acceptance and discount, foreign exchange guarantee, other businesses approved by China Banking Regulatory Commission.

Characteristic businesses: one-stop service of domestic and foreign currency, providing foreign exchange deposit, settlement, financing and financial management of domestic and foreign currency to clients.

NTBank 南通农商银行

江苏南通农村商业银行股份有限公司
Jiangsu Nantong Rural Commercial Bank Company Limited

南通农村商业银行是在有着60多年历史的南通市郊农村信用社和通州市农村信用社进行股份制改造的基础上，优化股权结构而成立的一家专注于“三农”和中小企业融资服务的银行。南通农商银行下辖88家支行、1家营业部，服务网点覆盖崇川区、港闸区、通州区、开发区、高新区以及滨海工业园区，现有员工近1 200人。

Nantong Rural Commercial Bank is a bank which was established on the basis of shareholding reform by optimizing ownership structure of Nantong Suburb Rural Credit Cooperative and Tongzhou City Rural Credit Cooperative with a history of more than 60 years. It focuses on serving “issues of agriculture, farmer and rural area” and providing financial services for medium and small size enterprises. With a staff of nearly 1 200, Nantong Rural Commercial Bank has set up 88 branches, 1 business department and outlets covering Chongchuan District, Gangzha District, Tongzhou District, Development Zone, High-tech Zone and Binhai Industrial Park.

无锡农村商业银行股份有限公司
Wuxi Rural Commercial Bank Company Limited

无锡农村商业银行（原江苏锡州农村商业银行）成立于2005年6月。2010年7月，经中国银监会批准正式更名。无锡农商行是无锡市区唯一的地方性法人银行，现下辖1家营业部，111家本地支行、分理处，6家异地支行（楚州、靖江、如皋、如皋港、丰县、仪征），另外控股2家村镇银行（铜山、姜堰），入股2家农村商业银行（淮安、东海）。截至2014年12月末，全行总资产1 040.0507939亿元，存款总额780.1435317亿元，贷款总额496.3249902亿元。该行是SWIFT（环球金融电讯协会）在中国的总行级成员之一，与花旗银行、渣打银行、美联银行、东京三菱银行等国际性跨国银行建立了账户行关系，形成了一个能与全球209个国家和地区的9 000多家银行机构、证券机构和企业客户进行实时清算的国际结算网络。

Wuxi Rural Commercial Bank Company Limited (former Jiangsu Xizhou Rural Commercial Bank) was established in June, 2005. In July, 2010, it was officially renamed with the approval of CBRC. Wuxi Rural Commercial Bank is the only regional legal person bank in Wuxi with 1 business department, 111 branches and sub-branches in Wuxi and 6 offsite branches (Chuzhou, Jingjiang, Rugao, Rugaogang, Fengxian and Yizheng). In addition, it also holds over 2 village banks (Tongshan and Jiangyan) and hold shares of 2 rural commercial banks (Huaian and Donghai). By the end of 2014, its total assets have reached RMB 104.00507939 billion with total balance of deposits of RMB 78.01435317 billion and balance of loans of RMB 49.63249902 billion. This bank is one of the members of head office level in SWIFT (Society for Worldwide Interbank Financial Telecommunication) and has established business relations with international banks including Citibank, Standard Chartered Bank, Wachovia, Bank of Tokyo-Mitsubishi etc. and has formed international settlement network which can conduct real time settlement with more than 9 000 banks, security institutions and enterprises of 209 countries around the world.

江苏宜兴农村商业银行
JIANGSU YIXING RURAL COMMERCIAL BANK

江苏宜兴农村商业银行股份有限公司
Jiangsu Yixing Rural Commercial Bank Company Limited

江苏宜兴农村商业银行由宜兴农村合作银行于2010年11月改制组建而成，是经中国银行业监督管理会批准，由自然人、境内金融机构、境内非金融企业法人共同发起设立的永久存续的股份制银行业金融机构，现下辖1家营业部，84家本地支行（分理处），2家异地支行（高淳、溧水），拥有员工1 000多人。截至 2014 年末，资产总额 431.25 亿元，各项存款余额 355.84 亿元，各项贷款余额 263.22 亿元。

Jiangsu Yixing Rural Commercial Bank Company Limited was restructured in November, 2010 from Yixing Rural Credit Cooperative Bank with the approval of CBRC. It is a long-standing joint-stock banking financial institution jointly set up by natural person, domestic financial institution and domestic non-financial enterprise legal person. It has set up 1 business department, 84 local branches (sub-branches), 2 offsite branches (Gaochun and Lishui) with a staff of more than 1 000. By the end of 2014, its total assets have reached RMB 43.125 billion, with total balance of deposits of RMB 35.584 billion and total balance of loans of RMB 26.322 billion.

江南农村商业银行
JIANGNAN RURAL COMMERCIAL BANK

江苏江南农村商业银行股份有限公司

Jiangsu Jiangnan Rural Commercial Bank Company Limited

江南农村商业银行是经国务院同意、中国银监会批准设立的全国首家地市级股份制农村商业银行，是江苏省农信系统内首家存款突破千亿元的法人机构，是中国银监会确定的二级资本债券和资产证券化发行试点单位。截至2014年末，全行注册资本达到人民币52.94亿元，总资产1 937亿元，各项存款余额1 356亿元，各项贷款余额905亿元，在岗员工3 300余人。2014年全行跨区经营步伐进一步加快，在无锡宜兴、镇江丹阳、泰州靖江和淮安淮安区新设4家异地支行，截至目前，营业网点已达227家。

Jiangsu Jiangnan Rural Commercial Bank Company Limited is the first regional joint-stock rural commercial bank established with the permission of the State Council and the approval of CBRC. It is the first legal institution whose balance of deposits have exceeded RMB 100 billion in the rural credit system in Jiangsu province. It is also the experimental unit in tier 2 capital bond and asset securitization determined by the CBRC. By the end of 2014, the registered capital of the bank has reached RMB 5.294 billion with total assets of RMB 193.7 billion, total balance of deposits of RMB 135.6 billion and total balance of loans of RMB 90.5 billion and a staff of more than 3 300. In 2014, the bank has sped up its steps in cross district operation and has set up 4 offsite branches in Yixin in Wuxi, Danyang in Zhenjiang, Jingjiang in Taizhou and Huaian District in Huaian. Up to now, it has set up 227 outlets.

江苏兴化农村商业银行股份有限公司
Jiangsu Xinghua Rural Commercial Bank Co., Ltd.

江苏兴化农村商业银行股份有限公司是一家发展中的小型商业银行，总行位于经济发达的长三角北部城市——江苏省兴化市，公司注册资本为5.5亿元人民币，下辖61个营业网点，先后荣获“全国支农先进单位”、“全国农村支付环境建设先进集体”、江苏省“合作金融先进单位”、江苏省“文明行业”、兴化市“综合先进部门”、“服务地方经济突出贡献单位”、“人民满意机关”等殊荣。江苏兴化农村商业银行于2009年11月23日经江苏银监局批复，同意开办外汇业务，于2010年7月5日由国家外汇管理局江苏省分局批准，同意开办结售汇业务。2010年正式加入SWIFT组织，同年成为外汇交易市场成员。

外汇业务经营范围：吸收外币存款；发放外币贷款；办理国际结算；办理外汇汇款、外币兑换；结汇、售汇；经中国银行业监督管理机构批准的其他业务。

特色业务：本外币一站式服务，可以向客户提供本外币存款、结算、融资和理财等服务。

Jiangsu Xinghua Rural Commercial Bank Co., Ltd. is small scale commercial bank in developing, whose head office is located in Xinghua, Jiangsu Province, a northern city of economically developed Yangtze River Delta. Its registered capital is RMB 550 million, with 61 branches and has won the awards including “Notional Advanced Unit in Supporting Agriculture Development”, “Advanced Group in the Construction of National Rural Payment Environment”, “Advanced Unit in Cooperative Financing” and “Civilized Industry” in Jiangsu Province and “Comprehensive Advanced Unit”, “Units Making Standout Contribution in Serving Local Economy” and “Most Popular Organ” in Xinghua city, etc.. With the approval of Banking Supervision Bureau, Xinghua Rural Commercial Bank started to conduct foreign exchange transactions on November 23,

2009 and join in SEIFT in 2010 and became a member of foreign exchange transaction market in the same year.

Scope of business of foreign exchange transactions: absorbing foreign exchange deposits; granting foreign exchange loans; conducting international settlement; conducting foreign exchange remittance and foreign currency exchange, settlement, sale and purchase of foreign exchange; other businesses approved by China Banking Regulatory Commission.

Characteristic businesses: one-stop service of domestic and foreign currency, providing deposit, settlement and financing and financial management of domestic and foreign currency to clients.

江苏大丰农村商业银行
JIANGSU DAFENG RURAL COMMERCIAL BANK

江苏大丰农村商业银行股份有限公司
Jiangsu Dafeng Rural Commercial Bank Co., Ltd.

江苏大丰农村商业银行股份有限公司是经中国银行业监督管理委员会批准成立的大丰市区独立法人地方股份制商业银行，于2011年11月26日正式挂牌营业。自成立以来，经营稳健，各项业务取得快速发展，资产规模不断扩大，资产流动性逐步增强，资产结构比较合理，业务发展格局良好。该行以服务“三农”和中小企业为宗旨，以“规范，进取，诚信，和谐”为核心，全面创新服务、创新管理、创新理念，努力打造成大丰具有影响力的现代化商业银行。业务经营发展，实现全面跨越。确立品牌意识，提升服务水平。加强同业交流，提升业务功能。完善基础设施，加强员工培训。强化内控管理，提高风险控制能力。

外汇业务经营范围：外汇存款、外汇贷款、结售汇、外币兑换、国际结算、咨信调查、咨询见证业务

Jiangsu Dafeng Rural Commercial Bank Co., Ltd. Is approved by china banking regulatory commission of dafeng city independent legal local joint-stock commercial bank and stated from Nov 26 2011 officially open. Since its establishment, positive business, each business made rapid development, asset scale expands unceasingly, liquidity is gradually enhanced, assets structure is reasonable, good business development pattern. We have to service “three rural” and small and medium-sized enterprises for the purpose and the “specification, nterprising, honest.

Harmonious as the the core, comprehensive service innavation, management.

Innovation, innovative concept, efforts to build dafeng influential modern commercial bank.

Business development and achieve full span; Establish brand awareness and improve service lcverls; Streng then trade exchange and promote business functions;

Improve infrastructure and strengthen staff training;

Strengthening the management of internal control and risk control ability.

Scope of business of foreign exchange transactions: Foreign exchange proceeds deposit, foreign exchange loans, foreign exchange settlement and sale, foreign exchange, international settlement, credit information, consulting and witness business.

江苏射阳农村商业银行股份有限公司
Jiangsu Sheyang Rural Commercial Bank Company Limited

江苏射阳农村商业银行股份有限公司成立于2008年9月，是江苏长江以北第一家地方股份制商业银行，注册资本5.25亿元。全行现有在职员工571人。总行设13个管理部、5个直属部、2个办公室、23个业务中心，基层设有10家一级支行、11家二级支行、18家分理处共39个营业网点。

Jiangsu Sheyang Rural Commercial Bank Company Limited was established in September, 2008. It is the first joint-stock commercial bank in northern area of Jiangsu province with RMB 0.525 billion registered capital. It now has a staff of 571. Its Head Office has 13 administrative departments, 5 directly subordinated department, 2 offices, 23 business centers. On the primary level, it has 39 outlets including 10 tier one branches, 11 tier two branches and 18 sub-branches.

盐城农商银行
RURAL COMMERCIAL BANK OF YANCHENG

江苏盐城农村商业银行股份有限公司
Jiangsu Yancheng Rural Commercial Bank Co., Ltd.

江苏盐城农村商业银行股份有限公司是经中国银行业监督管理委员会批准成立的盐城市区独立法人地方股份制商业银行，于2010年5月26日正式挂牌营业。自成立以来，经营稳健，各项业务取得快速发展，资产规模不断扩大，资产流动性逐步增强，资产结构比较合理，业务发展格局良好。该行以服务“三农”和中小企业为宗旨，以“规范，进取，诚信，和谐”为核心，全面创新服务、创新管理、创新理念，努力打造盐城具有影响力的现代化商业银行。

外汇业务开展状况：业务经营发展，实现全面跨越。确立品牌意识，提升服务水平。加强同业交流，提升业务功能。完善基础设施，加强员工培训。强化内控管理，提高风险控制能力。

外汇业务经营范围：外汇存款、外汇贷款、结售汇、外币兑换、国际结算、咨信调查、咨询见证业务。

Jiangsu Yancheng Rural Commercial Bank Co., Ltd.. Is approved by China banking regulatory commission of Yancheng city independent legal local joint-stock commercial bank and stated from May 26 2015 officially open. Since its establishment，positive business，each business made rapid development，asset scale expands unceasingly，liquidity is gradually enhanced，assets structure is reasonable，good business development pattern.We have to service “three rural” and small and medium-sized enterprises for the purpose and the “specification，nterprising，honest harmonious” as the core，comprehensive service innavation，management Innovation，innovative concept，efforts to build Yancheng influential modern commercial bank.

Business development and achieve full span; establish brand awareness and improve service leverls; strengthen trade exchange and promote business functions;

improve infrastructure and strengthen staff training; strengthening the management of internal control and risk control ability foreign exchange proceeds deposit, foreign exchange loans, foreign exchange settlement and sale, foreign exchange, international settlement, credit information, consulting and witness business.

扬州农村商业银行
YANGZHOU RURAL COMMERCIAL BANK

江苏扬州农村商业银行股份有限公司
Jiangsu Yangzhou Rural Commercial Bank Company Limited

江苏扬州农村商业银行股份有限公司成立于2010年12月25日，全行注册资本为5.2亿元人民币，营业网点62家，员工总数850余人。2004年7月，郊区、邗江信用联社合并组建扬州市区农村信用合作联社。2004年12月，扬州市区农村信用合作联社正式挂牌成立。2010年12月，成功改制组建扬州农村商业银行。截至2014年底，资产总额208.91亿元，各项存款余额184.05亿元，各项贷款余额134.48亿元。

Jiangsu Yangzhou Rural Commercial Bank Company Limited was established on December 25, 2010. Its registered capital is RMB 0.52 billion, with 62 outlets and a staff of more than 850. In July, 2004, Yangzhou Rural Credit Cooperative Union was established through the merger of Jiaoqu and Hanjiang credit cooperative. In December, 2004, Yangzhou Rural Credit Cooperative was officially set up. In Deceber, 2010, it was successfully restructured into Yangzhou Rural Commercial Bank. By the end of 2014, its total assets have reached RMB 20.891 billion with total balance of deposits of RMB 18.405 billion and balance of loans of RMB 13.448 billion.

徐州淮海农村商业银行股份有限公司
Xuzhou Huaihai Rural Commercial Bank Company Limited

徐州淮海农村商业银行是经中国银监会批准，在原徐州市郊信用联社的基础上，由境内自然人、境内非金融机构企业法人共同发起设立的永久存续的股份制银行业金融机构，总部设在江苏省徐州市。目前拥有员工500余人、24个营业机构，其中包括1家营业部、23家支行，网点全部位于徐州市主城区。

Xuzhou Huaihai Rural Commercial Bank Company Limited is a long-standing joint-stock banking financial institution jointly established by domestic natural person and domestic non-financial institution enterprise legal person on the basis of former Xuzhou Suburb Credit Cooperative with the approval of CBRC. Its Head Office is located in Xuzhou, Jiangsu Province. It has a staff of more than 500. It has 24 business outlets including 1 business department and 23 branches. All the outlets are located within the main urban areas of Xuzhou city.

连云港东方农村商业银行
LIANYUNGANG ORIENT RURAL COMMERCIAL BANK

连云港东方农村商业银行股份有限公司
Lianyungang Dongfang Rural Commercial Bank Company Limited

连云港东方农村商业银行是一家全方位、多功能、综合性竞争实力雄厚的地方性金融机构。现有员工700多人，下设37家支行。

Lainyungang Dongfang Rural Commercial Bank is a comprehensive, multi-functional, competitive regional financial institution with a staff of more than 700 and 37 branches.

富阳农商银行
浙江农信 FUYANG RURAL COMMERCIAL BANK

浙江富阳农村合作银行
Zhejiang Fuyang Rural Commercial Bank

浙江富阳农村商业银行股份有限公司自2015年5月18日正式挂牌开业，前身是浙江富阳农村合作银行，自改制以来，按照股份合作制的要求，不断完善法人治理结构，董事会、监事会、行长经营层各负其责、相互制衡的法人治理经营机制已初步形成；不断完善内控制度建设，操作行为进一步得到了规范和完善；不断扩大经营规模，合项业务迅猛发展。

外汇业务在全行业务总量及地区国际结算量的占比均不高，市场份额在15%左右；产品种类比较单一，主要以传统结售汇、信用证和汇款业务为主。

外汇业务经营范围：外汇存款、外汇贷款、外汇汇款，国际结算、外汇拆借，资信调查、咨询和见证业务，经外汇管理机关批准的结汇、售汇业务。

Zhejiang Fuyang Rural Commercial Bank Company Limited since May 18, 2015 formally opened. Its predecessor was the Zhejiang Fuyang Rural Cooperative Bank, was founded in 2005.Currently there is 20 branches, 45 sub-branches and 18 savings bank. More than 1 000 employees, scope of business covers the entire district of Fuyang. Deposits and loans accounted for both more than 30% in Fuyang district, which is the largest local financial institutions.

Our bank's foreign exchange business in the whole line of business volume and area of international settlement volume ratio is not high, the market share is around 15%; products type is relatively single, mainly based on the traditional settlement, letter of credit and remittance business.

Scope of business of foreign exchange transactions: foreign exchange deposits, foreign currency loans, foreign exchange remittance, international settlement, foreign currency lending, credit investigation, consulting and business witness, foreign exchange settlement and sale business that approved by the exchange administration agencies.

建德市农村信用合作联社
Jiande Rural Credit Cooperatives Union

建德农信联社是经浙江银监局批准的股份制地方金融机构。全辖共有营业网点44家，是全市金融机构中服务网点最多，服务范围最广、从业人数最多、服务品质最优的金融机构。

建德农信联社于2014年3月正式对外开办国际业务，作为中国外汇交易中心的会员，直接参与全国银行间外汇市场的交易，拥有总行级别外汇牌价定价资格；先进的EBILLS国际业务系统、专业的外汇业务人才、独立的法人地位及扁平化管理模式，在建德市内赢得了良好的品牌声誉，是众多外汇企业外汇业务的首选银行。

外汇业务经营范围：外汇存款、外汇贷款，外汇汇款，国际结算，外汇拆借、资信调查、咨询和见证业务，经外汇管理机关批准的结汇、售汇业务。

Jiande Rural Credit Cooperatives Union is a regional financial institution of joint-stock system approved by Zhejiang Banking Supervision Bureau. There are 44 branches within the region, which made it the financial institution with the most business outlets, largest range of service, largest faculty, best service in the city.

Jiande Rural Credit Cooperatives Union started its international business from March, 2014. As the core member of China foreign exchange transaction center, the Union directly engages in the domestic interbank foreign exchange transactions and enjoy the qualification of head office level to price foreign exchange rates. Jiande Rural Credit Cooperatives Union enjoys good reputation in Jiande City with advanced EBILLS international operational system, professional staff in foreign exchange transactions, independent legal entities and Flat Management mode, which makes it the preferred bank among many foreign exchange enterprises in conducting foreign exchange transactions.

Scope of business of foreign exchange transactions：foreign exchange deposits, foreign exchange loans, foreign exchange remittance, international settlement, foreign exchange lending, credit investigation, consultation and attestation, settlement, sale and purchase of foreign exchange approved by foreign exchange administration.

临安市农村信用合作联社
LINAN RURAL CREDIT COOPERATIVES UNION

临安市农村信用合作联社
Linan City Rural Credit Cooperative Union

临安市农村信用合作联社成立于2008年4月，是一家股份合作制社区性地方金融机构，前身为成立于1987年的临安县农村信用合作社联合社。现设理监事会办、办公室、人事监察部、审计部、信贷部、业务发展部、电子银行部、国际业务部、合规风险部、财务会计部、科技信息部和保卫部12个部室，下辖1家营业部、16家信用社和48家分社，拥有员工821人。目前，该联社是临安市存贷规模最大、营业网点最多、服务群体最广的金融机构。截至2014年末，存贷款总量分别达到126.68亿元和89.96亿元。

Linan City Rural Credit Cooperative Union, established in April, 2008, is a joint-stock regional financial institution of community character. It was formerly known as Linan County Rural Credit Cooperative which was established in 1987. It now has set up 12 offices and department including Board of Supervisors Office, Personnel Supervision Department, Auditing Department, Credit Department, Business Development Department, E-banking Department, International Business Department, Compliance Risks Department, Financial Accounting Department, Science and Technology Department and Security Department, and has established 1 business department, 16 credit cooperatives, 48 branches with a staff of 821. At present, this Cooperative is the largest financial institution in terms of deposit and loan scale, number of outlets and service group. By the end of 2014, the total volume of deposit and loan have reached RMB 12.668 billion and RMB 8.996 billion respectively.

杭州联合农村商业银行股份有限公司
Hangzhou United Rural Commercial Bank Company Limited

杭州联合银行，全称杭州联合农村商业银行股份有限公司，由杭州联合农村合作银行整体改制而来，创立于2011年1月5日，同年3月12日正式挂牌开业，注册资本14.43亿元，总行位于浙江省杭州市。截至2014年12月末，全行资产总额1 079.35亿元，各项存款余额871.93亿元，各项贷款余额达627.28亿元。拥有员工2 200余名，下辖分支机构144家。在英国《银行家》杂志公布的2014年全球银行1 000强排名中，列第488位。

Hangzhou United Bank, with its full name as Hangzhou United Rural Commercial Bank Company Limited, established on January 5, 2011, was restructured from Hangzhou United Rural Cooperative Bank and started to business on March 12 of the same year. Its registered capital is RMB 1.443 billion, with its Head Office located in Hanghzou, Zhejiang province. By the end of 2014, its total assets have reached RMB 10.7935 billion, with RMB 87.193 billion balance of deposits and RMB 62.728 billion balance of loans. It has a staff of more than 2 200 with 144 branches. According to the rank of banks provided by the Banker, a Britain published magazine, this bank ranks No.488 among the 1 000 banks around the world.

浙江桐庐农村合作银行
Zhejiang Tonglu Rural Cooperative Bank

浙江桐庐农村合作银行于2008年3月26日正式挂牌开业，是经中国银监会批准设立的股份合作制地方金融机构，前身是成立于1954年的桐庐县农村信用社。目前，该行下辖1家营业部、16家支行、22家分理处，11家储蓄所，2家自助银行共52个网点机构，分布于全县各乡镇（街道）。

自挂牌开业以来，在浙江省农信联社和县委县政府的坚强领导下，桐庐农村合作银行秉承“立足地方，服务‘三农’”定位和“你我牵手，合作永久”的发展理念，内强素质，外优服务，传承发扬农信人“根、诚、活、家”企业文化，着力打造服务“三农”的主力银行、服务中小企业的伙伴银行、便民快捷的社区银行、个性鲜明的特色银行、稳健经营的平安银行和协调发展的和谐银行。该行因农因企所需，围绕“普行春江大地，惠及百姓民生”的普惠理念，大力实施推进普惠金融工程，相继推出“合家”系列之“合家富、合家乐、合家安、合家惠”贷款、巾帼创业贷款、“银政通”技改贷款等金融产品，在全县163个村级便民服务中心设立金融服务专柜，加快ATM、POS等自助便民设施布设，建立普惠金融便民服务站，推行移动办公进村入户，构建“基础金融不出村，综合金融不出镇”的金融服务体系。

在加快业务发展的同时，桐庐农村合作银行切实履行地方银行的社会责任，连续多年被评为“纳税大户”；出资2 700余万元用于慈善事业。该行先后被省农信联社评为“十佳信用联社”，被浙江省委、省政府授予“文明单位”，被评为县综合考评优秀单位、县服务企业最佳部门等荣誉称号。

外汇业务开展状况：浙江桐庐农村合作银行自2009年1月正式对外开办国际业务以来，业务稳健发展。截至2014年12月末，全县已有近267家外贸企业在该行开户，占全县外贸企业一半以上；2014年度国际业务结算量在桐庐县辖内外汇指定银行中排名第二。于2012年6月加入SWIFT（环球同业银行金融电讯协会）系统，且在美国纽约、法国巴黎及澳门分别开立有美元、欧元及港元的境外清算账户。

外汇业务经营范围：已开通美元、欧元、港元、英镑、日元、澳大利亚元及加拿大元七个外币币种，业务种类丰富，包括储蓄、汇款、信用证、托收、结售汇业务，各类融资产品和衍生产品，能为用户提供全方位的外汇服务。国际业务网上银行，让您足不出户，即可轻松办理外汇业务。

特色业务：出口商票融资，外币流动资金贷款，合作办理远期结售业务，速汇金业务，跨境人民币业务。

Zhejiang Tonglu Rural Cooperative Bank was formally listed to establish on March 26, 2008, and is the share cooperative local financial institution approved by China Banking Regulatory Commission (CBRC). And its predecessor was Tonglu County Rural Credit Cooperatives founded in 1954. At present, the bank comprises one business department, sixteen sub-branches, twenty two small local branches, eleven savings departments, two self-service banks, a total of fifty two branch institutions distributed in every town (street) across the county.

Since the bank was listed to establish, under the leadership of Zhejiang Rural Credit Association and the county party committee and government, Tonglu Rural Cooperative Bank adheres to the position of “Having a Foothold on the Local Area, Serving for Agriculture, Rural Areas and Farmers” and the development concept of “You and Me, Hand in Hand, Permanent Cooperation”, strengthens the internal quality and optimizes the outward service, inherits and develops its corporate culture of “Root, Sincerity, Living, Family”, and takes great pains to build the main bank serving for agriculture, rural areas and farmers, the companion-like bank serving for small and medium-sized enterprises, the convenient and quick community bank, the distinctive bank, the safe bank with prudent operation, and the harmonious bank of coordinated development. Due to the requirements of farmers and enterprises, around the inclusive idea of “Spreading across the Whole County, Benefiting People’s Livelihood”, the bank vigorously implements inclusive financial engineering, launches the financial products in succession such as the loans about “Family” series of “Family Wealth, Family Happiness, Family

Safety, Family Benefit", the start-up loans for female, the renovation loans for "Bank Securities Express", and has established one hundred and sixty three financial serve counters in village-level civilian service centers across the county, and speeds up the layout of self-help facilities such as ATM and POS, establishes the inclusive financial convenience service stations, promotes the mobile office to go into villages and households, and builds the financial service system of "Basic Financial Services in Village, Comprehensive Financial Services in Town".

When accelerating the business development, Tonglu Rural Cooperative Bank earnestly fulfills the social responsibility of local bank, and has been evaluated as "Taxpayer" for many years, and contributes more than twenty seven million yuan to the charities. The bank has been judged to be the honorary titles such as "Top Ten Credit Association" by Zhejiang Rural Credit Association, "Civilized Unit" by Zhejiang provincial party committee and government, the county-level outstanding unit of comprehensive evaluation and the county-level best department for serving enterprise.

The development situation of foreign exchange business:

Since Zhejiang Tonglu Rural Cooperative Bank formally opened the international business in January 2009, its international business has developed steadily. By the end of December 2014, nearly two hundred and sixty seven foreign trade enterprises in the county had opened an account in our bank, occupying over half of foreign trade enterprises in the county. And its amount of settlement about international business in 2014 ranked second in the designated foreign exchange banks within the scope of Tonglu County. In June 2012, it joined Society for Worldwide Inter-bank Financial Telecommunication (SWIFT), and opened the overseas clearing accounts of USD dollar, Euro and HK dollar in New York, America, Paris, France and Macau respectively.

The scope of foreign exchange business:

Our bank currently operates seven foreign currencies such as USD dollar, Euro, HK dollar, pound, Japanese yen, Australian dollar and Canadian dollar, and has various business lines including savings, remittance, letter of credit, collection, foreign exchange settlement and sale, and has all kinds of financing products and derivative products, can provide you with all-round foreign exchange services. The international Internet Banking business lets you keep indoors and conveniently handle foreign exchange businesses.

Characteristic business:

The financing of commercial paper presented by exporter, current funds loan of foreign currency, cooperatively handling forward settlement and sales business, Money Gram business, cross-border RMB business.

浙江萧山农村商业银行股份有限公司
Zhejiang Xiaoshan Rural Commercial Bank Company Limited

萧山农商银行全称浙江萧山农村商业银行股份有限公司，是经国务院银行业监督管理机构批准，由浙江萧山农村合作银行整体改制，企业法人、自然人共同发起设立的股份制地方性金融机构。截至2014年末，全行总资产 957.62 亿元，各项存款806.61亿元，各项贷款总额560.73亿元，下设 152家分支机构，其中一级支行（包括营业部）34 家、二级支行 9 家、分理处 109 家，并设有自助银行 4家，在岗员工 1 696 名，是萧山存贷规模最大、机构网点最密、客户层面最广、支农贡献最高、缴纳税收最多的本土银行。

Xiaoshan Rural Commercial Bank, with its full name as Zhejiang Xiaoshan Rural Commercial Bank Company Limited, is restructured from Zhejiang Xiaoshan Rural Cooperative Bank. It is a regional joint-stock financial institution jointly started by enterprise legal person and natural person through the approval of the Banking Supervision Administrative of the State Council. By the end of 2014, the total assets of the bank is RMB 95.762 billion, with RMB 80.661 billion total deposit and RMB 56.073 billion total loans. It has set up 152 branches, with 34 tier one branches, 9 tier two branches, 109 sub-branches and 4 self-service banks with a staff of 1696. It is the largest local bank in Xiaoshan in terms of deposit and loan scale, number of outlets, range of customers, contribution of branches and payment of taxes.

余杭农村商业银行
YUHANG RURAL COMMERCIAL BANK
浙江农信

浙江杭州余杭农村商业银行股份有限公司
Zhejiang Hangzhou Yuhang Rural Commercial Bank Company Limited

浙江杭州余杭农村商业银行股份有限公司是经中国银行业监督管理委员会批准，由原浙江杭州余杭农村合作银行整体改制设立的股份制地方金融机构，注册资本14.4 亿元，内设 21 个部（室），下辖1家营业部，19 家支行，100家分理处，现有从业员工1 500 余人。2014 年12月末，存、贷款总量分别达到507.73 亿元和313.50 亿元，名列全区银行机构首位和“浙江农信”系统前列，是余杭区资金实力最强、服务覆盖面最广的银行机构。

Zhejiang Hangzhou Yuhang Rural Commercial Bank Company Limited (short for Yuhang Rural Commercial Bank) is a regional joint-stock financial institution restructured from Zhejiang Hangzhou Yuhang Rural Cooperative Bank with the approval of CBRC. Its registered capital is RMB 1.44 billion with 21 departments/offices, 1 business department, 19 branches, 100 sub-branches and a staff of more than 1 500. By the end of 2014, the total deposits and loans have reached RMB 50.773 billion and RMB 31.350 billion respectively, which ranks No.1 among the banking institutions and ranks the top in “Zhejiang Rural Credit Cooperatives” system. It is the largest bank in Yuhang in terms of capital strength and service range.

Anbank 安吉农商银行

浙江安吉农村商业银行股份有限公司
Zhejiang Anji Rural Commercial Bank Company Limited

浙江安吉农村商业银行股份有限公司于2013 年改制成立，前身是安吉县农村信用合作联社，现有注册资本6亿元，从业人员615人，下辖营业机构38 家，其中支行21家，分理处16家。网点遍布全县各个乡镇，是安吉县银行业金融机构中营业网点覆盖面最广、存贷规模最大、就近办理业务最方便、为社员和社区服务的地方性股份制金融机构。截至2014年末，安吉农商银行各项资产达156亿元，各项存款达130.6亿元，各项贷款达99亿元；存贷规模和市场占有率均居全县银行业金融机构首位。

Zhejiang Anji Rural Commercial Bank Company Limited was restructured from Anji County Rural Credit Cooperative Union in 2013 with a registered capital of RMB 0.6 billion and a staff of 615. It has 38 business outlets, including 21 branches and 16 sub-branches. Its outlets have covered all the villages and towns of the county. It is a regional joint-stock financial institution of most extensive coverage, largest deposit and loan scale, most convenient in conducting business for providing services for commune members and community among the banking financial institutions in Jian county. By the end of 2014, the total assets of Jian Rural Commercial Bank has reached RMB 15.6 billion with RMB 13.06 billion deposits and RMB 9.9 billion loans. Its deposit and loan scale and market share all rank the top in the banking financial institutions in the county.

浙江德清农村商业银行股份有限公司
Zhejiang Deqing Rural Commercial Bank Company Limited

浙江德清农村商业银行股份有限公司是于2012年6月18日经浙江银监局批准在原德清农村合作银行的基础上发起设立的股份制地方金融机构，注册资本70 000万元。目前全辖共有营业网点40家（包括1家营业部，15家支行，24家分理处），内设职能部门17个，从业员工人数达600余人。截至2014年末，全行资产总额209.6268亿元，本外币存款余额172.1182亿元，本外币贷款余额122.1346亿元。

Zhejiang Deqing Rural Commercial Bank Company Limited, established on June 18, 2012, is a joint-stock regional financial institution restructured from Deqing Rural Cooperative Bank with the approval of Banking Supervision Bureau of Zhejiang Province. Its registered capital is RMB 700 000 000. At present, it has 40 outlets (including 1 business department, 15 branches and 24 sub-branches) and 17 functional departments with a staff of more than 600. By the end of 2014, the total assets of the bank is RMB 20.96268 billion with total deposits (domestic and foreign currency) RMB 17.21182 billion and total loans (domestic and foreign currency) RMB 12.21346 billion.

南浔银行
浙江农信 Nanxun Bank

浙江南浔农村商业银行股份有限公司
Zhejiang Nanxun Rural Commercial Bank Company Limited

南浔银行于2011年1月6日挂牌开业，是在原浙江南浔农村合作银行的基础上组建的，由企业法人、自然人投资入股的股份制银行，是浙江首家农村商业银行。目前下辖1家营业部，22家支行，26家分理处，全行从业员工729人。注册资本1 025 694 678元。截至2014年末，全行总资产235.78073亿元，存款余额202.19395亿元，贷款余额135.36692亿元。

Bank of Nanxun (full name: Zhejiang Nanxun Rural Commercial Bank Company Limited) started its business on January 6, 2011. Reconstructed from Zhejiang Nanxun Rural Cooperative Bank, it is a joint-stock bank invested by enterprise legal persona and natural person, the first rural commercial bank in Zhejiang. At present, it has set up 1 business department, 22 branches, 26 sub-branches with a staff of 729. Its registered capital is RMB 1 025 694 678. By the end of 2014, the total assets of the bank is RMB 23.578073 billion with RMB 20.219395 billion balance of deposits and RMB 13.536692 billion.

浙江海宁农村商业银行股份有限公司
Zhejiang Haining Rural Commercial Bank Company Limited

浙江海宁农村商业银行股份有限公司前身是海宁市农村信用合作联社，是海宁历史最悠久，网点覆盖最齐全、存贷款规模最大的金融机构。海宁农商银行下辖1家营业部和11家支行，共有69个网点。截至2014年12月末，各项存款258.18亿元，各项贷款160.33亿元。

Zhejiang Haining Rural Commercial Bank Company Limited is a financial institution of longest history, most extensive coverage and largest deposit and loan scale in Haining. Haining Rural Commercial Bank has 1 business department, 11 branches and 69 outlets in total. By the end of 2014, its total deposits have reached RMB 25.818 billion and its total loans have reached RMB 16.033 billion.

海盐县农村信用合作联社
Haiyan County Rural Credit Cooperative Union

海盐县农村信用合作联社是一家股份合作制社区性金融机构，历经人民公社管理、农行管理、与农行脱钩和县级法人改制，现下辖1家营业部，8家信用社，33个营业网点，15个自助银行，在岗员工500余人。

Haiyan County Rural Credit Cooperative Union is a joint-stock financial institution of community nature. It has experienced the management of People's Commune and the Agriculture Bank of China and then separated from Agriculture Bank of China and was restructured by legal person of county level. Now, it has 1 business department, 8 credit cooperatives, 33 outlets, 15 self-service banks with a staff of more than 500.

嘉善农商银行
JIASHAN RURAL COMMERCIAL BANK
浙江农信

浙江嘉善农村商业银行股份有限公司
Zhejiang Jiashan Rural Commercial Bank Company Limited

浙江嘉善农村商业银行股份有限公司成立于2013年10月，由原浙江嘉善农村合作银行股东和员工发起，依法设立的股份制农村商业银行。下辖1家营业部和14家支行，共33个网点，员工532名。

Zhejiang Jiashan Rural Commercial Bank Company Limited is a joint-stock rural commercial bank jointly launched by the shareholders and staff of former Zhejiang Jiashan Rural Cooperative Bank and was established in October, 2013. It has 1 business department, 14 branches with 33 outlets and a staff of 532.

平湖农村合作银行
PINGHU RURAL COOPERATIVE BANK
浙江农信

浙江平湖农村合作银行
Zhejiang Pinghu Rural Commercial Bank Company Limited

浙江平湖农村合作银行是一家股份合作制的社区性地方金融机构，于2005年8月20日正式挂牌成立，是在平湖农村信用社基础上，由1 500多位法人和自然人入股而成，是平湖市服务网点最多、分布最广、规模最大、实力最强的金融机构。截至2014年末，各项存款余额176.7亿元，各项贷款余额114.5亿元。

Zhejiang Pinghu Rural Cooperative Bank is a regional joint-stock financial institution, which started its business on August 20, 2005. Established on the basis of Pinghu Rural Credit Cooperative, it is formed with the investment of more than 1 500 legal person and natural person. It is the largest financial institution in terms of the number of outlets, area of distribution, scale and strength. By the end of 2014, its total balance of deposits is RMB 17.67 billion and its total balance of loans is RMB 11.45 billion.

禾城农商银行
浙江农信 HECHENG RURAL COMMERCIAL BANK

浙江禾城农村商业银行股份有限公司
Zhejiang Hecheng Rural Commercial Bank Company Limited

浙江禾城农村商业银行股份有限公司于2013年4月21日由原浙江禾城农村合作银行改制成立，是嘉兴市首家股份制农村商业银行，设有13个职能部门和13家支行（营业部）、67个服务网点，全辖共有在岗员工700余人，是嘉兴市本级服务网点最多、分布最广、人员最多的金融机构。

Zhejiang Hecheng Rural Commercial Bank Company Limited established on April 21, 2013 from restructuring from former Zhejiang Hecheng Rural Cooperative Bank, is the first joint-stock rural commercial bank in Jiaxing. It has 13 functional departments, 13 branches (business departments), 67 service centers with a staff of more than 700. It is the largest financial institution in Jiaxing in terms of the number of outlet, coverage and number of staff.

桐乡市农村信用合作联社
TONGXIANG RURAL CREDIT COOPERATIVES UNION
浙江农信

桐乡市农村信用合作联社
Tongxiang City Rural Credit Cooperative Union

桐乡市农村信用合作联社是一家桐乡市辖内的农户、个体工商户、企业法人和其他经济组织入股组建的股份合作制社区性金融机构，于2004年12月9日创立，2005年2月21日挂牌成立。目前下辖13家信用社和1家营业部，营业网点总数达58个，机构网点环绕全市、遍布城乡，是全市网点分布最广的金融机构。

Tongxiang City Rural Credit Cooperative Union is a joint-stock cooperative financial institution of community nature jointly established by the peasants, individually-owned businesses, enterprise legal person and other economic units within its jurisdiction. It was established on December 9, 2004 and was officially opened on February 21, 2005. At present, it has 13 credit cooperatives and 1 business department with 58 outlets in total covering all the urban and rural areas of the city, which makes it the financial institution with the most extensive coverage in the city.

椒江农村合作银行
浙江农信 JIAOJIANG RURAL COOPERATIVE BANK

浙江台州椒江农村合作银行
Zhejiang Taizhou Jiaojiang Rural Cooperative Bank

浙江台州椒江农村合作银行于2005年9月23日挂牌开业，其前身为椒江区农村信用联社及其所辖的信用社。目前，网点总数38个，其中支行12家、营业部1家、分理处25家，员工500余名人，是椒江区域内营业网点最多、支农力度最大、与百姓最贴近的银行。

Zhejiang Taizhou Jiaojiang Rural Commercial Cooperative Bank, formerly known as Jiaojiang District Rural Credit Cooperative Union and Affiliated Cooperative, was officially opened on September 23, 2005. At present, the bank has 38 outlets in total with 12 branches, 1 business department, 25 sub-branches and a staff of more than 500. It is the bank of largest number of outlets, most supportive to agriculture industry and closest to the general public in Jiaojiang district.

浙江东阳农村商业银行股份有限公司
Zhejiang Dongyang Rural Commercial Bank Company Limited

浙江东阳农村商业银行股份有限公司是由东阳市农村信用合作联社改制而成，于2015年2月2日试营业，3月5日正式挂牌开业，注册资本6.68亿元，下设17个部室、1家营业部、16家支行、52家分理处、10家离行式自助银行和1家金融便民服务点（有人值守自助银行），共有在职干部职工800余名，是东阳市资金实力最强、职工队伍最庞大、服务机构最多的金融机构，截至2014年末，全行资产达到222.94亿元，各项存款余额191.66亿元，各项贷款余额130.89亿元。

Zhejiang Dongyang Rural Commercial Bank Company Limited is restructured from Dongyang City Rural Credit Cooperative Union. It started its trial business on February 2, 2015 and officially started its business on March, 5. With RMB 0.668 billion registered capital, it has set up 17 departments/offices, 1 business department, 16 branches, 52 sub-branches, 10 self-service bank and 1 convenient financial service center (self-service bank with a personnel in duty), with a staff of more than 800. It is the largest financial institution in Dongyang in terms of capital strength, staff and the number of outlets. By the end of 2014, the total assets of the bank has reached RMB 22.294 billion with RMB 19.166 billion total balance of deposit and RMB 13.089 billion balance of loans.

义乌农商银行
YIWU RURAL COMMERCIAL BANK
浙江农信

浙江义乌农村商业银行股份有限公司
Zhejiang Yiwu Rural Commercial Bank Company Limited

浙江义乌农村商业银行股份有限公司由浙江义乌农村合作银行整体改制而来，公司注册资本10.85亿元，创立于2012年5月22日，并于2012年7月18日正式挂牌开业。目前，经营网点达83个，员工人数实际在岗1 200余人。截至2014年12月末，全行各项存款余额409亿元，各项贷款余额305亿元。

Zhejiang Yiwu Rural Commercial Bank Company Limited is restructured from Zhejiang Yiwu Rural Cooperative Bank. Its registered capital is RMB 1.085 billion. It was established on May 22, 2012 and officially started its business on July 18, 2012. At present, the bank has 83 outlets with a staff of more than 1 200. By the end of 2014, the total assets of the bank has reached RMB 40.9 billion with RMB 30.5 billion balance of deposits.

浙江永康农村商业银行股份有限公司

Zhejiang Yongkang Rural Commercial Bank Company Limited

浙江永康农村商业银行股份有限公司是由浙江永康农村合作银行整体改制而成，下设1家营业部、17家支行、34家分理处和12家离行式自助银行，营业网点遍布永康城乡。

Zhejiang Yongkang Rural Commercial Bank Company Limited was restructured from Zhejiang Yongkang Rural Cooperative Bank with 1 business department, 17 branches, 34 sub-branches and 12 off-bank self-service banks, whose outlets cover the urban and rural areas of Yongkang.

青田农村商业银行
QINGTIANRURAL COMMERCIAL BANK

浙江青田农村商业银行股份有限公司
Zhejiang Qingtian Rural Commercial Bank Company Limited

青田农商银行始创于1954年，2005年改制为一级法人联社。2014年12月由青田县农村信用合作联社改制为青田农村商业银行，下辖17家支行，20家分理处，3家流动服务点，24家24小时自助银行。截至2014年末，各项存款余额达到81.72亿元，各项贷款余额56.28亿元；是青田县县域内存贷规模较大、营业网点最多、服务领域最广、税收贡献最大的地方性金融机构。

Qingtian Rural Commercial Bank was first started in 1954 and was restructured into a tier one legal person cooperative in 2005. In December, 2014, Qingtian County Rural Credit Cooperative Union was restructured into Qingtian Rural Commercial Bank with 17 branches, 20 sub-branches, 3 mobile service centers and 24 self-service banks 24 hours a day. By the end of 2014, its total balance of deposits is RMB 8.172 billion and total balance of loans is RMB 53 628 billion, which make it the largest regional financial institution in Qingtian County in terms of deposits and loans scale, the number of outlets, range of service and tax contributions.

临海农商银行

浙江农信 LINHAI RURAL COMMERCIAL BANK

浙江临海农村商业银行股份有限公司
Zhejiang Linhai Rural Commercial Bank Company Limited

临海农商银行辖有1家营业部，34家支行，39家分理处，766家村级金融服务点，便利店，营业网点遍及全市每个镇，街道。截至2015年2月末，存款余额204.47亿元，贷款余额114.53亿元，存、贷款总量和市场份额均居临海金融同业首位，是临海市唯一一家存款超过200亿元的金融机构。

Linhai Rural Commercial Bank has 1 business department, 34 branches, 39 sub-branches, 766 village financial service centers, convenient stores, whose outlets cover every town and street of the whole city. By the end of February, 2015, its balance of deposits have reached RMB 20.447 billion and its balance of loans have reached RMB 11.453 billion. Its total amount of deposits and loans as well as its markets share all rank the top in the financial institutions in Linhai. It is the only financial institution in Linhai whose deposits exceed RMB 20 billion.

浙江农信 龙湾农商银行 LONGWAN RURAL COMMERCIAL BANK

浙江温州龙湾农村商业银行股份有限公司
Zhejiang Wenzhou Longwan Rural Commercial Bank Company Limited

龙湾农商银行于2013年4月由龙湾农村合作银行成功改制而成。截至2014年末，各项存款171.25亿元，各项贷款130.22亿元，各项存贷款位居全区前列，成为当地经济发展的重要力量。龙湾农商银行的SWIFT码是：LWBKCNSH。

龙湾农商银行国际业务自2007年开办以来，业务产品不断创新、数量不断增加，常规的有国际结算、贸易融资、结售汇业务、跨境人民币业务等，还有市场热门的最新外汇产品，国际业务经过几年的发展，国际业务品种齐全。

外汇业务经营范围：外汇存款、外汇贷款、外汇汇款、国际结算、结售汇、外汇拆借、资信调查、咨询和见证业务、速汇金业务等。

Longwan Rural Commercial Bank was founded in April, 2013 from Longwan Rural Cooperative Bank. By the end of 2014, the bank's total deposit balance has reached RMB17.1 billion, the total loan balance has reached RMB13.2 billion. All the loans and deposits rank the top of the banks in Longwan. We are becoming the key force in local economic development. Swift code:LWBKCNSH.

Our bank have carried out the service of foreign exchange business since 2007, up to now, we provide various of services, regularly including international settlement, trade financing, foreign exchange settlement and sale, cross-border RMB business, and other popular services.

Foreign exchange business scope

Foreign currency deposits, foreign currency loans, foreign exchange remittances, international settlement, foreign exchange settlement and sale, foreign exchange lending, credit investigation, consultation and witness services, MoneyGram business, etc..

宁波市北仑区农村信用合作联社
Ningbo City Beilun District Rural Credit Cooperative Union

宁波市北仑区农村信用合作联社是由辖内自然人、企业法人和其他经济组织自愿入股组成股份合作制社区性地方金融机构，是北仑区创建时间最长、机构网点分布最多、服务对象最广泛的一家金融机构。

Ningbo City Beilun District Rural Cooperative Union is a joint-stock regional financial institution of community nature established by the voluntary investment of natural person, enterprise legal person and other economic units within its jurisdiction. It is a financial institution with longest history, most extensive distribution of outlets and broadest service targets in Beilun district.

慈溪农村商业银行
浙江农信 CIXI RURAL COMMERCIAL BANK

宁波慈溪农村商业银行股份有限公司
Ningbo Cixi Rural Commercial Bank Company Limited

宁波慈溪农村商业银行股份有限公司由宁波慈溪农村合作银行改制组建，经中国银行业监督管理机构批准成立，是具有独立法人资格的地方性银行机构，成立于2014年12月。目前，慈溪农村商业银行设有1家总部，1家营业部，26家支行，103家分理处，网点遍布慈溪。行总部设立14个部室，2014 年末，在职员工 1 390 人。截至2014年11月末，全行总资产521.4655亿元，各项存款余额435.6206亿元，各项贷款余额306.5270亿元，经营规模、网点设置、资金实力均居本市银行业首位，经营效益、信贷资产质量居全省农信系统前茅，资本充足率、拨备覆盖率等核心监管指标优于监管要求标准。

Ningbo Cixi Rural Commercial Bank Company Limited is a regional banking institution with independent legal personality. It was restructured from Ningbo Cixi Rural Cooperative Bank with the approval of CBRC in December, 2014. At present, Cixi Rural Commercial Bank has 1 Head Office, 1 business department, 26 branches and 103 sub-branches covering the whole Cixi. Its Head Office has 14 department offices. By the end of 2014, it has a staff of 1 390. By the end of November, 2014, its total assets have reached RMB 52.14655 billion with RMB 43.56206 billion balance of deposits and RMB 30.6527 billion balance of loans. Its business scale, the number of outlets and its capital strength all rank the top in the banking industry in the city. Its operational effectiveness and credit assets quality are among the top in the rural credit system of the province. Its core supervision indexes including capital adequacy ratio and provision coverage, etc. are all superior to the supervision requirement standard.

宁波市市区农村信用合作联社
Ningbo City Urban Area Rural Credit Cooperative Union

宁波市市区农村信用合作联社的前身是宁波江北信用联社，成立于1988年11月，经过行社脱钩体制改革，于1998年1月合并宁波市海曙、江东两区信用社组建市区信用联社，本联社是一家由农民、农村工商户和各类经济组织入股，为农民、农业和农村经济发展服务的社区性地方金融机构，现辖内有10家信用社、1家营业部和52家分支机构，网点遍布江北、江东、海曙三区各城乡街道，现有在编职工560多人。

Ningbo City Urban Rural Credit Cooperative Union was restructured from Ningbo Jiangbei Credit Union, which was established in November, 1988 through the structural reform of separation between banks and cooperatives. With the merger of Haishu Credit Cooperative and Jiangdong Credit Cooperative in Ningbo, the Urban Rural Cooperative Union was founded in January, 1998. This Union is a regional financial institution of community nature jointly invested by peasants, rural industrial and commercial units and various kinds of economic units for providing services for peasants, agriculture industry and rural economic development. It has 10 credit cooperatives, 1 business department and 52 branches within its jurisdiction. Its outlets cover all the urban and rural areas of the three districts including Jiangbei, Jiangdong and Haishu with a staff of more than 560.

宁波鄞州农村合作银行

Ningbo Yinzhou Rural Cooperative Bank

鄞州银行前身是诞生于20世纪50年代的鄞州全区52家农村信用社，1987年，经中国人民银行总行批准成为全国最早与农业银行脱离行政隶属关系的六家农村信用联社之一；1998年，经原中国人民银行浙江省分行批准，成为沪、浙、闽地区首家实施一级法人核算管理试点的信用联社；2001年11月，实施组建农村合作银行的试点，并于2003年3月25日获批复同意开业，同年4月8日正式对外挂牌营业。

Yinzhou Bank was established on the basis of 52 rural credit cooperatives in Yinzhou founded in the 1950s. It is one of the earliest six rural credit unions in China which separated their administrative subordination relationship with Agriculture Bank of China with the approval of People's Bank of China in 1987; in 1998, with the approval of Zhejiang Province Branch of People's Bank of China, it became the first credit union in Shanghai, Zhejiang and Fujian areas carrying out tier one legal person accounting management experimental unit; in November, 2001, it became the experimental unit in establishing rural cooperative bank and was approved to be opened on March 25, 2003 and its operation was officially started on April 8 of the same year.

宁波余姚农村合作银行
Ningbo Yuyao Rural Cooperative Bank

宁波余姚农村合作银行是一家于2004年12月31日经中国银行业监督管理委员会批准，由辖内自然人、企业法人和其他经济组织自愿入股组成的股份合作制社区性地方金融机构，前身是余姚市农村信用合作社联合社及所辖农村信用社。目前，本行下辖21家支行、1家营业部、64家分理处、4家储蓄所，共有营业网点90个，是余姚市金融系统中网点分布最广的金融机构。

Ningbo Yuyao Rural Cooperative Bank is a joint-stock regional financial institution of community nature restructured from Yuyao City Rural Credit Cooperative Union and Affiliated Rural Credit Cooperative. It was established on December 31, 2004 with the approval of CBRC by the voluntary joint investment of natural person, enterprise legal person and other economic units within its jurisdiction. At present, the bank has 21 branches, 1 business department, 64 sub-branches, 4 savings banks with 90 outlets, which make it the financial institution with broadest distribution of outlets in the financial system of Yuyao.

瓯海农商银行
OUHAI RURAL COMMERCIAL BANK
浙江农信

浙江温州瓯海农村商业银行股份有限公司
Zhejiang Wenzhou Ouhai Rural Commercial Bank Company Limited

瓯海农商银行前身为瓯海区农村信用合作联社和瓯海农村合作银行，成立于1954年，于2005年6月19日改制为合作银行，2014年7月14日改制为农商银行。现有下辖1家营业部、20家支行和26家分理处，乡镇金融网点和服务覆盖面达100%，在编员工817人。

国际业务部成立于2006年，近几年业务稳健快速发展，2014年国际结算量7亿美元，各项外币存款3.09亿美元，各项贷款764万美元。已开立境外代理行4家，分别是工行美国纽约分行、中行法兰克福分行、法兴银行、中行香港分行。现积极拓展境外代理行，以便于境外资金清算；同时已加入中国外汇交易中心。

外汇业务经营范围：吸收公众存款；发放短期贷款；办理国内结算业务；从事同业拆借；从事银行卡业务；外汇汇款等；经中国银行业监督管理机构批准的其他业务。

Ouhai Rural Commercial Bank, formerly known as Ouhai Rural Credit Cooperative Union and Ouhai Rural Cooperative Bank, was founded in 1954, and transformed to Cooperative Bank on June 19, 2005 and to Commercial Bank on July 14, 2014. It currently has 1 Head Office Banking Operation Department, 20 branches, 26 sub-branches and 817staff, with 100% coverage of township financial network and services.

Our International Business Department was established in 2006, with stable and rapid development during recent years. In 2014, the volume of international settlement had reached 700 million US Dollars, with 309 million USD Dollars balance of foreign currency deposits and 7.64 million USD Dollars balance of loans. Our bank has established correspondent relations with 4 foreign banks including Industrial and

Commercial Bank of China （New York), Bank of China (Frankfurt am Main), Societe Generale, Bank of China (Hong Kong). It is now making great efforts to expand the network of correspondent banks abroad in order to facilitate international settlement. In the meantime, the bank has joined China Foreign Exchange Trade System.

Absorption of deposits; short-term loan business; domestic settlements; inter-bank lending/borrowing; bank card business; foreign currency remittance; and other businesses under the approval of PBOC and CBRC.

瑞丰银行

BANK OF RUIFENG

浙江绍兴瑞丰农村商业银行股份有限公司

Zhejiang Shaoxing Ruifeng Rural Commercial Bank Company Limited

瑞丰银行是一家经中国银行业监督管理委员会批准，由辖内自然人、农村工商户、企业法人和其他经济组织自愿入股组成的股份有限公司，成立于2011年1月18日，总部位于浙江绍兴，前身是绍兴县农村合作银行。现有注册资本11.98亿元，员工1 800余人，总部设有19个管理部，下设25个职能中心（大队），辖内拥有23家支行和81家分理处共计营业网点106个，以及11家无人银行，分布在柯桥区各个镇（街）、绍兴市区和义乌，同时在嵊州作为主发起行设立嵊州瑞丰村镇银行。截至2014年末，全行总资产733.68亿元，存款总额534.26亿元，贷款总额388.13亿元。

Ruifeng Bank is a limited liability company established by the voluntary joint investment of natural person, rural industrial and commercial units, enterprise legal person and other economic units with the approval of CBRC. It was established on January 18, 2011 with its Head Office in Shaoxing, Zhejiang Province. It was restructured from Shaoxing County Rural Cooperative Bank. It now has a registered capital of RMB 1.198 billion and a staff of more than 1 800. Its Head Office has 19 administrative departments with 25 functional centers (teams), and with its jurisdiction, the bank has 23 branches and 81 sub-branches with 106 outlets in total and 11 self-service banks distributed in the towns (streets) of Keqiao District, Shaoxing City and Yiwu. Meanwhile, Shengzhou Ruifeng Village Bank has been established with this bank as the main originator. By the end of 2014, the total assets of the bank has reached RMB 73.368 billion with RMB 53.426 billion total deposits and RMB 38.813 billion total loans.

新昌农商银行
XINCHANG RURAL COMMERCIAL BANK

浙江新昌农村商业银行股份有限公司
Zhejiang Xinchang Rural Commercial Bank Company Limited

浙江新昌农村商业银行股份有限公司位于新昌县七星街道七星路18号，建办于1988年7月，始名新昌县农村信用合作社联合社，1999年12月县内8家农村合作基金会并入，2000年3月新昌南明城市信用社并入，2005年1月改制为浙江新昌农村合作银行，2013年11月改制为浙江新昌农村商业银行股份有限公司。下辖1家营业部，9家支行、30个营业网点，遍布全县城乡，是新昌县内存贷规模最大、网点最多的银行。

Zhejiang Xinchang Rural Commercial Bank Company Limited is located at No.18, Qixing Road, Qixing Street, Xinchang County. It was established in July, 1988 with the original name of Xinchang County Rural Credit Cooperative Union. With the merger of 8 rural cooperative foundations within the county in December, 1999 and the merger of Xinchang Nanming Urban Credit Cooperative in March, 2000, it was restructured into Zhejiang Xinchang Rural Cooperative Bank in January, 2005 and was restructured into Zhejiang Xinchang Rural Commercial Bank Company Limited in November, 2013. It has set up 1 business department, 9 branches with 30 outlets covering the urban and rural areas of the whole county. It is the largest bank in Xinchang county in terms of deposit and loan scale and the number of outlets.

诸暨农商银行
浙江农信 ZHUJI RURAL COMMERCIAL BANK

浙江诸暨农村商业银行股份有限公司
Zhejiang Zhuji Rural Commercial Bank Company Limited

浙江诸暨农村商业银行股份有限公司于2013年1月6日正式挂牌开业，本行是由原浙江诸暨农村合作银行整体改制并更名组建而成的一家地方性股份制商业银行，其前身是原诸暨市信用联社及辖属的农村信用社。下辖1家营业部、23家支行、49家分理处，营业网点遍布全市各镇乡街道，现有员工1 000余名。诸暨农商银行是诸暨市存贷款规模最大、人员网点最多、综合实力最强的一家金融机构。截至2014年12月，各项存款余额达257.39亿元，贷款余额186.56亿元。

Zhejiang Zhuji Rural Commercial Bank Company Limited started its business on January 6, 2013. This bank is a regional joint-stock commercial bank restructured and renamed from Zhejiang Zhuji Rural Cooperative Bank, which was formerly the Zhuji Credit Union and Affiliated Rural Credit Cooperative. It has set up 1 business department, 23 branches, 49 sub-branches. Its outlets have covered the streets of the whole city, towns and counties with a staff of more than 1 000. Zhuji Rural Commercial Bank is the largest financial institution in Zhuji in terms of deposits and loans scale, staff and comprehensive strength. By the end of 2014, its total balance of deposits have reached RMB 25.739 billion and total balance of loans RMB 18.656 billion.

黄岩农村合作银行
HUANGYAN RURAL COOPERATIVE BANK
浙江农信

浙江台州黄岩农村合作银行
Zhejiang Taizhou Huangyan Rural Cooperative Bank

浙江台州黄岩农村合作银行是由辖区内的农民、农村工商户、企业法人和其他经济组织入股的股份合作制社区性地方金融机构，自农村信用社建立以来已有60多年历史，现下辖1家营业部、20家支行、18家分理处，共有员工548人。

Zhejiang Taizhou Huangyan Rural Cooperative Bank is a joint-stock cooperative regional financial institution of community nature jointly invested by the peasants, rural industrial and commercial units, enterprise legal person and other economic units with its jurisdiction. It has a history of more than 60 years since its establishment as a rural credit cooperative. It now has set up 1 business department, 20 branches, 18 sub-branches with a staff of 548.

路桥农村合作银行
浙江农信 Luqiao Rural Cooperative Bank

浙江台州路桥农村合作银行

Zhejiang Taizhou Luqiao Rural Commercial Bank Company Limited

路桥农村合作银行于2005年3月18日正式挂牌开业，是台州市首家成立的农村合作银行。目前，下辖1家营业部、17家支行，45个营业网点，是路桥区域内营业网点最多的银行。截至2014年6月，全行各项存款余额达170亿元，各项贷款余额115.7亿元。

Luqiao Rural Cooperative Bank was officially opened on March 18, 2005. It is the first rural cooperative bank established in Taizhou. At present, it has set up 1 business department, 17 branches with 45 outlets, which is the bank with the largest number of outlet in Luqiao District. By June, 2014, its total balance of deposits have reached RMB 17 billion and its total balance of loans have reached RMB 11.57 billion.

温岭农村合作银行
WENLING RURAL COOPERATIVE BANK
浙江农信

浙江温岭农村合作银行
Zhejiang Wenling Rural Cooperative Bank

浙江温岭农村合作银行于2005年6月23日挂牌开业，其前身为温岭市农村信用社。现下设20家支行（营业部）、54家分理处，共846名员工。

Zhejiang Wenling Rural Cooperative Bank was officially opened on June 23, 2005. It was formerly known as Wenling City Rural Credit Cooperative. It now has set up 20 branches (business departments), 54 sub-branches with a staff of 846.

浙江苍南农村商业银行股份有限公司
Zhejiang Cangnan Rural Commercial Bank Company Limited

浙江苍南农村商业银行股份有限公司是一家股份制地方性金融机构，其前身为浙江苍南农村合作银行，现辖1家营业部、21家支行、54个营业网点、5个金融服务点，机构金融服务能力覆盖全县12个乡镇，是苍南县存贷款规模最大、信贷支农最多、纳税贡献度最高、网点最多、服务范围最广的金融机构。

Zhejiang Cangnan Rural Commercial Bank Company Limited is a joint-stock regional financial institution. It was formerly known as Zhejiang Cangnan Rural Cooperative Bank. It now has set up 1 business department, 21 branches with 54 outlets and 5 financial service centers. Its financial services are provided in 12 villages and towns in the county. It is the largest financial institution in Cangnan county in terms of deposit and loan scale, credit loans for peasants, contribution in taxes, number of outlet and range of services.

浙江乐清农村商业银行股份有限公司
Zhejiang Yueqing Rural Commercial Bank Company Limited

乐清农商银行全称浙江乐清农村商业银行股份有限公司，前身乐清农村合作银行成立于2005年，2014年更名为乐清农商银行，下辖1家总行营业部、19家支行和37家分理处，营业网点和自助银行达100家，农村金融覆盖率达100%，截至2014年12月31日，本行资产总额297.60亿元，各项存款247.37亿元，各项贷款189.79亿元。

The full name of Leqing Rural Commercial Bank is Zhejiang Yueqing Rural Commercial Bank Company Limited. It was formerly known as Yueqing Rural Cooperative Bank, which was established in 2005. In 2014, it was renamed as Yueqing Rural Commercial Bank. It has set up 1 Head Office Business Department, 19 branches, 37 sub-branches with 100 outlets and self-service banks. Its rural financial coverage rate has reached 100%. By the end of 2014, the total assets of the bank has reached RMB 29.76 billion with total deposits of RMB 24.737 billion and total loans of RMB 18.979 billion.

浙江瑞安农村商业银行股份有限公司
Zhejiang Ruian Rural Commercial Bank Company Limited

瑞安农商银行是由原来的瑞安农村合作银行改制而成，注册资本10.03亿元，现辖12家支行、1家营业部，共80个网点，拥有800余名员工。网点机构遍布城乡，网点数量居瑞安市同行业首位，是瑞安市资本雄厚，功能齐全，产品丰富、服务优良、营业网点最多、从业人员最多的唯一法人金融机构。

Ruian Rural Commercial Bank is restrucutured from Ruian Rural Cooperative Bank with a registered capital of RMB 1.003 billion. It now has set up 12 branches, 1 business department with 80 outlets in total and a staff of more than 800. Its outlets have covered urban and rural areas and its number of outlets ranks the top in the same industry in Ruian. It is the only legal person financial institution in Ruian which has strong capital strength, multiple functions, abundant products and high-quality services with the most number of outlets and staff.

鹿城农商银行
LUCHENG RURAL COMMERCIAL BANK

浙江温州鹿城农村商业银行股份有限公司
Zhejiang Wenzhou Lucheng Rural Commercial Bank Company Limited

浙江温州鹿城农村商业银行股份有限公司，简称鹿城农商银行，是一家经银监会批准、注册在温州市的股份制金融机构，是在温州市郊农村信用社的基础上，不断推进体制改革和法人治理发展而来，有60多年的经营历史。2005年6月22日完成一级法人体制改革更名为鹿城农村合作银行，2013年6月13日完成股份制改革更名为鹿城农商银行。现下辖1家营业部，10家中心支行，共有51个营业网点，119个自助网点，356台ATM，对鹿城区各街道（镇）的金融服务覆盖面达100%，目前在岗员工800多人。目前已开业村镇银行数有21家。

Zhejiang Wenzhou Lucheng Rural Commercial Bank Company Limited, short for Lucheng Rural Commercial Bank, is as joint-stock financial institution established with the approval of CBRC and registered in Wenzhou. It is founded on the basis of Wenzhou Suburb Rural Credit Cooperative and developed with continuous structural reform and corporate governance with an operation history of more than 60 years. Tier one legal person structural reform was completed on June 22, 2005 and was renamed into Lucheng Rural Cooperative Bank. Joint-stock reform was completed on June 13, 2013 and was renamed into Lucheng Rural Commercial Bank. With a staff of more than 800, it now has set up 1 business department, 10 central branches with 51 outlets, 119 self-service outlets and 356 ATMs, whose financial service covers 100% of the streets (towns) of Lucheng district. At present, it has set up 21 villages banks.

文成县农村信用合作联社
Wencheng County Rural Credit Cooperative Union

文成县农村信用合作联社（简称文成联社）是一家股份合作制金融机构，于2005年改制为县一级法人联社，实行独立核算。改制后，构建了由社员代表大会、理事会、监事会和经营管理层（即三会一层）组成的相互协调、相互制约的法人治理结构。是文成县金融服务覆盖面最广、服务客户数量最多、纳税贡献最大的地方金融机构。

Wencheng County Rural Credit Cooperative Union (short for Wencheng Cooperative Union) is joint-stock financial institution. It was restructured into Tier one legal person cooperative union of county level in 2005 and is implementing independent accounting. After the restructure, a legal person governance structure of intercoordination and interaction is formed by commune member's representative assembly, board of directors, and board of supervisors and management layer. It is the largest regional financial institution in Wencheng county in terms of financial service coverage, number of clients and taxes contributed.

浙江绍兴恒信农村合作银行
Zhejiang Shaoxing Hengxin Rural Cooperative Bank

浙江绍兴恒信合作银行总部设在绍兴市区，是一家由农户、个体工商户、中小企业自愿入股组成的股份合作制性质的社区性地方金融机构，其前身最高成立于1952年，历经了从农村信用社到信用社联合社、信用联社、合作银行等三次重大体制变革，2008年改制为合作银行。经过60年的发展，浙江绍兴恒信农村合作银行形成了辐射绍兴市区的机构体系和业务网络，全辖共有营业网点31家。

Zhejiang Shaoxing Hengxin Rural Cooperative Bank, with its Head Office in the urban area of Shaoxing, is a joint-stock regional financial institution of community nature established by the joint investment of peasants, individual-owned business, medium and small-sized enterprises. It was originally established in 1952 and have experienced three structural reforms from a rural credit cooperative into a credit cooperative union and then into a credit union and then into a cooperative bank in 2008. With more than 60 years of development, Zhejiang Shaoxing Hengxin Rural Cooperative Bank has formed a structural system and business network which cover the urban area of Shaoxing with 31 outlets within its jurisdiction.

浙江嵊州农村合作银行
Zhejiang Shengzhou Rural Cooperative Bank

嵊州农村合作银行于2004年11月改制而成立股份制合作金融机构，于2005年1月29日正式挂牌开业。截至2013年12月底，全行存款余额139.18亿元，贷款余额94.62亿元，存、贷款余额均位居全市金融机构首位。全行现有营业网点50个，其中15个支行（部）、33个分理处、2个储蓄所。营业网点遍布全市，是嵊州市营业网点最多、覆盖面积最广的银行业金融机构。近几年来，该行通过开展"优质文明服务年"、"优质服务深化年"等活动，不断深化全员"服务至上"的经营理念。自2012年9月开始开办国际业务，2014年结算量规模为13 672万美元。

Zhejiang Shengzhou Rural Cooperative Bank has been reconstructed into a joint-stock financial institution since November 2004, and officially went into operation on 19th January, 2005.Up to December 2013, the total balance of deposits and loans has reached 13.918billion and 9.462 billion respectively, which ranked first place among other financial institution in Shengzhou. At present there are 50 business fields spreading all over the city, of which consist of 15 branches, 33 sub-branches and 2 saving agencies. As a dominating competitive local bank, it takes the largest market share. In recent years, the bank has been committed to the programs "the year of promoting high-quality" and "the year of up-grading high quality" so as to improve all staffs service-oriented management concept. The international business department started in September 2012, and the total settlement amount has reached US 136.72 million in 2014.

Remittance, letter of credit, collection, financing etc..

长兴农村合作银行

浙江农信 CHANGXING RURAL CREDITL COOPERATIVES UNION

浙江长兴农村合作银行
Zhejiang Changxing Rural Cooperative Bank

长兴农村合作银行，位于“太湖明珠”长兴县，是在农村信用社第二轮改革中第一家经中国银行业监督管理委员会批准成立的地方金融机构，前身是长兴农村信用合作联社。长兴农村合作银行在60余年的发展历程中，始终与长兴百姓紧密相伴，目前已壮大为全县银行业存贷款规模第一的金融机构，服务超过30万客户，是长兴县网点最多、服务最全、实力最强、贡献最大的金融机构。

Changxing Rural Cooperative Bank is located in Changxing County known as “Pearl of Taihu Lake”. Restructured from Changxing Rural Credit Cooperative Union, it is the first regional financial institution established with the approval of CBRC in the second round of reform of rural credit cooperative. In the past over 60 years of development history, Changxing Rural Cooperative Bank has been working closely with people in Changxing and has become the largest financial institution in the county in terms of deposit and loan scale, the number of outlet, range of service, capital strength and contribution with more than 300 thousand customers.

浙江舟山普陀农村商业银行股份有限公司
Zhejiang Zhoushan Putuo Rural Commercial Bank Company Limited

浙江舟山普陀农村商业银行股份有限公司是经中国银行业监督管理委员会浙江监督局批准，在原浙江舟山普陀农村合作银行的基础上发起设立的股份制地方性金融机构。2013年10月正式挂牌，注册资本为500 492 190元人民币。目前有营业网点48家，员工500余人，总行内设12个职能部门，1个工会办，下设1家营业部、11家支行。

Zhejiang Zhoushan Putuo Rural Commercial Bank Company Limited is a joint-stock regional financial institution established on the basis on former Zhejiang Zhoushan Putuo Rural Cooperative Bank with the approval of Zhejiang Supervision Bureau of CBRC. It is officially opened in October, 2013 with registered capital of RMB 500 492 190. It now has set up 48 outlets with a staff of more than 500. Its Head Office has 12 functional departments, 1 labor union office, 1 business department and 11 branches.

浙江金华成泰农村商业银行股份有限公司
Zhejiang JinhuaChengtai Rural Commercial Bank Company Limited

浙江金华成泰农村商业银行股份有限公司
Zhejiang Jinhua Chengtai Rural Commercial Bank Company Limited

浙江金华成泰农村商业银行股份有限公司秉承着金华市区农村信用联社60年的发展历史，由浙江金华成泰农村合作银行整体改制而成，总行位于八一南街123号，现有存贷款规模200亿元，下辖52家网点机构，遍布金华市本级的婺城区、金东区、开发区和金义都市新区，是金华市本级营业网点最多、城乡金融服务面最广、支持“三农”力度最大、与广大农民和中小企业感情最深的金融机构。

Zhejiang Jinhua Chengtai Rural Commercial Bank Company Limited, Jinhua Chengtai Rural Commercial Bank for short, Which has 60-year history of Rural credit cooperative union and has reformed from Zhejiang Jinhua Chengtai rural cooperative bank since 2014. The head office is located in 123, South Bayi Road, Jinhua City, Zhejiang Province, China. Currently, it owns 20 billion yuan of deposits and loans, 52 branches across the Wucheng District, Jindong District, Jinyi Development Zones. It is the financial institution that has the most branches in Jinhua city, provides the most extensive service and support for urban and rural and “three rural”, establishes the deepest feelings with the majority of farmers, small and medium-sized enterprises.

浙江武义农村合作银行
Zhejiang Wuyi Rural Cooperative Bank

浙江武义农村合作银行，简称武义合作银行是在武义县农村信用合作联社的基础上改制成立的地方性银行。武义合作银行设总行营业部、10家支行和17家分理处，营业网点遍布武义县城乡，是武义县辖内存贷款总规模最大、营业网点分布最广的银行。

Zhejiang Wuyi Rural Cooperative Bank, short for Wuyi Cooperative Bank, is a regional bank restructured from Wuyi County Rural Credit Cooperative Union. Wuyi Cooperative Bank has set up Head Office Business Department, 10 branches and 17 sub-branches. Its outlets have covered urban and rural areas of Wuyi County, which make it the largest bank in Wuyi in terms of deposits and loans scale and the number of outlet.

浙江兰溪农村合作银行
Zhejiang Lanxi Rural Cooperative Bank

浙江兰溪农村合作银行是在兰溪市农村信用合作联社的基础上组建而成的一家股份合作制地方性金融机构，总行位于兰溪市标志性建筑信联大厦（市丹溪大道18号），网点覆盖全市城乡，是兰溪市资金实力最强、经营规模最大、营业网点最多、服务范围最广的金融机构。

Zhejiang Lanxi Rural Cooperative Bank is a joint-stock regional financial institution established on the basis of Lanxi City Rural Credit Cooperative Union. Its Head Office is located at Xinlian Mansion (No.18, Danxi Main Street), a landmark building in Lanxi. Its outlets have covered the urban and rural areas of the whole city, which makes the bank the largest bank in Lanxi in terms of capital strength, business scale, number of outlet and range of service.

江山农商银行
JIANGSHAN RURAL COMMERCIAL BANK
浙江农信

浙江江山农村商业银行股份有限公司
Zhejiang Jiangshan Rural Commercial Bank Company Limited

浙江江山农村商业银行股份有限公司前身浙江江山农村合作银行成立于2008年6月，目前下辖42个营业网点，其中：营业部1家，支行6家，分理处32家，金融服务点1个，24小时无人银行2个，共有员工500多人。

Zhejiang Jiangshan Rural Commercial bank Company Limited was restructured from Zhejiang Jiangshan Rural Cooperative Bank, which was established in June, 2008. It now has set up 42 outlets with 1 business department, 6 branches, 32 sub-branches, 1 financial service center, 2 24-hour self-service banks with a staff of more than 500.

宁波奉化农村商业银行股份有限公司
Ningbo Fenghua Rural Commercial Bank Company Limited

奉化农商银行是在奉化市农村信用合作联社基础上组建的，2013年7月23日，获得中国银监会同意筹建的批复，10月15日宁波银监局批复开业，奉化农商银行根植奉化，下设1家营业部、18家支行、32家分理处，机构网点遍布于全市各镇（街道），拥有从业人员600余人，是奉化市银行业中资金实力最强、机构网点最多、分布最广的金融机构。

Fenghua Rural Commercial Bank was restructured from Fenghua City Rural Credit Cooperative Union with the approval of CBRC on July 23, 2013. It was opened on October 15 on the approval of Ningbo Banking Supervision Bureau. Fenghua Rural Commercial Bank is rooted in Fenghua, with 1 business department, 18 branches, 32 sub-branches. Its outlets has covered towns and street of the city with a staff of more than 600. It is the largest financial institution in Fenghua in terms of capital strength, number of outlet and range of distribution.

安徽马鞍山农村商业银行股份有限公司
Anhui Maanshan Rural Commercial Bank Company Limited

马鞍山农商银行是安徽省首家、全国第一家地级市农商银行，其前身是马鞍山农村合作银行，与2005年12月20日成立（改制前为马鞍山农村信用联社），2009年，马鞍山农村合作银行再改制为马鞍山农商银行2014年，该行资产规模314.38亿元、存款238亿元、贷款172亿元；资本充足率14.21%，不良贷款率1.45%，拨备覆盖率173.46%，各项监管指标保持良好水平。

Maanshan Rural Commercial bank is the first prefecture-level rural commercial bank in Anhui and the whole country. Its was restructured from Maanshan Rural Cooperative Bank, which was established on December 20, 2005 (it was known as Maanshan Rural Credit Cooperative Union before the restructure). In 2009, Maanshan Rural Cooperative Bank was again restructured into Maanshan Rural Commercial Bank in 2014. The capital scale of the bank is RMB 31.438 billion with RMB 23.8 billion deposits and RMB 17.2 billion loans; its capital adequacy ratio is 14.21%, non-performing loan ratio is 1.45% and its provision coverage is 173.46%, so all its supervision indexes has been remaining on a healthy level.

福州农商银行
RURAL COMMERCIAL BANK OF FUZHOU

福建福州农村商业银行股份有限公司
Fujian Fuzhou Rural Commercial Bank Company Limited

福州农商银行成立于2011年1月11日，是在有着62年发展历史的福州市城区农村信用社基础上改制而成的股份制商业银行，是福州市历史最悠久的金融机构之一。现下辖1家营业部，27家支行，37家分理处，43家离行式自助银行。2012年6月，在闽侯县发起设立了福州地区第一家村镇银行——闽侯民本村镇银行。截至2014年12月末，全行资产总额236.64亿元，存款余额达205.7亿元，各项贷款余额达133.19亿元。

Fujian Fuzhou Rural Commercial Bank is a joint-stock commercial bank established on January 11, 2011 from restructuring from Fuzhou Urban Area Rural Credit Cooperative, which has a history of 62 years. It is one of the oldest financial institution in Fuzhou. It now has set up 1 business department, 27 branches, 37 sub-branches and 43 off-bank self-service banks. In June, 2012, it launched to establish the first village bank in Minhou County, that is Minhou Minben Village Bank—the first village bank in Fuzhou. By the end of 2014, its total assets have reached RMB 23.664 billion with balance of deposits of RMB 20.57 billion and balance of loans of RMB 13.319 billion.

德化县农村信用合作联社
DEHUA RURAL CREDIT UNION

德化县农村信用合作联社
Dehua County Rural Cooperative Bank

德化县农村信用合作联社是由自然人、企业法人和其他经济组织入股组成的社区性地方金融机构。拥有26个网点、200多名员工。

Dehua County Rural Credit Cooperative Union is a regional financial institution of community nature jointly invested by natural persons, enterprise legal persons and other economic units. It has set up 26 outlets with a staff of more than 200.

惠安县农村信用合作联社

惠安县农村信用合作联社
Huian County Rural Credit Cooperative Union

惠安农村信用社成立于1952年，是一家总行级独立法人金融机构，总部位于惠安县，下辖42个营业网点（其中1家营业部、19家信用社、22家分社）、68家自助银行（其中28家离行式）、249个农信便民点，员工400多人，截至2014年底，存款规模达103.09亿元，贷款规模75.57亿元，双双位居本地各银行业金融机构首位。现已成为当地存贷规模最大、机构网点最多、服务千家万户、助推小微企业、社会贡献度高的一支重要金融劲旅。

Huian County Rural Credit Cooperative Union was established in 1952. It is an independent legal person financial institution of Head Office level with its Head Office locating in Huian county. It has set up 42 outlets (including 1 business department, 19 credit cooperatives and 22 branches), 68 self-service banks (including 28 off-bank self-service banks), 249 rural credit convenient centers with a staff of more than 400. By the end of 2014, its deposit scale has reached RMB 10.309 billion and loan scale has reached RMB 7.557 billion, both rank the top in the banking financial institutions in Huian. It now has become an important financial institution which provides service for thousands of customers and provides support for small and micro businesses and makes great contributions to the society in Huian with largest deposit and loan scale and most number of outlet.

南安农村商业银行
RURAL COMMERCIAL BANK OF NANAN

福建南安农村商业银行股份有限公司
Fujian Nanan Rural Commercial Bank Company Limited

福建南安农村合作银行是经中国银行业监督管理委员会批准成立的福建省第一家农村合作银行，成立于2006年9月28日，前身是诞生于20世纪50年代初的南安市农村信用社。半个多世纪以来，南安市农村信用社始终坚持“立足‘三农’、服务‘三农’”的宗旨，以支农兴农富农为己任，经过几代人的不懈努力，已发展成为综合性、多功能、现代化的地方性金融机构。截至2014年末，该行资产总额247亿元，各项存款余额203.35亿元，各项贷款余额126.5亿元，全年实现各项营业收入17.25亿元，增幅28%；实现账面利润5.46亿元，增幅18.69%。资本充足率15.57%，贷款拨备余额6.82亿元，拨贷比5.4%，拨备覆盖率达到361.5%，贷款损失准备充足率822.5%，全行抗风险能力指标保持较高水平。截至2015年2月末，该行共有在岗员工近1 000人，下设14个职能部门、1家营业部、44家支行、52家分理处，机构网点遍布南安城乡。

Fujian Nanan Rural Cooperative Bank, established on September 28, 2006, is the first rural cooperative bank in Jujian established with the approval of CBRC. It was restructured from Nanan City Rural Credit Cooperative established in the 1950s. For over the half century, Nanan City Rural Credit Cooperative has been persisting on the principle of “rooted on agriculture, rural areas and farmers and serving for agriculture, rural areas and farmers” and shoulder the responsibility of supporting and boosting agriculture and enriching farmers. With the efforts of several generations, it has developed into a regional financial institution of comprehensiveness, multi-function and modernization. By the end of 2014, its total assets have reached RMB 24.7 billion with balance of deposit of RMB 20.335 billion and balance of loans of RMB 12.65 billion.

Its operation revenue of one year has reached RMB 1.725 billion with a growing rate of 28%; its book profit has reached RMB 0.546 billion with a growing rate of 18.6%. The risk resistance capacity indexes of the bank remain high with 15.57% of capital adequacy ratio, RMB 0.682 billion loan provision balance， 5.4% provision rate, 361.5% provision coverage and 822.5% loan loss reserves rate. By the end of February, 2015, the bank has set up 14 functional departments, 1 business department, 44 branches, 52 sub-branches covering urban and rural areas of Nanan with a staff of nearly 1 000.

泉州农村商业银行
RURAL COMMERCIAL BANK OF QUANZHOU

泉州农村商业银行股份有限公司
Quanzhou Rural Commercial Bank Co., Ltd.

泉州农商银行于2011年3月15日开业，注册资本10.1亿元，该行创建了具有本土特色浓重的“刺桐红”和“银博士”双品牌及拳头产品。改制四年来，该行目前合并资产总额已达215亿元，是改制前的5.4倍；合并各项存款从34亿元增加到140亿元，是改制前的4.12倍；合并各项贷款从26亿元增加到103亿元，是改制前的4倍。目前共有营业网点51个，实现大泉州服务全覆盖，首次突破了农商银行以县为服务范围的限制，成为全国唯一试点，也成为泉州“金改”的重要成果。同时在省内外发起设立14家村镇银行，服务范围从改制之前的4个区扩大到省内6个设区市的25个县（市、区），是改制前的6.25倍，并延伸到长三角的上海、珠三角的珠海，其中宁德7家村镇银行成为全国唯一一片集中连片发起设立村镇银行的试点。此举得到福建省委尤权书记、泉州郑新聪市长等领导以批示形式的肯定。

该行国业部成立于2011年1月，并于2013年1月正式对外开办外汇业务，是福建农信系统67家行社中第一家开办外汇业务的农商银行。2013年该行国际结算量2 423万美元，结售汇2 377万美元，均位居福建农信系统第一。2014年国际结算量和结售汇量双双突破1亿美元，分别达到10 346万美元、10 060万美元，其中结售汇量位居福建农信系统第一。

经过2年多的发展，该行国际业务产品创新持续加强，客户群体迅速扩大，境外合作银行不断增加，在福建农信系统内第一家办理了贸易项下跟单托收业务，取得福建农信系统单证业务零的突破，并在信用证通知、信用证交单等产品创新上创造了多项福建农信系统第一；境外账户行扩展到7家，账户行广泛分布欧美、亚太地区；与15个境内外银行建立RMA关系；福建农信系统允许开办的美元、欧元、日元和港元等四个外币品种，该行均具备了独立经营能力，同时在系统内首家实现了对公日元业务的突破。

外汇业务经营范围：外汇存款业务、外汇贷款业务、外汇汇款业务、国际结算业务、外币兑换业务、同业外汇拆借业务及资信调查、咨询、见证等七项外汇业务。

特色业务：出口信保融资、速汇金快速。

Quanzhou Rural Commercial Bank Co., Ltd. started business on March 15, 2011, with a registered capital of 1.01 billion RMB. This bank has created a dual-brand, “Red Erythrina” and “Dr. Silver”, with strong local characteristics and high-quality financial products. In the past four years after restructuring, at the end of 2014, the bank’s total assets reached 21.5 billion RMB, which is 5.4 times higher than before the restructuring. The deposits increased from 3.4 billion RMB to 14 billion RMB, or 4.12 times. The loans increased from 2.6 billion RMB to 10.3 billion RMB, or 4 times. The bank currently has 51 branches and covers all districts of Quanzhou city. Quanzhou Rural Commercial Bank Co., Ltd. also for the first time broke its own limits of service scope to become a pilot of the whole country and achieved an important progress in “Quanzhou Financial Reform”. After restructuring, the bank services coverage expanded from 4 areas in Quanzhou City to 25 areas in 6 cities in Fujian Province, an increase of 6.25 times. As well, the bank has set up 14 rural banks inside and outside Fujian Province, thereby extending its service area to Shanghai of the Yangtze River Delta Region, and also to Zhuhai of the Pearl River Delta Region. Especially the establishment of 7 rural banks in Ningde City at one time became the only pilot project of “Banking Concentration” in China. This action was highly commended by Mr. Quan You, the Chinese Communist Party Secretary of Fujian Province and Mr. Xincong Zheng, the Mayor of Quanzhou City.

The International Business Department of the bank was established in January 2011, and started business officially as from January 2013. It is the first Rural Commercial Bank which opened international business in 67 banks of the Fujian Rural Credit Union. During 2013 the bank’s International Settlements and Foreign exchange has amounted to USD 24.23 million and USD 23.77 million to occupy the first place in Fujian Rural Credit Union. In 2014 the bank’s International Settlements and Foreign exchange both exceeded USD 100 million, reaching USD 103.46 million and USD 100.6 million, its foreign exchange volume ranking No.1 in Fujian Rural Credit Union.

After a two-year rapid development, Quanzhou Rural Commercial Bank has continued to strengthen its international business products through innovation, expanding its customer basement, increasing the quantity of its foreign cooperative banks. The bank handled the first documentary collection business in Fujian Rural Credit Union, and obtained a breakthrough in documents business. Its business in notification of L/C, negotiation of L/C etc. also reached top level in Fujian Rural Credit Union. The bank has increased its overseas co-accounts banks up to 7 banks, widely distributed in Europe, America and the Asia-Pacific region, and has established RMA relationships with 15 domestic and overseas banks in the world. Currently, the bank has the capacity to operate foreign business independently for 4 currencies which include USD , Euro, JPY, HKD, and it is also the first bank which obtained breakthrough in institution business of JPY in Fujian Rural Credit Union.

Scope of business of foreign exchange transactions: foreign currency deposits, foreign currency loans, foreign exchange remittance business, international settlement, foreign currency exchange business, interbank foreign exchange lending business and credit investigation, consulting, witness.

Characteristic business: Financing Based on Export Credit Insurance, Money Gram.

厦门农商银行
RURAL COMMERCIAL BANK OF XIAMEN

厦门农村商业银行股份有限公司
Xiamen Rural Commercial Bank Company Limited

厦门农商银行2012年7月完成改制挂牌开业，是一家具有独立法人资格的银行机构。前身为全国首家地市级统一法人联社——厦门市农村信用合作联社，继承了厦门市农村信用社60多年的发展历史、服务特色和文化传统。

本行以“打造特色银行、铸就百年基业”为企业愿景，以“扎根海西、丰农裕商”为企业使命，秉承服务“三农”、社区村居民和中小微企业的经营宗旨，金融服务辐射全市近50%的户籍人口，用近90%的信贷资金投向当地小微企业和社区村居民，有力推动了地方经济发展。开业以来，不断加快品牌化经营、区域化布局、综合化发展步伐，充分发挥全省农信社系统资源优势、厦门特区区位优势和两岸金融中心对台优势，力争建设成为立足闽南、辐射海西、服务民生具有核心竞争力的特色银行、效益银行。

外汇业务开展状况：外汇业务为该行的新兴业务，我们有着专业的工作团队，全方位提供结算、信用证及外币资金各类业务，本外币一起助推厦门的中小企业发展。

外汇业务经营范围：外汇存款，外汇贷款，外汇汇款，外币兑换，国际结算，同业外汇拆借，资信调查、咨询、见证业务，外汇担保，外汇借款，外汇票据的承兑和贴现，自营外汇买卖和代客外汇买卖。

Xiamen Rural Commercial Bank (or “XRCB”) was established on July 16th 2012, which was reincorporated from Xiamen Rural Credit Cooperatives of more than 60 years history. At present, XRCB has registered capital of RMB 1.483 billion, established a business network of more than 60 outlets, and employs more than 1 000 staff.

International business is a highly-promoted new business in XRCB. With the professional work team, XRCB now provides foreign currency remittance, loan, collection, letter of credit and other services in deposit, settlement and trade financing areas, to promote the development of medium and small enterprises of Xiamen.

Deposits, loans, remittance, foreign exchange, international settlement, foreign exchange, sales, valet foreign exchange trading, foreign exchange loans, foreign exchange guarantee, credit investigation, inquiry, witness business.

漳州农商银行

RURAL COMMERCIAL BANK OF ZHANGZHOU

福建漳州农村商业银行股份有限公司

Fujian Zhangzhou Rural Commercial Bank Company Limited

漳州农商银行是漳州“本土银行”，股东全部来源于地方民营企业、个人，其中15%的股份来自地方国有企业。目前拥有员工400多人，27个营业网点分布在漳州芗城、龙文、漳浦、龙海及台商投资区。

Fujian Zhangzhou Rural Commercial Bank is a “local bank” of Zhangzhou with shareholders all coming from local private enterprises, individuals, among which 15% of its shares coming from local state-owned enterprises. At present, it has 27 outlets distributing in Xiangcheng, Longwen, Zhangpu, Longhai and Taiwan Businessman Investment Zone of Zhangzhou with a staff of more than 400.

福清汇通农商银行
RURAL COMMERCIAL BANK OF FU QING HUITONG

福建福清汇通农村商业银行股份有限公司
Fujian Fuqing Huitong Rural Commercial Bank Company Limited

福建福清汇通农村商业银行股份有限公司成立于2012年1月，其前身是福清市农村信用合作联社，是一家历史悠久的金融机构。2011年底完成股份制改革，2012年1月正式改制为福建汇通福清农村商业银行股份有限公司。

Fujian Fuqing Huitong Rural Commercial Bank Company Limited was established in January, 2012. It was restructured from Fuqing City Rural Credit Cooperative Union, which is a financial institution with a long history. Its join-stock system reform was completed at the end of 2011 and it was officially restructured into Fujian Fuqing Huitong Rural Commercial Bank Company Limited in January, 2012.

新余农商银行
XINYU RURAL COMMERCIAL BANK

新余农村商业银行股份有限公司
Xinyu Rural Commercial Bank Company Limited

新余农村商业银行股份有限公司是在原江西新余农村合作银行基础上改制成立的股份制商业银行。目前，新余农商银行设置了21个职能部门，下辖分宜、渝水、城南、城北、高新、孔目江和仙女湖支行7家一级支行，下村、良山、罗坊3家二级支行，1家营业部，54个营业网点遍布新余市城乡。截至2014年12月底，存款余额183.52亿元，贷款余额138.61亿元，存贷款市场份额连续七年居全市银行业第1位，是新余市营业网点最多、客户资源最广、业务规模最大、社会贡献最突出的银行金融机构。

Xinyu Rural Commercial Bank Company Limited is a joint-stock commercial bank restructured from Jiangxi Xinyu Rural Cooperative Bank. At present, Xinyu Rural Commercial Bank has set up 21 functional departments, 7 tier one branches, including Fenyi, Yushui, Chengnan, Chengbei, Gaoxin, Kongmujiang and Xiannuhu and 3 tier two branches, including Xiacun, Liangshan and Luofang, 1 business department, 54 outlets covering the city and county of Xinyu. By the end of 2014, its balance of deposits have reached RMB 18.352 billion and its balance of loans have reached RMB 13.861 billion. Its market share for deposits and loans rank No.1 in the banking business of the city for 7 years successively, and it is the banking financial institution Xinyu with largest number of outlet, most extensive range of client resources, biggest business scale and most prominent social contribution.

南昌农村商业银行股份有限公司
Nanchang Rural Commercial Bank Company Limited

南昌农村商业银行股份有限公司成立于2009年1月16日，3月26日挂牌，是全省首家在农村信用社基础上改制组建的农村商业银行，下辖1家营业部、40家支行、30家分理处，现有员工近1 000人，主要服务南昌市东湖区、西湖区、青山湖区、青云谱区、高新区、红谷滩新区、经济技术开发区等7个行政区。

Nanchang Rural Commercial Bank Company Limited was founded on January 16, 2009 and was officially opened on March 26. It is a rural commercial bank restructured from the first rural credit cooperative in the province. It has set up 1 business department, 40 branches, 30 sub-branches with a staff of nearly 1 000. It mainly provides services in 7 administrative districts in Nanchang including Donghu District, Xihu District, Qingshanhu District, Qingyunpu District, High-tech Zone, Honggutan New Zone, Economic and Technology Development Zone.

景德镇农商银行
Jingdezhen Rural Commercial Bank

景德镇农村商业银行股份有限公司
Jingdezhen Rural Commercial Bank Company Limited

景德镇农商银行是由农村信用社逐步改制组建而成，2007年10月，景德镇市农村信用合作联社成立，2010年11月29日成功改制为景德镇农商银行，成为全省第一家设区市农村商业银行。景德镇农商银行目前辖有 1家营业部、16家支行、55家分理处共计72个营业网点，是景德镇市服务区域最广、客户资源多、业务规模最大的地方银行机构。截至2014年末，资产总额170.37亿元，各项存款余额 132.77 亿元，各项贷款余额 86.10 亿元。

Jingdezhen Rural Commercial Bank was gradually restructured from rural credit cooperative. Jingdezhen Rural Credit Cooperative Union was established in October, 2007, and it was restructured into Jingdezhen Rural Commercial Bank on November 29, 2010, and became the first district city rural commercial bank in the province. Jingdezhen Rural Commercial Bank currently has 72 outlets including 1 business department, 16 branches and 55 sub-branches, which make it the largest regional banking institution in Jingdezhen in terms of service area, client resources and business scale. By the end of 2014, its total assets have reached RMB 17.037 billion with RMB 13.277 billion total balance of deposits and RMB 8.31 billion balance of loans.

吉安农商银行
JIAN RURAL COMMERCIAL BANK

吉安农村商业银行股份有限公司
Jian Rural Commercial Bank Company Limited

吉安农村商业银行股份有限公司是由原吉州、青原两区农村信用社合并改制而成的股份制银行，于2011年12月16日挂牌开业。现有内设部室13个，一级支行5家、二级支行5家、分理处21家，全行在编在岗员工480余人，机构网点遍布吉安城乡，金融服务覆盖各个区域，是当地营业网点最多、客户资源最广、存贷规模最大、经营机制最活的金融机构。

Jian Rural Commercial Bank Company Limited (short for Jian Rural Commercial Bank) is a joint-stock bank merged and restructured from Jizhou Rural Credit Cooperative and Qingyuan Rural Credit Cooperative. It was officially opened on December 16, 2011. So far, it has set up 13 department offices, 5 tier one branches, 5 tier two branches, 21 sub-branches with a staff of more than 480. Its outlets have covered all the urban and rural areas of Jian and its financial service has covered each field. It is the financial institution of most number of outlet, most extensive sources of customers, largest scale of deposit and loan scale and most flexible operational mechanism in Jian.

抚州农村商业银行股份有限公司
Fuzhou Rural Commercial Bank Company Limited

抚州农商银行是经中国银行业监督管理委员会批准，在对抚州市城郊农村信用合作联社和临川区农村信用合作联社进行合并重组和股份制改造的基础上，吸收新的自然人和企业法人作为发起人组建而成，是抚州市首家地方性股份制商业银行。

Fuzhou Rural Commercial Bank is the first regional joint-stock commercial bank in Fuzhou established with the approval of CBRC and on the basis of merging, restructuring and shareholding reform of Fuzhou Suburb Rural Credit Cooperative Union and Linchuan District Rural Credit Cooperative Union through absorbing natural persons and enterprise legal persons as originators.

赣州农商银行
GAN ZHOU RUAL COMMERCIAL BANK

赣州农村商业银行股份有限公司
Ganzhou Rural Commercial Bank Company Limited

2012年5月9日，赣州市首家农村商业银行——赣州农商行盛大开业，标志着章贡区农村信用合作联社改制成功。截至2013年9月底，赣州农商行共有员工300多人，内设部室15个，营业网点24个，搭建起现代股份制银行的管理架构，是赣州主城区网点最多、服务范围最广的金融机构。

On May 9, 2012, the first rural commercial bank in Ganzhou—Ganzhou Rural Commercial Bank was set up, which signifies the success of restructure of rural credit cooperative union in Zhanggong District. By the end of September, 2013, Ganzhou Rural Commercial Bank has built up a management structure of a joint-stock bank with a staff of more than 300 and 15 department offices, 24 outlets, which make it the largest bank in Ganzhou in terms of the number of outlet and range of service.

鹰潭农村商业银行股份有限公司
Yingtan Rural Commercial Bank Company Limited

鹰潭农商银行是在对原月湖区农村信用合作联社、贵溪市农村信用合作联社和余江县农村信用合作联社进行合并重组和股份制改造的基础上，吸收新的自然人和企业法人作为发起人而新设合并的地方性股份制商业银行，是全省首家经国务院同意、中国银监会批准成立的市级股份制农商银行。2012年11月26日，鹰潭农村商业银行正式挂牌开业，总部设在鹰潭市信江南路1号，注册资本5.72亿元，下辖1家营业部、18家支行、59家分理处，是鹰潭市营业网点最多、服务地域最广、服务机制最为灵活的银行机构。

Yingtan Rural Commercial Bank is a regional joint-stock commercial bank established on the basis of merging, restructuring and shareholding reform of former “Yuehu District Rural Credit Cooperative Union”, “Guixi City Rural Credit Cooperative Union” and “Yujiang County Rural Credit Cooperative Union” through absorbing natural persons and enterprise legal persons as originators. It is the first joint-stock rural commercial bank of city level in the province approved by the State Council and CBRC. Yingtan Rural Commercial Bank was officially opened on November 26, 2012. Its Head Office is located at No. 1 South Xinjiang Road, Yingtan City. Its registered capital is RMB 0.572 billion with 1 business department, 18 branches and 59 sub-branches. It is the banking institution with most number of outlet, most extensive range of service and most flexible service mechanism in Yantan.

山东邹平农村商业银行股份有限公司
Shandong Zouping Rural Commercial Bank Company Limited

山东邹平农村商业银行股份有限公司是经中国银行业监督管理委员会批准设立的股份制金融机构，2009年2月27日正式挂牌开业，是山东省首批农村商业银行。

Shandong Zouping Rural Commercial Bank Company Limited is a joint-stock financial institution established with the approval of CBRC. It was officially opened on February 27, 2009, which is the first rural commercial banks in Shandong Province.

山东齐河农村商业银行股份有限公司
Shandong Qihe Rural Commercial Bank Company Limited

齐河农村商业银行股份有限公司的前身是齐河农村合作银行。齐河农村合作银行成立于2010年，是德州市首家农村合作银行。齐河农村商业银行注册资本金3.35亿元，下设1家营业部，21家支行，12家分理处。

Shandong Qihe Rural Commercial Bank Company Limited was restructured from Qihe Rural Cooperative Bank, which was established in 2010, the first rural cooperative bank in Dezhou city. It has a registered capital of RMB 0.335 billion with 1 business department, 21 branches and 12 sub-branches.

山东禹城农村商业银行股份有限公司
Shandong Yucheng Rural Commercial Bank Company Limited

山东禹城农村商业银行是在原禹城市农村信用合作联社基础上发起设立的股份制商业银行，注册资本3.82亿元，2013年12月7日正式开业，是德州市第一家获批开业的农村商业银行。

Shandong Yucheng Rural Commercial Bank is a join-stock commercial bank established on the basis of former Yucheng City Rural Credit Cooperative Union. It has a registered capital of RMB 0.382 billion. It was officially opened on December 7, 2013, which is the first approved rural commercial banks in Dezhou.

山东东营胜利农村合作银行

Shandong Dongying Shengli Rural Commercial Bank Company Limited

山东东营胜利农村合作银行位于东营市东营区庐山路1028号，2006年6月26日正式挂牌开业，是在原东营区农村信用合作社联合社基础上组建的地方性股份合作制银行，注册资本44 115万元。现下设职能部室10个，下辖营业部1家，支行16家，分理处16家，共33处营业网点，拥有员工496名。

Shandong Dongying Rural Cooperative Bank is located at Lushan Road, Dongying District, Dongying City. It was officially opened on June 26, 2006. It is a regional joint-stock cooperative bank established on the basis of former Dongying District Rural Credit Cooperative Union with a registered capital of RMB 441 150 000. It has set up 10 department offices and 33 outlets including 1 business department, 16 branches and 16 sub-branches with a staff of 496.

曹县农村信用合作联社
Cao County Rural Credit Cooperative Union

曹县农村信用合作联社（以下简称曹县联社）于2005年12月成立一级法人，现有从业人员577人，下设12个职能部室、3个公司部、1个营业部、38个基层网点，是全县营业网点最多，资金实力最强，服务范围较广的县域金融机构，是曹县人民自己的银行。近年来，在省联社及菏泽办事处的正确领导下，在社会各界以及广大客户的大力支持下，曹县联社以科学发展观统揽全局，围绕省联社“一二三四六”的发展目标，始终坚持以服务“三农”为己任，不断创新工作思路，改进工作方法，强化内部管理，加强科技、队伍、企业文化等各项建设，真抓实干，全力推动，各项业务全面迅速发展。截至2014年5月末，各项存款103.64亿元，较年初增加9.42亿元；各项贷款余额71.16亿元，较年初增加9.49亿元。实现各项收入3.41亿元，增幅33.12%；实现经营利润1.51亿元，增幅44.91%。先后荣获“省级劳动关系和谐企业”、“省级‘富民兴鲁’劳动奖章”，“市级职业道德先进单位”、“十佳爱心企业”、“支持维权先进单位”、“十佳服务地方经济发展先进单位”等荣誉称号，并连续多年被评为系统内市级考评先进单位，曹县联社现已经发展成为全县最具发展潜力和最具社会影响力的金融机构。

Cao County Rural Credit Cooperative Union (hereinafter refer to as Cao County Cooperative Union) established its Tier one legal person in December, 2005 and has set up 12 department offices, 3 Corporation Divisions, 1 business department and 38 outlets of basic level with a staff of 577. It is a local bank and is the largest financial institution in the county in terms of capital strength and range of services. For the past few years, under the right leadership of provincial rural credit cooperative and Heze Office and the strong support of all sectors of society and large number of customers, Cao County Cooperative Union has been consistently dedicating to providing services for “agriculture, farmer and rural area”, and keep innovating new ideas of working, improving working methods, reinforcing interior management, strengthening construction in various aspects including technology, staff and cooperative culture, etc. and work hard with every effort to promote the rapid and overall development of all the businesses through centering on the “one-two-three-four-six” development objective made by the provincial rural credit cooperative. By the end of May, 2014, its total deposits have reached RMB 10.364 billion, an increase of RMB 0.942 billion compared with that of the beginning of the year; its total balance of loans have reached RMB 7.116 billion, an increase of RMB 0.949 billion compared with that of the beginning of the year; RMB 0.341 billion total income has been realized with an increase of 33.12%; RMB 0.151 billion operating profit has been realized with an increase of 44.91%. Many honorary titles have been earned, including “Harmonious Labor Relations Enterprise of the Province”, “Enrich the Public and Revitalize Shandong Labor Medal of the Province”, “The Municipal Ethics Advanced Unit”, “Top Ten Charitable Enterprises”, “Advance Unit in Supporting Safeguarding Legal Rights”, “Top ten Advanced Units in Serving Local Economic Development”, etc. and has won the title of advanced unit in municipal Evaluation within the system for many years successively. Now, Cao County Cooperative Union has become the financial institution with most potential and social influence in Cao County.

菏泽农村商业银行股份有限公司
Heze Rural Commercial Bank Company Limited

菏泽农商银行股份有限公司是在原菏泽市牡丹区农村信用社、菏泽市高新技术开发区农村信用社、菏泽市经济技术开发区农村信用社以及原城市信用社的基础上改制组建的，由企业法人和自然人股东共同发起设立的，股本金总额7亿元。2014年5月4日，中国银行业监督管理委员会正式批准筹建，2014年10月24日获准开业。菏泽农商银行的创立实现了从股份合作制的农村信用合作联社向股份商业银行的成功跨越。

Heze Rural Commercial Bank Company Limited is established by restructuring on the basis of former Heze City Mudan District Rural Credit Cooperative, Heze City High-tech Development Zone Rural Credit Cooperative, Heze City Economic and Technology Development Zone Rural Credit Cooperative and former City Credit Cooperative. It is founded by the joint investment of enterprise legal persons and natural persons. Its equity capital is RMB 0.7 billion in total. It was approved on May 4, 2014 by CBRC and was officially opened on October 24, 2014.The establishment of Heze Rural Commercial Bank has realized the successful restructuring from a joint-stock rural credit cooperative to a joint-stock commercial bank.

山东济南润丰农村合作银行
Shandong Jinan Runfeng Rural Commercial Bank Company Limited

山东济南润丰农村银行是一家城区农村合作金融机构，目前该行拥有营业网点95处，总部在山东济南，员工数1 200余人，市场定位主要是服务城区中小企业和社区居民。

Shandong Jinan Runfeng Rural Cooperative Bank is a suburb rural cooperative financial institution. At present, it has set up 95 outlets. Its Head Office is in Jinan, Shandong with a staff of more than 1 200. It mainly provides services for medium and small-sized enterprises and community residents.

山东圣泰农村合作银行
Shandong Shengtai Rural Commercial Bank Company Limited

山东圣泰农村合作银行是山东省首批农村信用社改革试点单位之一，是由辖区内56家企业法人、1 202名自然人发起设立的股份合作制银行，注册资金10 600万元，总部设在山东省济宁市，2005年8月20日挂牌成立。

Shandong Shengtai Rural Cooperative Bank is one of the earliest test units in rural credit cooperative reform in Shandong. It is a joint-stock cooperative bank established by the launch of 56 enterprise legal persons and 1 202 natural persons. Its registered capital is RMB 106 000 000 with its Head Office locating in Jining, Shandong. It was officially opened on August 20, 2005.

聊城农商银行
LIAOCHENG RURAL COMMERCIAL BANK

聊城农村商业银行股份有限公司
Liaocheng Rural Commercial Bank Company Limited

聊城农村商业银行股份有限公司是经中国银行业监督管理委员会批准、在原聊城市东昌府区农村信用合作联社基础上改制设立的股份制地方性银行机构，于2013年12月28日正式挂牌开业。聊城农商银行实行一级法人、统一核算、分级管理、授权经营的管理体制，全行注册资本5.02亿元，服务范围覆盖聊城市东昌府区、经济技术开发区、高新技术产业开发区、江北水城旅游度假区4个区，辖41处营业网点，其中1家营业部，40家支行，员工809名。

Liaocheng Rural Commercial Bank Company Limited is a regional joint-stock bank restructured on the basis of former Liaocheng City Dongchangfu District Rural Credit Cooperative Union with the approval of CBRC. It was officially opened on December 28, 2013. Liaocheng Rural Commercial Bank carries on the management system of Tier one legal person, unified accounting, level-to-level administration and authorized operation. Its registered capital is RMB 0.502 billion. Its services covers 4 districts of Liaocheng, including Dongchengfu District, Economic and Technology Development Zone, High-tech Industrial Development Zone and Jiangbei Shuicheng Tourist Resort. Within its jurisdiction, 41 outlets including 1 business department, 40 branches has been set up with a staff of 809.

山东临沂兰山农村合作银行
Shandong Linyi Lanshan Rural Commercial Bank Company Limited

山东临沂兰山农村合作银行成立于2005年10月29日，是经中国银行业监督管理委员会批准成立的，由辖内农民、农村工商户、企业法人及其他经济组织自愿入股，以“立足城乡，面向‘三农’，面向社区，面向中小企业”为市场定位，以服务农民、农业和农村经济发展为宗旨和经营方向的股份合作制地方性金融企业。现辖1家营业部、16个部室、31家支行、60家分理处，共有干部职工1 200余人。

Shandong Linyi Lanshan Rural Cooperative Bank, established on October 29, 2005, is a regional joint-stock financial enterprise established with the voluntary investment of peasants, rural industrial and commercial units, enterprise legal persons and other economic units with the approval of CBRC. Its market positioning is “rooted in urban and rural areas, facing ‘agriculture, rural areas and farmers’, and facing the community and medium and small enterprises” and regard serving farmers, agriculture and rural economic development as its orientation and operation direction. It now has set up 1 business department, 16 department offices, 31 branches, 60 sub-branches with a staff of more than 1 200.

山东荣成农村商业银行股份有限公司
Shandong Rongcheng Rural Commercial Bank Company Limited

山东荣成农村商业银行股份有限公司成立于2010年12月，是经中国银行业监督管理委员会批准设立的股份制地方性金融机构，是威海市成立的第一家农村商业银行，其前身为诞生于20世纪50年代初的荣成市农村信用合作社。现辖71个营业网点，员工782人。2014年末，全行存贷款规模分别达189亿元和140亿元，是荣成市经营规模最大、服务范围最广、资金实力最强的银行。

Shandong Rongcheng Rural Commercial Bank Company Limited is a regional joint-stock financial institution established in December, 2010 with the approval of CBRC. It is the first rural commercial bank established in Weihai. It was restructured from Rongcheng City Rural Credit Cooperative established in the 1950s. Now, it has set up 71 outlets within its jurisdiction and has a staff of 782. By the end of 2014, its deposit and loan scale have reached RMB 18.9 billion and RMB 14 billion respectively, which make it the largest bank in Rongcheng in terms of operational scale, range of service and capital strength.

威海农商银行
RURAL COMMERCIAL BANK OF WEIHAI

山东威海农村商业银行股份有限公司
Shandong Weihai Rural Commercial Bank Co., Ltd.

山东威海农村商业银行股份有限公司前身是威海市环翠区农村信用合作联社。目前，所辖网点47个，从业员工600余名，资产规模、营业网点、服务范围、资金实力均居本市银行业前列。

威海农商银行秉承“稳健经营，稳步发展”的经营理念，坚持“四个面向”的市场定位，遵循“每一步，心相伴”的服务宗旨，不断加大地方经济的支持力度，为威海市民提供优质高效的金融服务，倾力打造“服务‘三农’、服务社区、贴心周到的便民银行”，努力实现创建一流现代化商业银行的奋斗目标。成立以来，先后获得“省级先进单位”、威海市“文明单位”和“优秀单位”等称号，为建设美丽幸福新威海作出了积极贡献。

外汇业务开展状况：威海农商银行以烟台农商行为外汇清算行（SWIFT：ZFRBCNBQ）。自2012年开始开办外汇业务，外汇业务发展迅速，信誉良好。

外汇业务经营范围：外汇存款，外汇贷款，外汇汇款，外币兑换，国际结算，结汇、售汇，同业外汇拆借，外汇担保，外汇借款，外汇票据的承兑和结算。

Shandong Weihai Rural Commercial Bank Co., Ltd., its predecessor is Weihai Huancui district rural credit cooperative association. At present, have 47 network, employed more than 600 employees, asset scale, outlets, scope of services, financial strength are ranked among the top banks in the city.

Shandong weihai rural commercial bank Co., Ltd. adhering to the “prudent management, steady development” business philosophy, adhere to the “four dimensions” market positioning, follow the “every step, accompanied by heart” service tenet, increasing the support of the local economy, to provide quality and efficient financial services to citizens of weihai, bend force to build the “three rural service, community service, good and thoughtful convenient bank", to create first-class modern commercial bank's goals. Since its establishment, awarded "provincial advanced unit", weihai city "civilized unit" and "outstanding unit" and so on the title, to build beautiful happy new weihai made a positive contribution.

Foreign exchange clearing bank:yantai rural commercial bank Co., Ltd. (Swift：ZFRBCNBQ). Run foreign exchange business since 2012，the foreign exchang business deveopment is rapid，reputalbe.

Scope of business of foreign exchange trancactions: foreign exchange deposits; foreign exchange loans; foreign exchange remittance; foreign exchange; the international settlement; foreign exchange settlement and sale; trade foreign currency lending; foreign exchange guarantee; foreign borrowing; bill acceptance and settlement of foreign exchange.

文登市农村信用合作联社
Wendeng City Rural Credit Cooperative Union

文登市农村信用社成立于1953年12月；1994年5月与农行分门办公；2001年7月收购原城市信用社；2005年12月成立一级法人联社。现有在职职工528人，辖联社营业部1家，信用社24家，分社、储蓄所15家。

Wendeng City Rural Credit Cooperative Union was established in December, 1953; it separated itself from Agriculture Bank of China in May, 1994; it took over former City Credit Cooperative in July, 2001; Tier one legal person Cooperative was set up in December, 2005. It now has set up 1 business department, 24 credit cooperatives and 15 branches and savings banks within its jurisdiction with a staff of 528.

山东昌乐农村商业银行股份有限公司
Shandong Changle Rural Commercial Bank Company Limited

山东昌乐农村商业银行股份有限公司是在原昌乐县农村信用合作联社的基础上发起设立的，注册资本30 012 万元人民币，现辖营业网点33个，自助银亭10个，离行式自助银行3个，社区金融服务点9个，综合业务网络遍布城乡，从业人员480余人，是昌乐县营业网点和从业人员最多、服务范围最广、资金规模最大的综合性、多功能地方性金融机构。截至2014年末，全行各项存款余额101.43亿元，各项贷款余额70.46亿元，存贷款规模稳居全县首位。

Shandong Changle Rural Commercial Bank Company Limited was established on the basis of Changle County Rural Credit Cooperative Union. It has a registered capital of RMB 300 120 000, and 33 outlets, 10 self-service bank houses, 3 off-premise self-service banks and 9 community financial service center. It comprehensive business network has covered the whole urban and rural areas with a staff of more than 480. It is the largest comprehensive and multi-functional regional financial institution in terms of the number of outlets, the number of staff, the range of service and capital scale. By the end of 2014, its total balance of deposit has reached RMB 10.143 billion and its total balance of loan has reached RMB 7.046 billion, whose deposit and loan scale is the largest in the county.

山东高密农村商业银行股份有限公司
Shandong Gaomi Rural Commercial Bank Company Limited

高密农村商业银行是由原高密市农村信用合作联社于2012年9月改制成立的股份制商业银行，注册资本40 299万元人民币，同年12月18日挂牌开业。目前，下辖49个营业网点，共有干部职工637人。截至2014年末，全行各项存款126.64亿元，各项贷款96.2亿元。该行各项存款余额、增量，各项贷款余额、增量，存、贷款市场占有率、上缴税金等各项主要业务指标均居当地金融机构居第一位。

Shandong Gaomi Rural Commercial Bank Company Limited is a joint-stock commercial bank restructured from Gaomi City Rural Credit Cooperative Union in September, 2012. Its registered capital is RMB 402 990 000 and the bank started its business operation on December 18, 2012. At present, the banks has started 49 outlets with a staff of 637. By the end of 2014, the total deposit of the bank is RMB 12.664 billion and the total loan of the bank is RMB 9.62 billion. The business index including balance and increase rate of the total deposit, and balance, increase rate of loan, market share of deposit and loan, paid taxes are all rank No.1 among the local financial institutions.

山东诸城农村商业银行股份有限公司
Shandong Zhucheng Rural Commercial Bank Company Limited

山东诸城农村商业银行股份有限公司位于山东省诸城市，于2012年8月由山东诸城农村合作银行改制成立。山东诸城农村合作银行创立于2005年并于2012年12月正式揭牌开业，前身是成立于1954年的诸城市农村信用社。截至2014年末，全行总资产186亿元，下辖14个职能部室，1家营业部，5个公司事业部，37家支行；在岗员工683人，各项存款162亿元，各项贷款110亿元。

Shandong Zhucheng Rural Commercial Bank Company Limited, located in Zhucheng, Shandong Province, was restructured from Shandong Zhucheng Rural Credit Cooperative Bank. Shandong Zhucheng Rural Credit Cooperative Bank, which was restructured from Zhucheng Urban Rural Credit Cooperative founded in 1954, was established in 2005 and started its business from December of the same year. By the end of 2014, its total assets is RMB 18.6 billion. The bank has set up 14 departments/offices, 1 business department, 5 enterprise business divisions and 37 branches with a staff of 683 and RMB 16.2 billion total deposits and RMB 11 billion total loans.

山东莱州农村商业银行股份有限公司
Shandong Laizhou Rural Commercial Bank Company Limited

山东莱州农村商业银行股份有限公司于2009年2月26日正式挂牌成立，该行作为农村信用社经由银行化、股份制改革新成立的一家商业银行，被列为全省首批农村商业银行试点单位。

Shandong Laizhou Rural Commercial Bank Company Limited was officially opened on February 26, 2009. As a commercial bank which has experienced banking reform and joint-stock reform from a rural credit cooperative, it was listed as the first rural commercial bank test units of the province.

山东龙口农村商业银行股份有限公司
Shandong Longkou Rural Commercial Bank Company Limited

山东龙口农村商业银行股份有限公司在是原山东龙口农村合作银行的基础上改制成立的，2011年11月11日正式开业，注册资本170 000万元，辖13个部室、30家支行、31家分理处、1家营业部，在岗干部员工806人。

Shandong Longkou Rural Commercial Bank Company Limited was restructured on the basis of former Shandong Longkou Rural Cooperative Bank and was officially opened on November 11, 2011 with a registered capital of RMB 1.7 billion. It has set up 13 department offices, 30 branches, 31 sub-branches, 1 business department with a staff of 806.

山东张店农村商业银行股份有限公司
Shandong Zhangdian Rural Commercial Bank Company Limited

山东张店农村商业银行前身——山东张店农村合作银行是经中国银行业监督管理委员会批准成立的山东省首批农村合作银行，是由辖内自然人、企业法人和其他经济组织入股组成的股份合作制社区性地方金融机构。2004年10月18日挂牌开业。2011年3月28日更名为山东张店农村商业银行股份有限公司。

Formerly know as Shandong Zhangdian Rural Cooperative Bank, Shandong Zhangdian Rural Commercial Bank is a regional joint-stock cooperative financial institution of community nature jointly invested by natural persons, enterprise legal persons and other economic units with the approval of CBRC. It was officially opened on October 18, 2004 and was renamed into Shandong Zhangdian Rural Commercial Bank Company limited on March 28, 2011.

山东寿光农村商业银行股份有限公司
Shandong Shouguang Rural Commercial Bank Company Limited

寿光农商银行2009年3月3日由山东寿光农村合作银行正式改制而成，是全省农信系统率先成立农村商业银行的3家行社之一，也是全省首家省内、省外同时设立村镇银行的金融机构。注册资本9.09亿元，辖81个营业网点，其中，营业部1家、全功能网点23个、特色网点11个、基础网点46个，员工902人。同时，分别在天津华明、安徽芜湖、河北任丘、临沂苍山、天津宁河等发起设立5家村镇银行。截至2014年底，全行资产总额278.5亿元，各项存款余额233.8亿元，各项贷款余额164.1亿元。

Shouguang Rural Commercial Bank was established on March 3, 2009 through restructuring from Shandong Shouguang Rural Cooperative Bank. It is one of the three banks which first established rural commercial bank in the rural credit system in the province and it is also the first financial institution in the province which set up village bank in and outside the province. Its registered capital is RMB 0.909 billion. With a staff of 902, the bank has set up 81 outlets, including 1 business department, 23 global function branch, 11 characteristic branch and 46 basic branches. Meanwhile, the bank has also set up 5 village banks including Huaming in Tianjing, Wuhu in Anhui, Renqiu in Hebei, Cangshan in Linfen and Ninghe in Tianjing. By the end of 2014, the total assets of the bank has reached RMB 27.85 billion with total balance of deposits of RMB 23.38 billion and total balance of loans of RMB 16.41 billion.

山东广饶农村商业银行股份有限公司
Shandong Guangrao Rural Commercial Bank Company Limited

广饶农村商业银行是在广饶农村合作银行基础上以发起方式设立的，是东营市首家、全省第四家农村商业银行，注册资本5.2亿元。

Guangrao Rural Commercial Bank was established with the initiation mode on the basis of Guangrao Rural Cooperative Bank. It’s the first rural commercial bank in Dongying and the forth rural commercial bank in the province with a registered capital of RMB 0.52 billion.

山东临沂河东农村合作银行
Shandong Linyi Hedong Rural Cooperative Bank

山东临沂河东农村合作银行的前身是临沂市河东区农村信用社，成立于20世纪50年代，是经中国银监会批准成立的以区为单位的统一法人单位，是由辖区内自然人、企业法人和其他经济组织自愿入股组成的股份制合作制金融机构。注册资本26 347万元，营业网点42个，共有员工507人。是临沂市经中国银监会批复的第二家股份合作制银行。2007年6月29日正式成立。

Shandong Linyi Hedong Rural Cooperative Bank, formerly known as Linyi City Hedong District Rural Credit Cooperative, was founded in the 1950s and is a unified legal person unit with district as unit with the approval of CBRC. It is a joint-stock cooperative financial institution voluntarily invested by natural persons, enterprise legal persons and other economic units with its jurisdiction. Its registered capital is RMB 263 470 000 with 42 outlets and a staff of 507. It is the second joint-stock cooperative bank approved by Linyi Banking Regulatory Commission and was officially opened on June 29, 2007.

山东博兴农村商业银行股份有限公司
Shandong Boxing Rural Commercial Bank Company Limited

博兴农村商业银行是在原山东博兴农村合作银行的基础上以发起方式设立的，下设12个职能部室、1家营业部、18家支行、15家分理处，在岗员工376人，是博兴县营业网点最多、服务范围最广、资金规模最大的综合性银行业金融机构。

Boxing Rural Commercial Bank was established with the initiation mode on the basis of former Shandong Boxig Rural Cooperative Bank. It has set up 12 functional offices, 1 business department, 18 branches and 15 sub-branches with a staff of 376. It is a comprehensive banking financial institution in Boxing with most number of outlet, most extensive range of services and largest capital scale.

山东临淄农村商业银行
RURAL COMMERCIAL BANK OF SHANDONG LINZI

山东临淄农村商业银行股份有限公司
Shandong Linzi Rural Commercial Bank Company Limited

山东临淄农村商业银行股份有限公司是在原临淄区农村信用合作联社的基础上改制成立，注册资本52 350万元，设13个职能部室，29家支行，26家分理处。

Shandong Linzi Rural Commercial Bank Company Limited was restructured on the basis of former Linzi Rural Credit Cooperative Union. With a registered capital of RMB 523 500 000, it has set up 13 functional offices, 29 branches and 26 sub-branches.

青岛农商银行
QINGDAO RURAL COMMERCIAL BANK

青岛农村商业银行股份有限公司
Qingdao Rural Commercial Bank Company Limited

青岛农村商业银行股份有限公司是经国务院同意、中国银监会批准，在青岛市农村信用社（农村合作银行）的基础上，以新设合并方式组建而成的股份制商业银行。截至2014年末，注册资本50亿元，全行拥有营业网点343家，从业员工5 000余人，资产总额达到1 451亿元；各项存款余额达到1 201亿元；各项贷款余额达到862亿元，是青岛市营业网点和从业人员最多，服务范围最广的综合性、多功能地方法人银行。

青岛农商银行的前身是有着60余年发展历史的青岛市农村信用社。自1951年青岛市第一家农村信用社成立以来，青岛农商银行锐意改革、砥砺奋进，完成了从信用合作社到信用联社再到股份制农村商业银行的历史性跨越。2012年6月，原华丰、城阳、黄岛、即墨四家农村合作银行，胶州、胶南、平度、莱西4家农村信用联社及青岛市联社共9家单位，正式组建成立青岛农商银行。现发展成为一家实力雄厚、经营稳健、科技先进、产品多元的金融企业。

Qingdao Rural Commercial Bank Company Limited is a joint-stock commercial bank consolidated from Qingdao Rural Credit Cooperative (Rural Cooperative Bank) with the approval of the State Council and CBRC. By the end of 2014, the registered capital of the bank is RMB 5 billion. The bank has established 343 outlets with a staff of more than 5 000. Its total assets have reached RMB 145.1 billion and its total balance of deposits have reached RMB 120.1 billion and total balance of loans have reached RMB 86.2 billion. It is the largest comprehensive, multifunctional regional legal person bank in Qingdao in terms of the number of outlet, staff and range of service.

Qingdao Rural Commercial Bank was restructured from Qingdao Rural Credit Cooperative with a history of more than 60 years. Since the establishment of the first rural credit cooperative in 1951, Qingdao Rural Commercial Bank has been reforming with keen determination, advancing with courage and has completed its historical leap from a credit cooperative to credit cooperative union and then to joint-stock rural commercial bank. In June, 2012, Qingdao Rural Commercial Bank was established through the merger of 9 units including 4 rural cooperative banks (Huafeng, Chengyang, Huangdao and Jimo) and 4 Rural Credit Cooperative Union (Jiaozhou, Jiaonan, Pingdu and Laixi) and Qingdao Union. It has now developed into a financial enterprise of enormous potentiality, stable operation, advanced technology and multiple products.

山东聊城润昌农村商业银行股份有限公司
Shandong Liaocheng Runchang Rural Commercial Bank Company Limited

山东聊城润昌农村商业银行股份有限公司是在原冠县农村信用合作联社基础上，经中国银行业监督管理委员会批准成立的地方性股份制银行机构，是聊城市首家、山东省第五家农村商业银行。2010年10月29日，冠县农村信用社正式更名为聊城润昌农村商业银行。现有23个基层营业网点。

Shandong Liaocheng Ruichang Rural Commercial Bank Company Limited is a regional joint-stock banking institution restructured from former Guan County Credit Cooperative Union with the approval of CBRC. It is the first rural commercial bank in Liaocheng and the fifth rural commercial bank in Shandong province. On October 29, 2010, Guan County Credit Cooperative Union was officially renamed into Liaocheng Ruichang Rural Commercial Bank and has set up 23 outlets of basic level.

山东安丘农村商业银行股份有限公司
Shandong Anqiu Rural Commercial Bank Company Limited

山东安丘农村商业银行股份有限公司在安丘市农村信用合作联社的基础上改制成立，全行注册资本22 700万元，设有11个职能部室，所辖36家支行、22家分理处、1家营业部，在岗干部员工655人，是安丘营业网点最多、服务范围最广、资产规模最大的农村银行业金融机构。

Shandong Anqiu Rural Commercial Bank Company Limited was restructured on the basis of Anqiu Rural Credit Cooperative Union. With a registered capital of RMB 227 000 000, it has set up 11 functional offices, 36 branches, 22 sub-branches, 1 business department with a staff of 655. It is the largest rural banking financial institution in Anqiu in terms of the number of outlet, range of service and capital scale.

山东青州农村商业银行股份有限公司
Shandong Qingzhou Rural Commercial Bank Company Limited

山东青州农村商业银行股份有限公司创立于2001年6月，前身是青州市农村信用合作联社。下辖营业网点74个，在岗员工760余人，是青州市资产规模最大、营业网点最多、综合实力最强的地方性金融机构。截至2014年末，全行各项存款余额208亿元，各项贷款达到144亿元。

Shandong Qingdao Rural Commercial Bank Company Limited, established in June, 2001 was restructured from Qingzhou Rural Credit Cooperative Union. It has set up 74 outlets with a staff of more than 760. It is the largest regional financial institution in Qingzhou in terms of capital scale, the number of outlet and comprehensive strength. By the end of 2014, the total deposits of the bank has reached RMB 20.8 billion and its total loans have reached RMB 14.4 billion.

山东费县农村商业银行股份有限公司
Shandong Fei County Rural Commercial Bank Company Limited

费县农村商业银行是2011年12月16日在费县农村合作银行的基础上改制成立的，是临沂市首家农村商业银行。现有员工506人，下辖36个营业网点，是全县机构、人员和信贷规模最大的金融机构。

Fei County Rural Commercial Bank Company Limited was restructured from Fei County Rural Cooperative Bank on December 16, 2011. It is the first rural commercial bank in Linyi with a staff of 506 and 36 outlets. It is the largest financial institution in the county in terms of number of staff and credit scale.

潍坊农商银行
Weifang Rural Commercial Bank

潍坊农村商业银行股份有限公司
Wiefang Rural Commercial Bank Company Limited

潍坊农村商业银行股份有限公司是根据省、市农村金融机构改革意见，在原潍城、奎文、坊子、寒亭四区农村信用合作联社基础上以新设合并方式发起设立的股份制商业银行，于2012年7月28日召开创立大会、11月15日挂牌开业，服务范围覆盖辖内潍城、奎文、坊子、寒亭、高新、滨海、峡山七个区，下设14家一级支行、1家营业部，109家二级支行，注册资本21.25亿元，在岗员工1 863人。截至2014年末，全行资产总额412亿元，其中各项贷款余额215.8亿元，负债总额377亿元，其中各项存款余额335亿元。

Wiefang Rural Commercial Bank Company Limited is a joint-stock commercial bank established through merger of four rural credit cooperative unions including Weicheng, Kuiwen, Fangzi and Hanting according to the opinion on reforming provincial and urban rural financial institutions. Its opening ceremony was launched on July 28, 2012 and started its business on November 15. It provides services for 7 districts including Weicheng, Kuiwen, Fangzi, Hanting, Gaoxin, Binhai and Xiashan with 14 tier one branches, 1 business department, 109 tier two branches. It has a registered capital of RMB 2.125 billion and a staff of 1863.By the end of 2014, the total assets of the bank has reached RMB 41.2 billion with balance of loans of RMB 21.58 billion, and total indebtedness of RMB 37.7 billion with balance of deposits of RMB 33.5 billion.

烟台农村商业银行股份有限公司
Yantai Rural Commercial Bank Co., Ltd.

烟台农村商业银行股份有限公司是在烟台市原芝罘、莱山、开发区、福山、牟平5家城区信用社的基础上整合组建起来的股份制商业银行，于2012年12月26日正式获得中国银行业监督管理委员会山东监管局开业批复（银监鲁准〔2012〕915号），2013年1月18日正式挂牌开业。烟台农商银行册资本25亿元，所有者权益34.55亿元，资本充足率为15.81%。截至2014年底，烟台农商银行辖内11家一级支行，57家二级支行，43家分理处。

外汇业务：外汇存款；外汇贷款；外汇汇款；外汇拆借；国际结算；资信调查、咨询和见证业务。

Yantai Rural Commercial Bank Co.,Ltd. was established on Jan 8th 2013,which formerly existed as Rural Credit Cooperative Union of Yantai Zhifu, Rural Credit Cooperative Union of Yantai Laishan, Rural Credit Cooperative Union of Yantai Development Zone, Rural Credit Cooperative Union of Yantai Fushan, Rural Credit Cooperative Union of Yantai Muping,with a registered capital of 2.5 billion Yuan (about 403 million dollars). The bank has 11 first-level branches, 57 second-level branches, and 1767 employees.

Principal Banking Services: bills of exchange, letters of credit,corporate finance, correspondent banking, money markets, mortgaes, documentary credit, factoring,saving accounts-personal, saving account-specialty, foreign exchange, home equity loans,international settlements, internet banking,etc..

山东临朐农村商业银行股份有限公司
Shandong Linqu Rural Commercial Bank Company Limited

山东临朐农村商业银行股份有限公司是在原临朐县农村信用合作联社的基础上发起设立的，注册资本22 558.5万元人民币，下辖1家营业部、49家支行，在岗员工612人，是临朐县营业网点最多、服务范围最广、资产规模最大的综合性、多功能地方金融机构。截至2014年末，各项存款余额123.96亿元，各项贷款余额83.93亿元。

Shandong Linqu Rural Commercial Bank Company Limited is established on the basis of Linqu Rural Credit Cooperative Union. With RMB 225 585 000 registered capital, the bank has set up 1 business department, 49 branches with a staff of 612. It is the largest comprehensive and multifunctional regional financial institution in Linqu in terms of the number of outlet, range of service and capital scale. By the end of 2014, its total balance of deposits have reached RMB 12.396 billion and its total balance of loans have reached RMB 8.393 billion.

山东昌邑农村商业银行股份有限公司
SDRC CHANGYI RURAL COMMERCIAL BANK CO., LTD.

山东昌邑农村商业银行股份有限公司
Shandong Changyi Rural Commercial Bank Company Limited

山东昌邑农村商业银行股份有限公司（以下简称昌邑农商银行）于2012年12月挂牌成立，是在原昌邑市农村信用合作联社基础上改制组建的股份制商业银行，现有在岗员工604人，营业网点58个，包括营业部1家、一级支行20家、二级支行10家、三级支行27家，是昌邑市存贷款余额最高、营业机构和从业人员最多、服务范围最广的商业银行。截至2014年末，各项存款余额129.18亿元，各项贷款余额87.51亿元，居昌邑金融机构首位。

Shandong Changyi Rural Commercial Bank Company Limited (hereinafter refer to as Changyi Rural Commercial Bank), established in December, 2012, was founded by the restructuring of Changyi City Rural Credit Cooperative Union. It now has a staff of 604, 58 branches, 1 business department, 20 tier one branches and 10 tier two branches and 27 tier three branches, which make the bank the largest commercial bank in term of balance of deposits and loans, branches, staff and range of service. By the end of 2014, its balance of deposits have reached RMB 12.918 billion and its balance of loans have reached RMB 8.751 billion, which ranks No.1 in the financial institutions in Changyi.

武汉农村商业银行股份有限公司
Wuhan Rural Commercial Bank Company Limited

武汉农村商业银行是国务院、中国银监会批准成立的全国第一家副省级省会城市农村商业银行，于2009年9月9日正式开业。目前，全行200余个网点遍布城乡各地，并先后在湖北省内设立了咸宁分行、宜昌分行、黄冈分行，在江苏、广东、云南、海南、湖北五省设立了30余家村镇银行。截至2014年12月末，全行总资产519.90202亿元，存款总额1 202.05773亿元，贷款总额840.34485亿元。

Wuhan Rural Commercial Bank, starting its business on September 9, 2009, is the first subsidiary provincial level provincial capital rural commercial bank approved by the State Council and CBRC. At present, the bank has set up more than 200 branches covering cities and towns and has set up Xianning Branch, Yichang Branch, Huangguang branch in Hunan province and more than 30 village banks in five provinces including Jiangsu, Guangdong, Yunnan, Hainan and Hubei. By the end of 2014, the total assets of the bank has reached RMB 51.990202 billion with total deposits of RMB 120.205773 billion and total loans of RMB 84.034485 billion.

浏阳农商银行

湖南浏阳农村商业银行股份有限公司
Hunan Liuyang Rural Commercial Bank Company Limited

浏阳农商银行，全称为湖南浏阳农村商业银行股份有限公司，其前身是诞生于20世纪50年代的浏阳市农村信用社。是浏阳市资金实力最强、服务网点最多、经营规模最大的金融机构，也是该市唯一一家法人银行。

Liuyang Rural Commercial Bank, with its full name as Hunan Liuyang Rural Commercial Bank Company Limited, is formerly known as Liuyang City Rural Credit Cooperative established in the 1950s. It is the largest financial institution in Liuyang in terms of capital strength, number of outlet and operational scale and is the only legal person bank in the city.

东莞农村商业银行股份有限公司
Dongguan Rural Commercial Bank Company Limited

东莞农村商业银行是经中国银行业监督管理委员会批准，在东莞市农村信用合作联社基础上整体改制设立的，具有独立法人资格的总行级地方性股份制商业银行，总部设在广东省东莞市。改制后，原东莞农信社的全部资产、负债、机构和人员依法由设立后的东莞农村商业银行承继，注册资本43.13亿元，下设135家支行、390家分理处。

Dongguan Rural Commercial Bank is a regional joint-stock commercial bank of Head Office level with independent legal person qualification established by restructuring on the basis of Dongguan City Rural Credit Cooperative Union. Its Head Officc is located in Dongguan, Guangdong. After the restructuring, the total assets, liabilities, institution and staff of former Dongguan Rural Credit Cooperative are all inherited by Dongguan Rural Commercial Bank. With a registered capital of RMB 4.313 billion, it has set up 135 branches and 390 sub-branches.

南海农商银行
NANHAI RURAL COMMERCIAL BANK

广东南海农村商业银行股份有限公司
Guangdong Nanhai Rural Commercial Bank Company Limited

南海农商银行的前身是南海农村信用社，至今已有60多年发展历史，是南海区内唯一一家法人银行机构。2011年12月成功完成改制，更名为南海农商银行。现已经成长为南海区从业人员及营业网点最多、信贷规模最大、服务范围最广的银行，是华南地区具有较强竞争力和影响力的中小银行之一。截至2014年末，营业网点42个，资产总额1205.72亿元，各项存款余额925.51亿元，各项贷款余额631.43亿元。

Nanhai Rural Commercial Bank was formerly known as Nanhai Rural Credit Cooperative, with a history of more than 60 years, which is the only legal person banking institution in Nanhai. Its restructuring was completed in December, 2011 and was renamed into Nanhai Rural Commercial Bank. It has now become the largest bank in Nanhai in terms of staff, number of outlet, credit loan scale and range of service, which is one of the small and medium banks which strong competitiveness and influence in Southern China. By the end of 2014, it has set up 42 outlets and its total assets have reached RMB 120.572 billion with total balance of deposits of RMB 92.551 billion and total balance of loans of RMB 63.143 billion.

广东顺德农村商业银行股份有限公司
Guangdong Shunde Rural Commercial Bank Company Limited

广东顺德农村商业银行股份有限公司总部位于广东省佛山市顺德区，前身是始建于1952年，具有60多年发展历史的顺德农村信用合作社，是顺德历史最悠久的合作制金融机构之一。2009年12月23日，佛山顺德农村商业银行股份有限公司正式开业；2012年11月13日，正式更名为广东顺德农村商业银行股份有限公司。目前，该行设有分支机构328家，从业人员3 900多人。在2014年度英国《银行家》杂志全球1 000家大银行综合排名第339位，在国内银行综合排名第37位。截至2014年末，该行总资产跨越两千亿元大关，达2 069.44亿元，各项存款余额1 403.32亿元，各项贷款余额1 018.59亿元，人民币存贷款市场份额稳居顺德同业首位。2014年实现经营利润44.27亿元，缴纳税收11.4亿元。截至2014年末，资本净额达216亿元。外汇业务发展迅速，已与全球500多家知名银行总行建立了代理行关系，代理网络遍布全球五大洲。

The Head office of Guangdong Shunde Rural Commercial Bank Company Limited is located in the Shunde District, Foshan City, Guangdong Province. It was restructured from Shunde Rural Credit Cooperative established in 1952, with a history of more than 60 years, which make it one of the cooperative financial institutions with longest history in Shunde. Foshan Shunde Rural Commercial Bank Company limited officially started its business on December 23, 2009, and was renamed into Guangdong Shunde Rural Commercial Bank Company Limited on November 13，2012. At present, this bank has set up 328 branches with a staff of more than 3 900. According to the rank of banks provided by the Banker, a Britain published magazine, this bank ranks No.339 among the 1 000 banks around the world, and ranks No.37 among banks in China. By the end of 2014, the total assets of the bank have exceeded RMB 200 billion and reached RMB 206.944 billion, with RMB 140.332 billion total balance of deposits and RMB 101.859 billion balance of loans, and its market shares for RMB deposits and loans has been remaining the top among the same business in Shunde. In 2014, it has realized RMB 4.427 billion operation profits and paid RMB 1.14 billion taxes. By the end of 2014, its net capital has reached RMB 21.6 billion. Its foreign exchange business has been developing rapidly and the bank has established agency relationship with more than 500 banks around the world and its agency network has covered five continents of the world.

广州农商银行
GUANGZHOU RURAL COMMERCIAL BANK

广州农村商业银行股份有限公司

Guangzhou Rural Commercial Bank Company Limited

广州农村商业银行的前身是始建于1951年，至今已有50多年发展历史的广州市农村信用合作社。1998年9月，广州市农村信用合作社联合社成立。2006年11月，广州市农村信用合作联社开业，顺利完成统一法人体制改革。2009年12月11日，广州农村商业银行股份有限公司正式开业，总行设在广州。截至2014年末，下辖营业网点600余个，遍布广州城乡，网点数列广州地区银行同业机构首位。截至2014年12月末，该行资产规模4 666.08亿元，存款总额3 544.39亿元，各项贷款总额1 859.81亿元。在2014年英国《银行家》发布的“全球1 000家大银行”榜单居第210位，国内上榜银行第24位。

Guangzhou Rural Commercial Bank was restructured from Guangzhou Rural Credit Cooperative established in 1951 with more than 50 years of history. In September, 1998, Guangzhou Rural Credit Cooperative Union was founded. In November, 2006, Guangzhou Rural Credit Cooperative Union started its business and smoothly completed its structural reform into a unified legal person. On December 11, 2009, Guangzhou Rural Commercial Bank Company Limited officially started its business with its Head Office in Guangzhou. By the end of 2014, the bank has set up more than 600 outlets covering urban and rural areas of Guangzhou and its number of outlcts rank the top in the banking industry in Guangzhou. By the end of 2014, its total assets have reached RMB 466.608 billion with RMB 354.439 billion total balance of deposit and RMB 185.981 billion balance of loan. According to the rank of banks provided by the Banker, a Britain published magazine, this bank ranks No.210 among the top 1 000 banks around the world and ranks No.24 among banks in China.

惠州农村商业银行股份有限公司
Huizhou Rural Commercial Bank Company Limited

惠州农村商业银行股份有限公司为股份有限公司形式的农村商业银行，实行一级法人、统一核算、分级管理、授权经营的管理体制，注册资本近12亿元，总资产达150亿元，从业人员1 200多人；共有营业网点108个，基本覆盖惠州4个区城乡。

Huizhou Rural Commercial Bank Company Limited is a rural commercial bank with the form of limited liability company. It carries on the management system of tier one legal person, unified accounting, level-to-level management and authorized operation. Its registered capital is nearly RMB 1.2 billion and has a total asset of RMB 15 billion and a staff of more than 1 200. It has set up 109 outlets, covering urban and rural areas of 4 districts in Huizhou.

江门融和农商银行
Jiangmen Ronghe Rural Commercial Bank
融财富·和万家

江门融和农村商业银行股份有限公司
Jiangmen Ronghe Rural Commercial Bank Company Limited

江门融和农村商业银行由成立于1952年的广东省江门市区农村信用合作联社于2011年整体改制而成。截至2014年末，各项存款余额209亿元，同比增长11.60%，居江门市区第4位；资产总额273 亿元，增长13.48%；各项财务收入17亿元，同比增长27.02%，资本充足率13.92%，拨备覆盖率277.74%，流动性比率46.6%。

江门融和农村商业银行SWIFT码为：JRRCCNBJ。

该行自2009年9月开展自营外汇业务，目前代理行40余家，已在香港中银、香港工银行亚洲、纽约中银等银行开立账户行，可开展美元、港元、欧元、日元、加拿大元、澳大利亚元以及新加坡元的清算以及结售汇业务；可提供美元、港元资金拆借、贸易融资以及福费廷买入业务。

外汇业务经营范围：外汇存款、外汇贷款、外汇汇款、国际结算、同业外汇拆借、代客外汇买卖、外汇票据贴现，即期结售汇业务并代理速汇金公司速汇金业务。

Jiangmen Ronghe Rural Commercial Bank was founded in 2011 from Jiangmen Rural Credit Cooperative Union which founded in 1952. By the end of 2014，the bank's total Deposit Balance has reached RMB 20.9 billion, with year-on-year growth of 11.60 percent，Ranking the fourth in jiangmen's all finance institutions; whose total assets has reached RMB 27.3 billion, with year-on-year growth of 13.48 percent; The financial income has reached RMB 1.7 billion, with year-on-year growth of 27.02 percent, the capital adequacy ratio has reached 13.92 percent，the provision coverage ratio has reached 277.74% and liquidity ratio has reached 46.6%.

Swift code: JRRCCNBJ.

Since in the year 2009 on September, the bank have carried out the service of foreign exchange business, up to now, it has set up corresponding relationship with more than forty banks from all over the world, at the same time it has opened accounts with Bank of China HongKong Ltd., ICBC Asia and Bank of China New York branch etc., it can provide clearing and foreign exchange of 7 currencies, including USD dollar, Hong Kong dollar, euro, yen, Canadian dollar, Australian dollar and Singapore dollar; also provide foreign exchange interbank lending, trade finance and forfaiting buying business with USD and HKD .

Foreign currency deposits, foreign currency loans, foreign exchange remittances, international settlement, foreign exchange interbank lending, valet foreign exchange trading, foreign exchange bills discounted, spot foreign exchange business and as a agent of MoneyGram to conduct MoneyGram business.

江门新会农村商业银行股份有限公司
Jiangmen Xinhui Rural Commercial Bank Company Limited

江门新会农村商业银行股份有限公司由成立于1952年的原江门市新会区农村信用合作联社改制成立，于2011年12月12日正式挂牌营业。

新会农商银行注册资本13.8亿元人民币，资产总额接近430亿元，下辖122个营业网点，拥有职工1 500多人，提供定活期存款、企业贷款、个人信贷、结算业务、国际结算、国外保函、代收代付、代理业务、电子银行、理财服务、保管箱等多种金融服务。截至2014年末，新会农商银行在新会区存、贷款份额排名均为第一，是江门市区规模最大、发展最快、服务覆盖面最广的农村金融机构。

江门新会农村商业银行股份有限公司国际业务于2013年12月12日正式对外开办，截至2014年末，外币存款余额为3 708.19万美元，办理国际结算量4.58亿美元，结售汇量达3.12亿美元，外币贷款余额为7 986万美元。

外汇业务经营范围：江门新会农村商业银行股份有限公司外汇业务经营范围：外汇存款、外汇贷款、外汇汇款、国际结算、同业外汇拆借、代客外汇买卖、外汇票据贴现。

Jiangmen Xinhui Rural Commercial Bank Company Limited (hereafter referred to as XHRCB), evolved from Jiangmen Xinhui Rural Credit Cooperative which was established in 1952, ran for business on 12th December 2011.

The registered capital of XHRCB is 1.38 billion RMB, and the total assets approach 34 billion RMB. XHRCB has 122 branches and more than 1 500 employees. We provide fixed term deposit, current deposit, enterprise loan, personal credit, settlement service, international settlement, international letter of guarantee, bill payments, agent service, e-banking, financing service, safe deposit box and other financial services. At the end of 2014, XHRCB ranked NO.1 in both deposit and loan market share of Xinhui. XHRCB is a rural financial institution that is the largest, fastest growing, and has the widest coverage of services in Jiangmen downtown.

The international business department of Jiangmen Xinhui Rural Commercial Bank Company Limited run for business on 12th December 2013. At the end of 2014, the balance held on deposit of the bank's foreign currency was USD 37.08 million, the amount of international settlement service was USD 458 million, the amount for foreign exchange trading was USD 312 million, and the balance held on foreign currency loan was USD 79.86 million.

The service of international business in Jiangmen Xinhui Rural Commercial Bank Company Limited includes: foreign exchange deposit, foreign exchange loan, remittance, international settlement, inter-bank foreign exchange borrowing (lending), valet foreign exchange trading, discounting bill of foreign exchange.

揭阳农村商业银行
JIEYANG RURAL COMMERCIAL BANK

广东揭阳农村商业银行股份有限公司
Guangdong Jieyang Rural Commercial Bank Company Limited

揭阳榕城农村商业银行成立于2010年6月29日，是在原揭阳市区农村信用合作联社的基础上组建而成的股份制地方性金融机构，前身是始建于1952年，具有50多年发展历史的揭阳农村信用合作社，是揭阳历史最悠久的合作制金融机构之一。揭阳榕城农村商业银行总行设在揭阳市东山区。目前，总行内设14个部门，下辖13家支行、46家分理处，分布在揭阳市榕城、东山、试验区三个市辖区，是市区营业网点最多的金融机构。

Jieyang Rural Commercial Bank is a regional joint-stock financial institution founded on the basis of former Jieyang City Rural Credit Cooperative Union on June 29, 2010. It is formerly known as Jieyang Rural Credit Cooperative founded in 1952 with a history of more than 50 years, which is one of the cooperative financial institutions of longest history in Jieyang. Jieyang Rongcheng Rural Commercial Bank has its Head Office located in Dongshan District of Jieyang. At present, its Head Office has set up 14 department with 13 branches, 46 sub-branches under its jurisdiction, which are distributed in 3 districts including Rongcheng, Dongshan and Shiyan. It is the financial institution with most number of outlet in the city.

珠海农商银行
ZRCB

珠海农村商业银行股份有限公司
Zhuhai Rural Commercial Bank Co., Ltd.

珠海农村商业银行股份有限公司是珠海地区历史最悠久、营业网点最多、服务最基层的本土法人银行。珠海农商银行在2014年4月正式推出国际业务，同年被评为珠海市最具成长性外汇银行奖及年度珠海辖区银行执行外汇管理规定情况考核被评为A类银行。

珠海农商银行将充分发挥多元化金融服务和跨境金融服务优势，借助横琴区位优势和“先行先试”的政策优势，进一步加强海外代理行渠道，打破银行传统模式，走创新之路，打造全球最好的社区零售银行。

Zhuhai Rural Commercial Bank Co., Ltd. is the oldest local corporate banking with the most outlets and basic service in Zhuhai. In April, 2014, Zhuhai rural commercial bank officially launched international business, and was rated as the most progressive of foreign exchange bank and was awarded as class A bank in the annual assessment of bank implementation of the foreign exchange management in Zhuhai in the same year.

Zhuhai rural commercial bank will give full play to the advantages of diversified financial services and cross-border financial services, and with the help of the location advantages of Hengqin free trade area and the “pilot” policy advantages to further strengthen the channels of overseas correspondent banks, breaking the traditional model of bank, taking the road of innovation, and to create the best community retail bank in the world.

广东农信 GDRC | 新兴农商银行 XINXING RURAL COMMERCIAL BANK

广东新兴农村商业银行股份有限公司
Guangdong Xinxing Rural Commercial Bank Company Limited

广东新兴农村商业银行是在原新兴县农村信用合作联社的基础上组建而成的股份制地方性金融机构，其前身是始建于1952年，具有60多年发展历史的新兴县农村信用社，是新兴县历史最悠久的金融机构之一。新兴农商银行于2012年11月1日正式挂牌开业，是云浮市第1家成功改制的农商银行。新兴农商银行内设13个部门，下辖26家支行、3家离行式自助银行。广东新兴农村商业银行是新兴县资产规模最大、网点覆盖面最广、从业人员最多的金融机构。

Guangdong Xinxing Rural Commercial Bank Company Limited is a regional joint-stock financial institution established on the basis of former Xinxing Rural Credit Cooperative Union. It was originally established as Xinxing Rural Credit Cooperative in 1952 with a history of more than 60 years, which is one of the financial institutions of longest history in Xinxing County. Xinxing Rural Commercial Bank was officially opened on November 1, 2012, which is the first rural commercial bank successfully restructured in Yunfu city. Xinxing Rural Commercial Bank has set up 13 departments, with 26 branches and 3 off-bank self-service banks. Guangdong Xinxing Rural Commercial Bank is the largest financial institution in Xinxing County in terms of capital scale, coverage of outlet and number of staff.

深圳农村商业银行
Shenzhen Rural Commercial Bank

深圳农村商业银行成立于2005年12月9日，是经中国银监会批准，在深圳市农村信用社基础上改制组建而成的股份制农村商业银行。截至2014年底，全行总资产折合人民币1 590.26亿元，2014年度实现净利润人民币26.15亿元，净资产收益率（ROE）22.29%。在英国《银行家》杂志2014年发布的“世界银行1 000强”中，排名第434位。截至2014年底，全行近200个营业网点遍布深圳全市，网点数量居深圳银行同业首位。截至2014年底，广西地区支行共有8个营业网点，村镇银行共有19个营业网点。

Restructured from Shenzhen Rural Credit Cooperative, Shenzhen Rural Commercial Bank is a joint-stock rural commercial bank established on December 9, 2005 with the approval of CBRC. By the end of 2014, the total assets of the bank has reached RMB 159.026 billion. In 2014, the bank has realized RMB 2.615 billion net profits with net ROE of 22.29%. According to the rank of banks provided by the Banker, a Britain published magazine, this bank ranks No.434 among the top 1 000 banks around the world. By the end of 2014, the nearly 200 outlet of the bank has covered the whole Shenzhen city. Its number of outlet ranks the top among the banks in Shenzhen. By the end of 2014, the bank has set up 8 branches in Guangxi and its village bank has established 19 outlets.

CDRCB 成都农商银行

成都农村商业银行股份有限公司
Chengdu Rural Commercial Bank Company Limited

2010年1月15日，成都农商银行挂牌开业。2011年注册资本达到100亿元，位居全国农商银行首位。目前，全行拥有32家分支机构，635个营业网点，并投资设立了39家村镇银行以及邦银金融租赁公司。

成都农商银行以服务“三农”、中小企业和地方经济建设为使命，不断开拓创新，经营实力进一步增强，发展步伐逐步加快。在英国《银行家》评选的2014年全球1 000家大银行中排名第277位，先后荣获“2014年区域性商业银行最佳网上银行”、“最具发展潜力中小银行”等多项荣誉。

2012年，成都农商银行成立国际业务部，开展出口跟单托收、进口押汇、对公结售汇等数十项外汇业务。截至2015年4月底，已与国内外629家银行机构建立代理行关系，覆盖范围超过80个国家和地区。

外汇业务经营范围：即期结售汇、外汇贷款、外币汇款、资本项下外汇业务、外币现钞、国际结算等。

Chengdu Rural Commercial Bank was officially opened on January 15, 2010. Its registered capital has reached RMB 10 billion in 2011, ranking the first in the rural commercial banks in China. At present, the bank has set up 32 branches with 635 outlets and has invested in 39 village banks and Bangyin Financial Leasing Company.

Chengdu Rural Commercial Bank dedicated to serving “agriculture, rural areas and farmers”, medium and small enterprises and local economic construction. With continuous expansion and innovation, its economic strength has improved and its development pace has sped up. In the 1 000 banks selected by “The Banker”, a British magazine, this bank ranks 277. And the bank has received many awards including “Best Online Bank of Regional Commercial Bank in 2014”, “The Most Potential Medium and

Small Banks”.

In 2012, Chengdu Rural Commercial Bank has set up International Business Department and started more than 10 foreign exchange businesses including export documentary collection, import bill advance, settlement and sale of exchange to the public, etc. By the end of April, 2015, the bank has established agency relationship with 629 domestic and foreign banks covering 80 countries and regions.

Scope of business of foreign exchange transactions: at sight settlement and sale of exchange, foreign exchange transaction under capital, foreign exchange cash, international settlement, etc..

附录一

2014年中国外汇管理大事记

2014 NIAN ZHONGGUO WAIHUI GUANLI DASHIJI

1月

10日

《国家外汇管理局关于进一步改进和调整资本项目外汇管理改革政策的通知》（汇发[2014]2号）发布，通过简化融资租赁公司对外债权管理，简化境外投资者受让境内不良资产外汇管理等措施，进一步深化资本项目外汇管理改革，推进简政放权，促进贸易投资便利化。

21日

《国家外汇管理局关于印发〈外债转贷款外汇管理规定〉的通知》（汇发[2014]5号）发布，参照国内外汇贷款管理方式，取消账户开立、还本付息和结售汇等环节的限制，转贷款债务人逐笔登记转变为债权人集中登记，简化外债转贷款外汇管理。

2月

26日

易智付科技（北京）有限公司、北京银联商务有限公司、网银在线（北京）科技有限公司、拉卡拉支付有限公司、资和信电子支付有限公司5家支付机构通过验收，成为第二批开展跨境电子商务外汇支付业务试点机构。

3月

5日

《国家外汇管理局关于边境地区贸易外汇管理有关问题的通知》（汇发[2014]12号）发布，规范和便利边境贸易结算，促进我国与周边国家边境贸易健康发展。

20日

《国家外汇管理局关于核定2014年度境内机构短期外债余额指标有关问题的通

知》（汇发[2014]14号）发布，2014年4月8日施行，核定部分中资银行2014年度指标，指标调整应重点向服务中小企业的银行倾斜，并适当关注中资企业的对外短期融资需求。

4月

8日

《国家外汇管理局关于发布〈金融机构外汇业务数据采集规范（1.0版）〉的通知》（汇发[2014]18号）发布，为加强外汇业务数据采集管理，便利金融机构数据报送提供了制度保障。

16日

《国家外汇管理局关于印发〈涉外收支交易分类与代码（2014版）〉的通知》（汇发[2014]21号）发布，根据国际货币基金组织最新国际统计标准（《国际收支与国际投资头寸手册（第六版）》），全面修订2004年实施的《涉外收支交易分类与代码》。

18日

国家外汇管理局印发《跨国公司外汇资金集中运营管理规定（试行）》的通知（汇发[2014]23号），2014年6月1日起施行，创新跨国公司账户体系；进一步简化单证审核；便利跨国公司融通资金；资本金、外债结汇采负面清单管理；加强统计监测防控风险。

22日

《国家外汇管理局 海关总署关于印发〈银行调运外币现钞进出境管理规定〉的通知》（汇发[2014]24号）发布，进一步规范银行调运外币现钞进出境管理。

5月

4日

根据《国际收支和国际投资头寸手册（第六版）》要求，完成国际收支网上申报系统、监测分析系统、资本项目信息系统、账户系统等系统的交易编码转换上线工作。

12日

《关于发布〈跨境担保外汇管理规定〉的通知》（汇发[2014]29号）发布，合理界定跨境担保的外汇管理范围和监管责任边界，取消或大幅度缩小跨境担保的数量控制范围和登记范围，以登记为主要管理手段，取消所有事前审批，简化和明确跨境担保外汇管理。

6月

23日

《国家外汇管理局关于印发〈银行对客户办理人民币与外汇衍生产品业务管理规定〉的通知》（汇发[2014]34号）发布，自8月1日起实施支持产品创新、完善实需管理、简化市场准入等外汇衍生产品市场发展新措施，更好满足市场主体管理汇率风险需求。

25日

《银行办理结售汇业务管理办法》（中国人民银行令[2014]2号）发布，降低银行结售汇市场准入条件，简化市场准入管理。

7月

1日

《中国人民银行关于银行间外汇市场交易汇价和银行挂牌汇价管理有关事项的通知》（银发[2014]188号）发布，取消银行对客户美元挂牌买卖价差限制，由银行根据市场供求自主定价，实现人民币对所有外币挂牌汇价管理的完全市场化。

4日

《国家外汇管理局关于在部分地区开展外商投资企业外汇资本金结汇管理方式改革试点有关问题的通知》（汇发[2014]36号）发布，将外商投资企业外汇资本金意愿结汇改革试点扩大到天津滨海新区等其他16个国家级经济、金融改革发展试验区，便利外商投资企业经营与资金运作需要。

《国家外汇管理局关于境内居民通过特殊目的公司境外投融资及返程投资外汇管理有关问题的通知》（汇发[2014]37号）发布，对返程投资外汇管理政策进行了大幅改革，进一步便利境内居民跨境投融资活动。

10日

中国外汇交易中心发布《银行间外汇市场职业操守和市场惯例指引》和《银行间外汇市场职业操守和市场惯例专业委员会工作章程》，促进公平竞争、诚信有序的外汇市场发展环境。

9月

1日

《对外金融资产、负债及交易统计制度》正式实施。

11日

《国家外汇管理局关于调整银行执行外汇管理规定情况考核周期的通知》（汇发[2014]42号）发布，进一步提高银行执行外汇管理规定情况考核工作的有效性。

22日

国家外汇管理局发布《关于公布废止和失效34件外汇管理规范性文件的通知》（汇发[2014]44号），2014年9月25日施行，宣布废止和失效外汇管理规范性文件34件，其中废止18件、宣布失效16件。

26日

《国际收支和国际投资头寸手册（第六版）》系列解读材料发布，以方便社会公众和申报主体学习了解最新要求，更好地配合国际收支统计制度和系统建设实施工作。

10月

10日

正式启动对外金融资产负债及交易数据、个人外币现钞存取数据和银行自身外债数据（新接口）采集。

12月

5日

《国家外汇管理局关于调整金融机构进入银行间外汇市场有关管理政策的通知》（汇发[2014]48号）发布，自2015年1月1日起取消对金融机构进入银行间外汇市场的事前准入许可，进一步发挥市场机制的调节作用。

9日

国家外汇管理局管理检查司与人民银行征信中心签署合作备忘录，自2015年1月1日起处罚的企事业单位实质性外汇违规信息将纳入金融业信用信息基础数据库。

15日

国家外汇管理局配合公安机关在浙江侦破“9.16”特大地下钱庄案。

25日

《国家外汇管理局关于印发〈银行办理结售汇业务管理办法实施细则〉的通知》（汇发[2014]53号）发布，进一步便利银行办理结售汇业务。

附录二

中国外汇指定银行通讯录

ZHONGGUO WAIHUI ZHIDING YINHANG TONGXUNLU

政策性银行及大型商业银行

中国工商银行股份有限公司

通讯地址：中国北京市西城区复兴门内大街55号

邮编：100140

客服电话：95588

中国农业银行股份有限公司

联系地址：北京东城区建国门内大街69号

邮编：100005

客服电话：95599

中国银行股份有限公司

总行地址：中国北京市复兴门内大街1号

邮编：100818

服务热线：95566

中国建设银行股份有限公司

总行地址：中国北京西城区金融大街25号

邮编：100033

客户服务热线：95533

交通银行股份有限公司

总部地址：中国上海市浦东新区银城中路188号

邮编：200120

服务热线：95559

中信银行股份有限公司

地址：北京市东城区朝阳门北大街9号

邮编：100010

客户中心：95558

招商银行股份有限公司

地址：深圳市福田区深南大道7088号招商银行大厦

邮编：518040

服务热线：95555

中国光大银行

地址：北京市西城区太平桥大街25号中国光大中心

邮编：100033

客户服务热线：95595

华夏银行股份有限公司

地址：北京市东城区建国门内大街22号华夏银行大厦

邮编：100005

电话：95577

广发银行股份有限公司

地址：广东省广州市东风东路713号

邮编：510080

电话：95508

平安银行股份有限公司

地址：中国广东省深圳市深南东路5047号

邮编：518001

服务热线：95511

兴业银行股份有限公司

办公地址：中国福州市湖东路154 号

邮编：350003

客服热线：95561

中国民生银行股份有限公司

联系地址：中国北京市西城区复兴门内大街 2 号民生银行大厦

邮编：100031

24小时客服热线：95568

对公专线：400-689-5568

上海浦东发展银行

通信地址：上海市中山东一路12号

邮编：200002

服务热线：95528

恒丰银行股份有限公司

地址：中国·烟台市南大街248号

邮编：264000

客服热线：400-813-8888

浙商银行股份有限公司

地址：浙江省杭州市庆春路 288号

邮编：310006

客服电话：95527

渤海银行股份有限公司

地址：天津市河西区马场道201-205号

邮编：300204

服务咨询电话：400-888-8811

中国进出口银行

地址：北京西城区复兴门内大街30号

邮编：100031

电话：(010)83579988

中国农业发展银行

地址：北京市西城区月坛北街甲2号

邮编：100045

电话：010-68085370

国家开发银行

地址：中国北京市西城区复兴门内大街18号

邮编：100031

电话：010-68306688

中国邮政储蓄银行

地址：北京市西城区金融大街3号

邮编：100808

客服电话：95580

城市商业银行

北京银行股份有限公司

总行地址：北京市西城区金融大街丙17号

邮编：100033

客服电话：95526

上海银行股份有限公司

办公地址：中国上海市浦东新区银城中路168号

邮编：200120

客服热线：95594

天津银行股份有限公司

地址：天津市河西区友谊路15号

邮编：300201

客服电话：4006960296

重庆银行股份有限公司

地址：重庆市渝中区邹容路153号

邮编：400010

联系电话：（023）63836229

重庆三峡银行股份有限公司

办公地址：重庆市渝中区民权路 107 号

邮编：400010

客服热线：96968

河北银行股份有限公司

地址：河北省石家庄市平安北大街28号

邮编：050011

客服电话：400-612-9999或0311-96368

唐山银行股份有限公司

地址：唐山市新华西道66号

邮编：063000

客服电话：0315-96368

廊坊银行股份有限公司

地址：河北省廊坊市广阳道31号

邮编：065000

电话：400-620-0099、0316-96368

邯郸银行股份有限公司

地址：河北省邯郸市滏东北大街245号远大国门B座（北院）
　　　河北省邯郸市和平路东段367号（南院）

邮编：056005

客户服务：96368（邯郸）4000196368（全国）

晋商银行股份有限公司

地址：山西省太原市长风西街丽华大厦A座

邮编：030021

电客户服务热线：95105588

包商银行股份有限公司

地址：内蒙古自治区包头市青山区钢铁大街6号

邮编：014030

客服热线：95352

内蒙古银行股份有限公司

总行地址：呼和浩特市赛罕区腾飞南路33号

邮编：010010

客服电话：40005-96019

鞍山银行股份有限公司

地址：鞍山市铁东区五一路15号

邮编：114001

电话：0412-2214300

锦州银行股份有限公司

地址：辽宁省锦州市松山新区科技路68号

邮编：121013

电话：4006696178、96178（锦州）

抚顺银行股份有限公司

地址：辽宁省抚顺市新抚区永宁街2号

邮编：113008

24小时服务热线、电话银行：024-96663

辽阳银行股份有限公司

联系地址：辽阳市白塔区民主路21号

邮政编号：111000

客服热线：0419-96678、400-800-8555

营口银行股份有限公司

地址：辽宁省营口市沿海产业基地新海大街99号16F

邮编：115000

电话：40078-96178

丹东银行股份有限公司

注册地址：辽宁省丹东市振兴区鸭绿江大街 198-1 号

邮编：118000

服务热线：4007096658

盛京银行股份有限公司

地址：沈阳市沈河区北站路109号

邮编：110013

服务热线：024-96666、400-699-6666

阜新银行股份有限公司

地址：辽宁省阜新市细河区中华路51号

邮编：123000

客服电话：96665

葫芦岛银行股份有限公司

地址：辽宁省葫芦岛市龙湾大街33号

邮编：125000

客服电话：96656（辽宁省内），40011-96656（全国）

大连银行股份有限公司

地址：大连市中山区中山路88号

邮编：116001

客户服务热线：4006640099

朝阳银行股份有限公司

地址：辽宁省朝阳市朝阳大街三段4号

邮编：122000

客服：96667

吉林银行股份有限公司

地址：中国长春市东南湖大路1817号

邮编：130033

客户服务电话：400-88-96666（全国），96666（吉林省）

哈尔滨银行股份有限公司

地址：中国哈尔滨市道里区尚志大街160号

邮编：150010

客服热线：4006095537

龙江银行股份有限公司

地址：黑龙江省哈尔滨市道里区友谊路436号

邮编：150018

电话：400-645-8888

南京银行股份有限公司

地址：中国江苏省南京市中山路288号

邮编：210008

电话：96400（江苏），4008896400（全国）

江苏银行股份有限公司

总行地址：中国江苏省南京市洪武北路55号

邮编：210005

客服热线：95319

苏州银行股份有限公司

地址：江苏省苏州市园区钟园路728号

邮编：215028

客服热线：96067

杭州银行股份有限公司

办公地址：中国·杭州市庆春路46号

邮编：310003

客户服务热线：95398/400-8888-508

绍兴银行股份有限公司

办公地址：中国·绍兴市中兴南路1号

邮编：312000

客服热线：0575-96528（绍兴），4000896528（全国）

湖州银行股份有限公司

地址：湖州市南街471—475号

邮编：313000

电话：4008096528、0572—96528

金华银行股份有限公司

地址：中国·浙江省金华市金东区光南路668号

邮编：321015

电话：400-711-6668

嘉兴银行股份有限公司

地址：浙江省嘉兴市建国南路409号

邮编：314000

服务咨询电话：0573-96528、4008396528

温州银行股份有限公司

地址：浙江省温州市车站大道华海广场196号

邮编：325088

客服热线：上海：962699、其他地区：0577-96699

台州银行股份有限公司

地址：浙江省台州市市府大道699号

邮编：318000

电话：0576-89036978

宁波银行股份有限公司

地址：中国浙江宁波市宁南南路700号

邮编：315100

客服热线：95574

浙江稠州商业银行股份有限公司

地址：浙江省义乌市江滨路义乌乐园东侧

邮编：322000

电话：（0571）96527、4008096527

浙江泰隆商业银行股份有限公司

地址：浙江省台州市路桥区南官大道188号

邮编：318050

客户服务热线：0576-96575、全国服务热线：400-88-96575

浙江民泰商业银行股份有限公司

地址：中国浙江省温岭市三星大道168号

邮编：317500

电话：0576-86109988

宁波东海银行股份有限公司

通讯地址：宁波市江东区民安东路268号国际金融服务中心A座5—7楼

邮编：315042

电话：0574-81872233

徽商银行股份有限公司

地址：合肥市安庆路79号徽商银行大厦

邮编：230001

服务电话：4008896588，安徽省内直拨：96588

福建海峡银行股份有限公司

地址：福建福州六一北路158号福建海峡银行

邮编：350011

联系电话：400-893-9999

泉州银行股份有限公司

地址：福建省泉州市丰泽区云鹿路3号

邮编：362000

联系电话：400-88-96312、（全国）96312（福建）

厦门银行股份有限公司

地址：厦门市思明区湖滨北路101号

邮编：361012

客服热线：400-858-8888

南昌银行股份有限公司

地址：南昌市中山路159号

邮编：330008

服务投诉电话：0791-96266（400-78-96266）

九江银行股份有限公司

地址：江西省九江市长虹大道619号

邮编：332000

客服热线：95316

赣州银行股份有限公司

地址：赣州市八一四大道31号

邮编：341000

联系电话：0797-96296

齐鲁银行股份有限公司

地址：中国·济南市顺河街176号

邮编：250001

服务热线：4006096588

临商银行股份有限公司

地址：山东省临沂市兰山区北京路37号

邮编：276000

服务热线：4006996588

青岛银行股份有限公司

地址：青岛市香港中路68号华普大厦

邮编：266071

电话：96588（青岛）、400-66-96588（全国）

日照银行股份有限公司

地址：日照市烟台路197号

邮编：276826

电话：0633-96588（日照）、（0086）400-68-96588（全国）

威海市商业银行

地址：威海市宝泉路9号财政大厦

邮编：264200

电话：96636（省内）、4000096636（境内）

潍坊银行股份有限公司

地址：潍坊市胜利东街5139号

邮编：261041

客服热线：0536-96588、400-61-96588

烟台银行股份有限公司

地址：山东省烟台市海港路25号

邮编：264000

服务热线：4008311777

齐商银行股份有限公司

地址：山东省淄博市张店区金晶大道105号

邮编：255025

客服热线：400-86-96588

东营银行股份有限公司

地址：山东省东营市东营区井冈山路808号

邮编：257000

电话：0546-96588、4006296588

德州银行股份有限公司

地址：德州市经济技术开发区三八东路1266号

邮编：253077

客服热线：（40084）96588

济宁银行股份有限公司

地址：山东省济宁市金宇路6号

邮编：272000

客服热线：4006770537

莱商银行股份有限公司

地址：山东省莱芜市龙潭东大街137号

邮编：271100

电话：40066-96629

郑州银行股份有限公司

地址：郑州市郑东新区商务外环22号郑银大厦

邮编：450046

客服热线：967585（河南地区）、4000967585（全国地区）

洛阳银行股份有限公司

地址：洛阳市洛龙区开元大道256号

邮编：471000

客户服务：（0379）96699

汉口银行股份有限公司

地址：中国·武汉建设大道933号

邮编：430015

客户服务：96558（武汉）、4006096558（全国）

湖北银行股份有限公司

地址：武汉市汉正街湖北银行大厦

邮编：430071

客服热线：96599 省内、400-85-96599 全国

长沙银行股份有限公司

地址：湖南长沙市芙蓉中路1段433号

邮编：410005

客户服务：0731-96511

华融湘江银行股份有限公司

地址：中国湖南长沙市天心区芙蓉南路一段828号鑫远杰座大厦

邮编：410004

服务热线：96599

珠海华润银行股份有限公司

地址：珠海市吉大九洲大道东1346号珠海华润银行大厦

邮编：519015

电话：96588（广东省外请加拨0756）、4008800338

广州银行股份有限公司

地址：广州市天河区珠江东路30号

邮编：510620

电话：400-83-96699

广东南粤银行股份有限公司

地址：广东省湛江市开发区乐山大道60号

邮编：524005

电话：4000-961818（全国）、961818（广东）

东莞银行股份有限公司

地址：东莞市莞城区体育路21号东莞银行大厦

邮编：523011

服务热线：96228（省内）、4001196228（省外）

广东华兴银行股份有限公司

注册地址：广东省汕头市金砂路92号嘉信大厦

邮编：515041

服务热线：4008308001

柳州银行股份有限公司

地址：广西柳州市中山西路12号

邮编：545001

客服电话：0772-96289

桂林银行股份有限公司

地址：桂林市中山南路76号

邮编：541002

全国热线：400-86-96299；广西专线：96299

广西北部湾银行股份有限公司

地址：广西壮族自治区南宁市青秀路10号

邮编：530028

电话银行：86-771-96288

成都银行股份有限公司

地址：四川成都市西御街16号

邮编：610015

电话：400-68-96511/028-96511

乐山市商业银行股份有限公司

地址：中国四川乐山市春华路南段439号金融大厦

邮编：614000

服务热线：96811（省内）、4001196811（省外）

德阳银行股份有限公司

地址：四川省德阳市蒙山街14号

邮编：618000

服务热线：96836

南充市商业银行

地址：四川省南充市顺庆区滨江中路一段97号26栋

邮编：637000

联系电话：400-16-96869、028-96869

贵阳银行股份有限公司

地址：贵州省贵阳市中华北路77号

邮编：550004

客服电话：40011-96033

富滇银行股份有限公司

地址：中国·昆明市拓东路41号

邮编：650011

服务热线：0871-96533、4008896533

西安银行股份有限公司

地址：西安市高新路60号

邮编：710075

客服电话：029-96779、4008696779

长安银行股份有限公司

地址：西安高新技术产业开发区高新四路13号朗臣大厦

邮编：710075

电话：（029）96669

兰州银行股份有限公司

地址：兰州市酒泉路211号

邮编：730030

省内电话：96799　省外电话：40088-96799

甘肃银行股份有限公司

地址：甘肃省兰州市城关区甘南路122号

邮编：730000

电话：96666

青海银行股份有限公司

地址：青海省西宁市城西区黄河路36号

邮编：810001

联系电话：0971-96399/400-888888-3

宁夏银行股份有限公司

办公地址：中国宁夏回族自治区银川市金凤区北京中路157号

邮编：750002

服务热线：区内：96558；区外：400-80-96558

乌鲁木齐市商业银行

地址：新疆乌鲁木齐市新华北路108号市商业银行大厦

邮编：830002

电话：0991-8805337

昆仑银行股份有限公司

注册地址：新疆克拉玛依市世纪大道7 号

邮编：834000

客服和投诉电话：40066-96569

新疆汇和银行股份有限公司

地址：奎屯市团结南街56号

邮编：833200

服务热线：4008009666

农村商业银行（合作银行、信用联社）

北京农村商业银行股份有限公司

地址：北京市朝阳区朝阳门北大街16号

邮编：100020

服务热线：96198；400-66-96198（全国）

上海农村商业银行股份有限公司

地址：上海市浦东新区银城中路8号

邮编：200120

客服热线：021-962999

天津农村商业银行股份有限公司

地址：河西区马场道59号国际贸易中心A座

邮编：300203

客服电话：022-96155、4006096155

天津滨海农村商业银行股份有限公司

地址：天津市空港经济区西三道158号金融中心一号楼

邮编：300308

客服热线：4006068698

重庆农村商业银行股份有限公司

地址：重庆市江北区洋河东路10号

邮编：400020

客户服务热线：966866

山西尧都农村商业银行股份有限公司

地址：山西省临汾市尧都区向阳西路中段

邮编：041000

服务热线：96518

吉林九台农村商业银行股份有限公司

地址：吉林省九台市新华大街504号

邮编：130500

服务热线：0431-96888

吉林珲春农村商业银行股份有限公司

地址：吉林省珲春市新安路1598号

邮编：133300

电话：0433-7523311

延边农村商业银行股份有限公司

地址：吉林省延吉市友谊路185号

邮编：133000

客户服务热线：96888

长春农村商业银行股份有限公司

地址：吉林省长春市二道区自由大路5755号

邮编：130033

服务热线：96888

黑河农村商业银行股份有限公司

地址：黑河市兴安街186号

邮编：164300

客户服务热线：96388

江苏常熟农村商业银行股份有限公司

地址：江苏省常熟市新世纪大道58号

邮编：215500

客服电话：0512-962000、4009962000

江苏张家港农村商业银行股份有限公司

地址：江苏省张家港市人民中路66号

邮编：215600

服务热线：96065

江苏江阴农村商业银行股份有限公司

地址：江苏省江阴市澄江中路1号

邮编：214431

客服热线：0510-96078

江苏紫金农村商业银行股份有限公司

地址：南京市建邺区梦都大街136号

邮编：210019

电话：（86）025-88866666

江苏邳州农村商业银行股份有限公司

地址：江苏省邳州市建设中路16号（信合大厦）

邮编：221300

电话：0516-86234450

江苏丹阳农村商业银行股份有限公司

地址：丹阳市金陵西路152号

邮编：212300

电话：0511-86519256

江苏海安农村商业银行股份有限公司

注册地址：江苏省海安县海安镇长江中路 88号

邮编：226600

客服热线：96008

江苏盱眙农村商业银行股份有限公司

地址：江苏省盱眙县金鹏大道2号

邮编：211700

客服热线（电话银行）：96008

江苏江都农村商业银行股份有限公司

地址：扬州市江都区龙城路21号

邮编：225200

电话：0514-86995122

江苏海门农村商业银行股份有限公司

地址：江苏省海门市解放中路137号

邮编：226100

24小时客服热线：96008

江苏启东农村商业银行股份有限公司

地址：江苏省启东市人民中路599号

邮编：226200

服务热线：0513-83316806

江苏如东农村商业银行股份有限公司

地址：江苏省如东县掘港镇范堤路2号

邮编：226400

电话：0513-84118604

江苏如皋农村商业银行股份有限公司

地址：如皋市如城镇海阳路195号

邮编：226500

电话：0513-87616020

昆山农村商业银行

地址：江苏省昆山市前进东路828号

邮编：215301

服务热线：0512-96079 (网银业务)

江苏太仓农村商业银行股份有限公司

地址：太仓市城厢镇太平南路27号

邮编：215400

电话：0512-53530688

江苏吴江农村商业银行股份有限公司

地址：江苏省苏州市吴江区中山南路1777号

邮编：215200

服务热线：96068（江苏省内）、400-86-96068（江苏省外）

江苏姜堰农村商业银行股份有限公司

地址：江苏省泰州市姜堰区姜堰大道128号

邮编：225500

客服热线：96008

江苏靖江农村商业银行股份有限公司

地址：靖江市骥江路179号

邮编：214500

客服电话：96008

江苏南通农村商业银行股份有限公司

地址：南通市通州区金沙镇建设路1号

邮编：226300

客服热线：96008

无锡农村商业银行股份有限公司

地址：江苏无锡市滨湖区金融二街9号

邮编：214131

电话：0510-82832118

江苏宜兴农村商业银行股份有限公司

地址：江苏省宜兴市宜城街道学前路 28号

邮编：214200

客服热线：96008

江苏江南农村商业银行股份有限公司

地址：江苏省常州市和平中路413号

邮编：213004

电话：89995001

江苏兴化农村商业银行股份有限公司

地址：江苏省兴化市五里东路2号金融大厦

邮编：225700

电话：0523-83328800、83328801

江苏大丰农村商业银行股份有限公司

联系地址：江苏省大丰市金丰南大街10号

邮编：224100

电话：0515-83929003

江苏射阳农村商业银行股份有限公司

地址：江苏省盐城市射阳县解放路385号

邮编：224300

电话：0515-82396008、82334030

江苏盐城农村商业银行股份有限公司

地址：盐城市大庆中路98号

邮编：224005

服务热线：0515-88880000

江苏扬州农村商业银行股份有限公司

地址：江苏扬州市鸿大路1号

邮编：225000

电话：0514-82990333

徐州淮海农村商业银行股份有限公司

地址：徐州市文亭街28号

邮编：221000

电话：0516-85608403

连云港东方农村商业银行股份有限公司

地址：江苏连云港市新浦区郁洲南路10号

邮编：222100

客服热线：96008

浙江富阳农村合作银行

地址：浙江省富阳市桂花西路187号

邮编：311400

联系电话：0571-63334386

建德市农村信用合作联社

地址：浙江省杭州市建德新安江新安东路126号

邮编：311600

电话：0571-64153142

临安市农村信用合作联社

地址：临安市锦城镇城中街442号

邮编：311300

客服热线：96596

杭州联合农村商业银行股份有限公司

地址：杭州市建国中路99号

邮编：310009

客服热线：96592

浙江桐庐农村合作银行

地址：浙江省桐庐县城南街道迎春南路278号

邮编：311501

服务热线：4008896596

浙江萧山农村商业银行股份有限公司

地址：杭州市萧山区人民路258 号

邮编：311201

客服热线：4008896596

浙江杭州余杭农村商业银行股份有限公司

地址：杭州市余杭区临平南大街72号

邮编：311100

客服热线：4008896596

浙江安吉农村商业银行股份有限公司

地址：浙江省安吉县递铺镇玉华路150号

邮编：313300

电话银行：4008896596

浙江德清农村商业银行股份有限公司

地址：浙江省德清县武康镇永安街119、121号

邮编：313200

服务热线：4008896596

浙江南浔农村商业银行股份有限公司

地址：浙江省湖州市南浔区人瑞路1188号

邮编：313009

24小时客服电话：40088-96596

浙江海宁农村商业银行股份有限公司

地址：浙江省海宁市海昌路225号

邮编：314400

客服热线：96596、4008896596

海盐县农村信用合作联社

地址：浙江省海盐县武原街道枣园西路176号

邮编：314300

服务热线：96596

浙江嘉善农村商业银行股份有限公司

地址：浙江省嘉兴市嘉善县罗星街道晋阳东路168号

邮编：314100

客服热线：96596

浙江平湖农村合作银行

地址：浙江省平湖市当湖东路112-150号

邮编：314200

电话：0573-85135897

浙江禾城农村商业银行股份有限公司

地址：浙江省嘉兴市中山西路735号

邮编：314031

电话：0573-82716445

桐乡市农村信用合作联社

地址：浙江省桐乡市梧桐街道校场东路59号

邮编：314500

服务电话：96596、0573-88037895

浙江台州椒江农村合作银行

地址：椒江区工人东路322号

邮编：318000

办公室电话：0576-88882932

浙江东阳农村商业银行股份有限公司

地址：浙江省东阳市双岘路18号

邮编：322100

电话银行：96596、4008896596

浙江义乌农村商业银行股份有限公司

总行地址：浙江省义乌市稠州北路488号

邮编：322000

客户服务电话：4008896596 或 96596 或0579-85562008

浙江永康农村商业银行股份有限公司

地址：浙江省永康市九铃东路3259号

邮编：321300

客户服务热线：96596

浙江青田农村商业银行股份有限公司

地址：青田县鹤城镇鹤城东路180号

邮编：323900

电话：0578-6833720

浙江临海农村商业银行股份有限公司

地址：浙江省临海市古城街道巾山中路2号

邮编：317000

客服热线：96596、4008896596

浙江温州龙湾农村商业银行股份有限公司

地址：浙江省温州市龙湾区永宁西路555号

邮编：325024

客户热线：400-8296596、96596

宁波市北仑区农村信用合作联社

地址：浙江省宁波市北仑区新矸街道新大路177号

邮编：315800

客服热线：96596

宁波慈溪农村商业银行股份有限公司

总部地址：慈溪市浒山街道南城路25号

邮编：315300

客户服务热线：96596、4008896596

宁波市市区农村信用合作联社

地址：宁波市江北区育才路15号

邮编：315000

客服热线：96596

宁波鄞州农村合作银行

地址：浙江宁波市鄞州区民惠路88号

邮编：315100

客服：96561

宁波余姚农村合作银行

地址：宁波市余姚市新建路69号

邮编：315400

电话：0574-62628888

浙江温州瓯海农村商业银行股份有限公司

地址：浙江省温州市鹿城区车站大道福森大厦

邮编：325000

电话：0577-88369598

浙江绍兴瑞丰农村商业银行股份有限公司

地址：浙江绍兴柯桥笛扬路1363号

邮编：312030

电话：0575-84788101

浙江新昌农村商业银行股份有限公司

地址：浙江绍兴市新昌县七星街道七星路18号金融大厦

邮编：312500

热线：0575-86626666

浙江诸暨农村商业银行股份有限公司

地址：诸暨市大桥东路2号

邮编：311800

电话：0575-87013622、87014046

浙江台州黄岩农村合作银行

地址：黄岩洞天路88号

邮编：318020

服务热线：96596、4008896596

浙江台州路桥农村合作银行

地址：路桥区西路桥大道328号

邮编：318050

电话：400-88-96596、96596

浙江温岭农村合作银行

地址：浙江省温岭市城东街道下保路100号

邮编：317500

电话：400-88-96596、96596

浙江苍南农村商业银行股份有限公司

地址：浙江省苍南县灵溪镇人民大道425号

邮编：325800

24小时热线：96596

浙江乐清农村商业银行股份有限公司

地址：浙江省乐清市伯乐西路99号

邮编：325600

服务热线：4008896595、96596

浙江瑞安农村商业银行股份有限公司

地址：浙江省瑞安市安阳街道万松东路148号

邮编：325200

服务热线：4008057702、96596

浙江温州鹿城农村商业银行股份有限公司

地址：温州市车站大道547号信合大厦A幢

邮编：325000

联系电话：0577 - 88077070

文成县农村信用合作联社

地址：浙江省温州市文成县大峃镇建设路162号

邮编：325300

服务热线：96596

浙江绍兴恒信农村合作银行

地址：绍兴市中兴中路159号

邮编：312000

电话：0575-85208928

浙江嵊州农村合作银行

地址：浙江省官河路398号

邮编：312400

电话：0575-83181288

浙江长兴农村合作银行

地址：长兴县太湖街道明珠路1298号

邮编：313100

服务热线：4008896595

浙江舟山普陀农村商业银行股份有限公司

地址：舟山市普陀区沈家门街道滨港路164号

邮编：316100

客服热线：4008896596、96596

浙江金华成泰农村商业银行股份有限公司

地址：浙江省金华市八一南街123号

邮编：321017

客户服务热线：96596或4008896596

浙江武义农村合作银行

地址：武义县武阳中路37号

邮编：321200

服务热线：96596

浙江兰溪农村合作银行

地址：兰溪市丹溪大道18号

邮编：321100

电话：0579-88882529

浙江江山农村商业银行股份有限公司

地址：浙江省江山市江滨路188号

邮编：324100

服务热线：96596

宁波奉化农村商业银行股份有限公司

地址：奉化市中山路27号

邮编：315500

客服热线：96596

安徽马鞍山农村商业银行股份有限公司

地址：马鞍山市红旗南路1659号

邮编：243000

电话：0555-8360876

福建福州农村商业银行股份有限公司

地址：福州市鼓楼区福飞南路118号心连心金融大厦

邮编：350003

服务电话：96336

德化县农村信用合作联社

地址：福建省泉州市德化县龙浔镇德新街153号

邮编：362500

电话：0595-23522343

惠安县农村信用合作联社

地址：福建省惠安县螺城镇建设南路118号

邮编：362100

电话：0595-87393115

福建南安农村商业银行股份有限公司

地址：南安市成功街889号

邮编：362300

电话：0595-86397826

泉州农村商业银行股份有限公司

地址：福建省泉州市东湖街800号

邮编：362000

客服热线：96335

厦门农村商业银行股份有限公司

地址：福建省厦门市湖里区东港北路31号港务大厦

邮编：361000

个人业务咨询电话：40083-96336

公司业务咨询电话：0592-2682023

行政办公咨询电话：0592-2682002

福建漳州农村商业银行股份有限公司

地址：漳州市芗城区水仙大街53号

邮编：363000

电话：0596-2680572

福建福清汇通农村商业银行股份有限公司

地址：福清市融城镇江滨路78号新亚商业城A楼

邮编：350300

电话：0591-85213768

新余农村商业银行股份有限公司

地址：江西省新余市仰天岗东大道259号

邮编：338000

电话：0790-6424009

南昌农村商业银行股份有限公司

地址：南昌市洪都北大道

邮编：330077

服务热线：962268

景德镇农村商业银行股份有限公司

地址：江西省景德镇市新风路4号

邮编：333000

电话：0798-8380033

吉安农村商业银行股份有限公司

地址：吉安市吉州区大桥西路7号

邮编：343000

服务热线：962268

抚州农村商业银行股份有限公司

地址：抚州市临川大道中段

邮编：344100

服务热线：962268

赣州农村商业银行股份有限公司

地址：赣州市章江南大道10号

邮编：341000

服务热线：0791-962268

鹰潭农村商业银行股份有限公司

地址：鹰潭市月湖区信江南路1号

邮编：335000

服务热线：962268

山东邹平农村商业银行股份有限公司

地址：邹平县城三八街14号

邮编：256200

电话：0543-4355385

山东齐河农村商业银行股份有限公司

地址：齐河县城齐鲁大街215号

邮编：251100

电话：0534-5325309

山东禹城农村商业银行股份有限公司

地址：禹城市汉槐街181号

邮编：251200

电话：0534-7227880

山东东营胜利农村合作银行

地址：东营市东营区宁阳路与庐山路交叉路口东南角

邮编：257000

电话：0546-8217377

曹县农村信用合作联社

地址：山东省菏泽市曹县青岛路中段曹县农村信用合作联社

邮编：274400

电话：0530－3569678

菏泽农村商业银行股份有限公司

地址：菏泽市牡丹区中华路789号

邮编：274000

电话：0530-5337813

山东济南润丰农村合作银行

地址：济南市经十一路72号

邮编：250001

电话：0531-82079016

山东圣泰农村合作银行

地址：济宁市中区建设路110号

邮编：272000

电话：0537-2326217

聊城农村商业银行股份有限公司

地址：聊城市东昌府区柳园南路3号

邮编：252000

客服电话：400-88-96668

山东临沂兰山农村合作银行

地址：临沂市兰山区解放路215号

邮编：276000

电话：0539-8237796

山东荣成农村商业银行股份有限公司

地址：荣成市成山大道中段15号

邮编：264300

电话：0631-7553207

山东威海农村商业银行股份有限公司

地址：山东省威海市海滨中路56号

邮编：264200

电话：0631-96668 、5286018

文登市农村信用合作联社

地址：文登市龙山路68号

邮编：264400

电话：0631-8454145

山东昌乐农村商业银行股份有限公司

地址：昌乐县城新昌路78号

邮编：262400

电话：0536-6279033

山东高密农村商业银行股份有限公司

地址：高密市立新街89号

邮编：261500

电话：0536-2339387

山东诸城农村商业银行股份有限公司

地址：山东省诸城市密州路15-1号

邮编：262200

电话：0536-6185700

山东莱州农村商业银行股份有限公司

地址：莱州市光州西路356号

邮编：261400

电话：0535-2211630

山东龙口农村商业银行股份有限公司

地址：龙口市南山路东、港城大道北侧101号

邮编：265700

电话：0535-8514004

山东张店农村商业银行股份有限公司

地址：张店柳泉路256号

邮编：255000

电话：0533-3588035

山东寿光农村商业银行股份有限公司

地址：寿光市银海路19号

邮编：262700

电话：0536-5224989

山东广饶农村商业银行股份有限公司

地址：广饶县城花苑路285号

邮编：267300

电话：0546-6923222

山东临沂河东农村合作银行

地址：临沂市河东区府前街

邮编：276000

电话：0539-8385095

山东博兴农村商业银行股份有限公司

地址：博兴县博城五路522号

邮编：256500

电话：0543-2322017

山东临淄农村商业银行股份有限公司

地址：临淄区齐兴路88号

邮编：255400

电话：0533-71918888

青岛农村商业银行股份有限公司

地址：青岛市崂山区香港东路109号

邮编：266061

电话：96668（青岛）、400-11-96668（全国）

山东聊城润昌农村商业银行股份有限公司

地址：聊城市东昌府区东昌东路95号

邮编：252000

电话：0635-8261255

山东安丘农村商业银行股份有限公司

地址：安丘市兴安路143号

邮编：262100

电话：0536-4226757

山东青州农村商业银行股份有限公司

地址：青州市驼山中路3188号

邮编：262500

电话：0536-3260350

山东费县农村商业银行股份有限公司

地址：费县中山路168号

邮编：273400

电话：0539-5227481

潍坊农村商业银行股份有限公司

地址：山东省潍坊市北宫东街5007号

邮编：261000

电话银行：40088-96668

烟台农村商业银行股份有限公司

地址：烟台市芝罘区西盛街26号

邮编：264000

电话：0535-6695786

山东临朐农村商业银行股份有限公司

地址：临朐县临九路农信大厦

邮编：262600

电话：0536-3169837

山东昌邑农村商业银行股份有限公司

地址：昌邑市北海路136号

邮编：261300

电话：0536-7224273

武汉农村商业银行股份有限公司

地址：武汉市江岸区建设大道618号

邮编：430015

客服热线：96555

湖南浏阳农村商业银行股份有限公司

地址：湖南省浏阳市浏阳大道1号

邮编：410300

电话：0731-83611373

东莞农村商业银行股份有限公司

地址：东莞市东城区鸿福东路2号

邮编：523123

客服热线：0769-961122

广东南海农村商业银行股份有限公司

地址：广东省佛山市南海区桂城南海大道北26号农商银行大厦

邮编：528200

客服热线：96138

广东顺德农村商业银行股份有限公司

地址：广东省佛山市顺德区大良新城区拥翠路2号

邮编：528300

客服热线：0757-22223388

广州农村商业银行股份有限公司

地址：广州市天河区珠江新城华夏路1号

邮编：510623

客服热线：95313

惠州农村商业银行股份有限公司

地址：广东省惠州市惠州大道（江北段）82号

邮编：516003

客服热线：96138

江门融和农村商业银行股份有限公司

地址：广东省江门市蓬江区东华一路30号

邮编：529000

服务热线：96138

江门新会农村商业银行股份有限公司

地址：广东省江门市新会区会城中心南路30号

邮编：529100

服务热线：0750-6327777、96138

广东揭阳农村商业银行股份有限公司

地址：揭阳市东山区建阳路联泰花园一幢

邮编：522031

客服热线：96138

珠海农村商业银行股份有限公司

地址：珠海市香洲兴业路223号农商银行大厦

邮编：519000

客服热线：96138

广东新兴农村商业银行股份有限公司

地址：广东省云浮市新兴县新城镇新洲大道南8号

邮编：527400

客服热线：96138

深圳农村商业银行

地址：深圳市罗湖区深南东路3038号合作金融大厦

邮编：518001

电话：961200（深圳） 4001-961200（全国）

成都农村商业银行股份有限公司

地址：成都市武侯区科华中路88号

邮编：610014

服务热线：028-962711、4006028666

附录三

外汇管理常用法规

WAIHUI GUANLI CHANGYONG FAGUI

外汇管理常用法规[1]

第一部分　综合类常用法规目录

1. 中华人民共和国外汇管理条例（国务院令第532号）

2. 结汇、售汇及付汇管理规定（银发[1996]210号）

3. 境内机构外币现钞收付管理暂行办法（[96]汇管函字第211号）

4. 境内外汇划转管理暂行规定（[97]汇管函字第250号）

第二部分　经常项目外汇管理常用法规目录

一、货物贸易外汇管理

5. 国家外汇管理局、海关总署关于进行“口岸电子执法系统”出口收汇核销联网核查试点的通知（汇发[2001]7号）

6. 海关总署、对外贸易经济合作部、国家税务总局、国家工商行政管理总局、国家外汇管理局、国家质量监督检验检疫总局关于在全国范围内对口岸电子执法系统入网用户进行资格审查的通知（署通发[2001]188号）

7. 国家外汇管理局、海关总署关于进一步加强加工贸易深加工结转售付汇及核销管理有关问题的通知（汇发[2001]64号）

8. 国家外汇管理局、海关总署关于在全国范围内试运行“口岸电子执法系统”出口收汇系统的通知（汇发[2001]102号）

9. 国家外汇管理局关于正式运行“口岸电子执法系统”出口收汇系统的通知（汇发[2001]140号）

10. 国家外汇管理关于对深加工结转项下以人民币结算办理出口核销所需凭证请示的批复（汇复[2002]175号）

---

① 资料来源：国家外汇管理局官方网站，http://www.safe.gov.cn/。

11. 国家外汇管理局关于印发《出口收汇核销管理办法实施细则》和《出口收汇核销管理操作规程》的通知（汇发[2003]107号）

12. 国家外汇管理局、国家税务总局关于“出口收汇核报系统”的核销数据传送及退税数据使用有关问题的通知（汇发[2003]126号）

13. 国家外汇管理局关于下发“境内银行涉外收付相关凭证管理规定”的通知（汇发[2004]45号）

14. 国家外汇管理局关于进一步简化出口收汇核销手续有关问题的通知（汇发[2005]73号）

15. 国家税务总局、国家外汇管理局关于试行申报出口退税免予提供纸质出口收汇核销单的通知（国税函[2005]第1051号）

16. 国家税务总局、国家外汇管理局关于远期收汇出口货物出口退税有关问题的通知（国税发[2006]168号）

17. 国家外汇管理局关于实行网上公布结汇关注企业名单有关问题的通知（汇发[2007]33号）

18. 国家外汇管理局关于实施《出口收结汇联网核查办法》有关问题的通知（汇发[2008]31号）

19. 国家外汇管理局、商务部、海关总署关于印发《出口收结汇联网核查办法》的通知（汇发[2008] 29号）

20. 国家外汇管理局关于货物贸易项下违反外汇管理行为有关处罚问题的通知（汇发[2008] 34号）

21. 国家外汇管理局综合司关于凭纸质出口报关单办理贸易收结汇有关问题的通知（汇综发[2008]118号）

22. 国家外汇管理局综合司关于在出口与收汇主体不一致情况下实施联网核查有关问题的通知（汇综发[2008]122号）

23. 国家外汇管理局综合司关于出口收结汇联网核查系统正式运行的通知（汇综发[2008]128号）

24. 国家外汇管理局综合司关于发布《进出口收付汇核销业务应急预案》的通知（汇综发[2008]144号）

25. 国家外汇管理局关于下发《出口收结汇联网核查操作规程》的通知（汇发[2008] 42号）

26. 国家外汇管理局关于改进出口收结汇联网核查管理有关问题的通知（汇发[2009]10号）

27. 海关总署、国家外汇管理局关于加强进口付汇、出口收汇进出口货物报关单管理和加强防伪鉴别措施的联合通知（署监[1996]28号）

二、服务贸易、收益及经常转移外汇管理

28. 关于下发《贸易进口付汇核销监管暂行办法》的通知（[97]汇国发字第01号）

29. 关于下发《进口付汇核销贸易真实性审核规定》的通知（[98]汇国函字第199号）

30. 关于完善售付汇管理的通知（汇函[1998]27号）

31. 关于印发《规范进出口代理业务的若干规定》的通知（[1998]外经贸政发第725号）

32. 关于转发《海关总署、中国人民银行、国家外汇管理局关于试点和推广进出口报关单联网核查系统的通知》的通知（汇发[1998]68号）

33. 关于保税仓库外汇管理有关问题的通知（汇发[1998]97号）

34. 国家外汇管理局关于印发《深加工结转（转厂）售付汇及核销操作程序》的通知（汇发[1999]78号）

35. 国家外汇管理局关于进口付汇核销报审手续有关问题的通知（汇发[2001]98号）

36. 国家外汇管理局关于进一步调整进出口核销管理政策有关问题的通知（汇发[2002]65号）

37. 国家外汇管理局关于印发《贸易进口付汇核销管理操作规程》的通知（汇发[2002]113号）

38. 国家外汇管理局、海关总署关于对凭进口货物报关单证明联办理售付汇及核销实行分类管理的通知（汇发[2003]15号）

39. 国家外汇管理局、海关总署关于纸质进出口报关单及相关电子底账有关问题的通知（汇发[2003]14号）

40. 国家外汇管理局关于境内机构对外贸易中以人民币作为计价货币有关问题的通知（汇发[2003]29号）

41. 国家外汇管理局关于印发《进出口收付汇逾期未核销行为处理暂行办法》的通知（汇发[2003]40号）

42. 海关总署、国家外汇管理局关于将“进口报关单联网核查系统”迁移到中国电子口岸运行有关问题的通知（署电发[2003]249号）

43. 国家外汇管理局关于印发《边境贸易外汇管理办法》的通知（汇发[2003]113号）

44. 国家外汇管理局关于规范凭收汇凭证办理进口付汇核销手续有关问题的通知（汇发[2004]76号）

45. 国家外汇管理局关于印发《货到汇款项下贸易进口付汇自动核销管理规定》的通知（汇发[2004]82号）

46. 国家外汇管理局关于个人对外贸易经营有关外汇管理问题的通知（汇发[2004]86号）

47. 国家外汇管理局关于印发《进口付汇逾期未核销备查管理规定》的通知（汇发[2004]101号）

48. 国家外汇管理局关于印发《进口付汇差额核销管理办法》的通知（汇发[2004]116号）

49. 国家外汇管理局关于进一步简化贸易进口付汇及核销手续有关问题的通知（汇发[2005]67号）

50. 国家外汇管理局关于印发《个人外汇管理办法实施细则》的通知（汇发[2007]1号）

51. 国家外汇管理局综合司关于发布《进出口收付汇核销业务应急预案》的通知（汇综发[2008]144号）

52. 关于非贸易项下结汇、售汇及付汇管理有关问题的通知［（96）汇管函字第209号］

三、个人外汇管理

53. 个人外汇管理办法（中国人民银行令[2006]第3号）

54. 关于加强对引进无形资产售付汇管理有关问题的通知［（98）汇管函字第092号］

55. 国家外汇管理局关于外汇指定银行办理利润、股息、红利汇出有关问题的通知（汇发[1998]29号）

56. 国家外汇管理局关于中资外汇指定银行外汇利润结汇的通知（汇发[1999]189号）

57. 国家外汇管理局关于修改《加强对引进无形资产售付汇管理有关问题的通知》并转发国家版权局国权[1999]15号文的通知（汇发[1999]283号）

58. 国家外汇管理局关于修改《关于外汇指定银行办理利润、股息、红利汇出有关问题的通知》的通知（汇发[1999]308号）

59. 国家外汇管理局关于简化外商投资企业技术引进售付汇管理手续的通知（汇发[1999]319号）

60. 国家外汇管理局关于旅行社旅游外汇收支管理有关问题的通知（汇发[2001]3号）

61. 国家外汇管理局、农业部关于印发《远洋渔业企业远洋渔业外汇收支管理暂行规定》的通知（汇发[2001]49号）

62. 关于加强技术引进合同及售付汇管理的补充通知（外经贸技发[2001]98号）

63. 国家外汇管理局关于国际海运业外汇收支管理有关问题的通知（汇发[2001]58号）

64. 国家外汇管理局关于对旅行社代售国际机票业务兑换外汇有关问题的批复（汇复[2001]213号）

65. 国家税务总局、国家外汇管理局关于加强外国公司船舶运输收入税收管理及国际海运业对外支付管理的通知（国税发[2001]139号）

66. 关于加强技术进口合同售付汇管理的通知（外经贸技发[2002]50号）

67. 国家外汇管理局关于下发《非贸易售付汇及境内居民个人外汇收支管理操作规程》（试行）的通知（汇发[2002]29号）

68. 国家外汇管理局关于旅行社组织境内居民赴香港、澳门地区旅游有关外汇管理问题的通知（汇发[2002]31号）

69. 国家外汇管理局关于调整专利权许可用汇审核凭证等有关问题的通知（汇发[2002]34号）

70. 国家外汇管理局关于调整中国公民出境旅游购汇政策的通知（汇发[2002]55号）

71. 国家税务总局、国家外汇管理局关于加强外国公司船舶运输收入税收管理

及国际海运业对外支付管理的补充通知（国税发[2002]107号）

72. 国家外汇管理局关于旅游外汇管理有关问题的通知（汇发[2002]84号）

73. 国家外汇管理局关于旅行社组织内地居民赴香港澳门旅游有关外汇管理问题的补充通知（汇发[2002]109号）

74. 国家外汇管理局关于现行法规中没有明确规定的非贸易项目售付汇有关问题的通知（汇发[2003]35号）

75. 国家外汇管理局关于跨国公司非贸易售付汇管理有关问题的通知（汇发[2004]62号）

76. 国家外汇管理局关于企业和预算外单位公务出国用汇管理有关问题的通知（汇发[2004]117号）

77. 国家外汇管理局综合司关于调整部分服务贸易项下售付汇政策有关问题的通知（汇综发[2006]73号）

78. 国家外汇管理局关于调整经常项目外汇管理政策的通知（汇发[2006]19号）

79. 国家外汇管理局、国家税务总局关于服务贸易等项目对外支付提交税务证明有关问题的通知（汇发[2008]64号）

80. 国家外汇管理局、海关总署关于印发《携带外币现钞出入境管理暂行办法》的通知（汇发[2003]102号）

四、外汇账户管理法规

81. 国家外汇管理局关于印发《携带外币现钞出入境管理操作规程》的通知（汇发[2004]21号）

82. 个人外汇管理办法（中国人民银行令[2006]第3号）

83. 国家外汇管理局关于印发《个人外汇管理办法实施细则》的通知（汇发[2007]1号）

84. 国家外汇管理局综合司关于境外个人购汇管理有关问题的通知（汇综发[2008]159号）

85. 境内外汇账户管理规定（银发[1997]416号）

86. 境外外汇账户管理规定（[97]汇政发字第10号）

87. 国家外汇管理局关于调整经常项目外汇管理政策的通知（汇发[2006]19号）

88. 国家外汇管理局综合司关于下发《经常项目外汇账户和境内居民个人购汇操作规程》的通知（汇综发[2006]32号）

89. 国家外汇管理局关于境内机构自行保留经常项目收入的通知（汇发[2007]49号）

90. 国家外汇管理局关于通过外汇账户办理外汇业务有关问题的通知（汇发[2008]60号）

第三部分　资本项目外汇管理常用法规目录

一、外商直接投资外汇管理

91.《国家外汇管理局关于下发〈外商投资企业外汇登记管理暂行办法〉的通知》（汇资函[1996]187号）

92.《关于加强外商投资企业审批、登记、外汇及税收管理有关问题的通知》（外经贸法发[2002]575号）

93.《财政部、国家外汇管理局关于进一步加强外商投资企业验资工作及健全外资外汇登记制度的通知》（财会[2002]1017号）

94.《国家外汇管理局关于完善外商直接投资外汇管理工作若干问题的通知》（汇发[2003]30号）

95.《国家外汇管理关于境内居民通过境外特殊目的公司融资及返程投资外汇管理有关问题的通知》（汇发[2005]75号）

96.《关于外国投资者并购境内企业的规定》（商务部2006年第10号令）

97.《国家外汇管理局综合司关于完善外商投资企业外汇资本金支付结汇管理有关业务操作问题的通知》（汇综发[2008]142号）

二、境外直接投资

98.《国家外汇管理局关于境内企业境外放款外汇管理有关问题的通知》（汇发[2009]24号）

99.《国家外汇管理局关于发布〈境内机构境外直接投资外汇管理规定〉的通知》（汇发[2009]30号）

三、外债管理

100.《外债管理暂行办法》（国家发展计划委员会[2003]第28号令）

101.《国家外汇管理局关于实施〈境内外资银行外债管理办法〉有关问题的通

知》（汇发[2004]59号）

102.《国家外汇管理局关于完善外债管理有关问题的通知》（汇发[2005]74号）

四、对外担保管理

103.《境内机构对外担保管理办法》（银发[1996]302号）及其《实施细则》（[97]汇政发字第10号）

104.《国家外汇管理局关于调整境内银行为境外投资企业提供融资性对外担保管理方式的通知》（汇发[2005]61号）

五、贸易信贷管理

105.《国家外汇管理局关于实行企业货物贸易项下外债登记管理有关问题的通知》（汇发[2008]30号）

106.《国家外汇管理局关于对企业货物贸易项下对外债权实行登记管理有关问题的通知》（汇发[2008]56号）

107.《国家外汇管理局关于完善企业货物贸易项下外债登记管理有关问题的通知》（汇发[2008]73号）

六、合格境外机构投资者（QFII）

108.《合格境外机构投资者境内证券投资管理办法》（中国证券监督管理委员会、中国人民银行、国家外汇管理局2006年第36号令）

109.《合格境外机构投资者境内证券投资外汇管理规定》（国家外汇管理局2009年第1号公告）

110.《国家外汇管理局 国家税务总局关于服务贸易等项目对外支付提交税务证明有关问题的通知》（汇发[2008]64号）（QFII收益汇出的核准依据）

七、合格境内机构投资者（QDII）

111.《中国人民银行、中国银行业监督管理委员会、国家外汇管理局关于发布〈商业银行开办代客境外理财业务管理暂行办法〉的通知》（银发[2006]121号）

112.《国家外汇管理局关于印发〈商业银行代客境外理财业务外汇管理操作规程的通知〉》（汇综发[2006]135号）

113.《合格境内机构投资者境外证券投资管理试行办法》（中国证券监督管理

委员会2007年第46号令）

114.《国家外汇管理局关于基金管理公司和证券公司境外证券投资外汇管理有关问题的通知》（汇发[2009]47号）

115.《保险资金境外投资管理暂行办法》（中国保险监督管理委员会、中国人民银行、国家外汇管理局 2007年第2号令）

116.《中国银行业监督管理委员会、国家外汇管理局关于印发〈信托公司受托境外理财业务管理暂行办法〉的通知》（银监发[2007]27号）

八、H股管理

117.《国家外汇管理局　中国证监会关于进一步完善境外上市外汇管理有关问题的通知》（汇发[2002]77号）

118.《国家外汇管理局关于完善境外上市外汇管理有关问题的通知》（汇发[2003]108号）

119.《国家外汇管理局关于境外上市外汇管理有关问题的通知》（汇发[2005]6号）

九、个人财产对外转移

120.《个人财产对外转移售付汇管理暂行办法》（中国人民银行公告[2004]第16号）

121.《国家税务总局　国家外汇管理局关于个人财产对外转移提交税收证明或者完税凭证有关问题的通知》（国税发[2005]13号）

122.《国家外汇管理局　外交部　公安部　监察部　司法部关于实施〈个人财产对外转移售付汇管理暂行办法〉有关问题的通知》（汇发[2005]9号）

第四部分　国际收支统计与监测常用法规目录

123.《国际收支统计申报办法》（1995年8月30日国务院批准，1995年9月14日中国人民银行行长第2号令发布）

124.《国家外汇管理局关于下发〈国际收支统计申报办法实施细则〉的通知》（汇发［2003］21号）

125.《通过金融机构进行国际收支统计申报业务操作规程（试行）》（汇发

［2009］35号、汇发［2009］37号、汇发［2009］43号、汇发［2009］45号）

126.《国家外汇管理局关于下发“境内银行涉外收付相关凭证管理规定”的通知》（汇发［2004］45号）

127.《国家外汇管理局关于下发〈国际收支统计间接申报核查制度（试行）〉的通知》（汇发［2003］1号）

128. 国家外汇管理局国际收支司《关于下发〈金融机构对境外资产负债及损益申报业务操作规程〉的通知》［（96）汇国发字第13号］

129. 国家外汇管理局国际收支司《关于下发〈汇兑业务统计申报操作规程〉的通知》［（96）汇国发字第16号］

130.《国家外汇管理局关于印发〈贸易信贷调查制度〉和〈贸易信贷调查实施方案〉的通知》（汇发[2006]67号）

131.《国家外汇管理局综合司关于境内金融机构补充申报直接投资数据有关事项的通知》（汇综发[2008]24号）

132.《国家外汇管理局综合司关于境内银行报送非居民账户数据的通知》（汇综发[2008]51号）

133. 国家外汇管理局《关于中资金融机构试行报送外汇资产负债统计报表的通知》（汇发[2008]52号）

134.《国家外汇管理局关于中资金融机构报送外汇资产负债统计报表的通知》（汇发[2009]6号）

135.《国家外汇管理局综合司关于跨境贸易人民币结算中国际收支统计申报有关事宜的通知》（汇综发[2009]90号）

第五部分　金融机构外汇业务管理常用法规目录

一、银行结售汇业务

136.《外汇指定银行办理结汇、售汇业务管理暂行办法》（中国人民银行令［2002］第4号）

137.《中国人民银行关于结售汇业务管理工作的通知》（银发［2004］62号）

138.《国家外汇管理局关于调整银行即期结售汇业务市场准入和退出管理方式的通知》（汇发[2007]20号）

139.《外币代兑机构管理暂行办法》（中国人民银行令［2003］第6号）

140.《国家外汇管理局关于在北京、上海开展个人本外币兑换特许业务试点的通知》（汇发[2008]38号）

141.《中国人民银行关于扩大外汇指定银行对客户远期结售汇业务和开办人民币与外币掉期业务有关问题的通知》（银发[2005]201号）

142.《国家外汇管理局关于外汇指定银行对客户远期结售汇业务和人民币与外币掉期业务有关外汇管理问题的通知》（汇发[2006]52号）

143.《国家外汇管理局关于调整银行结售汇头寸管理办法的通知》（汇发[2005]69号）

144.《国家外汇管理局关于调整银行结售汇综合头寸管理的通知》（汇发[2006]26号）

145.《国家外汇管理局关于银行自身资本与金融项目结售汇审批原则及程序的通知》（汇发[2004]61号）

146.《国家外汇管理局关于印发〈银行结售汇统计制度〉的通知》（汇发[2006]42号）

147.《国家外汇管理局关于规范银行外币卡管理的通知》（汇发［2004］66号）

148.《国家外汇管理局关于印发〈银行执行外汇管理规定情况考核办法〉的通知》（汇发［2009］33号）

149.《中国人民银行关于进一步改善银行间外汇市场交易汇价和外汇指定银行挂牌汇价管理的通知》（银发［2005］250号）

150.《国家外汇管理局关于调整非工作日美元对人民币现汇和现钞挂牌买卖价差的批复》（汇复[2007]440号）

二、保险外汇业务管理

151. 国家外汇管理局、中国保险监督管理委员会关于发布施行《保险业务外汇管理暂行规定》的通知（汇发[2002]95号）

152. 国家外汇管理局关于报送保险外汇监管报表有关问题的通知（汇发[2003]27号）

153. 国家外汇管理局关于印发《保险业务外汇管理操作规程》的通知（汇发[2003]118号）

154. 国家外汇管理局关于保险公司开办境内外汇同业拆借业务有关问题的通知（汇发[2003]105号）

155. 国家外汇管理局关于出口信用保险业务外汇收付有关问题的通知（汇发[2004]29号）

156. 国家外汇管理局关于简化对保险机构外汇业务审核手续有关问题的通知（汇发[2004]85号）

157. 国家外汇管理局关于调整部分保险业务外汇管理政策有关问题的通知（汇发[2006]23号）

158. 保险外汇资金境外运用管理暂行办法（中国保监会令2004年第9号）

159. 关于印发《保险外汇资金境外运用管理暂行办法实施细则》的通知（保监发[2005]77号）

三、证券、财务公司等外汇业务管理

160.《国家外汇管理局关于外资参股基金管理公司有关外汇管理问题的通知》（汇发[2003]44号）

161.《国家外汇管理局关于信托投资公司购汇补充外汇资本金有关问题的通知》（汇发[2001]159号）

162.《国家外汇管理局关于汽车金融公司有关外汇管理问题的通知》（汇发[2004]72号）

163.《境内企业内部成员外汇资金集中运营管理规定》（汇发[2009]49号）

附录四

金融机构外汇业务管理

JINRONG JIGOU WAIHUI YEWU GUANLI

金融机构外汇业务管理①

我国对金融机构外汇业务的监管由外汇管理、银行业监督管理等部门分别负责。根据《中国人民银行法》、《商业银行法》、《外汇管理条例》等规定，人民银行履行银行结售汇业务的市场准入管理职责，具体由外汇管理部门负责。商业银行其他外汇业务，如外汇与外汇间的买卖等，由银行业监督管理部门负责。外汇管理部门还负责保险经营机构、证券公司、财务公司等非银行金融机构外汇业务资格审批。非银行金融机构外汇业务的范围包括外汇保险、发行或代理发行外币有价证券、买卖或代理买卖外币有价证券、即期结售汇业务等。对金融机构监管的另一类重要内容是其为客户办理外汇收支业务的合规性考核制度。

第一节　银行结售汇业务管理

一、银行结售汇业务管理概述

银行结售汇业务是一项政策性、行政性较强的业务。银行在办理结售汇业务时，需按照外汇管理规定对企业和个人结售汇交易背景的真实性和合规性审核。同时，银行办理结售汇业务的净差额须通过银行间外汇市场平盘，对人民币汇率和外汇储备产生影响，并通过基础货币投放影响货币政策和宏观经济政策。因此，需要对银行结售汇业务进行特殊监管。

银行经营结售汇业务需遵循以下管理要求：一是事先向外汇管理部门取得结售汇业务资格，未取得资格者不得经营结售汇业务；二是为客户办理结售汇业务时审核规定的有效凭证和商业单据；三是按规定对超限额的结售汇综合头寸及时通过银行间外汇市场进行平盘；四是按规定制定并公布挂牌汇价；五是建立独立的结售汇会计科目，并制定相应的结售汇单证保留制度；六是履行国际收支申报、结售汇统计、结售汇综合头寸统计、大额交易备案以及其他相关统计义务。

---

① 资料来源：国家外汇管理局官方网站，http://www.safe.gov.cn/。

专栏

银行结售汇业务的定义与分类

银行结售汇业务是指银行为客户办理的人民币与外币之间兑换业务。结汇是指客户将外汇卖给银行，售汇是指客户向银行购买外汇。

银行结售汇业务属于外汇零售市场，是银行与企业或个人之间进行的柜台式外汇买卖所形成的市场。与此相对的是银行间外汇市场，是指银行及其他金融机构之间进行结售汇头寸平补的市场。银行为客户办理结售汇业务会形成相应的头寸盈缺，多余的头寸需要在银行间外汇市场抛出，短缺的头寸需要补进。

银行办理的结售汇业务可以区分为代客结售汇业务和自身结售汇业务。代客结售汇业务是指银行为客户办理的结售汇业务。自身结售汇业务是指银行因自身贸易进出口、服务贸易收支、收益和利润支付以及资本与金融项目投资需要等产生的结售汇业务。银行应区分代客结售汇业务与自身结售汇业务，分别管理、核算和统计。

二、银行结售汇业务市场准入管理

（一）即期结售汇业务

对于总行级机构，实行核准制的准入管理方式。银行总行应提交的申请材料：一是证明银行具备金融业务经营资格的材料，包括《金融许可证》复印件或银监部门批准农村合作金融机构经营外汇业务的许可文件；二是经营结售汇业务的内部管理规章制度。

对于银行分支机构，实行由银行上级行自行授权、事前报告所在地外汇局的备案制准入管理方式。银行分支机构只需事前向所在地外汇局提交包含相关监管信息要素的《银行经营结售汇业务备案表》并经外汇局确认备案后，即可开办业务。如果银行分支机构因重大违规行为受到外汇局处罚，则自执行处罚决定之日起，一定时期内其授权行和该机构均不得授权下辖机构开办结售汇业务。

银行结售汇业务资格区分为对公和对私业务资格。银行可根据自身经营需要分别或者一并申请。取得对私结售汇业务资格后，应按照《个人外汇管理办法》及其实施细则的管理规定，具备与国家外汇管理局个人结售汇管理信息系统的网络接入条件，依法合规办理个人结售汇业务。

银行经营结售汇业务期间，如发生机构更名、营业地址变更等情况，应在规定期限内持《变更备案表》向所在地外汇局备案。银行停止经营结售汇业务，应提前由停办业务行或者授权其开办结售汇业务的上级行持《停办备案表》向所在地外汇局备案。

（二）远期结售汇业务和人民币与外币掉期业务

目前，已开办的人民币外币衍生产品包括远期结售汇业务和人民币与外币掉期业务。

在市场准入方面，只要银行拥有即期结售汇业务资格，在近两年的结售汇业务经营中没有发生重大外汇违规行为，并且具有银监部门核准的衍生产品交易业务资格，即可向外汇局申请开办远期结售汇业务。申请人民币与外币掉期业务，则应办理远期结售汇业务6个月以上。银行申请这两项业务，应提交其具有衍生产品交易业务资格的法定证明文件，并提供相应的内部管理规章制度。银行分支机构申请上述业务需要事先取得其法人的书面授权。

对于远期结售汇业务，主要管理要求包括：（1）银行应按照“了解你的客户”的经营原则，不得为没有任何实际经济背景、意在进行汇率投机的客户办理远期结售汇业务。（2）远期合约到期时，银行凭客户提供的相应有效凭证为其办理结售汇。（3）凡可办理即期结售汇的外汇收支，均可用于办理远期结售汇履约。（4）应按约定远期交易价格的合约本金全额交割，不得差额交割。（5）远期合约到期时客户如违约，按照商业原则处理。（6）客户可以通过掉期业务调整远期合约的履约期限（提前履约或展期），合约金额、展期次数和期限由客户与银行自行协商。（7）客户对象为境内机构和居民个人，但居民个人仅限于办理符合规定的人民币购汇境外投资或理财项下的远期结汇业务。

对于人民币与外汇掉期业务，主要管理要求包括：（1）客户掉期近端（指掉期中的第一次资金交换）换出外汇资金，应属于能办理即期结汇的外汇资金；掉期远端（指掉期中的第二次资金交换）换出的外汇资金，限于近端换入的外汇资金，或能办理即期结汇的外汇资金。（2）客户可以通过掉期业务直接以人民币换入外汇，换入外汇资金的支付使用应符合外汇管理规定。（3）客户可以对掉期合约全额或部分金额进行履约期限调整（提前履约或展期），展期次数和期限由客户与银行自行协商。（4）为客户办理人民币与外币间的掉期业务暂不涉及利率互换。（5）客户对象为境内机构和居民个人，但居民个人仅限于办理符合规定的人民币购汇境外投资或理财项下的近端换入外汇、远端换出外汇的掉期业务。（6）因客户掉期业务违约形成的银行外汇或人民币敞口，银行可自行纳入结售汇综合头寸进行平盘，由此产生的损益由银行自行与客户处理。

（三）个人结售汇业务市场准入管理

目前，国内办理个人（含居民、非居民）本外币兑换的途径主要有三条：一是可办理外币兑换业务的银行网点；二是主要设立于酒店、机场内与银行签约的外币代兑机构；三是正在试点的个人本外币兑换业务特许经营机构。这三类网点构成了一个多层次的个人外币兑换服务网络，不同的服务主体根据自身所处的地理位置、优势服务于不同的客户群体。为便于客户识别，外汇局要求所有可办理个人本外币兑换业务的经营机构都需要在其营业场所的显著位置悬挂（张贴）个人外币兑换服务统一标识。

1. 外币代兑机构代兑业务管理

外币代兑机构是指与具有结售汇业务经营资格的银行签订协议，经银行授权办理外币兑换业务的境内企业法人机构，或由所属法人机构授权的境内非独立法人机构。主要分布在涉外酒店宾馆、机场及其他交通枢纽。

代兑机构的业务范围主要为非居民个人和居民个人办理外币现钞或旅行支票兑换人民币服务。其中，为非居民个人办理每人每日累计不超过等值500美元（含）的人民币兑换外币现钞的兑回业务；设立在境内关外场所的外币代兑机构，上述限额可调高至等值1 000美元（含）。

外汇分支局对银行授权外币代兑机构办理外币兑换业务实行事前备案管理。

2. 个人本外币兑换特许业务管理

个人本外币兑换特许业务是指境内非金融类的一般工商企业经国家外汇管理局批准，为个人办理的人民币与外币之间的货币兑换业务，包括现钞和旅行支票兑换等。

其业务范围包括：（1）年度总额内境内个人结售汇业务，办理兑入或兑出每人每日累计不得超过等值5 000美元（含）；（2）年度总额内境外个人结汇业务，办理兑入每人每日累计不得超过等值5 000美元（含）；境外个人办理无结汇水单的兑出业务，每人每日累计不得超过等值500美元（含），对设立在境内关外场所的网点，该限额可调高至等值1 000美元（含）。

特许经营机构可使用自身品牌，自主经营、自负盈亏，可自行选择合作银行，也可根据自身服务能力状况选择挂牌交易的货币种类，并参照中国人民银行汇价管理有关规定确定挂牌交易汇价。

三、银行结售汇综合头寸管理

银行结售汇综合头寸是指外汇指定银行持有的因人民币与外币间交易而形成的外汇头寸，由银行办理符合外汇管理规定的对客户结售汇业务、自身结售汇业务和参与银行间外汇市场交易所形成。

银行结售汇综合头寸管理遵循以下原则：一是按权责发生制[①]计算头寸。银行与客户签订远期结售汇合约后，即银行承担汇率风险时，即可将其计入结售汇综合头寸。二是限额管理。为防止银行囤积外汇和过量抛售外汇，下限一般为零，上限由外汇局核定。外汇局根据国际收支状况、银行的结售汇业务量和本外币资本金（或者营运资金）以及资产状况等因素，核定银行的头寸限额。三是按天管理。每个交易日结束时银行的结售汇综合头寸应保持在外汇局核定的限额内。对于临时超过核定限额的，银行应在下一个交易日结束前调整至限额内。四是要求银行定期将统计与会计科目进行核对。

四、银行自身结售汇业务管理

银行在经营活动中，除了为客户办理结售汇业务外，其本身也会产生一些结售汇业务需求，比如资本金本外币转换、外汇利润转换为人民币或用人民币购汇支付外方股东利润、支付境外系统服务费等。这些交易与一般工商企业具有共性，但也

---

① 权责发生制是指凡在当期已经实现的收入和已经发生或应当负担的费用，不论款项是否收付，都应当作为当期的收入和费用；凡是不属于当期的收入和费用，即使款项已在当期收付，也不应当作为当期的收入和费用。

有一些特殊性。比如：企业办理结售汇业务往往由银行履行审核职责，银行是由自己审核还是由外汇局审核，需要视具体情况进行明确；企业的经常项目资金、资本金、外债等都实行专门的账户管理，但银行为了结算需要应能够自由开立外汇账户。

对银行自身结售汇的管理要点包括：（1）银行外汇利润应在财务年度终了或在董事会批准当年分配方案后一定期限内，经外汇局审核后办理结汇。银行向境外股东或母行汇出利润，经外汇局审核后办理。（2）银行资本金或营运资金本外币转换，由银行的总行或总部（外国银行分行除外）统一向外汇局申请。银行申请时要求提供申请本外币转换的测算依据。（3）银行经营外汇业务形成的外汇债权，一般应由债务人以自有外汇或以人民币购汇偿还。但如果银行得到企业的人民币资金，而且由于银行与债务人法律纠纷等原因，不能由债务人自行办理购汇，可由银行向外汇局提出代债务人购汇申请，由外汇局批准后办理。银行申请代债务人购汇，应主要满足债务真实合规、获得的债务人资金合法等两项条件。

五、银行对客户挂牌汇价管理

挂牌汇价是指银行对客户办理结售汇业务执行的汇率，包括现钞（汇）买入价和卖出价。现钞（汇）买入价是银行从客户买入外币现钞（汇）的价格，也就是客户办理现钞（汇）结汇的汇率；现钞（汇）卖出价是银行向客户卖出外币现钞（汇）的价格，也就是客户办理现钞（汇）售汇的汇率。通常来说，银行向客户报出的现汇买入价要高于现钞买入价，而银行向客户报出的现汇卖出价与现钞卖出价相同。因此，银行对客户挂牌三种汇价，分别是现汇买入价、现钞买入价、现汇（钞）卖出价。

按照现行外汇管理规定，银行对客户挂牌人民币对美元汇价实行最大买卖价差幅度管理。当日现汇最高卖出价与现汇最低买入价区间应包含当日中国外汇交易中心公布的中间价，并且买卖价差不得超过中间价的1%；现钞最高卖出价与现钞最低买入价区间应包含当日中国外汇交易中心公布的中间价，且买卖价差不得超过中间价的4%。在上述价差幅度内，银行可自行调整美元现汇和现钞的买卖价。银行可自行决定对客户人民币对非美元货币挂牌现汇和现钞买卖价，现行外汇管理没有浮动区间管理。

专栏

现钞和现汇的区别

现钞和现汇是外汇的两种不同形式。现汇是指从国外银行汇到国内的外币存款以及外币汇票、本票、旅行支票等银行可以通过电子划算直接入账的国际结算凭证。现钞指的是外币钞票。由于现汇可以直接进行电子结算，并且入账后即变为生息资产，因此决定了银行买入现汇时的价格要比现钞高。同时，银行买入现钞后一般要积累到一定数额后，才将其运送并存入外国银行调拨使用，银行为此要承担相应的利息损失以及现钞调运过程中的运费、保险费等支出，因此银行从客户买入现钞所出的价格低于买入现汇的价格。

由此可知，在进行跨境贸易、投资等国际结算时，现汇的安全性、便捷性和规模性较现钞具有明显优点。现钞多用于零星小额支付，特别是在银行结算没有介入的主要针对个人消费者的商业服务网点，现钞要比现汇方便。

六、银行结售汇统计

银行结售汇统计根据银行结售汇管理需要建立，由外汇指定银行进行统计，定期报送外汇局。

银行结售汇统计采集的是报表数据，非逐笔数据；内容包括银行自身和代客结售汇数据，不包括银行间市场本外币交易数据、外币与外币间转换产生的套汇数；统计报表包含即期、远期和掉期。银行结售汇统计需要按旬和月报送。已联通国家外汇管理局专网的银行（或已开办因私购汇业务的银行）可直接登录国家外汇管理局专门的服务器报送；没有联通的，可将电子文件通过通讯平台、报盘、传真等方式报送至所在地外汇局，由所在地外汇局代为导入国家外汇管理局服务器。

七、银行卡外汇业务管理

为支持银行卡外汇业务的发展，落实经常项目可兑换，结合信用卡交易先消费后还款、便于真实性审核的特点，国家外汇管理局2003年明确了银行卡正常的境外交易透支可事后购汇偿还的政策，并建立了银行卡外汇业务的管理框架。

在境内外币卡发行方面，境内金融机构可发行外币贷记单位卡，但卡内不能存有外汇资金；可以向在本行开有经常项目外汇账户的单位发行外币借记单位卡。

外币卡在境内使用时，个人外币卡在境内可以提取人民币现钞，也可以到发卡金融机构营业柜台，在其对外挂牌兑换的币种范围内提取外币现钞，但不得透支提取外币现钞，也不得在自动柜员机上提取外币现钞。个人卡提取外币现钞，应执行国家外汇管理局关于个人在境内提取外币现钞的相关规定。单位外币卡在境内不得提取外币现钞或人民币现钞。

境外卡在境内使用时，可提取人民币现钞，也可在银行柜台提取外币现钞，但不得在自动柜员机上提取外币现钞。非居民持境外卡在境内提取人民币现钞后，未用完部分，可到银行柜台兑回。

为防止境外大额提取外币现钞，进行资本非法转移，或从事其他金融犯罪活动，或从事赌博、走私活动，在银行卡管理中具体采取了以下措施：一是要求银行设置境外提现限额标准。二是要求银行在交易系统中进行商户类别码设置，持卡人在境外刷卡交易获取银行授权时，由银行系统自动拒绝不合规交易。三是为防止利用银行卡境外虚假消费进行套现，会同人民银行出台相关文件，要求发卡银行、中国银联等加强银行卡跨境交易尤其是大额跨境消费的监测。

八、银行执行外汇管理规定情况考核

为激励银行认真贯彻和实施外汇管理法规，督促银行依法合规经营，国家外汇管理局从2008年9月起对银行执行外汇管理规定情况进行考核。考核对象包括所有开办外汇业务的银行，考核周期为每年的1月1日至12月31日，考核内容包括业务合规、数据质量、内控制度和其他四个大项，涵盖了国际收支、经常项目、资本项目和外汇检查等各方面的外汇业务。

考核的具体工作由国家外汇管理局及其分支机构共同实施，外汇局以日常监管中发现银行存在的问题作为依据，并结合现场核查，进行各项目考核。考核结果由外汇局采取适当方式通知被考核银行，并视情况将对银行执行外汇管理规定的整体评估情况予以上报、公布。

考核工作为外汇管理部门及时了解外汇管理政策的实施效果，发现银行在执行外汇管理规定中存在的难点和问题，评估外汇管理政策的有效性提供了第一手资料，也为银行提升自身外汇业务经营的合规性，完善内控机制创造了条件。

九、银行结售汇业务改革展望

一是在总结北京、上海试点经验的基础上，扩大个人本外币兑换特许业务试点，以满足日益增长的个人本外币兑换业务需要。二是改革银行结售汇头寸管理，便利银行的风险控制。三是本着便利银行操作、均衡管理、风险可控的原则，对于银行的自身结售汇业务进一步梳理和规范。四是坚持和完善对银行执行外汇管理规定情况的考核制度，及时总结和评估考核效果，不断改进和完善考核工作。五是进一步研究丰富企业规避人民币汇率风险的衍生工具。

第二节　保险公司外汇业务管理

随着我国加入世界贸易组织以及金融体制改革的推进，保险行业作为金融业的重要组成部分，进入了快速发展时期。同时，我国对外经济规模不断扩大，与之相关的外汇保险需求不断增加。为适应新形势的发展需要，从2001年开始，国家外汇管理局与中国保险监督管理委员会，根据保险业的发展需求和行业自身特点，逐步规范保险业务外汇管理，支持保险市场的健康发展。根据现行法规，国家外汇局负责核准保险经营机构外汇业务资格，以及对保险业务项下的外汇收支、结汇、售汇和外汇账户实施监督管理。中国保监会按照《保险法》等有关规定对保险经营机构外汇保险的经营活动实施监督管理。

一、保险公司的外汇业务

（一）外汇保险业务

外汇保险是指根据保险合同约定，支付保险费、赔偿或给付保险金均以外币计价结算的商业保险。保险公司可开办下列全部或部分外汇保险业务：

- 外汇财产保险
- 外汇人身保险

- 外汇再保险
- 外汇海事担保
- 外汇投资
- 资信调查和咨询业务

（二）自身外汇收支业务

保险公司在经营过程中，除外汇保险项下外汇收支外，自身还可能发生与服务贸易、直接投资等活动相关的外汇收支，如外汇资本金、境外差旅费、咨询费、国际组织会员会费等。

二、外汇保险业务产生的背景

根据《外汇管理条例》规定：“中华人民共和国境内禁止外币流通，并不得以外币计价结算，但国家另有规定的除外。”这是维护人民币主权货币地位的必要措施。但随着我国对外开放步伐加快，境内机构和个人对外交往更加频繁，保险需求也日益多元化，出现了在一定条件下以外币计价结算的合理保险需求。为满足境内机构和个人的合理需求，在不影响人民币主权货币地位的前提下，外汇局允许符合一定条件的保险合同，可以外币进行计价结算。

三、外汇保险业务的条件

对于符合以下条件之一的财产保险，保险经营机构可以外汇收取保险费，支付赔偿或给付保险金，或进行保险合同结算：一是保险标的在中华人民共和国境内与境外之间移动；二是保险标的在中华人民共和国境外存在或者实现；三是保险标的在中华人民共和国境内，通过国际租赁、国际银团贷款或者其他国际融资形式存在或者实现；四是投保人和受益人均为境外法人或自然人。

对于符合下列条件之一的人身保险，可以外汇收取保险费，支付赔偿或给付保险金，或进行保险合同结算：一是投保人为境外法人或驻华机构，且受益人为境外自然人；二是境内居民个人在境外人身意外及医疗的保险。

四、保险公司外汇管理的主要内容

目前保险公司外汇管理的主要内容包括两个方面：一是对保险公司外汇保险业务的管理；二是保险公司自身外汇收支的管理。具体为：

- 外汇保险业务资格管理；
- 外汇保险项下外汇收支管理；
- 保险公司资本金本外币转换管理；
- 保险公司自身外汇收支管理。

（一）外汇保险业务资格管理

保险公司外汇保险业务资格管理包括市场准入、退出、经营范围变更等。保险经营机构从事外汇保险业务须经外汇局核准。保险经营机构应当首先按照规定准备有关申请资料后，向外汇局提出申请，外汇局依法审核同意后，保险经营机构方可从事外汇业务。经批准获得外汇业务经营资格的保险公司，应当在核准的业务范围内经营，不得擅自经营或者超范围经营外汇业务。保险经营机构可根据经营需要，扩大或停止办理外汇业务，在变更之前，应向外汇局提出申请，由外汇局依法审核。

（二）与外汇保险有关的外汇收支管理

外汇保险项下的外汇收支包括保费、赔偿、保险金、再保险保费、摊回赔偿、退保费等。保险公司外汇保险项下外汇收支的管理是按照真实性审核的原则办理。保险经营机构持相关凭证可直接在银行办理相应的收付手续。

（三）保险公司资本金本外币转换管理

随着我国保险市场对外开放，境外保险公司纷纷以合资或独资形式在境内设立保险经营机构。同时，为保证外汇保险业务正常开展，保险经营机构需要持有一定数额的外汇资本金。保险经营机构由此产生了资本金本外币间兑换需求。根据《外汇管理条例》，保险经营机构资本金本外币转换应经外汇管理机关批准。

保险经营机构根据公司经营实际需要，按照规定向外汇局提交申请资料，经外汇局依法审核同意后，持核准文件直接到银行办理本外币转换手续。

（四）自身外汇收支管理

保险公司自身外汇收支行为，如境外差旅费、咨询费、国际组织会员会费、在境外投资设立公司的投资款等，与一般境内机构的交易并无本质不同。因此，保险公司办理这类外汇收支时，则被视为一般的境内机构办理。不过，从国际上看，由于金融体系不健全、抗风险能力差等诸多问题，一些发展中国家在资本项目开放中发生了一些风险。国际货币基金组织研究表明，资本项目开放以后，有2/3以上成员国的金融体系都出现了不同程度的问题，有些甚至发生了危机。因此如何继续稳妥、有序地开放资本项目成为中国需要考虑的一个问题。

第三节　证券、财务公司等外汇业务管理

非银行金融机构主要包括存款类机构（如企业集团财务公司、汽车金融公司等），证券类机构（如证券公司、基金管理公司、信托公司等），以及其他类机构（如金融租赁公司等）。作为我国金融体系的有机组成部分，非银行金融机构经营方式灵活、业务种类繁多、服务范围广泛，在外汇资金融通方面正日益发挥着重要作用。但与此同时，我国非银行金融机构发展时间普遍较短，有关法律法规滞后、行业自律管理尚不健全，隐藏的风险不容忽视。因此，对非银行金融机构实施有效的外汇管理十分必要。非银行金融机构外汇业务管理由于各类非银行金融机构经营方式和范围差别较大、业务发展水平参差不齐，且需与资本项目整体可兑换水平相协调，因此，对不同非银行金融机构的外汇业务管理各有侧重。但总体上来看，对非银行金融机构的外汇管理均涉及相关外汇业务市场准入管理、开展外汇业务所涉及的账户及汇兑管理等方面。

一、证券公司外汇业务管理

目前，证券公司外汇业务包括：外币有价证券的经纪业务、外币资产管理业务、外汇同业拆借业务等。其中，绝大多数证券公司以外币有价证券的经纪业务（即B股经纪业务）为主。自1992年B股市场成立后，境内外投资者通过境内证券公司，以美元（上海）和港元（深圳）计价交易在上市的境内公司股票。但是，随着我国资本市场的逐步开放，证券公司外汇业务重心逐渐开始向跨境投资业务方向转移。

因此，其外汇业务运行是否平稳，不仅涉及广大投资者利益，而且关系到未来资本市场开放、资本项目可兑换的平稳推进，因此，对其外汇业务进行监管很有必要：一是有助于控制跨境证券投资的风险。通过市场准入的监管，规范证券机构跨境交易行为，明确外汇业务操作，有助于控制整体风险和开放风险。二是有助于发挥代位监管的职责。随着证券投资项下的开放，跨境交易主体不断增多，资金流动规模及频率加大等，为实现有效监管，监管部门有必要借助于证券经营机构，通过重点监管他们来实现全面监管和监测。

目前，对证券公司外汇业务的管理主要集中在外汇业务市场准入管理方面。基本内容包括：证券经营机构申请开展外汇业务须经外汇局批准取得经营外汇业务资格，须满足一定的外汇营运资金要求，并建立相应的内部控制及管理制度，对其从业人员也有相关的要求，开展境外证券投资须取得证监会的批准等。符合条件的，由外汇局核发《外汇业务经营许可证》，并要求每隔一定时期（目前为三年）重新核发一次。管理方式以审批为主，除初次准入、业务范围界定由总局审批外，其他大部分业务由分局办理。

二、企业集团财务公司外汇业务管理

企业集团财务公司是企业集团内部的金融服务机构，承担着加强集团资金集中管理和提高集团资金使用效率的重要职能。近年来，我国企业（特别是国有企业）改善经营效率、加强风险管理的需求日益强烈，财务公司迫切希望开展相关外汇业务。另外，随着国内外汇资金的不断增加，适当鼓励不同机构进入境内外汇市场，可以便利企业外汇资金使用，有效降低企业经营成本，而且从长远看，也有利于境内外汇市场发展，扩大市场参与者，真正发挥通过市场调节资源、发现价格（汇率）的作用。为此，根据我国外汇市场发展水平、企业集团和财务公司业务发展需要，目前允许财务公司开展的外汇业务主要是结售汇业务。

财务公司开展结售汇是一项创新业务，技术性强，操作较为复杂，必须本着风险可控、统筹安排的原则，在人员、制度、规范、技术保障等方面做到规范，也只有通过规范管理，才能促进业务的发展。

企业集团财务公司开展即期结售汇业务是指财务公司办理自身人民币和外币之间的兑换业务，以及财务公司对企业集团成员公司之间的人民币和外币之间的兑换业务，且由此形成的外汇头寸的平盘。此前，只有外汇指定银行才能开展即期结售汇业务。

财务公司结售汇业务管理的基本框架为：一是财务公司结售汇业务资格准入的审批。准入的审批对财务公司基本条件要求不高，即取得金融业务许可证、满足一定的外汇营运资金要求即可，但对其开展结售汇业务相关制度建设（如内部结售汇、国际收支申报制度等）、技术条件（如结售汇相关数据收发系统、国际收支申报系统等）和人员提出相关要求。二是结售汇头寸管理。取得结售汇业务资格的财务公司，可申请结售汇综合头寸，未申请结售汇综合头寸或结售汇综合头寸为零的财务公司，每日必须将持有的外汇头寸到外汇市场进行平盘或卖给外汇指定银行。三是外汇交易中心会员管理。取得结售汇业务资格的财务公司应向中国外汇交易中心申请成为其会员，并向国家外汇管理局备案。

附录五

外汇检查与法规适用

WAIHUI JIANCHA YU FAGUI SHIYONG

外汇检查与法规适用[①]

外汇检查是我国外汇管理的重要环节，是国家外汇管理局依法行政的重要表现。本章介绍了外汇检查的目的和意义、历史沿革、外汇处罚的依据、处罚种类及检查处理违反外汇管理行为程序。

第一节 概 要

外汇检查是国家外汇管理局及其分支局依据国家外汇管理法规、政策，依法对境内机构、个人的外汇收支或者外汇经营活动，以及境外机构、境外个人在境内的外汇收支或者外汇经营活动进行检查，并对违反外汇管理规定需依法追究行政法律责任的当事人进行调查、处理的具体行政行为。

一、外汇检查的目的和意义

我国目前实行的是经常项目可兑换，资本项目部分可兑换的外汇管理政策，在这种较宽松的外汇管理政策的环境下，高效的外汇检查工作对促进整个金融市场的健康稳定发展十分必要。一是对违反外汇管理规定的行为依法予以惩处，维护外汇市场秩序。二是通过检查促进外汇管理法规、政策不断完善，提高管理水平。三是了解外汇资金流动趋势及特点，防范跨境资金异常流动风险。四是通过检查为企业服务，帮助企业建立内控机制，规避风险。

二、我国外汇检查的历史沿革

1996年《中华人民共和国外汇管理条例》（以下简称《条例》）出台，并于1997年进行了修订。其中，法律责任一章规定了13种违法行为的行政处罚措施，成为外汇检查的直接法律依据。2008年8月5日，根据国际经济形势的变化和我国经济

① 资料来源：国家外汇管理局官方网站，http://www.safe.gov.cn/。

的发展情况，对《条例》进行了修订。新《条例》明确了外汇管理机关多项监督检查职权，同时针对新出现的违法违规行为制定了处罚条款，基本解决了检查手段和处罚依据不足的问题，健全和完善了外汇监管手段和措施。

随着国际收支形势的不断变化和外汇管理体制改革的不断深入，外汇检查工作由注重对资金流出的监管和检查转向对资金流入流出的均衡监管和检查。同时，不断完善检查方式，加强现场检查、非现场检查和非现场监管的结合力度，推进外汇市场信用体系建设，做到查处和宣传相结合。

三、外汇检查的依据和处罚种类

（一）外汇检查的法律依据

对违反外汇管理行为的定性和处罚，应当依据外汇管理法律、法规、规章和其他规范性文件规定的处罚条款，主要包括《中华人民共和国行政处罚法》、《中华人民共和国中国人民银行法》、《中华人民共和国商业银行法》、《中华人民共和国担保法》、《中华人民共和国保险法》、《中华人民共和国外汇管理条例》、《国际收支统计申报办法》等。

（二）外汇处罚的种类

外汇管理法律、法规、规章和其他规范性文件规定的行政处罚主要有：罚款、没收违法所得、强制收兑、警告、通报批判、责令整顿、撤销外汇账户、停办结售汇业务等。

第二节　外汇违法行为处罚

《条例》第三十九条至第四十八条规定了十类当事人违反外汇管理规定所应当承担的法律责任。

一、逃汇行为

第三十九条规定："有违反规定将境内外汇转移境外，或者以欺骗手段将境内资本转移境外等逃汇行为的，由外汇管理机关责令限期调回外汇，处逃汇金额30%

以下的罚款；情节严重的，处逃汇金额30%以上等值以下的罚款；构成犯罪的，依法追究刑事责任。”

违反规定将境内外汇转移境外主要表现为：将境内外汇转移境外时，未出具有效单（凭）证；或根据规定应办理登记的未登记，应获得事前批准的未批准、应进行事后备案的未备案；或转移境外的资金性质和金额，与向金融机构提供的单（凭）证或在外汇管理机关登记、批准或备案的内容不符等。

以欺骗手段将境内资本转移境外主要表现为：使用虚假单证或无真实、合法交易基础的单证办理对外支付、向外汇管理机关办理登记、批准和备案的；对外支付金额和资金性质与真实交易金额和性质不符的；凭借伪造、变造的虚假单证将境内资产携往境外等。

二、非法套汇行为

第四十条规定：“有违反规定以外汇收付应当以人民币收付的款项，或者以虚假、无效的交易单证等向经营结汇、售汇业务的金融机构骗购外汇等非法套汇行为的，由外汇管理机关责令对非法套汇资金予以回兑，处非法套汇金额30%以下的罚款；情节严重的，处非法套汇金额30%以上等值以下的罚款；构成犯罪的，依法追究刑事责任。”

套汇行为主要表现为将应在境内以人民币或外汇收付的货款、投资款等交易款项，以外汇或人民币进行收付，该行为客观上用外汇或外汇权益替代了人民币或人民币权益；以虚假、无效的交易单证等向经营结汇、售汇业务的金融机构骗购外汇等行为，客观上是非法套取外汇。其中“虚假、无效的交易单证”既包括作废的、伪造的或变造的交易单证，也包括无真实、合法交易基础，主要目的是为非法套汇而开具的交易单证，以及单证所列资金性质和（或）金额与实际交易不符的交易单证等。

三、非法汇入外汇、非法结汇行为

第四十一条规定：“违反规定将外汇汇入境内的，由外汇管理机关责令改正，处违法金额30%以下罚款；情节严重的，处违法金额30%以上等值以下罚款。”

非法结汇的，由外汇管理机关责令对非法结汇资金予以回兑，处违法金额30%以下罚款。

非法汇入外汇行为主要表现为：违反外汇管理规定将不允许调入境内的外汇汇入境内，如向境内汇入外汇资金时，应经批准的而未批准，或应登记的未登记，或违反了国家市场准入的规定；以伪造、变造等欺骗手段将境外外汇和资产调入境内的行为，如利用虚假单证或无真实、合法交易基础的单证将外汇资金汇入境内的行为。

“结汇”是指将外汇卖给经营结汇、售汇业务的金融机构的行为。非法结汇行为主要表现为：违反外汇管理规定将不允许结汇的外汇资金进行结汇；应经批准而未取得批准违反规定将外汇结汇的行为；在办理结汇时提供的单证不符合规定，如没有提供结汇单证或者提交单证不全，利用伪造、变造的虚假单证或无真实、合法交易基础的单证办理结汇的行为。

四、违反携带外汇出入境管理行为

第四十二条规定：“违反规定携带外汇出入境的，由外汇管理机关给予警告，可以处违法金额20%以下的罚款。法律、行政法规规定由海关予以处罚的，从其规定。”

违反携带外汇出入境管理行为主要表现为：将不符合外汇管理规定的外汇携带出入境；携带外汇出入境时，应登记的未登记，应事先批准的未批准；携带超过规定限额的外币现钞出入境时未按规定申报或未如实申报；以欺骗手段将外汇携带出入境，如利用虚假单证或无真实、合法交易基础的单证将外汇资金携带出入境。

五、违反外债管理规定的行为

第四十三条规定：“有擅自对外借款、在境外发行债券或者提供对外担保等违反外债管理的行为的，由外汇管理机关给予警告，处违法金额30%以下的罚款。”

违反外债管理规定行为主要表现为：擅自对外借款、在境外发行债券的行为和擅自提供对外担保的行为等。如未经许可擅自对外筹借政府贷款、国际金融组织贷款、国际商业贷款和其他形式的外债；未按照批准的金额、金融条件、形式和期限等对外借款；未经批准，或者未按照批准的金额、金融条件、形式、期限和发行市场等在境外发行债券等有价证券等。擅自提供对外担保的行为，即未经外汇管理机关批准，擅自提供对外担保；未按照批准的范围，包括担保金额、期限、履约等法律责任，提供对外担保；以伪造、变造等虚假单证骗取外汇管理机关对对外担保的批准的、未经核准擅自履约的，也应当以违反本条规定论处等。

六、非法使用外汇行为

第四十四条规定："违反规定，擅自改变外汇或者结汇资金用途的，由外汇管理机关责令改正，没收违法所得，并处违法金额30%以下的罚款；情节严重的，并处违法金额30%以上等值以下的罚款。有违反规定以外币在境内计价结算或者划转外汇等非法使用外汇行为的，由外汇管理机关责令改正，给予警告，可以处违法金额30%以下的罚款。"

非法使用外汇行为主要表现为：擅自改变外汇或者结汇资金用途的行为。即未经批准，擅自将已批准或规定了用途的外汇或结汇资金移作他用；以外币在境内计价结算的行为，即在国家明确规定可以以外币计价和结算的事项及范围之外，没有以本币即人民币进行计价和结算，而以外币进行计价和结算；非法划转外汇的行为，即违反国家有关规定或未经批准机关批准，将外汇在不同账户之间划转的行为。

七、非法买卖外汇行为

第四十五条规定："私自买卖外汇、变相买卖外汇、倒买倒卖外汇或者非法介绍买卖外汇数额较大的，由外汇管理机关给予警告，没收违法所得，并处违法金额30%以下的罚款；情节严重的，处违法金额30%以上等值以下的罚款；构成犯罪的，依法追究刑事责任。"

非法买卖外汇行为主要表现为：一是私自买卖外汇行为，即未经外汇管理机关批准，私自在经营结汇、售汇业务的金融机构和其他经批准的非金融机构以及中国外汇交易中心及其分中心等规定的场所以外买卖外汇；二是变相买卖外汇行为，即不直接进行外汇和人民币的买卖，而以其他形式，如借外汇以人民币偿还、借人民币以外汇偿还、以外汇和人民币互换等方式进行本外币之间的买卖；三是倒买倒卖外汇行为，即违反国家有关规定，以获取非法利益为目的，经营倒买倒卖外汇及外汇权益；四是非法介绍买卖外汇的行为，即违反国家有关规定，以获取非法利益为目的，作为中间人介绍买方和卖方私自进行外汇交易的行为，本项规定的违法行为主要针对非法介绍行为。

八、非法经营外汇业务行为

第四十六条规定："未经批准擅自经营结汇、售汇业务的，由外汇管理机关责令改正，有违法所得的，没收违法所得，违法所得50万元以上的，并处违法所得1倍以上5倍以下的罚款；没有违法所得或者违法所得不足50万元的，处50万元以上200万元以下的罚款；情节严重的，由有关主管部门责令停业整顿或者吊销业务许可证；构成犯罪的，依法追究刑事责任。"

未经批准经营结汇、售汇业务以外的其他外汇业务的，由外汇管理机关或者金融业监督管理机构依照前款规定予以处罚。

擅自经营结汇、售汇业务的行为主要表现为：任何机构或者个人未经外汇管理机关批准，擅自经营了结汇、售汇业务。

未经批准经营结汇、售汇业务以外的其他外汇业务行为主要表现为：未经外汇管理机关或银行业监督管理机构的批准，擅自经营了结汇、售汇业务以外的其他外汇业务。

九、金融机构违反收付汇、结售汇、外汇市场管理等行为

第四十七条规定："金融机构有下列情形之一的，由外汇管理机关责令限期改正，没收违法所得，并处20万元以上100万元以下的罚款；情节严重或者逾期不改正的，由外汇管理机关责令停止经营相关业务：

（一）办理经常项目资金收付，未对交易单证的真实性及其与外汇收支的一致性进行合理审查的；

（二）违反规定办理资本项目资金收付的；

（三）违反规定办理结汇、售汇业务的；

（四）违反外汇业务综合头寸管理的；

（五）违反外汇市场交易管理的。”

违反真实性审核管理行为主要表现为：金融机构在办理经常项目资金收付时，对客户提供的交易单证是否真实及其与外汇收支情况是否一致未尽到合理审查的义务。

违反资本项目资金收付管理行为主要表现为：金融机构未按有关规定办理资本项目资金收付。

违反结售汇管理行为主要表现为：不应该结汇、售汇的，进行了结汇、售汇；结汇和售汇适用的汇率不符合中国人民银行的规定；未审核或者留存相应的有效凭证和有效单据等。

违反综合头寸管理行为主要表现为：金融机构未按外汇管理机关要求准确计算外汇业务综合头寸、未按照外汇管理机关规定的内容、期限、形式和方式报送有关外汇业务综合头寸报表、未实行外汇业务综合头寸管理等。

违反外汇市场交易管理行为主要表现为：未经批准进入银行间外汇交易市场进行外汇交易；违反中国人民银行和外汇管理机关规定的外汇市场交易规则；擅自进行场外交易、以欺诈等手段进行外汇交易；擅自进行规定的交易币种、工具种类、方式和形式以外的外汇交易等。

十、境内外机构、个人违反国际收支统计申报、报送报表、提交单证、外汇登记等行为

第四十八条规定：“有下列情形之一的，由外汇管理机关责令改正，给予警告，对机构可以处30万元以下的罚款，对个人可以处5万元以下的罚款：

（一）未按照规定进行国际收支统计申报的；

（二）未按照规定报送财务会计报告、统计报表等资料的；

（三）未按照规定提交有效单证或者提交的单证不真实的；

（四）违反外汇账户管理规定的；

（五）违反外汇登记管理规定的；

（六）拒绝、阻碍外汇管理机关依法进行监督检查或者调查的。”

违反国际收支统计申报管理行为主要表现为：申报主体违反国际收支申报规定

应当进行申报的不申报，申报时瞒报、错报、漏报国际收支数据，不按照规定的时间、期限、形式和渠道等要求进行申报，包括金融机构代为申报和报送统计时发生的违反外汇管理规定的行为。

违反信息报表报送管理行为主要表现为报送义务主体不按照规定提供报表、报告等文件资料的行为。包括应当报送的不报送，报送的数据不及时、不准确、不完整，不按照规定的方式、渠道报送等。

违反真实性审核管理行为主要表现为不提交单证，出借、借用、串用单证，以及伪造、变造单证等。

违反外汇账户管理行为主要表现为：违反规定开立或者关闭外汇账户的，如应当经过事前批准而不获取批准的，应当报备而不报备的，或者提供虚假单证骗取开户等；违反规定的收支范围和单证要求使用外汇账户的，如超过外汇管理机关规定的账户收支范围办理外汇收付的；违反外汇账户限额管理规定的，如向外汇账户存入外汇超过外汇管理机关规定额度；出借、串用、借用外汇账户及其他违反外汇账户管理固定的行为。

违反外汇登记管理行为主要表现为：应当在外汇管理机关登记而不登记的；在外汇管理机关登记的内容不真实或不准确的；外汇登记超过规定期限，或者不按照规定内容、形式、方式进行外汇登记；伪造、变造和提供虚假单证骗取登记等。

妨碍外汇执法行为主要表现为：拒绝和阻碍外汇管理机关进入现场进行调查询问的；拒绝和阻碍外汇管理机关取证或者复制证据材料的；向外汇管理机关提供事实、证明文件、数据等情况不真实或者不准确的。

此外，新《条例》第四十九条还规定，境内机构违反外汇管理规定的，除对机构进行处罚外，对其直接负责的主管人员和其他直接责任人员，也应当给予处分。对金融机构负有直接责任的董事、监事、高级管理人员和其他直接责任人员给予警告，处5万元以上50万元以下的罚款，构成犯罪的，依法追究刑事责任。

外汇管理机关工作人员徇私舞弊、滥用职权、玩忽职守，构成犯罪的，要依法追究刑事责任。不构成犯罪的，依法给予处分。

第三节　检查处理违反外汇管理行为的程序

为保证依法行政，国家外汇管理局根据《中华人民共和国行政处罚法》、《中华人民共和国外汇管理条例》等规定，制定了《检查处理违反外汇管理行为办案程序》（以下简称《办案程序》），国家外汇管理局及分支局在检查处理违反外汇管理行为的过程中，严格依据有关法律法规及《办案程序》的规定进行。

一、检查处理违反外汇管理行为的原则

处罚法定原则、公正公开原则、处罚与教育相结合原则是行政处罚法的基本原则。检查处理违反外汇管理行为也遵循上述行政处罚法的基本原则，在检查处理过程中，遵循公正、公开、及时的原则，以事实为依据，以法律为准绳，坚持惩罚与教育相结合的原则。

二、检查处理违反外汇管理行为的回避

在检查处理违反外汇管理行为的过程中，外汇局负责人、外汇检查人员有下列情形之一的，当事人有权按规定提出回避要求，相关人员也可以主动申请回避：（1）是本案的当事人或者当事人的近亲属；（2）本人或者其近亲属与本案有利害关系；（3）是本案的证人或者鉴定人；（4）与本案当事人有其他关系，可能影响案件公正处理。

作出回避决定前，外汇局负责人和外汇检查人员不停止对违反外汇管理行为的调查和处理。

三、处罚的适用

（一）基本原则

1. 外汇局实施行政处罚，应当责令当事人限期改正违反外汇管理行为。

2. 对当事人同一个违反外汇管理行为，不得给予两次以上罚款的行政处罚。

（二）从轻处罚和减轻处罚的情节

违反外汇管理行为当事人有下列情形之一的，应当依法从轻或者减轻行政处罚：

1. 主动消除或者减轻违反外汇管理行为危害后果的；

2. 受他人胁迫从事违反外汇管理行为的；

3. 配合外汇局检查处理违反外汇管理行为有立功表现的；

4. 初次实施违反外汇管理行为且违反外汇管理行为情节轻微危害后果微小的；

5. 其他依法应当从轻或者减轻行政处罚的。

（三）不予处罚的情节

1. 违反外汇管理行为轻微并及时纠正，没有造成危害后果的，不予行政处罚。

2. 对在二年内未被发现的违反外汇管理行为，不再给予行政处罚。法律另有规定的除外。二年的期限，从违反外汇管理行为发生之日起计算，违反外汇管理行为有连续或者继续状态的，从行为终了之日起计算。

四、调查

外汇局可以进入经营外汇业务的银行、保险和证券等金融机构进行现场检查；可以进入涉嫌违反外汇管理行为发生场所调查取证；可以查阅复制与被调查违反外汇管理行为直接有关的交易单证等纸质、视听电子资料；可以查阅、复制被调查违反外汇管理行为的当事人和直接有关的单位、个人的财务会计资料及相关文件。

五、行政处罚决定的作出

（一）行政处罚告知书

在作出行政处罚决定前，外汇局应当制作行政处罚告知书印送当事人。当事人收到行政处罚告知书后反馈意见的，应当自收到行政处罚告知书之日起七日内反馈。对当事人提出的事实理由和证据，外汇局应当进行核实，当事人提出的事实理由证据成立的，应当采纳。外汇局不得因当事人申辩而加重处罚。

（二）听证告知

有下列情形之一的，外汇局在作出行政处罚决定之前，应当告知违反外汇管理行为的当事人有要求举行听证的权利：（1）拟给予暂停或者停止经营结汇售汇业务处罚的；（2）拟给予暂停或者停止经营外汇业务处罚的；（3）拟给予法人或者其他组织等值100万元人民币以上罚（没）款处罚的；（4）拟给予自然人等值10

万元人民币以上罚（没）款处罚的；（5） 法律、法规规定可以要求举行听证的其他情形。

（三）行政处罚决定

对于违反外汇管理行为事实清楚，据此定性和处罚的证据客观充分，调查取证程序合法、适当，依法应当给予行政处罚的，根据情节轻重及具体情况，作出行政处罚决定。

（四）不予行政处罚决定书的作出

终结调查的违反外汇管理行为，符合相关规定，决定不予行政处罚的，外汇局可以不进行行政处罚告知而直接制作不予行政处罚决定书印送当事人。

六、行政处罚决定书的执行

（一）行政处罚决定书的生效

行政处罚决定书自送达当事人之日起生效。

（二）当事人申请复议和诉讼

当事人对外汇局作出的行政处罚决定不服的，可以依法申请行政复议；对行政复议决定仍然不服的，可以依法向人民法院提起行政诉讼。

（三）缴纳罚没款

外汇局依法作出罚（没）款的行政处罚决定的，当事人应当自收到行政处罚决定书之日起十五日内，到指定的银行缴纳罚（没）款。

当事人逾期不缴纳罚（没）款的，作出行政处罚决定的外汇局可以采取下列措施：（一）申请人民法院强制执行；（二）每日按罚（没）款数额的百分之三加处罚款，法律另有规定的除外。

（四）延期、分期或者免除缴纳罚（没）款

当事人确有困难需要延期、分期或者免除缴纳罚（没）款的，当事人应当以书面方式向作出行政处罚决定的外汇局提出申请。延期或者分期缴纳罚（没）款期限最长不得超过5个月。

七、简易程序

（一）适用范围

违反外汇管理行为事实确凿并有法定依据，对个人处以五十元以下、对单位处以一千元以下罚款或者警告的，可以适用简易程序。

（二）具体程序

1. 向违反外汇管理行为当事人表明执法身份，口头告知其拟作出行政处罚的事实、理由依据及其依法享有的权利；

2. 对违反外汇管理行为当事人的陈述和申辩，应当充分听取。当事人提出的事实、理由或者证据成立的，应当采纳；

3. 填写行政处罚决定书并交违反外汇管理行为当事人；

4. 告知违反外汇管理行为当事人在规定期限内到指定银行缴纳罚款。

八、文书送达

外汇局送达文书材料，应当首先采取直接送达方式交给当事人，并由当事人在送达回执上签字或者盖章，注明签收日期。送达回执上的签收日期为送达日期。外汇局直接送达文书材料有困难的，可以委托送达、邮寄送达、公告送达或留置送达。

后 记

中国金融业的发展历程是在风雨洗礼中不断成长的。2010年，中国的外汇指定银行只有167家，至2015年，中国外汇指定银行已发展至271家，增加了104家。中国银行业外汇业务的长足发展由此可见一斑。

2015年初，经研究商榷，我们计划编纂《中国外汇指定银行年鉴（2015）》一书，目的是满足市场、行业的发展需求。由于这是第一部正式出版的《中国外汇指定银行年鉴》，没有可以参照的模式和依据，困难可想而知。

整整一个多月，策划方案没有出来。

为慎重起见，我们请教了多位业内权威，听取他们的意见和建议。令人欣慰的是，各位专家均对我们的想法给予了积极肯定。一是明确了目前业内尚没有这样一本工具书性质的读物；二是市场中客观存在着需求和发行空间。专家们的意见更加坚定了我们的信心，我们下定决心要把这样一件有意义的事情办好。

经过为期半年的不懈努力，《中国外汇指定银行年鉴 2015》终于要付梓出版了。在此，衷心感谢国家外汇管理局收支司副司长温建东先生为本书作序，感谢国家发改委学术委员会秘书长张燕生先生、对外经济贸易大学校长助理丁志杰先生、中央财经大学中国银行业研究中心主任郭田勇先生、商务部研究院研究员梅新育先生为本书撰写推荐寄语，感谢中国银行总行贸易金融部程军总经理、中国工商银行国际业务部高明总经理、中国农业银行国际业务部孙梅玉总经理、建设银行国际业务部杨爱民总经理、交通银行国际业务部刘阳总经理对本书编纂工作的大力支持和帮助。最后需要特别感谢的是北京中商国讯管理咨询有限公司总经理赵研先生和他的同事们在年鉴资料的收集、整理和翻译过程中所做的大量卓有成效的工作。正是因为有了大家的支持和共同努力，年鉴才能得以顺利出版。

由于我们能力所限，经验不足，年鉴难免存在缺陷和不足之处，我们真诚期待广大读者提出宝贵意见和建议，以便我们今后把年鉴编纂工作做得更好。

魏建玲

2015年8月23日